JavaScript™

Third Edition

ABSOLUTE
BEGINNER'S
GUIDE

Kirupa Chinnathambi

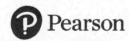
Pearson

JavaScript™ Absolute Beginner's Guide, Third Edition

ISBN-13: 978-0-13-795916-7
ISBN-10: 0-13-795916-8

Library of Congress Control Number: 2022914516

2 2022

Trademarks

Warning and Disclaimer

Special Sales

For information about buying this title in bulk quantities, or for special sales opportunities (which may include electronic versions; custom cover designs; and content particular to your business, training goals, marketing focus, or branding interests), please contact our corporate sales department at corpsales@pearsoned.com or (800) 382-3419.

For government sales inquiries, please contact governmentsales@pearsoned.com.

For questions about sales outside the U.S., please contact intlcs@pearson.com.

Editor-in-Chief
Mark Taub

Director, ITP Product Management
Brett Bartow

Acquisitions Editor
Kim Spenceley

Development Editor
Chris Zahn

Managing Editor
Sandra Schroeder

Project Editor
Mandie Frank

Copy Editor
Bart Reed

Indexer
Ken Johnson

Proofreader
Barbara Mack

Technical Editor
Trevor McCauley

Editorial Assistant
Cindy Teeters

Designer
Chuti Prasertsith

Compositor
codeMantra

Graphics
Vived Graphics

Pearson's Commitment to Diversity, Equity, and Inclusion

Pearson is dedicated to creating bias-free content that reflects the diversity of all learners. We embrace the many dimensions of diversity, including but not limited to race, ethnicity, gender, socioeconomic status, ability, age, sexual orientation, and religious or political beliefs.

Education is a powerful force for equity and change in our world. It has the potential to deliver opportunities that improve lives and enable economic mobility. As we work with authors to create content for every product and service, we acknowledge our responsibility to demonstrate inclusivity and incorporate diverse scholarship so that everyone can achieve their potential through learning. As the world's leading learning company, we have a duty to help drive change and live up to our purpose to help more people create a better life for themselves and to create a better world.

Our ambition is to purposefully contribute to a world where

- Everyone has an equitable and lifelong opportunity to succeed through learning

- Our educational products and services are inclusive and represent the rich diversity of learners

- Our educational content accurately reflects the histories and experiences of the learners we serve

- Our educational content prompts deeper discussions with learners and motivates them to expand their own learning (and worldview)

While we work hard to present unbiased content, we want to hear from you about any concerns or needs with this Pearson product so that we can investigate and address them.

- Please contact us with concerns about any potential bias at https://www.pearson.com/report-bias.html.

Credits

Figures 1.2a-c, 11.2-11.8, Chapter 35 – Screenshots of Chrome browser: Google LLC

Figures 1.2d, Chapter 43 - Screenshot of smileys: Twitter, Inc.

Figure 1.2e: GitHub, Inc.

Figures 1.2f, 34.1: Netflix, Inc.

Figures 1.5-1.8, Chapter 36 - Screenshot of an Excel sheet: Microsoft

Figures 5.1, 9.7, Chapter 41 - Screenshot of JavaScript file: Dropbox, Inc.

Figure 11.1: Randall Munroe

Chapter 43 – Screenshots of using an emoji and Character Viewer on Mac: Apple Inc

Many illustrations and screenshots use emojis from Twitter's Twemoji set: https://twemoji.twitter.com/

Cover Image: rozdesign/Shutterstock

Contents at a Glance

Reader Services

Register your copy of *JavaScript™ Absolute Beginner's Guide*, **Third Edition** at informit.com for convenient access to downloads, updates, and corrections as they become available. To start the registration process, go to informit.com/register and log in or create an account*. Enter the product ISBN, **9780137959167**, and click Submit. Once the process is complete, you will find any available bonus content under Registered Products.

*Be sure to check the box that you would like to hear from us in order to receive exclusive discounts on future editions of this product.

Table of Contents

About the Author

Kirupa Chinnathambi has spent most of his life trying to teach others to love web development as much as he does. In 1999, before blogging was even a word, he started posting tutorials on kirupa.com. In the years since then, he has written hundreds of articles, written a few books (none as good as this one, of course!), and recorded a bunch of videos you can find on YouTube. When he isn't writing or talking about web development, he spends his waking hours helping make developers happy and productive as a Product Manager at Google. In his non-waking hours, he is probably sleeping, joining Meena in running after their daughter Akira, protecting himself from Pixel (aka a T-rex in an unassuming cat's body)…or writing about himself in the third person.

You can find him on Twitter, Facebook, LinkedIn, and the interwebs at large. Just search for his name in your favorite search engine.

About the Technical Editor

Trevor McCauley: friend.

Dedication

To Meena!

(Who still laughs at the jokes found in these pages despite having read them a bazillion times!)

Acknowledgments

As I found out, getting a book like this out the door is no small feat. It involves a bunch of people in front of (and behind) the camera who work tirelessly to turn my ramblings into the beautiful pages you are about to see. To everyone at Pearson who made this possible, thank you!

With that said, there are a few people I'd like to explicitly call out. First, I'd like to thank Mark Taber for giving me this opportunity so many years ago, Kim Spenceley for carrying forward Mark's work in the second and third editions, Chris Zahn for meticulously ensuring everything is human-readable, Bart Reed for his excellent copyediting, Mandie Frank for keeping the project on track, and Loretta Yates for helping make the connections that made all of this happen. The technical content of this book has been reviewed in great detail by my long-time friends and online collaborators, Kyle Murray (1st edition), Trevor McCauley (1st, 2nd, and 3rd editions), Steve Mills (3rd edition), and Dillion Megida (3rd edition). I can't thank them enough for their thorough (and frequently, humorous!) feedback.

Lastly, I'd like to thank my parents for having always encouraged me to pursue creative hobbies like painting, writing, playing video games, and writing code. I wouldn't be half the rugged indoorsman I am today without their support. ☺

We Want to Hear from You!

As the reader of this book, *you* are our most important critic and commentator. We value your opinion and want to know what we're doing right, what we could do better, what areas you'd like to see us publish in, and any other words of wisdom you're willing to pass our way.

We welcome your comments. You can email or write to let us know what you did or didn't like about this book—as well as what we can do to make our books better.

Please note that we cannot help you with technical problems related to the topic of this book.

When you write, please be sure to include this book's title and author as well as your name and email address. We will carefully review your comments and share them with the author and editors who worked on the book.

Email: community@informit.com

INTRODUCTION

Have you ever tried learning to read, speak, or write in a language different from the one you grew up with? If you were anything like me, your early attempts probably looked something like the following:

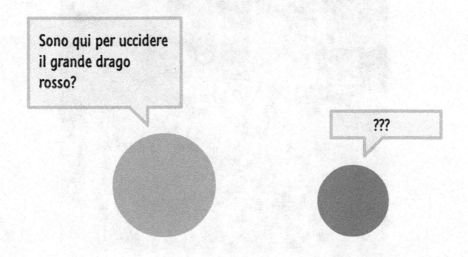

Unless you are Jason Bourne (or Roger Federer), you barely survived learning your first language. This is because learning languages is hard. It doesn't matter if you are learning your first language or a second or third. Being good at a language to a point where you are useful in a non-comical way takes a whole lotta time and effort.

It requires starting with the basics. It requires a boatload of practice and patience. It's one of those few areas where there really aren't any shortcuts for becoming proficient.

Parlez-Vous JavaScript?

Successfully learning a *programming* language is very similar to how you would approach learning a *real-world* language. You start off with the basics. Once you've gotten good at that, you move on to something a bit more advanced. This whole process just keeps repeating itself, and it never really ends. None of us ever truly stops learning. It just requires starting somewhere.

To help you with the "starting somewhere" part, that is where this book comes in. This book is filled from beginning to end with all sorts of good (and hilarious, I hope!) stuff to help you learn JavaScript.

Now, I hate to say anything bad about a programming language behind its back, but JavaScript is often pretty dull and boring, as you can see here:

```javascript
let number = 0;

function increaseCount(rate) {
  let newNumber += rate;
  number = newNumber;

  // do something totally interesting with number
  if (number < 200 * Math.PI) {
    console.log("number is: " + number);
  } else {
    console.log("number is still: " + number);
  }
}
increaseCount(3);
```

There is no other way to describe it. Despite how boring JavaScript might most certainly be, it doesn't mean that learning it has to be boring as well. As you make your way through the book, hopefully you will find the very casual language and illustrations both informative and entertaining. Infotaining, as some might say!

All this casualness and fun is balanced out by deep coverage of all the interesting and useful things you need to know about JavaScript. The goal is to get so familiar with JavaScript that you are able to figure out what techniques to use and when. By the time you reach the last chapter, you will be prepared to face almost any JavaScript-related challenge head-on without breaking a sweat.

Contacting Me/Getting Help

Putting aside the casualness for a moment, my primary goal for writing this book is to help you learn JavaScript. As you make your way through the content, it is natural to get stuck or have questions why something works the way it does...or doesn't. That's part of the learning process. For those moments when you've hit a brick wall, please don't hesitate to contact me. The easiest way to reach me is by posting on the forums at **https://forum.kirupa.com**.

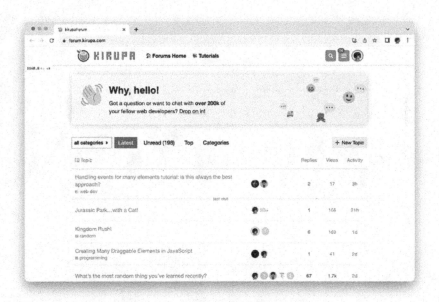

You won't just get to contact me; your question will also reach some awesomely knowledgeable and friendly developers from the 200k member community who will be happy to chime in as well.

And with that, flip the page—it's time to get started!

1

HELLO, WORLD!

The Hypertext Markup Language (HTML) is all about displaying things, and Cascading Style Sheets (CSS) is all about making things look good. Using the two of them, you can create some pretty nifty-looking stuff, such as the weather app you can see at **http://bit.ly/kirupaWeather**. Figure 1.1 shows what this weather app looks like.

FIGURE 1.1

An example of a layout designed entirely using CSS

Despite how nifty sites built using only CSS and HTML look, they are pretty static. They don't adapt or react to what we are doing. It's almost like watching a great *Seinfeld* episode over and over again. It's fun for a while, but it gets boring eventually. The web today isn't static. The sites we use often, such as those shown in Figure 1.2, have a certain level of interactivity and personalization that goes well beyond what HTML and CSS by themselves can provide.

FIGURE 1.2

Examples of various websites that rely heavily on JavaScript for their proper functioning

To make our content come alive, we will need some outside help. What we need is JavaScript!

What Is JavaScript?

JavaScript is a modern-day programming language that is a peer of HTML and CSS. In a nutshell, it allows us to add interactivity to our documents. Here's a short list of just some of the things we can do with JavaScript:

- Listen for events like a mouse click and then do something.
- Modify the HTML and CSS of our page after the page has loaded.
- Make things move around the screen in interesting ways.
- Create awesome games that work in the browser.
- Communicate data between the server and the client.
- Interact with a webcam, microphone, and other devices.
- Do things on a backend server via a framework such as Node or Deno.

This flexibility has made JavaScript one of the most popular programming languages ever, as you can see in Figure 1.3.

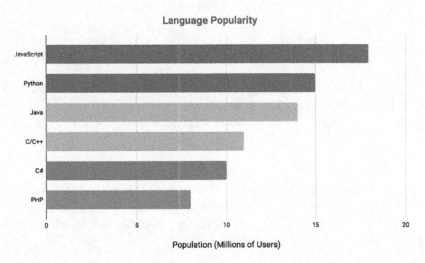

FIGURE 1.3

Chart of popular programming languages, where you can see that JavaScript is on top!

This growth in popularity isn't showing any signs of slowing down. We can find JavaScript powering apps running on a variety of devices well beyond what existed when JavaScript was first introduced many years ago (see Figure 1.4).

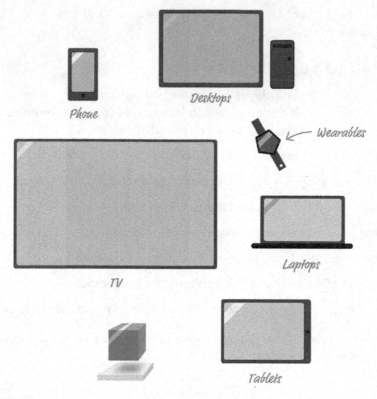

FIGURE 1.4

JavaScript can power apps running on a variety of devices.

This proliferation is partly helped by modern web frameworks like React, Vue, Next.js, Nuxt, and more, which build powerful abstractions on top of JavaScript that make creating rich and complex web apps easy, productive, and fun!

What JavaScript Looks Like

The way we write JavaScript is sort of like composing a formal letter—sort of. We put together words that often resemble everyday English to tell our browser what to do. The following example shows some old-fashioned, fresh outta-the-oven JavaScript:

```
let defaultName = "JavaScript";

function sayHello(name) {
  if (name == null) {
    alert("Hello, " + defaultName + "!");
```

```
  } else {
    alert("Hello, " + name + "!");
  }
}
```

Don't worry if you don't know what any of that means. Just pay attention to what the code looks like. Notice that we see a lot of English words such as function, if, else, alert, and name. In addition to the English words, we also have a lot of bizarre symbols and characters from the parts of our keyboard that we probably rarely use. We'll be using them plenty really soon, and we'll also fully understand what everything in this code does as well.

Anyway, that's enough background information for now. At this point, you might be expecting me to provide a history of JavaScript and the people and companies behind making it work, but I'm not going to bore you with stuff like that. Instead, I want you to get your hands dirty by writing some JavaScript. By the end of this chapter, I want you to have created something simple that displays some text in your browser.

Hello, World!

Right now, you might feel a bit unprepared to start writing code. This is especially true if you aren't all that familiar with programming in general. As you'll soon find out, JavaScript isn't nearly as annoying and complicated as it might seem to be. We're going to build our example together, so let's get started.

 TIP To start writing JavaScript, you need to have basic familiarity with building a web page, using a code editor, and adding some HTML and CSS. If you aren't too familiar with these basics, I encourage you not only to finish the example in this chapter but also to read the *optional* "Building Your First Interactive Web Page" chapter at **https://bit.ly/firstFullApp**.

The HTML Document

The first thing we need is an HTML document. This document will host the JavaScript we will be writing. Next, launch your favorite code editor. If you don't have one, I encourage you to use Visual Studio Code, which is the code editor you will be seeing used throughout this book. After you've launched your favorite code editor, go ahead and create a new file. In Visual Studio Code, you will see a tab labeled **Untitled-1**, similar to the screenshot in Figure 1.5.

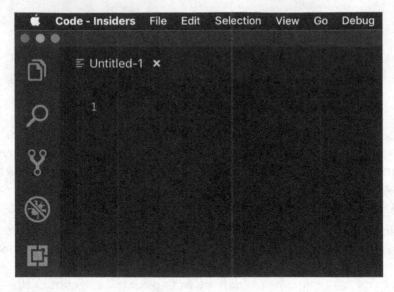

FIGURE 1.5

The Untitled-1 tab in Visual Studio Code

Save this newly created file by going to File | Save. You will be asked to give this file a name and specify where you would like to save it. Give this file the name **hello_world.htm** and save it to your **Desktop**. After you have saved this file, add the following HTML into it:

```html
<!DOCTYPE html>
<html>

<head>
  <meta charset="utf-8">
  <title>An Interesting Title Goes Here</title>

  <style>

  </style>
</head>

<body>
  <script>

  </script>
```

```
</body>

</html>
```

After you've added this HTML, save your document to confirm these changes. It's time to take a look at what our page looks like in a browser.

In either File Explorer or Finder, navigate to your Desktop folder and double-click **hello_world.htm**. You will see your default browser appearing and displaying the name of this file. You should see something that looks like what is shown in Figure 1.6.

FIGURE 1.6

Titled tab in Visual Studio Code

If everything worked out well, you should see a blank page! No, there isn't anything wrong here. While our page has content, there is nothing visible going on. That's fine because we'll fix that shortly. The key to making this fix is for you to go back to your code editor and focus on the <script> tag that you see toward the bottom of your HTML:

```
<script>

</script>
```

This tag acts as a container where you can place any JavaScript you want to run inside it. What we want to do is display the words **hello, world!** in a dialog that appears when you load your HTML page. To make this happen, inside your script region, add the following line:

```
<script>
  alert("hello, world!");
</script>
```

Save your HTML file and run it in your browser. What do you see once your page has loaded? You should see a dialog appear that looks like Figure 1.7.

```
hello, world!
                                                           Close
```

FIGURE 1.7

Your "hello, world!" dialog should look like this.

If this is your first attempt at writing JavaScript, congratulations! Now, let's look at what you just did.

Statements, Expressions, and Functions

We (well, mostly *you*) just wrote a very simple JavaScript **statement**. A statement is a logical set of instructions that tell your browser what to do. A typical application will have many, MANY statements. In our case, we just have one:

```
alert("hello, world!");
```

You can tell something is a statement by looking at the last character in it. It is usually a semicolon (;), just like what you see here.

Inside a statement, you will see all sorts of funky JavaScript jargon. Our code, despite being just one line, is no exception. You have this weird thing called alert that makes an appearance. This is an example of a common English word that behaves similarly in the JavaScript world. It is responsible for getting your attention by displaying some text.

To be more precise, the word alert is something known as a **function**. You will use functions all the time; a function is a *reusable* chunk of code that does something. The "something" it does could be defined by you, defined by some third-party library you are using, or it could be defined by the JavaScript framework itself. In our case, the code that gives your alert function the magical ability to display a dialog with a message you pass to it lives deep inside the browser. All you really need to know is that if you want to use the alert function, simply call it and pass in the text you want it to display. Everything else is taken care of for you.

Getting back to our example, the text you want to display is **hello, world!**, and notice how I am specifying it. I wrap the words inside quotation marks:

```
<script>
  alert("hello, world!");
</script>
```

Whenever you are dealing with text (more commonly known as **strings**), you will always wrap them inside a single quote or a double quote. I know that seems weird, but every programming language has its own quirks. This is one of the many quirks you will see as you further explore JavaScript. We'll look at strings in greater detail shortly; for now, just enjoy the view.

Let's go one step further. Instead of displaying **hello, world!**, change the text you are displaying to show your first and last names instead. Here is an example of what my code looks like when I use my name:

```
<script>
  alert("Kirupa Chinnathambi!");
</script>
```

If you run your application, you will see your name appear in the dialog (see Figure 1.8).

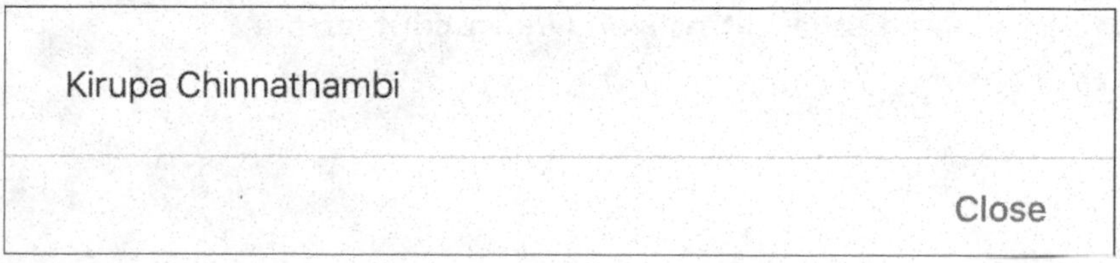

Kirupa Chinnathambi

Close

FIGURE 1.8

The dialog box now displays your name.

Pretty straightforward, right? You can replace the contents of your string with all sorts of stuff—the name of your pet, your favorite TV show, and so on—and JavaScript will display it.

 NOTE We bucketed a lot of the code we see in JavaScript as being **statements**. While that is true, there is a special type of statement called an **expression**. An expression defines a line of code that returns or generates a value. We'll cover expressions in later chapters, but I wanted to make you aware of them now, just as a heads-up.

THE ABSOLUTE MINIMUM

In this chapter, you created a simple example that helped get you familiar with writing JavaScript code. As part of this process, I threw a lot of concepts and terms at you. I certainly don't expect you to know or remember all of them now. In future chapters, we are going to pick each interesting part of what you've seen so far and elaborate on it in more detail. After all, I'm pretty sure you eventually want to do things in JavaScript that go beyond displaying some text in a ridiculously annoying way using the alert dialog.

Going forward, at the end of each chapter, you may even see a set of links to external resources written by me or others. These resources will give you more details or a different perspective on what you learned, along with opportunities to put your learning into practice with more involved examples. Think of what you see in this book as a jumping-off point for greater and more awesome things.

Additional resources:

? Ask a question: **https://forum.kirupa.com**

✔ Practice by building real apps: **https://bit.ly/coding_exercises**

🐣 Errors/known issues: **https://bit.ly/javascript_errata**

IN THIS CHAPTER

- Learn how to use values to store data
- Organize your code with variables
- Get a brief look at variable naming conventions

2

VALUES AND VARIABLES

In JavaScript, every piece of data we provide or use is considered to contain a value. In our example from the previous chapter, we might think of **hello, world!** as just some words we pass in to the `alert` function:

```
alert("hello, world!");
```

To JavaScript, however, these words have a specific representation under the covers. They are considered **values**. We may not have thought much about that when we were typing those words, but when we are in JavaScript Country, every piece of data we touch is considered a value.

Now, why is knowing this important? It is important because we will be working with values a whole lot. Working with them in a way that doesn't drive you insane is a good thing. There are just two things we need to simplify our life working with values:

- We need to identify them easily.
- We need to reuse them throughout our application without unnecessarily duplicating them.

Those two things are provided by what we are going to be spending the rest of our time on: **variables**. Let's learn all about them here.

Using Variables

A variable is an identifier for a value. Instead of typing **hello, world!**, every time we want to use that phrase in our application, we can assign that phrase to a variable and use that variable whenever we need to use **hello, world!** again. This will make more sense in a few moments—I promise!

There are several ways to use variables. For most cases, the best way is by relying on the `let` keyword followed by the name you want to give your variable, like so:

```
let myText
```

In this line of code, we declare a variable called `myText`. Right now, our variable has simply been **declared**. It doesn't contain anything of value. It is merely an empty shell.

Let's fix that by **initializing** our variable to a value like, say, **hello, world!**, as shown here:

```
let myText = "hello, world!";
```

At this point, when this code runs, our `myText` variable will have the value **hello, world!** associated with it. Let's put all of this together as part of a full example. If you still have **hello_world.htm** open from earlier, replace the contents of your

`<script>` tag with the following, or you can create a new HTML file and add the following contents into it:

```
<!DOCTYPE html>
<html>

<head>
  <meta charset="utf-8"">
  <title>An Interesting Title Goes Here</title>

  <style>

  </style>
</head>

<body>
  <script>
    let myText = "hello, world!";
    alert(myText);
  </script>
</body>

</html>
```

Notice that we are no longer passing in the **hello, world!** text to the `alert` function directly. Instead, we are now passing in the variable name `myText` instead. The end result is the same. When this script runs, an alert with **hello, world!** will be shown. What this change allows us to do is have one place in our code where **hello, world!** is being specified. If we wanted to change **hello, world!** to **The dog ate my homework!**, all we would have to do is just make one change to the phrase specified by the `myText` variable:

```
let myText = "The dog ate my homework!";
alert(myText);
```

Throughout our code, wherever we reference the `myText` variable, we will now see the new text appear. Although this is hard to imagine as being useful for something as simple as what we have right now, for larger applications, the convenience of having just one location where we can make a change that gets reflected everywhere is a major time-saver. You'll see more less-trivial cases of the value variables provide in subsequent examples.

More Variable Stuff

What we learned in the previous section will take us far in life. At least, it will in the parts of our life that involve getting familiar with JavaScript. We won't dive too much further into variables here—we'll do all of that as part of future chapters where the code is more complex and the importance of variables is more obvious. With that said, there are a few odds and ends we should cover before calling it a day.

Naming Variables

We have a lot of freedom in naming our variables however we see fit. Ignoring what names we should give things based on philosophical/cultural/stylistic preferences, from a technical point of view, JavaScript is very lenient on what characters can go into a variable name.

This leniency isn't infinite, so we should keep the following points in mind when naming our variables:

- Variables can be as short as one character, or they can be as long as you want—think thousands and thousands of characters.

- Variables can start with a letter, underscore, or dollar sign ($). They can't start with a number.

- Outside of the first character, our variables can be made up of any combination of letters, underscores, numbers, and $ characters. We can also mix and match lowercase and uppercase letters to our heart's content.

- Spaces are not allowed.

Here are some examples of valid variable names:

```
let myText;
let $;
let r8;
let _counter;
let $field;
```

```
let thisIsALongVariableName_butItCouldBeLonger;
let __$abc;
let OldSchoolNamingScheme;
```

To see if a variable name is valid, check out the really awesome and simple
JavaScript Variable Name Validator at **https://bit.ly/namevalidator**.

Outside of valid names, there are other things to focus on as well, such as naming
conventions, how many people commonly name variables, and other things you
identify with a name. We will touch on these items in other chapters.

More on Declaring and Initializing Variables

One of the things you will learn about JavaScript is that it is a very forgiving and
easy-to-work-with language.

Declaring a Variable Is Optional

For example, we don't have to use the `let` keyword to declare a variable. We
could just do something like the following:

```
myText = "hello, world!";
alert(myText);
```

Notice the `myText` variable is being used without formally being declared with the
`let` keyword. While not recommended, this is completely fine. The end result is that
we have a variable called `myText`. The only thing is that by declaring a variable this
way, we are declaring it globally. Don't worry if the last sentence makes no sense.
We'll look at what *globally* means when talking about variable scope later.

Declaring and Initializing on Separate Lines Is Cool

There is one more thing to call out, and that is this: The declaration and initialization of a variable do not have to be part of the same statement. We can break
them up across multiple statements:

```
let myText;
myText = "hello, world!";
alert(myText);
```

In practice, we will find ourselves breaking up our declaration and initialization of variables all the time.

Changing Variable Values and the const Keyword

Lastly, we can change the value of a variable declared via `let` to whatever we want, whenever we want:

```
let myText;

myText = "hello, world!";

myText = 99;

myText = 4 * 10;

myText = true;

myText = undefined;

alert(myText);
```

If you have experience working with languages that are more strict and don't allow variables to store a variety of data types, this leniency is one of the features people both love and hate about JavaScript. With that said, JavaScript does provide a way for you to restrict the value of a variable from being changed after you initialize it. That restriction comes in the form of the `const` keyword, which we can declare and initialize our variables with:

```
const siteURL = "https://www.google.com";
alert(siteURL);
```

By relying on `const`, we can't change the value of `siteURL` to something other than **https://www.google.com**. JavaScript will complain if we try to do that. There are some gotchas with using the `const` keyword, but it does a great job overall in preventing accidental modifications of a variable. We'll cover those pesky gotchas in bits and pieces when the time is right.

TIP Jump Ahead—Variable Scoping

Now that you know how to declare and initialize variables, a very important topic is that of **visibility**. You need to know when and where a variable you declared can actually be used in your code. The catch-all phrase for this is **variable scope**. If you are curious to know more about it, you can jump ahead and read Chapter 8, "Variable Scope."

THE ABSOLUTE MINIMUM

Values store data, and variables act as an easy way to refer to that data. There are a lot of interesting details about values, but those are details you do not need to learn right now. Just know that JavaScript enables you to represent a variety of values such as text and numbers without a lot of fuss.

To make your values more memorable and reusable, you declare variables. You declare variables using the `let` keyword and a **variable name**. If you want to initialize the variable to a default value, you follow all of that up with an equal sign (=) and the value you want to initialize your variable with.

? Ask a question: **https://forum.kirupa.com**

✔ Practice by building real apps: **https://bit.ly/coding_exercises**

🎇 Errors/known issues: **https://bit.ly/javascript_errata**

IN THIS CHAPTER

- Learn how functions help you better organize and group your code

- Understand how functions make your code reusable

- Discover the importance of function arguments and how to use them

FUNCTIONS

So far, all the code we've written really contained no structure. It was just… there:

```
alert("hello, world!");
```

There is nothing wrong with having code like this. This is especially true if our code is made up of a single statement. Most of the time, though, that will never be the case. Our code will rarely be this simple when we are using JavaScript in the real world for real-worldly things.

To highlight this, let's say we want to display the distance something has traveled (see Figure 3.1).

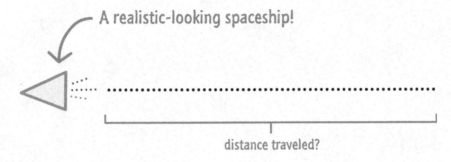

A realistic-looking spaceship!

distance traveled?

FIGURE 3.1

Distance traveled

If you remember from school, distance is calculated by multiplying the speed something has traveled by how long it took (see Figure 3.2).

$$distance = speed \times time$$

FIGURE 3.2

Calculating distance

The JavaScript version of that sort of looks like this:

```
let speed = 10;
let time = 5;
alert(speed * time);
```

We have two variables, named `speed` and `time`, and they each store a number. The `alert` function displays the result of multiplying the values stored by the `speed` and `time` variables. This is a pretty literal translation of the distance equation we just saw.

Let's say we want to calculate the distance for more values. Using only what we've seen so far, our code would look like this:

```
let speed = 10;
let time = 5;
alert(speed * time);

let speed1 = 85;
let time1 = 1.5;
alert(speed1 * time1);

let speed2 = 12;
let time2 = 9;

alert(speed2 * time2);
let speed3 = 42;
let time3 = 21;
alert(speed3 * time3);
```

I don't know about you, but as the legendary JavaScript developer and occasional basketball player Charles Barkley would say, this just looks **turrible**. Our code is unnecessarily verbose and repetitive. Like we saw earlier when we were learning about **variables**, repetition makes our code harder to maintain, and it also wastes our time.

This entire problem can be solved very easily by using what we'll be seeing a lot of here, **functions**:

```
function showDistance(speed, time) {
  alert(speed * time);
}
showDistance(10, 5);
showDistance(85, 1.5);
showDistance(12, 9);
showDistance(42, 21);
```

Don't worry too much about what this code does just yet. Just know that this smaller chunk of code does everything all those many lines of code did earlier, but without all the negative side effects. We'll learn all about functions and how they do all the sweet things they do, starting...right...now!

What Is a Function?

At a very basic level, a function is nothing more than a wrapper for some code. A function provides the following benefits:

- It groups statements together.
- It makes our code reusable.

We will rarely write or use code that doesn't involve functions, so it's important that we get familiar with them and learn all about how well they work.

A Simple Function

The best way to learn about functions is to just dive right in and start using them, so let's start off by creating a very simple function. Creating a function isn't very exciting. It just requires understanding some minor syntactical quirks, like using weird parentheses and brackets.

Here is an example of what a very simple function looks like:

```
function sayHello() {
  alert("hello!");
}
```

Just having a function defined isn't enough, though. Our function needs to be **called**, and we can do that by adding the following line afterwards:

```
function sayHello() {
  alert("hello!");
}
sayHello();
```

To see all this for yourself, create a new HTML document (call it **functions_sayhello.htm**) and add the following code to it:

```
<!DOCTYPE html>
<html>


<head>
```

```
    <meta charset="utf-8">
    <title>Say Hello!</title>
    <style>

    </style>
  </head>
  <body>
    <script>
      function sayHello() {
        alert("hello!");
      }
      sayHello();
    </script>
  </body>
</html>
```

If you have typed all this in and then preview your page in your browser, you will see **hello!** displayed. The only thing you need to know right now is that our code works. Let's look at why the code works next by breaking the `sayHello` function into individual chunks and viewing each in greater detail.

First, we see the `function` keyword leading things off, as shown in Figure 3.3.

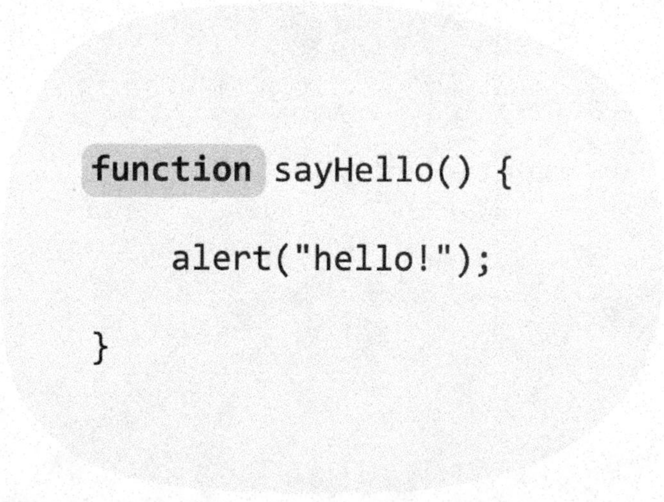

```
function sayHello() {

    alert("hello!");

}
```

FIGURE 3.3

The function keyword

This keyword tells the JavaScript engine that lives deep inside your browser to treat this entire block of code as something having to do with functions.

After the `function` keyword, we specify the actual name of the function, followed by some opening and closing parentheses, as you can see in Figure 3.4.

```
function sayHello() {

    alert("hello!");

}
```

FIGURE 3.4

The function name and parentheses

Rounding out our function declaration are the opening and closing brackets that enclose any statements we may have inside (see Figure 3.5).

```
function sayHello() {

    alert("hello!");

}
```

FIGURE 3.5

The opening and closing brackets

The final thing is the contents of our function—the statements that make our function actually functional (see Figure 3.6).

```
function sayHello() {

    alert("hello!");

}
```

FIGURE 3.6

The function's content

In our case, the content is the `alert` function, which displays a dialog with the word **hello!** in it.

The last thing to look at is the **function call** (see Figure 3.7). The function call is typically the name of the function we want to *call* (or *invoke*) followed again by the parentheses. Without our function call, the function we created doesn't do anything. It is the function call that wakes our function up and makes it do things.

```
function sayHello() {

    alert("hello!");

}

sayHello();
```

FIGURE 3.7

The function call

Now, what we have just seen is a very simple function. In the next couple sections, we are going to build on what we've just learned and look at increasingly more realistic examples of using functions.

Creating a Function That Takes Arguments

The previous sayHello example was quite simple:

```
function sayHello() {
  alert("hello!");
}
sayHello();
```

We call a function, and the function does something. That simplification by itself is not out of the ordinary. All functions work just like that. What is different is the details on how functions get invoked, where they get their data from, and so on. The first such detail we are going to look at involves functions that take **arguments**.

Let's start with a simple and familiar example:

```
alert("my argument");
```

What we have here is our `alert` function. We've seen it a few (or a few dozen) times already. What this function does is take what is known as an **argument** for figuring out what to actually display when it gets called. Calling the `alert` function with an argument of **my argument** results in the display shown in Figure 3.8.

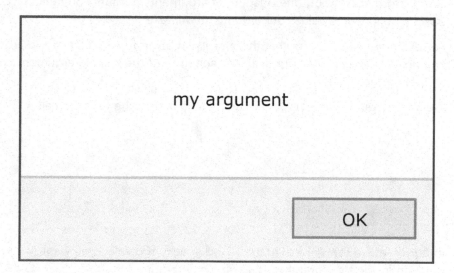

FIGURE 3.8

Displaying the argument

The argument is the stuff between our opening and closing parentheses when calling the `alert` function. The `alert` function is just one of many functions available to us that take arguments, and many of the functions we create will take arguments as well.

For example, earlier in this chapter we briefly looked at a function that takes arguments—our `showDistance` function:

```
function showDistance(speed, time) {
  alert(speed * time);
}
```

See, we can tell when a function takes arguments by looking at the function declaration itself:

```
function showDistance(speed, time) {
  alert(speed * time);
}
```

What used to be empty parentheses following the function name will now contain some information about the quantity of arguments our function needs, along with some hints on what values our arguments will take.

For example, we can infer that the showDistance function takes two arguments. The first argument corresponds to the speed, and the second argument corresponds to the time.

We specify our arguments to the function as part of the function call:

```
function showDistance (speed, time) {
  alert (speed * time);
}
showDistance(10, 5);
```

In our case, we call showDistance and specify the values we want to pass to our function inside the parentheses, as shown in Figure 3.9.

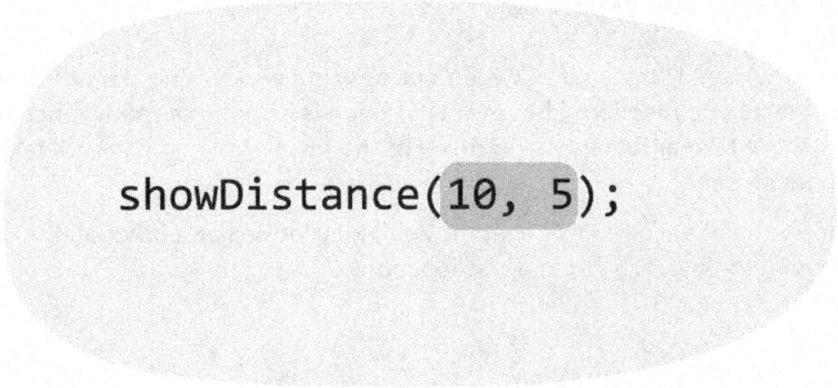

FIGURE 3.9

Values we want to pass to the function

Because we are providing more than one argument, we can separate the individual arguments by a comma. Oh, and before I forget to mention it, the order in which we specify our arguments matters.

Let's look at all of this in greater detail, starting with the diagram in Figure 3.10.

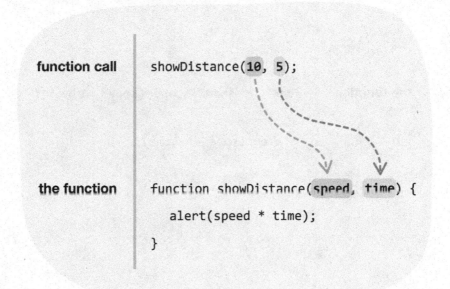

FIGURE 3.10

A diagram of the function call

When the showDistance function gets called, it passes in a **10** for the speed argument, and it passes in a **5** for the distance argument. That mapping, as shown in the diagram, is entirely based on order.

Once the values you pass in as arguments reach our function, the names we specified for the arguments are treated just like variable names, as shown in Figure 3.11. We can use these variable names to easily reference the values stored by the arguments inside our function without any worry in the world.

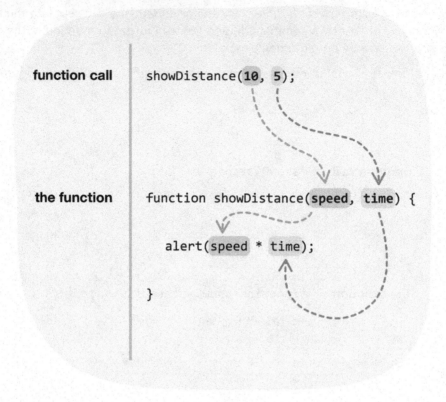

FIGURE 3.11

The argument names work like variables.

 NOTE Mismatched Number of Arguments

If a function happens to take arguments and we don't provide any arguments as part of our function call, provide too few arguments, or provide too many arguments, things can still work. We can code our function defensively against these cases, and in future chapters we will touch on that a bit.

In general, to make the code we are writing clearer, we should provide the required number of arguments for the function we are calling.

Creating a Function That Returns Data

The last function variant we will look at is one that returns some data back to whatever called it. Here is what we want to do. We have our showDistance function, and we know that it looks as follows:

```
function showDistance(speed, time) {
  alert(speed * time);
}
```

Instead of having our showDistance function calculate the distance and display it as an alert, we want to store that value for some future use. We want to do something like this:

```
let myDistance = showDistance(10, 5);
```

The myDistance variable will store the results of the calculation the showDistance function performs.

The Return Keyword

We return data from a function by using the return keyword. Let's create a new function called getDistance that looks identical to showDistance, with the only difference being what happens when the function runs to completion:

```
function getDistance(speed, time) {
  let distance = speed * time;
  return distance;
}
```

Notice that we are still calculating the distance by multiplying speed and time. Instead of displaying an alert, we instead return the distance (as stored by the distance variable).

To call the getDistance function, we can just call it as part of initializing a variable:

```
let myDistance = getDistance(10, 5);
```

When the `getDistance` function is called, it gets evaluated and returns a numerical value that then becomes assigned to the `myDistance` variable. That's all there is to it.

Exiting the Function Early

Once our function hits the `return` keyword, it stops everything it is doing at that point, returns whatever value you specified to the caller, and exits:

```
function getDistance(speed, time) {
  let distance = speed * time;
  return distance;

  if (speed < 0) {
    distance *= -1;
  }
}
```

Any code that appears after our `return` statement will not get reached. It will be as if that code never even existed.

In practice, we will use the `return` statement to terminate a function after it has done what we wanted it to do. That function could return a value to the caller, like we saw in the previous examples, or that function could simply just exit:

```
function doSomething() {
  let foo = "Nothing interesting";
  return;
}
```

Using the `return` keyword to return a value is optional. The `return` keyword can be used in a standalone manner, like we see here, to just exit the function. If a function does not specify anything to return, a default value of `undefined` is returned.

Function Expressions

The functions we've seen so far are of the **function declaration** (or **statement** or **definition**) variety. There is another common way to work with functions, and that is the **function expression** way. In this approach, our functions are typically unnamed and associated with a variable. This makes more sense with an example, so here we go:

```
const area = function(width, height) {
    return width * height;
}
alert(area(4, 5)); // displays "20"
```

We have a function called `area`, and we use it just like we would any function we've seen so far. The main visual difference is in how we write the function body. Getting into specifics, what we have here is an **anonymous function** assigned to the variable `area`. As we can imagine, it is *anonymous* because this function has no name. However, it doesn't have to be that way. We can totally name the function as part of a function expression, as shown here:

```
const area = function areaHelper(width, height) {
    return width * height;
}
alert(area(4, 5)); // still displays "20"
```

In this case, we still have a function assigned to the variable `area`. What is different is that our function has a name, and that name is `areaHelper`! This name isn't exposed outside of the function body itself. This means that the only way to call this function is via the `area` variable. If that is the case, why would we bother naming our function? There are two reasons:

- Debugging our code is easier when we encounter a named function.

- For more advanced scenarios, we may want to recursively call our function. The only way to do that is by referencing the function by name. (For an example of a recursive function, go here: **https://bit.ly/kirupaHanoi**)

What makes function expressions interesting is that they open the door for some really cool techniques we would otherwise not be able to do.

 TIP Immediately Invoked Function Expression (IIFE)

A function doesn't have to be invoked separately from when it gets defined. We can define a function that gets executed immediately, and such a function is known as an *immediately invoked function*

expression, or *IIFE* for short. The way we define an IIFE is by wrapping our function expression in a bunch of extra parentheses. Take a look at the following example:

```
(function() {
    let greeting = "Hello";
  alert(greeting);
})();
```

When this code runs, the word **Hello** is displayed in an alert dialog. What makes this unique is that we can't access the `greeting` variable at all. It is locked and kept private inside the IIFE, so this is a good way to have our code do something without having its internals publicly accessible.

THE ABSOLUTE MINIMUM

Functions are among a handful of things we will use in almost every single JavaScript application. They provide the much sought-after capability to help make our code reusable. Whether we are creating our own functions or using the many functions that are built into the JavaScript language, we will simply not be able to live without them.

What we have seen so far are examples of how functions are commonly used. There are some advanced traits that functions possess that I did not cover here. Those uses will be covered in the future—a distant future when we reach Chapters 9, 22, and 49. For now, everything you've learned will take you quite far when it comes to understanding how functions are used in the real world.

? Ask a question: **https://forum.kirupa.com**

✔ Practice by building real apps: **https://bit.ly/coding_exercises**

🎯 Errors/known issues: **https://bit.ly/javascript_errata**

4

CONDITIONAL STATEMENTS: IF, ELSE, AND SWITCH

From the moment you wake up, whether you realize it or not, you start making decisions. Turn the alarm off. Turn the lights on. Look outside to see what the weather is like. Brush your teeth. Put on your robe and wizard hat. Check your calendar. Basically…well, you get the point. By the time you step outside your door, you consciously or subconsciously will have made hundreds of decisions, with each one having a certain effect on what you ended up doing.

For example, if the weather looks cold outside, you might decide to wear a hoodie or a jacket. You can model this decision as shown in Figure 4.1.

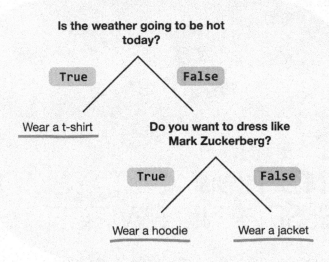

FIGURE 4.1

Modeling decisions

At each stage of making a decision, you ask yourself a question that can be answered as **true** or **false**. The answer to that question determines your next step and ultimately whether you wear a t-shirt, hoodie, or jacket. Going broader, every decision you and I make can be modeled as a series of **true** and **false** statements. This may sound a bit chilly (ha!), but that's generally how we, others, and pretty much all living things go about making choices.

This generalization especially applies to everything our computer does. This may not be evident from the code we've written so far, but we are going to fix that. In this tutorial, we will cover what are known as **conditional statements**. These are the digital equivalent of the decisions we make, where our code does something different depending on whether something is **true** or **false**.

The If/Else Statement

The most common conditional statement we will use in our code is the **if/else statement**, or just the **if statement**. The way this statement works is shown in Figure 4.2.

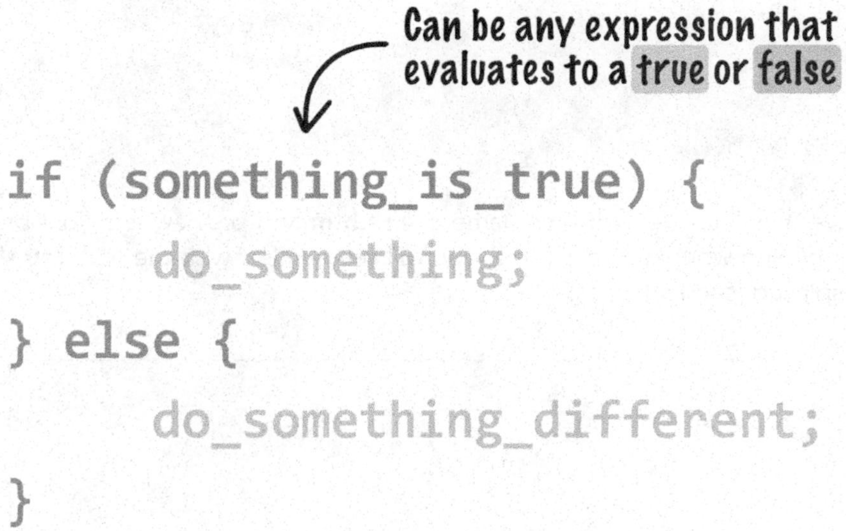

Can be any expression that
evaluates to a true or false

```
if (something_is_true) {
    do_something;
} else {
    do_something_different;
}
```

FIGURE 4.2

How the `if` statement works

To make sense of this, let's take a look at a simple example of an `if`/`else` statement in action. Create a new HTML document and add the following markup and code to it:

```
<!DOCTYPE html>
<html>

<head>
  <meta charset="utf-8">
  <title>If / Else Statements</title>
</head>

<body>
  <script>
    let safeToProceed = true;

    if (safeToProceed) {
      alert("You shall pass!");
    } else {
      alert("You shall not pass!");
    }
```

```
    </script>
  </body>

  </html>
```

Save this document with the name **if_else.htm** and preview it in your browser. If everything worked as expected, you will see an alert with the text **You shall pass!** displayed (see Figure 4.3).

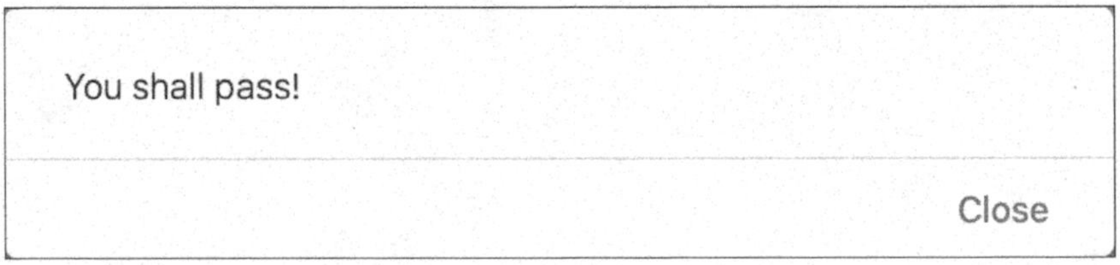

You shall pass!

Close

FIGURE 4.3

You will see this alert.

Here's the code from our example that's responsible for making this work:

```
let safeToProceed = true;

if (safeToProceed) {
  alert("You shall pass!");
} else {
  alert("You shall not pass!");
}
```

Our **expression** (the thing following the keyword `if` that ultimately evaluates to **true** or **false**) is the variable `safeToProceed`. This variable is initialized to **true**, so the *true* part of our `if` statement kicked in.

Now, go ahead and change the value of the `safeToProceed` variable from **true** to **false**:

```
let safeToProceed = false;

if (safeToProceed) {
  alert("You shall pass!");
```

```
} else {
    alert("You shall not pass!");
}
```

This time when you run this code, you will see an alert with the text **You shall not pass!** because our expression now evaluates to **false** (see Figure 4.4).

You shall not pass!

Close

FIGURE 4.4

*The alert you get when the expression evaluates as **false***

So far, all of this probably seems really boring. A large part of the reason for this is because we haven't turned up the complexity knob to focus on more realistic scenarios. We'll tackle that next by taking a deeper look at conditions.

Meet the Conditional Operators

In most cases, our expression will rarely be a simple variable that is set to **true** or **false** like it is in our earlier example. Our expression will involve what are known as **conditional operators**, which help us to compare between two or more expressions to establish a **true** or **false** outcome.

The general format of such an expression is shown in Figure 4.5.

```
if (expression operator expression) {
        do_something;
} else {
        do_something_different;
}
```

FIGURE 4.5

General format of a conditional operator expression

The **operator** (aka a **conditional operator**) defines a relationship between two expressions. The end goal is to return a **true** or a **false** so that our `if` statement knows which block of code to execute. The key to making all this work is the conditional operators themselves. They are shown in Table 4.1.

TABLE 4.1   Operators

Operator	When It Is True
==	If the first expression evaluates to something that is equal to the second expression
>=	If the first expression evaluates to something that is greater than or equal to the second expression
>	If the first expression evaluates to something that is greater than the second expression
<=	If the first expression evaluates to something that is less than or equal to the second expression
<	If the first expression evaluates to something that is less than the second expression
!=	If the first expression evaluates to something that is not equal to the second expression
&&	If the first expression and the second expression both evaluate to **true**
||	If either the first expression or the second expression evaluate to **true**

Let's take our general understanding of conditional operators and make it more specific by looking at another example, such as the following, with our relevant `if`-related code highlighted:

```
<!DOCTYPE html>
<html>

<head>
  <meta charset="utf-8">
  <title>Are you speeding?</title>
</head>

<body>
  <script>
    let speedLimit = 55;
```

```
    function amISpeeding(speed) {
      if (speed >= speedLimit) {
        alert("Yes. You are speeding.");
      } else {
        alert("No. You are not speeding. What's wrong with you?");
      }
    }


    amISpeeding(53);
    amISpeeding(72);
  </script>
</body>

</html>
```

Let's take a moment to understand what exactly is going on. We have a variable called speedLimit that is initialized to **55**. We then have a function called amISpeeding that takes an argument named speed. Inside this function, we have an if statement whose expression checks if the passed-in speed value is greater than or equal to (hello >= conditional operator!) the value stored by the speedLimit variable:

```
function amISpeeding(speed) {
  if (speed >= speedLimit) {
    alert("Yes. You are speeding.");
  } else {
    alert("No. You are not speeding. What's wrong with you?");
  }
}
```

The last thing our code does is actually call the amISpeeding function by passing in a few values for speed:

```
amISpeeding(53);
amISpeeding(72);
```

When we call this function with a speed of **53**, the speed >= speedLimit expression evaluates to **false**. The reason is that **53** is not greater than or equal to the stored value of `speedLimit`, which is **55**. This will result in an alert showing that you aren't speeding.

The opposite happens when we call `amISpeeding` with a speed of **72**. In this case, we are speeding and the condition evaluates to **true**. An alert telling us that we are speeding will also appear.

Creating More Complex Expressions

The thing we need to know about these expressions is that they can be as simple or as complex as we can make them. They can be made up of variables, function calls, or raw values. They can even be made up of combinations of variables, function calls, or raw values, all separated using any of the operators from Table 4.1. The only thing we need to ensure is that our expression ultimately evaluates to **true** or **false**.

Here is a slightly more involved example:

```
let xPos = 300;
let yPos = 150;

function sendWarning(x, y) {
  if ((x < xPos) && (y < yPos)) {
    alert("Adjust the position");
  } else {
    alert("Things are fine!");
  }
}

sendWarning(500, 160);
sendWarning(100, 100);
sendWarning(201, 149);
```

Notice what our condition inside `sendWarning`'s `if` statement looks like:

```
function sendWarning(x, y) {
        if ((x < xPos) && (y < yPos)) {
                alert("Adjust the position");
        } else {
                alert("Things are fine!");
```

```
        }
    }
```

There are three comparisons being made here. The first one is whether x is less than xPos. The second one is whether y is less than yPos. The third comparison is seeing if the **first statement and the second statement** both evaluate to **true** to allow the && operator to return a **true** as well. We can chain together many series of conditional statements, depending on what we are doing. The tricky thing, besides learning what all the operators do, is to ensure that each condition and sub-condition is properly insulated using parentheses.

All of what I am describing here and in the previous section falls under the umbrella of **Boolean logic**. If you are not familiar with this topic, I recommend you glance through the excellent QuirksMode article on this exact topic: **https://www.quirksmode.org/js/boolean.html**.

Variations on the If/Else Statement

We are almost done with the if statement. The last things we are going to look at are some of its relatives.

The if-only Statement

The first one is the solo if statement that doesn't have its else companion:

```
if (weight > 5000) {
    alert("No free shipping for you!");
}
```

In this case, if the expression evaluates to **true**, then great. If the expression evaluates to **false**, our code just skips over the alert and moves on to wherever it needs to go next. The else block is completely optional when working with if statements. To contrast with the if-only statement, we have the next relative.

The Dreaded If/Else-If/Else Statement

Not everything can be neatly bucketed into a single if or if/else statement. For those kinds of situations, we can chain if statements together by using the else if keyword. Instead of explaining this further, let's just look at an example:

```
if (position < 100) {
    alert("Do something!");
```

```
} else if ((position >= 200) && (position < 300)) {
  alert("Do something else!");
} else {
  alert("Do something even more different!");
}
```

If the first `if` statement evaluates to **true**, our code branches into the first alert. If the first `if` statement is **false**, our code evaluates the `else if` statement to see if the expressions in it evaluate to a **true** or **false**. This repeats until our code reaches the end. In other words, our code simply navigates down through each `if` and `else if` statement until one of the expressions evaluates to **true**.

```
if (condition) {
  ...
} else if (condition) {
  ...
} else if (condition) {
  ...
} else if (condition) {
  ...
} else if (condition) {
  ...
} else if (condition) {
  ...
} else {
  ...
}
```

If none of the statements have an expression that evaluates to **true**, the code inside the `else` block (if it exists) executes. If there is no `else` block, the code will just go on to the next set of code that lives beyond all these `if` statements. Between the more complex expressions and `if/else if` statements, you can represent pretty much any decision that your code might need to evaluate.

Phew! You have now learned all there is to know about the `if` statement. It's time to move on to a whole different species of conditional statement—the `switch` statement.

Switch Statements

In a world filled with beautiful `if`, `else`, and `else if` statements, the need for yet another way of dealing with conditionals may seem unnecessary. However, people who wrote code on room-sized machines and probably hiked uphill in the snow (with wolves chasing them) disagreed, so we have what are known as `switch` statements. What are they? We are going to find out!

Using a Switch Statement

Let's cut to the chase and look at the code first. The basic structure of a `switch` statement is as follows:

```
switch (expression) {
  case value1:
    statement;
    break;
  case value2:
    statement;
    break;
  case value3:
    statement;
    break;
  default:
    statement;
    break;
}
```

The thing to never forget is that a `switch` statement is nothing more than a conditional statement that tests whether *something* is true or false. That *something* is a variation of whether the **result of evaluating the `expression` equals a case value**. Let's make this explanation actually make sense by looking at a better example:

```
let color = "green";

switch (color) {
  case "yellow":
```

```
      alert("yellow color");
      break;
   case "red":
      alert("red color");
      break;
   case "blue":
      alert("blue color");
      break;
   case "green":
      alert("green color");
      break;
   case "black":
      alert("black color");
      break;
   default:
      alert("no known color specified");
      break;
}
```

In this simple example, we have a variable called `color` whose value is set to **green**:

```
let color = "green";
```

The `color` variable is also what we specify as our expression to the `switch` statement:

```
switch (color) {
   case "yellow":
      alert("yellow color");
      break;
   case "red":
      alert("red color");
      break;
   case "blue":
      alert("blue color");
      break;
```

```
    case "green":
      alert("green color");
      break;
    case "black":
      alert("black color");
      break;
    default:
      alert("no known color specified");
      break;
}
```

Our `switch` statement contains a collection of `case` blocks. Only one of these blocks will get hit, with its code getting executed. The way this chosen one gets picked is by matching a block's `case` value with the result of evaluating the expression. In our case, because our expression evaluates to a value of **green**, the code inside the `case` block whose `case` value is also **green** gets executed:

```
switch (color) {
  case "yellow":
    alert("yellow color");
    break;
  case "red":
    alert("red color");
    break;
  case "blue":
    alert("blue color");
    break;
  case "green":
    alert("green color");
    break;
  case "black":
    alert("black color");
    break;
  default:
    alert("no known color specified");
    break;
}
```

Note that **only** the code inside the **green** case block gets executed. That is thanks to the break keyword that ends that block. When our code hits the break, it exits the entire switch block and continues executing the code that lies below it. If you did not specify the break keyword, you will still execute the code inside the **green** case block. The difference is that you will then move to the next case block (the **black** one, in our example) and execute any code that is there. Unless you hit another break keyword, your code will just move through every single case block until it reaches the end.

With all of this said, if you were to run this code, you would see an alert window that looks like Figure 4.6.

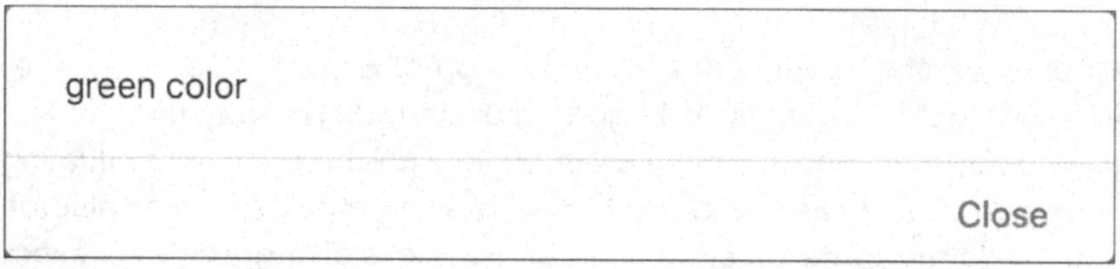

green color

Close

FIGURE 4.6

Alert window

You can alter the value for the color variable to another valid value to see the other case blocks execute. Sometimes, no case block's value will match the result of evaluating an expression. In those cases, your switch statement will just do nothing. If you wish to specify a default behavior, add a default block, like so:

```
switch (color) {
  case "yellow":
    alert("yellow color");
    break;
  case "red":
    alert("red color");
    break;
  case "blue":
    alert("blue color");
    break;
  case "green":
    alert("green color");
    break;
  case "black":
```

```
    alert("black color");
    break;
  default:
    alert("no known color specified");
    break;
}
```

Note that the `default` block looks a bit different from your other `case` statements. It actually doesn't contain the word **case**.

Similarity to an If/Else Statement

Earlier, we saw that a `switch` statement is used for evaluating conditions—just like the `if/else` statement we spent a bulk of our time on in this chapter. Given that this is a major accusation, let's explore this in further detail by first looking at how an `if` statement would look if it were to be literally translated into a `switch` statement.

Let's say we have an `if` statement that looks like the following:

```
let number = 20;

if (number > 10) {
  alert("yes");
} else {
  alert("nope");
}
```

Because the value of our number variable is **20**, our `if` statement will evaluate to **true**. Seems pretty straightforward. Now, let's turn this into a `switch` statement:

```
switch (number > 10) {
  case true:
    alert("yes");
    break;
  case false:
    alert("nope");
    break;
}
```

Notice that our expression is **number > 10**. The `case` value for the `case` blocks is set to **true** or **false**. Because **number > 10** evaluates to **true**, the code inside the **true** `case` block gets executed. While our expression in this case wasn't as simple as reading a color value stored in a variable like in the previous section, our view of how `switch` statements work still hasn't changed. Our expressions can be as complex as we would like. If they evaluate to something that can be matched inside a `case` value, then everything is golden...like a fleece!

Now, let's look at a slightly more involved example. This time, we will convert our earlier `switch` statement involving colors into equivalent `if/else` statements. Here's the `switch` statement we used earlier:

```
let color = "green";

switch (color) {
  case "yellow":
    alert("yellow color");
    break;
  case "red":
    alert("red color");
    break;
  case "blue":
    alert("blue color");
    break;
  case "green":
    alert("green color");
    break;
  case "black":
    alert("black color");
    break;
  default:
    alert("no color specified");
    break;
}
```

This `switch` statement converted into a series of `if/else` statements would look like this:

```
let color = "green";

if (color == "yellow") {
  alert("yellow color");
} else if (color == "red") {
  alert("red color");
} else if (color == "blue") {
  alert("blue color");
} else if (color == "green") {
  alert("green color");
} else if (color == "black") {
  alert("black color");
} else {
  alert("no color specified";
}
```

As we can see, `if/else` statements are very similar to `switch` statements, and vice versa. The `default` block becomes an `else` block. The relationship between the expression and the `case` value in a `switch` statement is combined into `if/else` conditions in an `if/else` statement.

Deciding Which to Use

In the previous section, we saw how interchangeable `switch` statements and `if/else` statements are. When we have two ways of doing something very similar, it is only natural to want to know when it is appropriate to use one over the other. In a nutshell, use whichever one you prefer. There are many arguments on the web about when to use `switch` versus an `if/else`, and the one thing is that they are all inconclusive.

My personal preference is to go with whatever is more readable. If you look at the comparisons earlier between `switch` and `if/else` statements, you'll notice that if you have a lot of conditions, the `switch` statement tends to look a bit cleaner. It is certainly less verbose and a bit more readable. What your cutoff mark is for deciding when to switch (ha!) between using a `switch` statement and an `if/else` statement is entirely up to you. I tend to draw the line at around four or five conditions.

Next, a `switch` statement works best when you are evaluating an expression and matching the result to a value. If you are doing something more complex involving weird conditions, value checking, and so on, you probably want to use something different. That could involve something even more different than an `if/else` statement, by the way! We will touch on those *different somethings* later.

To wrap all this up, the earlier guidance still stands: use whatever you like. If you are part of a team with coding guidelines, follow them instead. Whatever you do, just be consistent. It makes your life—as well as the life of anybody else who will be working with your code—a little bit easier. For what it's worth, I've personally never been in a situation where I had to use a `switch` statement. Your mileage may vary.

THE ABSOLUTE MINIMUM

While creating true artificial intelligence goes beyond the scope of this book, you *can* write code to help your application make choices. This code will almost always take the form of an `if/else` statement where you provide the browser with a set of choices it needs to make:

```
let loginStatus = false;


if (name == "Admin") {
  loginStatus = true;
}
```

These choices are fed by conditions that need to evaluate to **true** or **false**.

In this chapter, we learned the mechanics of how to work with `if/else` statements and their (sort of) related cousin, the `switch` statement. In future chapters, you'll see that we'll use these statements very casually, as if we've known them for years, so you'll be very familiar with how to write these statements by the time you reach the end of this book.

? Ask a question: **https://forum.kirupa.com**

✔ Practice by building real apps: **https://bit.ly/coding_exercises**

✊ Errors/known issues: **https://bit.ly/javascript_errata**

LOOPING WITH FOR, WHILE, AND DO...WHILE!

When we are coding something, there will be times when we want to repeat an action or run some code multiple times. For example, let's say we have a function called saySomething that we want to repeatedly call 10 times.

One way we could do this is by simply calling the function 10 times using copy and paste:

```
saySomething();
saySomething();
saySomething();
saySomething();
saySomething();
saySomething();
saySomething();
saySomething();
saySomething();
saySomething();
```

This works and accomplishes what we set out to do, but...we shouldn't do something like this. After all, duplicating code is never a good idea. If we had a nickel for every time you read that so far in this book, we'd have about four or five nickels (**#killing_it**).

Now, even if we do decide to duplicate some code a few times manually, this approach doesn't really work in practice. The number of times we will need to duplicate our code will vary based on some external factors, such as the number of items in a collection of data, some result from some web service, the number of letters in a word, and various other things that will keep changing. It won't always be a fixed number like 10. Often, the number of times we want to repeat some code could be very, VERY large. We don't want to copy and paste something a few hundred or thousand times in order to repeat it. That would be terrible.

What we need is a generic solution for repeating code with control over how many times the code repeats. In JavaScript, this solution is provided in the form of something known as a **loop**. There are three kinds of loops we can use to repeat some code:

- `for` loops
- `while` loops
- `do...while` loops

Each of these three loop variations allows us to specify the code we want to repeat (or loop) and a way to stop the repetition when a condition is met. In the following sections, you'll learn all about them.

NOTE Something Beyond alert!

We've been using the `alert` function these past few chapters to get our code to display something onscreen. In this chapter, we're going to look at one more way of displaying something on the screen that is a bit less intrusive. We're going to be using the `document.write` function:

```
document.write("Show this on screen!");
```

This function will print the text you provide to the page displayed in your browser without displaying a dialog that requires you to dismiss it every time it appears. You'll see why we want something that is more lightweight when you learn more about loops and how we may want to print many things to the screen.

The for Loop

One of the most common ways to create a loop is by using the `for` statement to create what's known as a **for loop**. A `for` loop allows us to repeatedly run some code until an expression we specify returns **false**. To help clarify this definition, let's look at an example.

If we had to translate our earlier `saySomething` example using `for`, it would look like this:

```
for (let i = 0; i < 10; i++) {
  saySomething();
}

function saySomething() {
  document.writeln("hello!");
}
```

If you want to follow along more actively and see this code for yourself, enter the following code inside some `<script>` tags in an HTML document:

```
<!DOCTYPE html>
<html>

<head>
  <meta charset="utf-8">
  <title>Loops!</title>
```

```
    <style>

    </style>
</head>

<body>
  <script>
    for (let i = 0; i < 10; i++) {
      saySomething();
    }

    function saySomething() {
      document.writeln("hello!");
    }
  </script>
</body>

</html>
```

Once your document is ready, save it and then preview it in your browser. After the page has loaded, what you would see is shown in Figure 5.1.

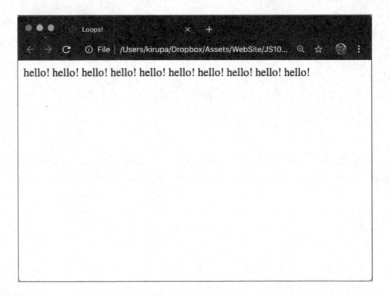

FIGURE 5.1

hello! is repeated across the page.

The word **hello!** will be repeated 10 times across your page. This is made possible thanks to the `for` loop, so we are going to thank it back by learning all about how it works. First, here is our star:

```
for (let i = 0; i < 10; i++) {
    saySomething();
}
```

This is a `for` loop. It probably looks very different from other statements you've seen so far, and that's because...well, it is very different. To understand the differences, let's generalize a `for` loop into the form shown in Figure 5.2.

```
for (start_point; condition; step) {

    // code to execute

}
```

FIGURE 5.2

A general, high-level `for` loop

This high-level view corresponds to the actual values from our example (see Figure 5.3).

```
for (let i = 0; i < 10; i++) {

    // code to execute

}
```

FIGURE 5.3

The actual values

These three differently colored regions each play a very important role in how your loop functions. In order to use a `for` loop well, we must know what each region accomplishes, so we will spend the next few minutes diving deeper into each section.

The Starting Point

In the first region, we define the **starting point** for our loop. A common thing to put here is some code to declare, and then we initialize a variable, similar to what we did in Figure 5.4.

```
for (let i = 0; i < 10; i++) {

    // code to execute

}
```

FIGURE 5.4

Declaring and initializing a variable

What we are telling JavaScript is to start our loop with the variable `i` initialized to **0**.

The Step

We are going to skip ahead to the **step** region next (see Figure 5.5).

In this stage, we specify how our starting point will evolve. For our example, what we are saying is that each time our loop runs, the value of `i` will be increased by 1. That is captured by the cryptic looking `i++`. We'll cover what the `++` means later when we look at how numbers and math in JavaScript work, but another way of representing this would be to say `i = i + 1`.

```
for (let i = 0; i < 10; i++) {

    // code to execute

}
```

FIGURE 5.5

The step

The Condition (aka How Long to Keep Looping)

Going back to the stage we skipped, we have the **condition** part of our loop, which determines when the loop will stop running (see Figure 5.6).

```
for (let i = 0; i < 10; i++) {

    // code to execute

}
```

FIGURE 5.6

The condition part of the loop

In our example, the condition is that our i variable is less than the value of **10**:

- If our i variable is less than 10, this expression evaluates to **true** and our loop **continues to run**.

- If our i variable becomes equal to or greater than 10, the condition is **false**, and our loop **terminates**.

Putting It All Together

Okay, now that we have looked at each part of our `for` loop in greater detail, let's use our newly gained knowledge to run through it all at once to see what is going on. Our full example, repeated from earlier, is as follows:

```
for (let i = 0; i < 10; i++) {
    saySomething();
}


function saySomething() {
    document.writeln("hello!");
}
```

When our `for` loop is initially hit at the starting point, the `i` variable is created and initialized to **0**. Next, we go to the condition part of the loop, which determines whether or not our loop should keep running. The condition checks whether the value of `i` is less than 10. Is 0 less than 10? Yes it is, so this condition evaluates to **true** and the code contained inside the loop runs. Once this is done, the step part of our loop kicks in. In this stage, the `i` variable is incremented by 1 to have a value of **1**. At this point, our loop has run through one cycle, commonly referred to as an **iteration**. Time to start the next iteration.

For the next iteration, the loop starts all over again, except the variable `i` isn't reinitialized. Its value is **1** from the previous iteration, so that carries over. For the condition, we recheck whether the new value is less than 10, which it is. The code inside our loop (basically the `saySomething` function) and the step part of the loop where `i` increments by 1 then happen. The value of `i` is then incremented by 1 to a value of **2**, and this iteration is done for the day, leaving the door open for the next iteration!

This process repeats iteration after iteration until the condition `i < 10` evaluates to **false**. Because the loop started with `i` being 0 and it is set to terminate when the value of `i` is less than 10, and because `i` increments by 1 in each iteration, this loop (and any code contained in it) will run 10 times before stopping. Phew!

Some for Loop Examples

In the previous section, we dissected a simple `for` loop and labeled all its inner workings. The thing about `for` loops and most everything in JavaScript is that a simple example doesn't always cover everything we might need. The best solution is to look at some more examples of `for` loops, and that's what we are going to be doing in the next few sections.

Breaking a Loop

Sometimes, we may want to end our loop before it reaches completion. The way we end a loop is by using the `break` keyword. Here is an example:

```
for (let i = 0; i < 100; i++) {
  document.writeln(i);

  if (i == 45) {
    break;
  }
}
```

When the value of `i` equals **45**, the `break` keyword stops the loop from continuing further. Although this example is a bit contrived, when we do run into a real-world case for ending our loop, we'll now know what to do.

Skipping an Iteration

There will be moments when we want our loop to skip its current iteration and move on to the next one. That is cleverly handled by the `continue` keyword:

```
let floors = 28;

for (let i = 1; i <= floors; i++) {
  if (i == 13) {
    // no floor here
    continue;
  }

  document.writeln("At floor: " + i + "<br>");
}
```

Unlike `break`, where our loop just stops and goes home, `continue` tells our loop to stop and move on to the next iteration. We will often find ourselves using `continue` when handling errors where we just want the loop to move on to the next item.

Going Backwards

There is no reason why our starting point *has* to have a variable initialized to 0 and then increment that variable upward:

```
for (let i = 25; i > 0; i--) {
    document.writeln("hello");
}
```

You can just as easily start high and then decrement until your loop condition returns **false**.

You may have heard that doing something like this increases your loop's performance. The jury is still out on whether **decrementing** is actually faster than incrementing, but feel free to experiment and see if you notice any performance benefits.

You Don't Have to Use Numbers

When filling out your `for` loop, you don't have to only use numbers:

```
for (let i = "a"; i != "aaaaaaaa"; i += "a") {
    document.writeln("hmm...");
}
```

You can use anything you want as long as your loop will eventually hit a point where it can end. Notice that in this example we are using the letter **a** as our currency for running this loop. At each iteration, the value of `i` is incremented with the letter **a**, and the loop stops when `i` equals **aaaaaaaa**.

Oh No He Didn't!

Oh yes! Yes, I did. I went there, took a picture, posted it on Facebook, and came back:

```
let i = 0;
let yay = true;

for (; yay;) {
  if (i == 10) {
    yay = false;
  } else {
    i++;
    document.writeln("weird");
  }
}
```

You don't have to fill out the three sections of your `for` loop in order to make it work. As long as, in the end, you manage to satisfy the loop's terminating condition, you can do whatever you want, just like the preceding example shows.

The Other Loops

Living in the shadow of the beloved `for` loop are the `while` and `do...while` loop variants. In the interest of completeness, let's quickly look at both of them.

The while Loop

The `while` loop repeats some code until its condition (another expression) returns **false**. Take a look at the following example:

```
let count = 0;

while (count < 10) {
  document.writeln("looping away!");

  count++;
}
```

In this example, the condition is represented by the count < 10 expression. With each iteration, our loop increments the count value by **1**:

```
let count = 0;

while (count < 10) {
  document.writeln("looping away!");

  count++;
}
```

Once the value of count becomes **10**, the loop stops because the count < 10 expression will return **false**. If you look at everything the while loop does, it does look like a great imitation of the for loop. Whereas the for loop formally requires you to define the starting, condition, and step stages, the while loop expects you to define those stages yourself in your own way.

The do...while Loop

Now, we get to the Meg Griffin of the loop variants. That would be the do... while loop, whose purpose is even less defined than while. Whereas the while loop had its conditional expression first before the loop would execute, the do... while loop has its conditional expression at the end.

Here is an example:

```
let count = 0;

do {
    document.writeln("I don't know what I am doing here! <br>");

    count++;
} while (count < 10);
```

The main difference between a `while` loop and a `do...while` loop is that the contents of a `while` loop could never get executed if its conditional expression is **false** from the very beginning:

```
while (false) {
  document.writeln("Can't touch this!");
}
```

With a `do...while` loop, because the conditional expression is evaluated only after one iteration, your loop's contents are guaranteed to run at least once:

```
do {
  document.writeln("This code will run once!");
} while (false);
```

That can come in handy in some situations. Now, before we wrap things up, there is just one last bit of information I need to tell you before we move on. The `break` and `continue` statements we saw earlier as part of the awesome `for` loop work similarly when used inside the `while` and `do...while` loop variants.

THE ABSOLUTE MINIMUM

So, there you have it—a look at `for` loops and how we can use them, along with very basic coverage of the `while` and `do...while` loops. Right now, we may not see ourselves using loops a whole lot. As we start getting into more involved situations involving collections of data, elements in your Document Object Model (DOM), text manipulation, and other stuff, we'll be using loops a whole lot more. Basically, keep all the information you've seen here really close by!

Additional resources:

? Ask a question: **https://forum.kirupa.com**

✔ Practice by building real apps: **https://bit.ly/coding_exercises**

🦖 Errors/known issues: **https://bit.ly/javascript_errata**

6

COMMENTING YOUR CODE...FTW!

Everything we write in our code editor might *seem* like it is intended for our browser's eyes only:

```javascript
let xPos = -500;

function boringComputerStuff() {
  xPos += 5;

  if (xPos > 1000) {
    xPos = 500;
  }
}
boringComputerStuff();
```

As we will soon find out, that isn't the case. There is another audience for our code, and that audience is made up of human beings.

Our code is often used or scrutinized by other people. This is especially true if you and I are working on a team with other JavaScript developers. We'll often be looking at their code, and they'll often be looking at our code. To make all this code look as efficient as possible, we need to ensure our code makes sense when someone other than us is looking at it. Even if you are working solo, this applies to you as well. That brilliant function that makes sense to you today might be gibberish when you look at it next week.

There are many ways of solving this problem. One of the best ways is by using something known as **comments**. In this short chapter, you will learn what comments are, how to specify them in JavaScript, and some good practices on how to use them.

What Are Comments?

Comments are the things we write as part of our code to communicate something to other humans:

```
// This is for not inviting me to your birthday party!
let blah = true;


function sweetRevenge() {
  while (blah) {
    // Infinite dialog boxes! HAHAHA!!!!
    alert("Hahahaha!");
  }
}
sweetRevenge();
```

In this example, the comments are marked by the // characters, and they provide some questionably useful information about the code being described.

The thing to keep in mind about comments is that they don't run and get executed like all the other code you write. **JavaScript ignores your comments**. It doesn't like you. It doesn't care what you have to say, so you don't have to worry about proper syntax, punctuation, spelling, and everything else you need to keep in mind when writing normal code. Comments exist only for us to help understand what a piece of code is doing.

There is one other purpose comments serve. We can use comments to mark lines of code that we don't want executed:

```
function insecureLogin(input) {
  if (input == "password") {
    // let key = Math.random() * 100000;
    // processLogin(key);
  }
  return false;
}
```

In this example, the following two lines can be seen in our code editor, but they won't run:

```
// let key = Math.random() * 100000;
// processLogin(key);
```

We'll often find ourselves using the code editor as a scratchpad, and comments are a great way to keep track of things we've tried in making our code work without affecting how your application ultimately runs.

Single-Line Comments

There are several ways to specify comments in our code. One way is by specifying **single-line comments** using the // characters followed by what we want to communicate. This is the comment variation we've seen several times already.

We can specify these comments in their own dedicated line:

```
// Return the larger of the two arguments
function max(a, b) {
  if (a > b) {
    return a;
  } else {
    return b;
  }
}
```

We can also specify these comments on the same line as a statement:

```
let zorb = "Alien"; // Annoy the planetary citizens
```

Where you specify comments is entirely up to you. Choose a location that seems appropriate for the comment you are writing.

Since I enjoy sounding like a broken record, I'll point this out one more time: our comments don't run as part of our application. Only you, me, and possibly Dupree can see them. If that last line made no sense, what you are telling me is that you did not see one of the greatest comedies of our generation. I highly encourage you to put this book down and take a few hours to rectify that.

Multiline Comments

The problem with single-line comments is that we have to specify the // characters in front of every single line we want to comment. That can get really tiring—especially if we are writing a long comment or commenting out a large chunk of code.

For those situations, we have another way of specifying comments. We have the /* and */ characters to specify the beginning and ending of what are known as **multiline comments**:

```
/*
let mouseX = 0;
let mouseY = 0;


canvas.addEventListener("mousemove", setMousePosition, false);

function setMousePosition(e) {
  mouseX = e.clientX;
  mouseY = e.clientY;
}
*/
```

Instead of adding // characters in front of each line like an animal, we can use the /* and */ characters to save us a lot of time and frustration.

In most applications, we'll use a combination of single-line and multiline comments, depending on what we are trying to document. This means we need to be familiar with both of these commenting approaches.

TIP JSDoc-Style Comments

When we are writing some code that we want used by others, we probably want an *easier way* to communicate what our code does beyond having people rummage through source code. That *easier way* exists, and it is made possible by a tool known as **JSDoc!** With JSDoc, we slightly modify how we write our comments:

```
/**
 * Shuffles the contents of your Array.
 *
 * @this {Array}
 * @returns {Array} The current array with the
contents fully shuffled.
 */
Array.prototype.shuffle = function () {
  let input = this;

  for (let i = input.length - 1; i >= 0; i--) {

    let randomIndex = Math.floor(Math.random() *
(i + 1));
    let itemAtIndex = input[randomIndex];

    input[randomIndex] = input[i];
    input[i] = itemAtIndex;
  }
  return input;
}
```

Once we have commented our files, we can use the JSDoc tool to export the relevant parts of our comments into an easily browsable set of HTML pages. This allows us to spend more time writing JavaScript while giving our users an easy way to understand what our code does and how to use various parts of it.

If you want to learn more on how to use JSDoc, check out the awesome "Getting Started" page at **https://jsdoc.app/about-getting-started.html** for more details.

Commenting Best Practices

Now that we have a good idea of what comments are and the several ways we can write them in JavaScript, let's talk a bit about how to properly use comments to help make our code easy to read:

- **Always comment code as you are writing it.** Writing comments is dreadfully boring, but it is an important part of writing code. It is much more time efficient for us (and others) to understand what our code does from reading a comment as opposed to deciphering line after line of JavaScript.

- **Don't defer comment writing for later.** Deferring comment writing for a later time is the grown-up equivalent of procrastinating on a chore. If we don't comment our code as we are writing it, we'll probably just skip commenting entirely. That's not a good thing.

- **Use more English and less JavaScript.** Comments are one of the few places when writing JavaScript where we can freely use English (or whatever language you prefer communicating in). Don't complicate the comments unnecessarily with code. Be clear. Be concise. Use words.

- **Embrace whitespace.** When scanning large blocks of code, we want to ensure our comments stand out and are clear to follow. That involves being liberal with the spacebar and Enter/Return key. Take a look at the following example:

```javascript
function selectInitialState(state) {
  let selectContent = document.querySelector("#stateList");
  let stateIndex = null;

  /*
      For the returned state, we would like to ensure that
      we select it in our UI. This means we iterate through
      every state in the drop-down until we find a match.
      When a match is found, we ensure it gets selected.
  */

  for (let i = 0; i < selectContent.length; i++) {

    let stateInSelect = selectContent.options[i].innerText;

    if (stateInSelect == state) {
      stateIndex = i;
    }
```

```
    }

    selectContent.selectedIndex = stateIndex;
}
```

Notice that the comment is appropriately spaced to distinguish it from the rest of the code. If your comments are strewn about in arbitrary locations where they are difficult to identify, that just unnecessarily slows you and whoever is reading your code down.

- **Don't comment obvious things.** If a line of code is self-explanatory, we shouldn't waste time explaining what it does unless there is some subtle behavior we need to call out as a warning. Instead, we should invest that time in commenting the less obvious parts of our code.

The best practices we see here will take us far in ensuring we write properly commented code. If you are working on a larger project with other people, I can assure you that your team already has some established guidelines on what proper commenting looks like. Take some time to understand those guidelines and follow them. You'll be happy. Your team will be happy.

THE ABSOLUTE MINIMUM

Comments are often viewed as a necessary evil. After all, would you rather take a few minutes documenting what *you* clearly already know, or would you rather implement the next cool piece of functionality? The way I like to describe writing comments is as follows: *It is a long-term investment.* The value and benefit of comments is often not immediately obvious. It becomes obvious when you start having other people looking over your code, and it becomes obvious when you have to revisit your own code after you've forgotten all about it and how it works. Don't sacrifice long-term time-savings for a short-term kick. Invest in single-line (//) and multiline (/* and */) comments now, before it's too late.

? Ask a question: **https://forum.kirupa.com**

✔ Practice by building real apps: **https://bit.ly/coding_exercises**

📝 Errors/known issues: **https://bit.ly/javascript_errata**

7

IN THIS CHAPTER

- Learn how to delay when your code runs
- Figure out several ways to run your code repeatedly without blocking your entire app

TIMERS

By default, our code runs synchronously. That is a fancy of way of saying that when a statement needs to execute, it executes immediately. There are no *ifs*, *ands*, or *buts* about it. The concept of delaying execution or deferring work to later isn't a part of JavaScript's default behavior. We kind of saw this when looking at loops earlier. The loop runs at lightning speed with no delay between each iteration. That is great for making quick calculations, but that isn't great if we want to make an update at a more measured (that is, slower) pace.

All of this doesn't mean the ability to stop work from running instantaneously doesn't exist! If we swerve just slightly off the main road, there are three functions that allow us to mostly do just that, and more: `setTimeout`, `setInterval`, and `requestAnimationFrame`. In this chapter, we will look at what each of these functions do.

Delaying with setTimeout

The `setTimeout` function allows us to delay executing some code. The way we use it is quite nice. This function allows us to specify what code to execute and how many milliseconds to wait before the code we specified executes. Putting that into JavaScript, we use something like this:

```
let timeoutID = setTimeout(someFunction, delayInMilliseconds);
```

As an example, if we wanted to call a function called `showAlert` after 5 seconds, the `setTimeout` declaration would look as follows:

```
function showAlert() {
  alert("moo!");
}

let timeoutID = setTimeout(showAlert, 5000);
```

Cool, right? Now, let's talk about something less interesting that we need to cover for the sake of completeness. That something has to do with the `timeoutID` variable that is initialized to our `setTimeout` function. It isn't there by accident. If we ever wanted to access this `setTimeout` timer again, we need a way to reference it. By associating a variable with our `setTimeout` declaration, we can easily accomplish that.

Now, you may be wondering why we would ever want to reference a timer once we've created it. There aren't too many reasons. The only reason I can think of would be to cancel the timer. For `setTimeout`, that is conveniently accomplished using the `clearTimeout` function and passing the timeout ID as the argument:

```
clearTimeout(timeoutID);
```

If you are never planning on canceling your timer, you can just use `setTimeout` directly without having it be part of the variable initialization.

With the technicalities out of the way, let's talk about when we would commonly use it in the real world: **user interface (UI) development**. When we are doing something related to the UI, deferring some action to a later time is strangely too common. Here are some examples that I ran into just in the past month:

- A menu slides in, and after a few seconds of the user no longer playing with the menu, the menu slides away.

- A long-running operation is unable to complete, and a `setTimeout` function interrupts that operation to return control back to the user.

- My favorite usage is using the `setTimeout` function to **detect whether users are active or idle: https://bit.ly/detectActivity**

If you do a search for `setTimeout` on Google, you'll see many more real-world cases where `setTimeout` proves very useful.

Looping with setInterval

The next timer function we are going to look at is `setInterval`. The `setInterval` function is similar to `setTimeout` in that it also allows us to execute code after a specified amount of time. What makes it different is that it doesn't just execute the code once. It keeps on executing the code in a loop forever.

Here is how we would use the `setInterval` function:

```
let intervalID = setInterval(someFunction, delayInMilliseconds);
```

Except for the function name, the way we use `setInterval` is identical to `setTimeout`. The first argument specifies the inline code or function we would like to execute. The second argument specifies how long to wait before our code loops again. Optionally, you can also initialize the `setInterval` function to a variable to store an interval ID—an ID that you can later use to do exciting things like cancel the looping. Yay!

Okay! Now that we've gone through all that, here is an example of the code at work, looping a function called `drawText` with a delay of 2 seconds between each loop:

```
<!DOCTYPE html>
<html>


<head>
```

```
  <meta charset="utf-8">
  <title>Show me some text!</title>
</head>

<body>
  <script>
    let thingToPrint = "";

    function drawText() {
      thingToPrint += "#";
      document.writeln(thingToPrint);
    }

    setInterval(drawText, 2000);
  </script>
</body>

</html>
```

If we wish to cancel the looping, we can use the appropriately named
clearInterval function:

```
clearInterval(intervalID);
```

Its usage is similar to its clearTimeout equivalent. We pass in the ID of the
setInterval timer instance that we optionally retrieved while setting up our
setInterval in the first place.

For the longest time, setInterval was the primary function you had for creating
animations in JavaScript. To get 30 or 60 frames a second, for example, you would
do something like the following by playing with the delay time value:

```
// 1000 divided by 60 is the millisecond value for 60fps
setInterval(moveCircles, 1000 / 60);
```

To see setInterval in action in some other realistic examples, check
out the bottom of the "Creating a Sweet Content Slider" article (**http://bit.ly/**

sliderTutorial) as well as the "Creating an Analog Clock Using the Canvas" article (**https://bit.ly/analogClock2**). They both feature `setInterval` quite prominently!

Animating Smoothly with requestAnimationFrame

Now we get to one of my favorite functions ever: `requestAnimationFrame`. The `requestAnimationFrame` function is all about synchronizing our code with a browser repaint event. Here's what this means: Our browser is busy juggling a billion different things at any given time. These things include fiddling with layout, reacting to page scrolls, listening for mouse clicks, displaying the result of keyboard taps, executing JavaScript, loading resources, and more. At the same time our browser is doing all of this, it is also redrawing the screen at 60 frames per second...or at least trying its very best to.

When we have code that is intended to animate something to the screen, we want to ensure our animation code runs properly without getting lost in the shuffle of everything else our browser is doing. Using the `setInterval` technique mentioned earlier doesn't guarantee that frames won't get dropped when the browser is busy optimizing for other things. To avoid our animation code from being treated like any other generic JavaScript, we have the `requestAnimationFrame` function. This function gets special treatment by the browser. This special treatment allows it to time its execution perfectly to avoid dropped frames, avoid unnecessary work, and generally steer clear of other side effects that plague other looping solutions.

The way we use this function starts off a bit similar to `setTimeout` and `setInterval`:

```
let requestID = requestAnimationFrame(someFunction);
```

The only real difference is that we don't specify a duration value. The duration is automatically calculated based on the current frame rate, whether the current tab is active or not, whether the device is running on battery or not, and a whole host of other factors that go beyond what we can control or understand.

Anyway, this usage of the `requestAnimationFrame` function is merely the textbook version. In real life, we'll rarely make a single call to `requestAnimationFrame` like this. Key to all animations created in JavaScript is an animation loop, and it is this loop that we want to throw `requestAnimationFrame` at. The result of that throw looks something like the following:

```
function animationLoop() {
  // animation-related code
```

```
    requestAnimationFrame(animationLoop)
}


// start off our animation loop!
animationLoop();
```

Notice that our `requestAnimationFrame` specifies that the `animationLoop` function gets called the next time the browser decides to repaint. It looks like the `requestAnimationFrame` function calls `animationLoop` directly, which isn't the case. That isn't a bug in the code. While this kind of circular referencing would almost guarantee a frozen/hung browser, `requestAnimationFrame`'s implementation avoids that. Instead, it ensures the `animationLoop` function is called just the right amount of times needed to ensure things get drawn to the screen to create smooth and fluid animations. It does so without freezing up the rest of your application functionality.

THE ABSOLUTE MINIMUM

If you think that timers fall under a more niche category compared to some of the other more essential things like the `if/else` statements and loops we looked at earlier, you would probably be right in thinking that. You can build many awesome apps without ever having to rely on `setTimeout`, `setInterval`, or `requestAnimationFrame`. That doesn't mean it isn't essential to know about them, though. There will be a time when you'll need to delay when your code executes, loop your code continuously, or create a sweet animation using JavaScript. When that time arrives, you'll be prepared...or at least know what to google for.

I've mentioned this a bunch of times so far, but JavaScript can be frustrating. Timers doubly so. If you ever run into any issues, I and other developers who have battled timers for a long time are here for you. The following resources can help.

- ? Ask a question: **https://forum.kirupa.com**
- ✔ Practice by building real apps: **https://bit.ly/coding_exercises**
- 📋 Errors/known issues: **https://bit.ly/javascript_errata**

VARIABLE SCOPE

Let's revisit something relating to variables we saw a few chapters ago. Each variable we declare has a certain level of visibility that determines when we can actually use it. In human-understandable terms, just because we declare a variable doesn't mean that it can be accessed from anywhere in our code. There are some basic things we need to understand, and this whole area of understanding falls under a topic known as **variable scope**.

In this chapter, I'm going to be explaining variable scope by looking at common cases that we've (mostly) already seen. This is a pretty deep topic, but we are just going to scratch the surface here. We'll see variable scope creep up in many subsequent tutorials where we will build on what we learn here.

Global Scope

We are going to start our exploration of scope at the very top with what is known as **global scope**. In real life, when we say that something can be heard globally, it means that we can be anywhere in the world and still be able to hear that... something:

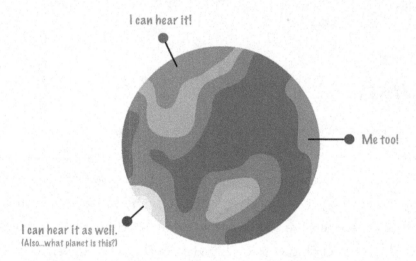

In JavaScript, much the same applies. If we say, for example, a variable is available globally, it means that any code on our page has access to read and modify this variable. We make something apply globally by declaring it in our code completely outside of a function.

To illustrate this, let's take a look at the following example:

```
<!DOCTYPE html>
<html>

<head>
  <meta charset="utf-8">
  <title>Variable Scope</title>
</head>
<body>
```

```
  <script>
    let counter = 0;

    alert(counter);
  </script>
</body>

</html>
```

Here, we are simply declaring a variable called counter and initializing it to **0**. By virtue of this variable being declared directly inside the <script> tag without being placed inside a function, the counter variable is considered to be **global**. What this distinction means is that our counter variable can be accessed by any code that lives in our document.

The following code highlights this:

```
<!DOCTYPE html>
<html>

<head>
  <meta charset="utf-8">
  <title>Variable Scope</title>
</head>

<body>
  <script>
    let counter = 0;
    function returnCount() {
      return counter;
    }

    alert(returnCount());
  </script>
</body>

</html>
```

In this example, the `counter` variable is declared outside of the `returnCount` function. Despite that, the `returnCount` function has full access to the `counter` variable. When the code runs, the `alert` function calls the `returnCount` function, which returns the value of the `counter` variable.

At this point, you are probably wondering why I am pointing this out. After all, we've been using global variables all this time without really noticing it. All I am doing here is formally introducing you to a guest that has been hanging around your party for a while.

Local Scope

Now, it gets a little interesting when we look at things that aren't globally declared. This is where understanding scope really starts paying dividends. As we saw earlier, a variable declared globally is accessible inside a function:

```
let counter = 0;


function returnCount() {
  return counter;
}
```

However, the opposite doesn't hold true. A variable declared inside a function will not work when accessed outside of the function:

```
function setState() {
  let state = "on";
}
setState();


alert(state) // undefined
```

In this example, the `state` variable is declared inside the `setState` function, and accessing the `state` variable outside of that function doesn't work. The reason is that the scope for our `state` variable is local to the `setState` function itself. A more generic way of describing this is to say that our `state` variable is just **local**.

 NOTE   Using Variables Without Declaring Them

If we initialize the `state` variable without formally declaring it, the scoping behavior is drastically different:

```
function setState() {
  state = "on";
}
setState();


alert(state) // "on"
```

In this case, even though our state variable makes its appearance inside the setState function first, not declaring it first with either let or const (or var, which is an older way of declaring variables) makes this variable live globally. In general, you don't want to declare a variable like this. Always prefix it with a let or const.

Miscellaneous Scoping Shenanigans

Since we are talking about JavaScript here, things would be too easy if we just left everything with variable scope as they stand now. In the following sections, I am going to highlight some quirks you need to be familiar with.

Block Scoping

Our code is made up of blocks—lots and lots of blocks. What exactly is a block? A **block** is a collection of JavaScript statements almost always wrapped by curly braces. For example, let's take a look at the following code:

```
let safeToProceed = false;


function isItSafe() {
  if (safeToProceed) {
    alert("You shall pass!");
  } else {
    alert("You shall not pass!");
  }
}


isItSafe();
```

JAVASCRIPT **ABSOLUTE BEGINNER'S GUIDE**

Counting the pair of curly braces, we see that there are three blocks. One block is the region contained by the `isItSafe` function itself:

```
let safeToProceed = false;

function isItSafe() {

  .

  .

  .

}
isItSafe();
```

The second block is the `if` statement region:

```
let safeToProceed = false;

function isItSafe() {
  if (safeToProceed) {

    .

    .

    .

  }
}
```

The third block is the region covered by the `else` statement:

```
let safeToProceed = false;

function isItSafe() {
  if (safeToProceed) {
    alert("You shall pass!");
  } else {

    .

    .

    .

  }
}
```

Any variable declared inside a block using `let` or `const` is local to that block and any child blocks contained inside it. To better understand this, take a look at the following code, which is a variation of the `isItSafe` function from earlier:

```
function isThePriceRight(cost) {
  let total = cost + 1;

  if (total > 3) {
    alert(total);
  } else {
    alert("Not enough!");
  }
}
isThePriceRight(4);
```

We declared the `total` variable as part of the function block. We are accessing this variable inside the `if` block. What do you think will happen? The `total` variable is totally (ha!) accessible here, because the `if` block is a child of the function block. To put it in the lingo of our times, the total variable is considered **in scope** of the `alert` function.

What about the following situation?

```
function isThePriceRight(cost) {
  let total = cost + 1;

  if (total > 3) {
    let warning = true;
    alert(total);
  } else {
    alert("Not enough!");
  }
  alert(warning);
}

isThePriceRight(4);
```

We have a variable called `warning` declared inside our `if` block, and we have an `alert` function that tries to print the value of `warning`. In this case, because we are trying to access the `warning` variable in a block that is outside the one the variable was originally declared in, our `alert` function won't actually display the value of **true**. Given where our `alert` function is, the `warning` variable is considered to be **out of scope**.

 NOTE Declaring Variables with the var Keyword!

A few paragraphs ago, I casually mentioned that variables were once declared with the `var` keyword. The `let` and `const` keywords are new additions to help you declare variables, and wherever you may have used `var` in the past, you should use `let` instead. We never discussed why `let` is preferable, and I said that we'll discuss it further when looking at variable scope. Well, here we are!

Variables declared with `var` scope to functions. They don't scope to blocks like our `if/else` ones. If we modify the example from earlier to have our `warning` variable be declared using `var` instead of `let`, our code will look as follows:

```
function isThePriceRight(cost) {
  let total = cost + 1;

  if (total > 3) {
    var warning = true;
    alert(total);
  } else {
    alert("Not enough!");
  }

  alert(warning);
}

isThePriceRight(4);
```

Earlier, the `alert` function for `warning` wouldn't display anything because the `warning` variable was out of scope when declared with `let`. With `var`, that isn't the case. You will see **true** displayed. This is because of the major difference between `let` and `var`. Variables declared with `var` are scoped at the function level: so as long as somewhere inside the function the variable is declared, that variable is considered to be in scope. Variables declared with `let`, as we saw earlier, are scoped to the block level.

The level of leniency provided by `var` in the scoping department is a little too much, and this leniency makes it easy to make variable-related mistakes. For this reason, my preference is for us to use `let` when it comes to declaring variables.

How JavaScript Processes Variables

If you thought the earlier block-scoping logic was weird, wait till you see this one. Take a look at the following code:

```
let foo = "Hello!";
alert(foo);
```

When this code runs, we can reasonably state that the value of **Hello!** will be displayed. We would reasonably be right. What if we made the following modification, where we move the variable declaration and initialization to the end?

```
alert(foo);
let foo = "Hello!";
```

In this situation, our code will error out. The foo variable is being accessed without being referenced. If we replace the let with a var, here is what our code would look like:

```
alert(foo);
var foo = "Hello!";
```

When this code runs, the behavior is different from what we saw earlier. We will see **undefined** displayed. What exactly is going on here?

When JavaScript encounters a scope (global, function, and so on), one of the first things it does is scan the full body of the code for any declared variables. When it encounters any variables, it initializes them by default with **undefined** for var. For let and const, it leaves the variables **completely uninitialized**. Lastly, it moves any variables it encounters to the top of the scope—the nearest block for let and const, the nearest function for var.

Let's dive in to see what this means. Our code initially looks like this:

```
alert(foo);
let foo = "Hello!";
```

When JavaScript makes a pass at this, the code gets turned into the following:

```
let foo;
alert(foo);
foo = "Hello!";
```

The `foo` variable, despite being declared at the bottom of our code, gets kicked up to the top. This is more formally known as **hoisting**. The thing about `let` and `const` is that when they get hoisted, they are left uninitialized. If we try to access an uninitialized variable, our code will throw an error and stop. If we modify our earlier example to use `var`, here is the way JavaScript would see things:

```
var foo = undefined;
alert(foo);
foo = "Hello!";
```

The variable still gets hoisted, but it gets initialized to **undefined**. This ensures our code still runs.

Here is the main takeaway from all of this: **be sure to declare and initialize your variables before actually using them**. While JavaScript has some affordances for dealing with cases where we don't do that, those affordances are just awfully confusing.

Closures

No conversation about variable scope can be wrapped up without discussing closures—that is, until right now. I am not going to explain closures here because it is a slightly more advanced topic that we will cover separately in the next chapter.

THE ABSOLUTE MINIMUM

Where our variables live has a major impact on where they can be used. Variables declared globally are accessible to our entire application. Variables declared locally will only be accessible to whatever scope they are found in. Within the range of global and local variables, JavaScript has a lot going on up its sleeve.

This chapter provided an overview of how variable scope can affect our code, and we'll see some of these concepts presented front and center in upcoming chapters.

? Ask a question: **https://forum.kirupa.com**

✔ Practice by building real apps: **https://bit.ly/coding_exercises**

🎫 Errors/known issues: **https://bit.ly/javascript_errata**

9

CLOSURES

By now, you probably know all about functions and all the fun things they do. An important part of working with functions, in JavaScript, and (possibly) life in general, is understanding the topic known as **closures**. Closures touch upon a gray area where functions and variable scope intersect.

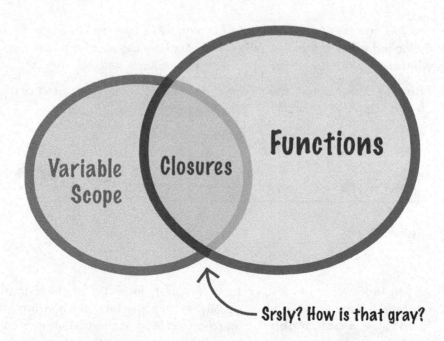

Srsly? How is that gray?

Now, I am not going to say any more about closures because this is something best explained by seeing code. Any words I add right now to define or describe what closures are will only serve to confuse things. In the following sections, we'll start off in familiar territory and then slowly venture into hostile areas where closures can be found.

Functions Within Functions

The first thing we are going to do is really drill down into what happens when you have functions within functions…and then the inner function gets returned. As part of that, let's quickly review functions.

Take a look at the following code:

```
function calculateRectangleArea(length, width) {
  return length * width;
}


let roomArea = calculateRectangleArea(10, 10);
alert(roomArea);
```

The `calculateRectangleArea` function takes two arguments and returns the multiplied value of those arguments to whatever called it. In this example, the **whatever called it** part is played by the `roomArea` variable.

After this code has run, the `roomArea` variable contains the result of multiplying 10 and 10, which is simply 100 (see Figure 9.1).

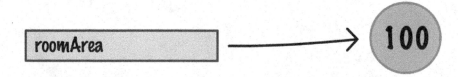

FIGURE 9.1

The result of `roomArea`

As you know, what a function returns can pretty much be anything. In this case, we returned a number. You can very easily return some text (aka a **string**), the **undefined** value, a **custom object**, and so on. As long as the code that is calling the function knows what to do with what the function returns, you can do pretty much whatever you want. You can even return another function. Return another function?!! Yes, let me elaborate on this.

Here is an example of a function returning a function:

```
function youSayGoodBye() {

  alert("Good Bye!");

  function andISayHello() {
    alert("Hello!");
  }

  return andISayHello;
}
```

We can have functions that contain functions inside them. In this example, we have our youSayGoodBye function that contains an alert and another function called andISayHello (see Figure 9.2).

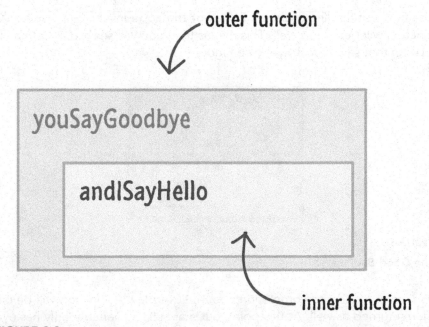

FIGURE 9.2

A function within a function

The interesting part is what the youSayGoodBye function returns when it gets called. It returns the andISayHello function:

```
function youSayGoodBye() {

  alert("Good Bye!");

  function andISayHello() {
    alert("Hello!");
  }

  return andISayHello;
}
```

Let's go ahead and play this example out. To call this function, initialize a variable that points to youSayGoodBye:

```
let something = youSayGoodBye();
```

The moment this line of code runs, **all of the code** inside your youSayGoodBye function will get run as well. This means that, you will see a dialog (thanks to the alert) that says **Good Bye!** (see Figure 9.3).

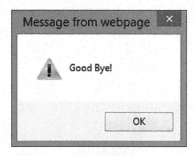

FIGURE 9.3

*The **Good Bye!** dialog*

As part of running to completion, the andISayHello function will be created and then returned as well. At this point, our something variable only has eyes for one thing, and that thing is the andISayHello function (see Figure 9.4).

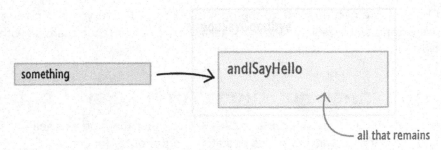

FIGURE 9.4

The `something` variable and the `andISayHello` function

The `youSayGoodBye` outer function, from the `something` variable's point of view, simply goes away. Because the `something` variable now points to a function, you can invoke this function by just calling it using the open and close parentheses like you normally would:

```
let something = youSayGoodBye();
something();
```

When you do this, the returned inner function (that is, `andISayHello`) will execute. Just like before, you will see a dialog appear, but this dialog will say **Hello**!, as shown in Figure 9.5, which is what the `alert` inside this function specified.

FIGURE 9.5

Hello!

All of this should probably be a review. The only thing you may have found new is realizing once a function returns a value, it is no longer around. The only thing that remains is the returned value.

Okay, we are getting close to the promised hostile territory. In the next section, we will extend what we've just seen by taking a look at another example with a slight twist.

When the Inner Functions Aren't Self-Contained

In the previous example, our andISayHello inner function was self-contained and didn't rely on any variables or state from the outer function:

```
function youSayGoodBye() {

  alert("Good Bye!");

  function andISayHello() {
    alert("Hello!");
  }

  return andISayHello;
}
```

In real scenarios, we will very rarely run into a case like this. We will often have variables and data that are shared between the outer function and the inner function. To highlight this, take a look at the following example:

```
function stopWatch() {
  let startTime = Date.now();

  function getDelay() {
    let elapsedTime = Date.now() - startTime;
    alert(elapsedTime);
  }

  return getDelay;
}
```

This example shows a very simple way of measuring the time it takes to do something. Inside the `stopWatch` function, we have a `startTime` variable that is set to the value of `Date.now()`:

```
function stopWatch() {
    let startTime = Date.now();

    function getDelay() {
        let elapsedTime = Date.now() - startTime;
        alert(elapsedTime);
    }

    return getDelay;
}
```

We also have an inner function called `getDelay`:

```
function stopWatch() {
    let startTime = Date.now();

    function getDelay() {
        let elapsedTime = Date.now() - startTime;
        alert(elapsedTime);
    }

    return getDelay;
}
```

The `getDelay` function displays a dialog containing the difference in time between a new call to `Date.now()` and the `startTime` variable declared earlier.

Back in the outer `stopWatch` function, the last thing that happens is that it returns the `getDelay` function before exiting. As we can see, the code here is very similar to the earlier example. We have an outer function, we have an inner function, and we have the outer function returning the inner function.

Now, to see the `stopWatch` function at work, add the following lines of code:

```javascript
let timer = stopWatch();

// do something that takes some time
for (let i = 0; i < 1000000; i++) {
  let foo = Math.random() * 10000;
}

// invoke the returned function
timer();
```

The full markup and code for this example looks like this:

```html
<!DOCTYPE html>
<html>

<head>
  <meta charset="utf-8">
  <title>Closures</title>

  <style>

  </style>
</head>

<body>
  <script>
    function stopWatch() {
      var startTime = Date.now();

      function getDelay() {
        var elapsedTime = Date.now() - startTime;
        alert(elapsedTime);
      }

      return getDelay;
```

```
    }

    let timer = stopWatch();

    // do something that takes some time
    for (let i = 0; i < 1000000; i++) {
        let foo = Math.random() * 10000;
    }

    // invoke the returned function
    timer();
  </script>
</body>

</html>
```

If you run this example, you'll see a dialog displaying the number of milliseconds it took between your timer variable getting initialized, your for loop running to completion, and the timer variable getting invoked as a function (see Figure 9.6).

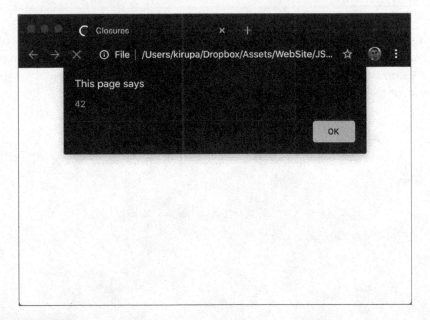

FIGURE 9.6

The `timer` variable invoked as a function

Explained in a different way, we have a stopwatch that we invoke, we begin some long-running operation, and then we invoke the stopwatch again to see how long the long-running operation took.

Now that we can see our little stopwatch example working, let's go back to the stopWatch function and see what exactly is going on. As mentioned earlier, a lot of what we see is similar to the youSayGoodBye/andISayHello example. There is a twist that makes this example different, and the important part to note is what happens when the getDelay function is returned to the timer variable.

Figure 9.7 is an incomplete visualization of what this looks like.

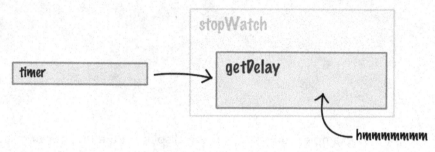

FIGURE 9.7

The stopWatch outer function is no longer active, and the timer variable is bound to the getDelay function.

The stopWatch outer function is no longer in play, and the timer variable is bound to the getDelay function. Now, here is the twist. The getDelay function relies on the startTime variable that lives in the context of the outer stopWatch function:

```
function stopWatch() {
  let startTime = Date.now();

  function getDelay() {
    let elapsedTime = Date.now() - startTime;
    alert(elapsedTime);
  }


  return getDelay;
}
```

When the outer `stopWatch` function goes away when `getDelay` is returned to the `timer` variable, what happens in the following line?

```
function getDelay() {
    let elapsedTime = Date.now() - startTime;
    alert(elapsedTime);
}
```

In this context, it would make sense if the `startTime` variable is actually undefined, right? But the example totally worked, so something else is going on here. That something else is the shy and mysterious closure. Here is a look at what happens to make our `startTime` variable actually store a value and not be undefined.

The JavaScript runtime that keeps track of all your variables, memory usage, references, and so on is really clever. In this example, it detects that the inner function (`getDelay`) is relying on variables from the outer function (`stopWatch`). When that happens, the runtime ensures that any variables in the outer function that are needed are still available to the inner function, **even if the outer function goes away**.

To help you visualize this properly, Figure 9.8 shows what the `timer` variable looks like.

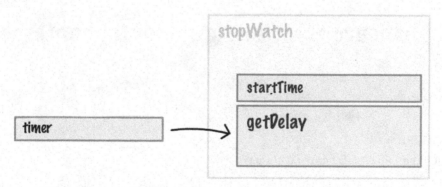

FIGURE 9.8

The `timer` variable

It is still referring to the `getDelay` function, but the `getDelay` function also has access to the `startTime` variable that existed in the outer `stopWatch` function. This inner function, because it **enclosed** relevant variables from the outer function into its bubble (aka scope), is known as a **closure** (see Figure 9.9).

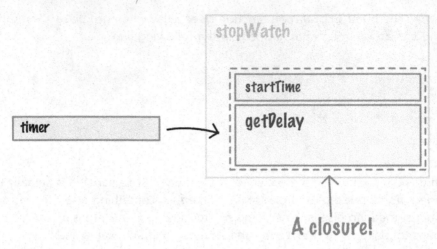

FIGURE 9.9

A closure defined diagrammatically

To define the closure more formally, we could say that it is a **newly created function that also contains its variable context** (see Figure 9.10).

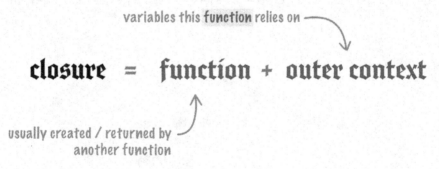

FIGURE 9.10

A more formal definition of a closure

To review this one more time using our existing example, the startTime variable gets the value of Date.now the moment the timer variable gets initialized and the stopWatch function runs. When the stopWatch function returns the inner getDelay function, the stopWatch function goes away. What doesn't go away are any shared variables inside stopWatch that the inner function relies on. Those shared variables are not destroyed. Instead, they are enclosed by the inner function (aka the closure).

THE ABSOLUTE MINIMUM

By looking at closures through examples first, you really missed out on a lot of boring definitions, theories, and hand waving. In all seriousness, closures are very common in JavaScript. You will encounter them in many subtle and not-so-subtle ways.

If there is only one thing you take out of all of this, remember the following: *The most important thing closures do is allow functions to keep on working even if their environment drastically changes or disappears.* Any variables that were in scope when the function was created are enclosed and protected to ensure the function still works. This behavior is essential for a very dynamic language like JavaScript, where you often create, modify, and destroy things on the fly. Happy days!

? Ask a question: **https://forum.kirupa.com**

✔ Practice by building real apps: **https://bit.ly/coding_exercises**

Errors/known issues: **https://bit.ly/javascript_errata**

10

WHERE SHOULD YOUR CODE LIVE?

Let's take a break from our regularly scheduled…programming (ha!). So far, all of the code we have written has been contained fully inside an HTML document:

```html
<!DOCTYPE html>
<html>

<head>
  <meta charset="utf-8">
  <title>An Interesting Title Goes Here</title>

  <style>
    body {
      background-color: #EEE;
    }

    h1 {
      font-family: sans-serif;
      font-size: 36px;
    }

    p {
      font-family: sans-serif;
    }
  </style>
</head>

<body>
  <h1>Are you ready for this?</h1>
  <p>Are you ready for seeing (or already having seen!)
     the most amazing dialog ever?</p>

  <script>
    alert("hello, world!");
  </script>
</body>

</html>
```

We are going to take a step back and revisit whether having this arrangement between HTML, CSS, and JS in the same document/file makes sense for all situations. To simplify how we talk about our document structure, let's replace the code view with a more, let's say, artistic view, involving some really nicely designed boxes (see Figure 10.1).

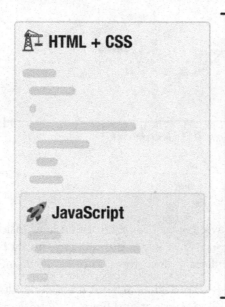

Everything is in a single file!

FIGURE 10.1

Our representation of a web page

In this world, the only thing that protects our HTML document from JavaScript is just a couple of `<script>` tags. Now, our JavaScript does not have to live inside our HTML document. We have another way we can use that involves a separate file where all our JavaScript will instead live (see Figure 10.2).

Our JavaScript is in a separate file!

FIGURE 10.2

Our JS now lives in its own separate file!

In this approach, we don't have any real JavaScript that lives inside our HTML document. We still have our `<script>` tag, but this tag **simply points to the JavaScript file** instead of containing line after line of actual JavaScript code.

The thing to note is that these approaches are not mutually exclusive. We can mix both approaches into an HTML document and have a hybrid approach, where we have an external JavaScript file as well as lines of JavaScript code fully contained inside our HTML document (see Figure 10.3).

To make things more interesting, we also have variations on the two approaches, such as having multiple `<script>` sections in an HTML document, having multiple JS files, and so on. In the following sections, we'll look at both of these approaches in greater detail and discuss when you would choose to use one approach over the other.

By the end of all this, you will have a good understanding of the pros and cons of each approach so that you can do the right thing with the JavaScript in your web pages and applications.

Onward!

Our JavaScript lives inside our HTML
document and also as part of a separate file!

FIGURE 10.3

A mixed approach where our JS content lives in several different places

Approach #1: All the Code Lives in Your HTML Document

The first approach we will look at is the one we've been using so far. This is the approach where all of our JavaScript lives inside a `<script>` tag alongside the rest of our HTML document:

```
<!DOCTYPE html>
<html>

<body>
  <h1>Example</h1>

  <script>
    function showDistance(speed, time) {
      alert(speed * time);
    }

    showDistance(10, 5);
```

```
    showDistance(85, 1.5);
    showDistance(12, 9);
    showDistance(42, 21);
  </script>
</body>

</html>
```

When our browser loads the page, it goes through and parses every line of HTML from top to bottom. When it hits the `<script>` tag, it will go ahead and execute all the lines of JavaScript as well. Once it has finished executing our code, it will continue to parse the rest of our document. This means the location of the `<script>` tag in our page is important. We will discuss that later when looking at Chapter 40, "Page Load Events and Other Stuff."

Approach #2: The Code Lives in a Separate File

The second approach is one where our main HTML document doesn't contain any JavaScript content. Instead, all of our JavaScript lives in a separate document. There are two parts to this approach. The first part deals with the JavaScript file. The second part deals with referencing this JavaScript file in the HTML. Let's look at both of these parts in greater detail.

The JavaScript File

The key to making this approach work is the separate file that contains our JavaScript code. It doesn't matter what we name this file, but its extension is typically **.js**. For example, my JavaScript file is called **example.js**.

Inside this file, the only thing we will have is JavaScript:

```
function showDistance(speed, time) {
  alert(speed * time);
}

showDistance(10, 5);
showDistance(85, 1.5);
showDistance(12, 9);
showDistance(42, 21);
```

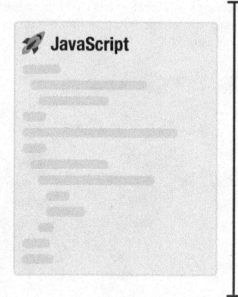

example.js

Everything we would normally put inside a <script> tag in the HTML will go here. Nothing else will go into this file. Putting anything else, such as arbitrary pieces of HTML and CSS, isn't allowed, and our browser will complain.

Referencing the JavaScript File

Once we have our JavaScript file created, the second (and final) step is to reference it in the HTML page. This is handled by our <script> tag. More specifically, it is handled by our <script> tag's src attribute, which points to the location of our JavaScript file:

```
<!DOCTYPE html>
<html>

<body>
  <h1>Example</h1>

  <script src="example.js"></script>
</body>

</html>
```

In this example, if our JavaScript file is located in the same directory as our HTML, we can use a relative path and just reference the filename directly. If our JavaScript file lives in another folder, we would alter our path accordingly:

```
<!DOCTYPE html>
<html>

<body>
  <h1>Example</h1>

  <script src="some/other/folder/example.js"></script>
</body>

</html>
```

In this case, our script file is nested inside three folders with the names **some**, **other**, and **folder**. We can completely avoid relative paths and use an absolute path as well:

```
<!DOCTYPE html>
<html>

<body>
  <h1>Example</h1>

  <script src="https://www.kirupa.com/js/example.js"></script>
</body>

</html>
```

Either a relative path or absolute path will work just fine. For situations where the path between our HTML page and the script we are referencing will vary (such as inside a template, a server-side include, a third-party library, and so on), we'll be safer using an absolute path.

SCRIPTS, PARSING, AND LOCATION IN THE DOCUMENT

A few sections earlier, I briefly described how scripts get executed. Your browser parses your HTML page starting at the top and then moves down line by line. When a `<script>` tag gets hit, your browser starts executing the code that is contained inside the tag. This execution is also done line by line, starting at the top. Everything else that your page might be doing takes a backseat while the execution is going on. If the `<script>` tag references an external JavaScript file, your browser first downloads the external file before starting to execute its contents.

This behavior, where your browser linearly parses your document, has some interesting side effects that affect where in your document you want to place your `<script>` tags. Technically, your `<script>` tags can live anywhere in your HTML document. There is a preferred place you should specify your scripts, though. Because of how your browser parses the page and blocks everything while your scripts are executing, **you want to place your `<script>` tags toward the bottom of your HTML document after all your HTML elements**.

If your `<script>` tag is toward the top of your document, your browser will block everything else while the script is running. This could result in users seeing a partially loaded and unresponsive HTML page if you are downloading a large script file or executing a script that is taking a long time to complete. Unless you really have a good need to force your JavaScript to run before your full document is parsed, ensure your `<script>` tags appear toward the end of your document, as shown in almost all the earlier examples. There is one other advantage to placing your scripts at the bottom of your page, but I will explain that much later when talking about the Document Object Model (DOM) and what happens during a page load.

So, Which Approach to Use?

We have two main approaches around where our code should live (see Figure 10.4).

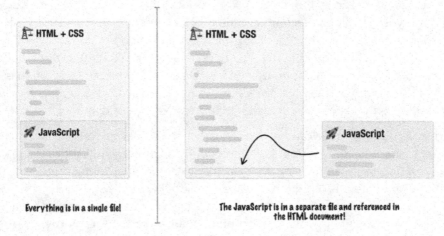

Everything is in a single file!

The JavaScript is in a separate file and referenced in the HTML document!

FIGURE 10.4

The two main approaches we have for dealing with our JS content

The approach you end up choosing depends on your answer to the following question: **Is the identical code going to be used across multiple HTML documents?**

Yes, My Code Will Be Used on Multiple Documents!

If the answer is **yes**, you probably want to put the code in an external file and then reference it across all the HTML pages you want it executing in. The first reason you want to do this is to avoid having code repeated across multiple pages (see Figure 10.5).

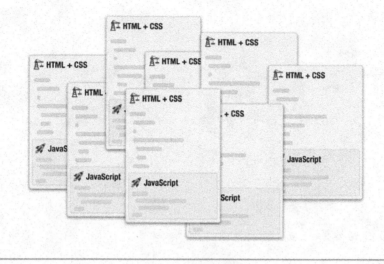

A whole lotta duplicate code!

FIGURE 10.5

Having duplicated code is a problem!

Duplicate code makes maintenance a nightmare, where a change to your script will require you updating every single HTML document with the exact change. If you are employing some sort of templating or server-side-includes (SSI) logic, where there is only one HTML fragment containing your script, then maintenance is less of an issue.

The second reason has to do with file size. When you have your script duplicated across many HTML pages, each time a user loads one of those HTML pages, they are downloading your script all over again. This is less of a problem for smaller scripts, but once you have more than a few hundred lines of code, the size starts adding up.

When you factor all your code into a single file, you don't have the issues I just outlined (see Figure 10.6).

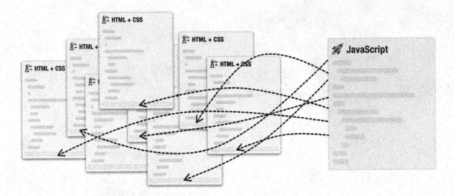

FIGURE 10.6

All your code in one place

Your code is easily maintainable because you update your code inside the one file only. Any HTML document that references this JavaScript file automatically gets the most recent version when it loads. By having all your code in one file, your browser will download the code only once and **deliver the cached version of the file on subsequent accesses**.

No, My Code Is Used Only Once on a Single HTML Document!

If you answered **no** to the earlier question around whether your code is going to be used across multiple HTML documents, you can do whatever you want. You can still choose to put your code into a separate file and reference it in your HTML document, but the benefits of doing that are less than what you saw earlier with the example involving many documents.

Placing your code entirely inside your HTML document is also fine for this situation. Most of the examples you will see in this book have all the code within the HTML document itself. Our examples aren't really going to be used across multiple pages, and they aren't going to be so large where readability is improved by putting all the code in a separate location.

THE ABSOLUTE MINIMUM

As you can see, even something as seemingly simple as determining where your code should live ends up taking many pages of explanation and discussion. Welcome to the world of HTML and JavaScript, where nothing is really black and white. Anyway, getting back to the point of this article, a typical HTML document will contain many script files loaded from an external location. Some of those files will be your own; some, however, will be created by a third party and included into your document.

Also, do you remember the hybrid approach, where your HTML document contains both a reference to a separate JavaScript file as well as actual code within the document? Well, that approach is pretty common as well. Ultimately, the approach you end up using is entirely up to you. Hopefully, this chapter gave you a taste of the information needed to make the right choice. In Chapter 40 we take a deeper look at what you saw here by looking at page loading–related events and certain special attributes that complicate things. However, don't worry about them for now.

? Ask a question: **https://forum.kirupa.com**

✔ Practice by building real apps: **https://bit.ly/coding_exercises**

📑 Errors/known issues: **https://bit.ly/javascript_errata**

IN THIS CHAPTER

- Learn how to go beyond alerts for displaying results
- Understand how the console works
- Learn the variety of logging solutions you have at your fingertips

11

CONSOLE LOGGING BASICS

When we are writing code, we will often find ourselves in one of two situations. One situation is where we wonder if the code we just wrote is going to run at all. In the other situation, we know our code runs, but it isn't running correctly. There is something wrong...*somewhere*.

In both of these situations, what we need is some extra visibility into what our code is doing. A timeless approach for bringing this visibility involves the alert function:

```
let myButton = document.querySelector("#myButton");
myButton.addEventListener("click", doSomething, false);


function doSomething(e) {
  alert("Is this working?");
}
```

Using the `alert` function isn't bad. It works fine for simple situations, but as our code starts to do more, relying on this function doesn't work as well. For starters, we'll probably go insane from dismissing the large number of dialogs that keep popping up while our code is running! We'll also want an easy way to persist the messages we are seeing. The fleeting nature of our `alert` dialogs makes any sort of long-term logging like that difficult.

In this chapter, we're going to look at one of the greatest inventions of all time that makes it easy to help us figure out what our code is doing. We are going to be learning about something known as the **console**.

Meet the Console

Even if you think you write the most perfect JavaScript, you'll be spending a fair amount of time in what is known as the **console**. If you've never used the console before, it is part of our browser's developer tools, where all sorts of text and stuff gets printed for us to see and (occasionally) interact with.

The console will look a little bit like what is shown in Figure 11.1.

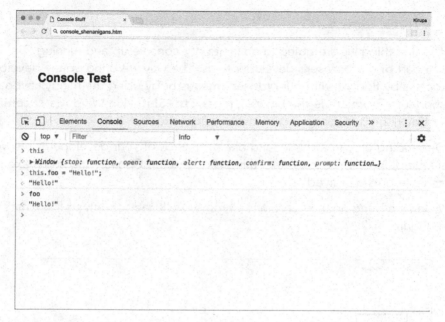

FIGURE 11.1

Meet the console.

At a very high level, the console helps with a bunch of things:

- We can read messages we have told our code to log and display.

- We can modify our application state by setting (or overwriting) variables and values.

- We can inspect the value of any DOM element, applied style, or code that is accessible and in scope.

- We can use it as a virtual code editor and write/execute some code, just for kicks.

In this chapter, we won't focus on all the things our console is capable of doing. Instead, we're just going to take it easy and gradually get comfortable with using the console to just display messages. We will cover all the crazy console-related things eventually, so don't worry.

Displaying the Console

The first thing we are going to do is get our console up and running. The console is a part of our browser's developer tools. The way we bring up the developer tools is by fiddling with our browser's menus or by using the handy keyboard shortcuts. From inside the browser, press **Ctrl+Shift+I** in Windows or **command+ option+I** on a Mac to bring up the developer tools.

Depending on your browser and platform, each of your developer tools will look a little different. The important thing is to find the Console tab and make sure the console gets displayed.

When we bring up the console in Chrome, we'll see something like what's shown in Figure 11.2.

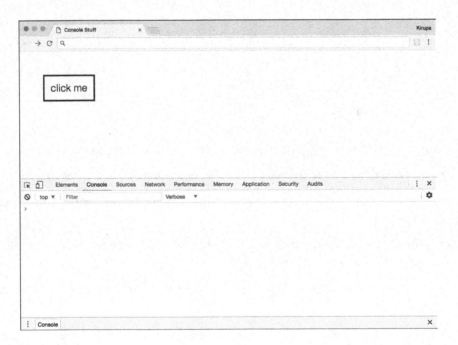

FIGURE 11.2

The Chrome console

I'll be using screenshots from Chrome when discussing the console. The thing I want to highlight is that it doesn't matter which browser you use. The console looks and functions pretty much the same on all browsers. Just bring up the console in your favorite browser and get ready to use it in the following sections.

If You Want to Follow Along

Now, you can just read the following sections and learn a whole bunch of console-related things without lifting a finger. If that is what you would like to do, then skip all of this and jump to the next section.

On the other hand, if you want to get your hands a bit dirty and see some of the console shenanigans for yourself on your screen, create a new HTML document and add the following HTML, CSS, and JavaScript into it:

```
<!DOCTYPE html>
<html>

<head>
  <title>Console Stuff</title>

  <style>
    #container {
      padding: 50px;
    }

    #myButton {
      font-family: sans-serif;
      font-size: 24px;
      font-weight: lighter;
      background-color: #FFF;
      border: 3px #333 solid;
      padding: 15px;
    }

    #myButton:hover {
      background-color: aliceblue;
    }
  </style>
</head>
<body>
  <div id="container">
    <button id="myButton">click me</button>
```

```
    </div>
    <script>

      let myButton = document.querySelector("#myButton");
      myButton.addEventListener("click", doSomething, false);

      function doSomething(e) {
        alert("Is this working?");
      }
    </script>
  </body>

</html>
```

What we have here is a really simple HTML page with a button that you can click. When you click the button, an alert dialog (the same one we described earlier) will appear. In the following sections, we'll modify this example to help bring some of the console-related things to life!

Console Logging 101

The first thing we are going to do is tell our console to display things onscreen. This is no different from what we did with the `alert` statement earlier, and it is almost just as easy. The key to all this is the **Console API**, which contains a bunch of properties and methods that allow us to display things to our console in a variety of ways. The first and probably most popular of these properties and methods is the `log` method.

Meet the log Method

At its most basic level, the `log` method is used as follows:

```
console.log("Look, ma! I'm logging stuff.")
```

We call it via the `console` object and pass in the text we want to display. To see this in action, we can replace the `alert` from our example with the following:

```
function doSomething(e) {
  console.log("Is this working?");
}
```

When you run this code, take a look at your console after clicking the **click me** button. If everything worked out properly, you will see the text "Is this working?" displayed, as shown in Figure 11.3.

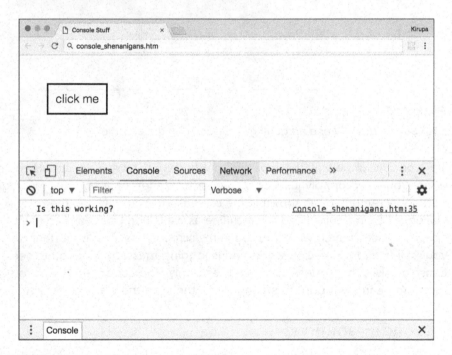

FIGURE 11.3

*The **click me** button and some text displayed!*

If you keep clicking the button, you'll see more instances of "Is this working?" getting logged, as shown in Figure 11.4.

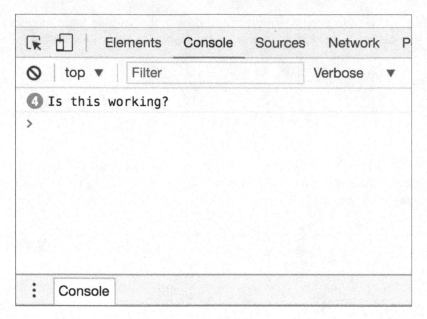

FIGURE 11.4

Each button click will end up getting represented in our console.

The specifics of how all this looks will depend on the developer tools you are using. You will probably just see a counter to the left of your initial message getting incremented, as shown in the screenshot. You may see the text "Is this working?" being duplicated on each line as well. Don't be alarmed if what you see doesn't exactly match what you see in my screenshots. The important detail is that your call to `console.log` works and is logging messages for you to see in the console. Also, these messages aren't read-only. You can select them. You can copy them. You can even print them and frame them on the wall behind you.

Going Beyond Predefined Text

Now that we've covered the basics, let's go a bit deeper. When using the console, we aren't limited to only printing some predefined text. For example, a common thing we might do is print the value of something that exists only by evaluating an expression or accessing a value. To see what I mean by this, make the following change to the `doSomething` function:

```
function doSomething(e) {
  console.log("We clicked on: " + e.target.id);
}
```

What we are doing here is telling our console to display the text "We clicked on" in addition to the `id` value of the element we clicked. If you preview these changes in your browser, click the **click me** button again and check out what is shown in the console (see Figure 11.5).

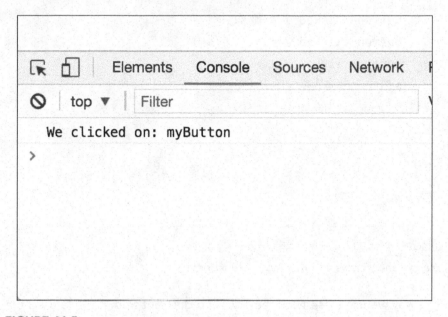

FIGURE 11.5

The `id` of the button you clicked is displayed!

The `id` value of the button you clicked is displayed in addition to the predefined text. Now, getting the `id` value of an element is probably not the most exciting thing you might want to print, but you can print pretty much anything that would look good when represented as text. That's powerful!

Displaying Warnings and Errors

It is time to look beyond the `log` method! Our `console` object provides us with the `warn` and `error` methods, which allow us to display messages formatted as warnings and errors, respectively, as shown in Figure 11.6.

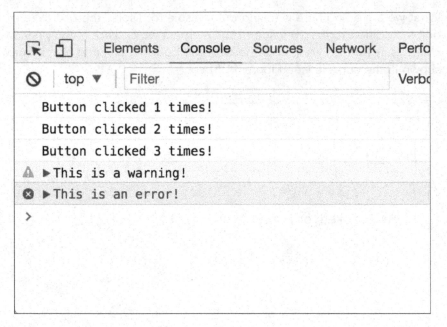

FIGURE 11.6

We can show errors and warnings...like a boss!

The way we use these two methods is no different from how we used the `log` method. Just pass in whatever you want to display. You can see an example of how to use these methods in the following snippet:

```
let counter = 0;

function doSomething(e) {
  counter++;

  console.log("Button clicked " + counter + " times!");

  if (counter == 3) {
    showMore();
  }
}

function showMore() {
```

```
    console.warn("This is a warning!");
    console.error("This is an error!");
}
```

When this code runs and our button is clicked three times, the `showMore` function gets called. Inside that function, all we have is our console warning and error:

```
function showMore() {
    console.warn("This is a warning!");
    console.error("This is an error!");
}
```

Now, there is something cool about warnings and errors that goes beyond just their appearance compared to their more boring `log` counterparts. You can expand them in the console and see the full stack trace of all the functions our code took before hitting them, as shown in Figure 11.7.

FIGURE 11.7

Seeing more details for our errors!

For large pieces of code with a lot of branching, this is really useful. The warn and error methods provide an excellent way for us to better understand the twisted paths our code took into getting into whatever state it ended up in!

NOTE   There Are More Console Methods

The warn and error methods are just two of the many methods the console provides for displaying our data in a specially formatted way.

THE ABSOLUTE MINIMUM

The console provides us with one of the best tools we have for understanding what our code is doing. Displaying messages is only one part of what the console allows us to do. Within our narrow focus of just displaying messages, there is a whole lot more that we can cover beyond what we've seen so far. We'll cover more things the console does later in the book, but the few console techniques we've seen here will take you and me far in helping us find and squash bugs in our code.

? Ask a question: **https://forum.kirupa.com**

✔ Practice by building real apps: **https://bit.ly/coding_exercises**

🐥 Errors/known issues: **https://bit.ly/javascript_errata**

OF PIZZA, TYPES, PRIMITIVES, AND OBJECTS

It's time to get serious. Srsly! In the past few chapters, we've been working with all kinds of values. We've worked with strings (text), numbers, booleans (aka **true** and **false**), functions, and various other built-in things that are part of the JavaScript language.

Following are some examples to jog your memory:

```
let someText = "hello, world!";
let count = 50;
let isActive = true;
```

Unlike other languages, JavaScript makes it really easy to specify and use these built-in things. We don't even have to think about or plan ahead to use any of them. Despite how simple using these different kinds of built-in things is, there is a lot of detail hidden from us. Knowing this detail is important because it will not only help us more easily make sense of our code, it may even help us to more quickly pinpoint what is going wrong when things aren't working the way they should.

Now, as you can probably guess, *built-in-things* isn't the proper way to describe the variety of values you can use in JavaScript. There is a more formal name for the variety of values you can use in your code, and that name is **types**. In this chapter, you are going to get a gentle introduction to what types are.

Let's First Talk About Pizza

No, I haven't completely lost it. Since I am always eating something (or thinking about eating something), I am going to try to explain the mysterious world of types by first explaining the much simpler world of pizza.

In case you haven't had pizza in a while, Figure 12.1 shows you what a typical pizza looks like.

If your pizza doesn't look like this,
take it back!™

FIGURE 12.1

An example of an amazing two-dimensional pizza!

A pizza doesn't just magically appear looking like this. It is made up of other ingredients—some simple and some not so simple.

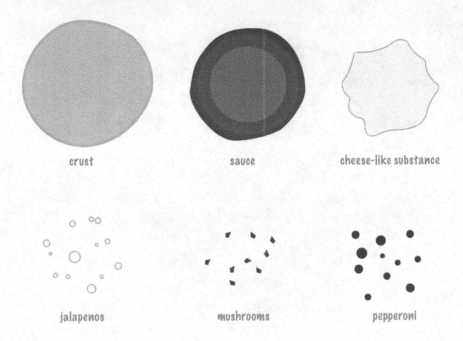

crust   sauce   cheese-like substance

jalapenos   mushrooms   pepperoni

The simple ingredients are easy to spot. These would be your **mushrooms** and **jalapenos**. The reason these ingredients are considered simple is because you can't break them apart any further.

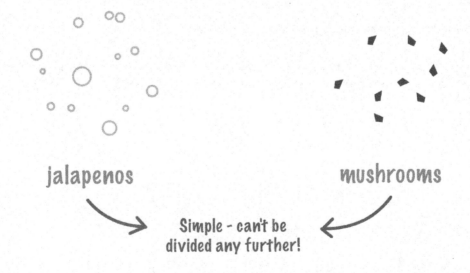

jalapenos   mushrooms

Simple - can't be
divided any further!

They aren't prepared. They aren't made up of other simple ingredients. Just like The Dude, they abide.

The not-so-simple, complex ingredients would be your **cheese**, **sauce**, **crust**, and **pepperoni**. These are more complex for all the reasons the simple ones are, um, simple. These complex ingredients are made up of **other ingredients**.

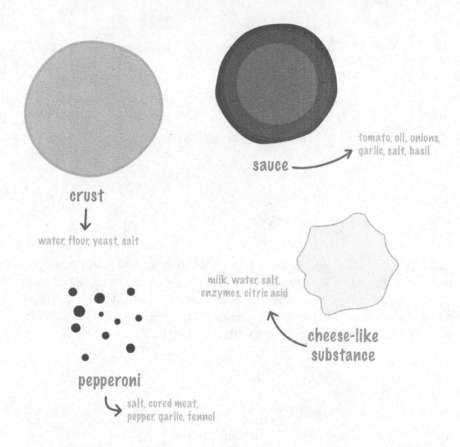

Unfortunately for all of us, there is no one simple ingredient called cheese or pepperoni out there. We need to combine, prepare, and add more ingredients to make up some of the complex ingredients we see here. There is a subtle wrinkle to point out about complex ingredients. Their composition isn't limited to just simple ingredients. Complex ingredients can themselves be made up of other complex ingredients. How scandalous!

From Pizza to JavaScript!

While this may be hard to believe, everything we learned about pizzas in the previous section was there for a purpose. The description of the simple and complex ingredients very neatly applies to types in JavaScript. Each individual ingredient could be considered a counterpart to a type that you can use (see Figure 12.2).

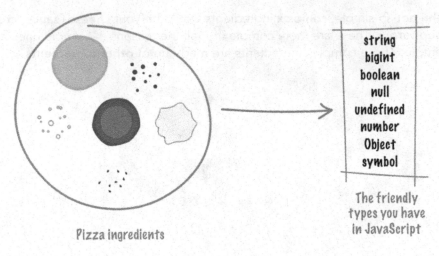

Pizza ingredients

The friendly
types you have
in JavaScript

FIGURE 12.2

A list of the simple types in JavaScript

Just like the cheese, sauce, pepperoni, mushrooms, and jalapenos in our version
of a pizza, the types in JavaScript are `string`, `number`, `boolean`, `null`, `unde-
fined`, `bigint`, `symbol`, and `Object`. Some of these types may be very familiar
to us already, and some of them may not be. While we will look at all these types
in much greater detail in future chapters, Table 12.1 provides a very brief summary
of what they do.

TABLE 12.1   Types

Type	What It Does
`string`	The basic structure for working with text.
`number`	As you can guess, it allows you to work with numbers.
`boolean`	Comes alive when you are using **true** and **false**.
`null`	Represents the digital equivalent of nothing...or **moo**.
`undefined`	While sort of similar to `null`, this is returned when a value should exist but doesn't—like when you declare a variable but don't assign anything to it.
`bigint`	Allows you to work with really large or really small numbers that go beyond what a typical "number" might support.
`symbol`	Something unique and immutable (can't be changed) that you can optionally use as an identifier for `Object` properties.
`Object`	Acts a shell for other types, including other objects.

Now, although each of the types is pretty unique in what it does, they can all be put into one of two groupings. Just like with our pizza's simple and complex ingredients, our types can be simple or complex as well. Except, in JavaScript terminology involving types, simple and complex are more formally known as **primitive** and **object**, respectively. Another way of saying this is that our types in JavaScript are either known as **primitive types** (or just **primitives**) and **object types** (or just **objects**).

Our primitive types are `string`, `number`, `boolean`, `null`, `bigint`, `symbol`, and `undefined`. Any values that fall under their umbrella can't be divided any further. They are the jalapenos and mushrooms of the JavaScript world. Primitives are pretty easy too. There is no depth to them, and we pretty much get what we see when we encounter one.

Our object types, represented by `Object` in Table 12.1, are a bit more mysterious, so the last thing we want to cover before unleashing the details about all these types is what objects in JavaScript actually are.

What Are Objects?

The concept of objects in a programming language like JavaScript maps nicely to its real-world equivalents. In the real world, we are literally surrounded by objects. Your computer is an object. A book on a shelf is an object. A potato is (arguably) an object. Your alarm clock is an object. A poster you got on eBay is also an object. I could go on forever, but (for everyone's sake) I'm going to stop here.

Some objects, such as a paperweight, don't do much.

Paperweight!
(It is not a rock!)

They just sit there. Other objects, like a television, go above and beyond the call of mere existence and do a lot of things.

A typical television takes input. It allows you to turn it on or off, change the channel, adjust the volume, and do all sorts of television-y things.

The thing to realize is that objects come in different shapes, sizes, and usefulness. Despite the variations, objects are all the same at a high level. They are an **abstraction**. They provide an easy way for you to use them without having to worry about what goes on under the covers. Even the simplest of objects hide a certain level of complexity that you and I don't have to worry about.

For example, it doesn't matter what goes on inside a TV, how the wires are connected, or what type of glue is used to hold everything together. Those are unnecessary details. All that we care about is that the TV does what it is told. When we want it to change the channel, the channel should change. When we adjust the volume, the volume should adjust. Everything else is just noise.

Basically, think of an object as a black box. There are some predefined/documented things it does. How it does them is something we can't easily see. How it does its magic is also something we don't really care about, as long as it works. We'll change that notion later when we learn to actually create the insides of an object, but let's relish this simple and happy world for now.

The Predefined Objects Roaming Around in JavaScript

Besides the built-in types we saw earlier, we also have a handful of predefined objects in JavaScript that we can use out of the box. These objects allow us to work with everything from collections of data to dates to even text and numbers. Table 12.2 lists these objects and what they do.

TABLE 12.2 Objects

Type	What It Does
Array	Helps store, retrieve, and manipulate a collection of data.
Boolean	Acts as a wrapper around the boolean primitive; still very much in love with **true** and **false**.
Date	Allows you to more easily represent and work with dates.
Function	Allows you to invoke some code, among other esoteric things.
Math	The nerdy one in the group. It helps you better work with numbers.
Number	Acts as a wrapper around the number primitive.
RegExp	Provides a lot of functionality for matching patterns in text.
String	Acts as a wrapper around the string primitive.

The way we use these built-in objects is a little bit different from how we use primitives. Each object has its own quirk about how we can use it as well. Explaining each object and how it is meant to be used is something I will save for later, but here is a very short snippet of commented code to show you what is possible:

```
// an array
let names = ["Jerry", "Elaine", "George", "Kramer"];
let alsoNames = new Array("Dennis", "Frank", "Dee", "Mac");

// a round number
let roundNumber = Math.round("3.14");

// today's date
let today = new Date();

// a boolean object
let booleanObject = new Boolean(true);

// infinity
let unquantifiablyBigNumber = Number.POSITIVE_INFINITY;

// a string object
let hello = new String("Hello!");
```

One thing you may find puzzling is the existence of the object form of the `string`, `boolean`, `symbol`, `bigint`, and `number` primitives. On the surface, the object form and primitive form of these types look very similar. Here is an example:

```
let movie = "Pulp Fiction";
let movieObj = new String("Pulp Fiction");


console.log(movie);
console.log(movieObj);
```

What you see printed will be identical. Below the surface, though, both `movie` and `movieObj` are very different. One is literally a primitive of type `string`, and the other is of type `Object`. This leads to some interesting (and possibly incomprehensible) behavior that I will gradually touch upon as we explore the handful of built-in types we've seen so far.

THE ABSOLUTE MINIMUM

If this feels like a movie or TV series that abruptly ended just as things were getting interesting, I don't blame you for thinking that way. Also, what's up with single seasons of TV shows pausing in the middle and continuing a "Part 2" a few months later? Anyway, I digress. The main takeaway is that our primitives make up the most basic types we can use in our code. Our objects are a bit more complex and are made up of other primitives or objects. We'll see more of that in upcoming chapters when we dive deeper. Beyond that, we learned the names for the common built-in types and some basic background material about them.

In subsequent chapters, we are going to get a deeper look at all these types and the nuances of working with them. Think of this chapter as the gentle on-ramp that suddenly drops you and me onto the rails of a crazy rollercoaster.

? Ask a question: **https://forum.kirupa.com**

✔ Practice by building real apps: **https://bit.ly/coding_exercises**

 Errors/known issues: **https://bit.ly/javascript_errata**

ARRAYS

Let's imagine you are jotting down a list on a piece of paper. Let's call the piece of paper **groceries**. Now, on the paper, you write a numbered list starting with zero with all the items that belong there, as shown in Figure 13.1.

0. Milk

1. Eggs

2. Frosted Flakes

3. Salami

4. Juice

That's some neat handwriting!

FIGURE 13.1

A list of items that resembles a grocery list

By simply creating a list of things, what you have right now is a real-world example of an array! The piece of paper, called **groceries**, would be your array. The items that you need to purchase are known as the array values.

In this chapter, you will learn all about what I like to go grocery shopping for. You may indirectly get an introduction to the very common built-in type, the array, as well.

Creating an Array

The popular way all the cool kids create arrays these days is to use opening and closing brackets. Here is our `groceries` variable that is initialized to an empty array:

```
let groceries = [];
```

We have our variable name on the left, and we have a pair of brackets on the right that initializes this variable as an empty array. This bracket-y approach for creating an array is better known as the **array literal notation**.

Now, we will commonly want to create an array with some items inside it from the very beginning. To create these non-empty arrays, we place the items we want inside the brackets and separate them by commas, like so:

```
let groceries = ["Milk", "Eggs", "Frosted Flakes", "Salami",
"Juice"];
```

Notice that our groceries array now contains **Milk**, **Eggs**, **Frosted Flakes**, **Salami**, and **Juice**. At this point, I need to emphasize how important the commas are. Without the commas, we'll just have one giant item instead of a series of individual items. All right, now that we've learned how to declare an array, let's go deeper and look at how we can actually use it to store and work with data.

Accessing Array Values

One of the nice things about an array is that we not only have easy access to it, but we also have easy access to each of the array values, similar to highlighting an item in our grocery list (see Figure 13.2).

0. Milk

1. Eggs

2. Frosted Flakes

3. Salami

4. Juice

FIGURE 13.2

Arrays enable you to access individual items selectively.

The only thing we need to know is what the procedure is for accessing an individual item.

Inside an array, each item is assigned a number, starting with zero. In Figure 13.2, **Milk** is given the value 0, **Eggs** the value 1, **Frosted Flakes** the value 2, and so on. The formal term for these numbers is the **index value**.

Let's say that our `groceries` array is declared as follows:

```
let groceries = ["Milk", "Eggs", "Frosted Flakes", "Salami",
"Juice"];
```

If we wanted to access an item from the array, all we need to do is pass in the index value of the item we are interested in:

```
groceries[1]
```

The index value is passed into our array using square brackets. In this example, we are referring to the **Eggs** value because the index position 1 refers to it. If we passed in a 2, we would return **Frosted Flakes**. We can keep passing in index values until we have no more values left.

The range of numbers we can use as our index values is one less than our array's length. The reason is that, as shown in the figures earlier, our index values start at zero. If our array only has five items, trying to display `groceries[6]` or `groceries[5]` will result in a message of **undefined**.

Let's go one step further. In most real-world scenarios, we will want to go through our array programmatically, as opposed to accessing each item individually.

We can take what I explained in the previous paragraph and use a `for` loop to accomplish this:

```
for (let i = 0; i < groceries.length; i++) {
  let item = groceries[i];
}
```

Notice the range of our loop starts at zero and ends just one before our array's full length (as returned by the `length` property). This works because, like I mentioned earlier, our array index values go from zero to one short of the value returned for the array's length. And, yes, the `length` property returns a count of all the items in our array!

Adding Items

Rarely will we leave our array in the state we initialized it in originally. We will want to add items to it. To add items to our array, we will use the push method:

```
groceries.push("Cookies");
```

The push method is called directly on our array, and we pass in the data we want to add to it. When we use the push method, our newly added data will always find itself at the end of the array.

For example, after running the code on our initial array, we will see **Cookies** added to the end of our groceries array (see Figure 13.3).

0. Milk

1. Eggs

2. Frosted Flakes

3. Salami

4. Juice

5. Cookies

FIGURE 13.3

*Our array is now larger with the addition of **Cookies** at the end.*

If we want to add data to the beginning of our array, we use the unshift method:

```
groceries.unshift("Bananas");
```

When data is added to the beginning of our array, the index value for all of the existing items increases to account for the newly inserted data (see Figure 13.4).

FIGURE 13.4

Our newly added item is inserted at the beginning.

The reason is that the first item in our array will always have an index value of 0. This means that the space originally occupied by the item currently at 0 needs to push itself and everything below it out to make room for the new data.

Both the `push` and `unshift` methods, besides adding the elements to the array when we use them, return the new length of the array as well:

```
console.log(groceries.push("Cookies")); // returns 6
```

Not sure why that is useful, but keep it under your hat in case you do need it. If you have a good use case for this, definitely let me know by posting on the forums at **https://forum.kirupa.com**!

Removing Items

To remove an item from the array, we can use the pop and shift methods. The pop method removes the last item from the array and returns it:

```
let lastItem = groceries.pop();
```

The shift method does the same thing on the opposite end of the array. Instead of the last item being removed and returned, the shift method removes and returns the first item from the array:

```
let firstItem = groceries.shift();
```

When an item is removed from the beginning of the array, the index positions of all remaining elements are decremented by one to fill in the gap (see Figure 13.5).

FIGURE 13.5

What happens when an item is removed from our array

One thing to note: When we are adding items to our array using `unshift` or `push`, the returned value from that method call is the new length of our array. That is not what happens when we call the `pop` and `shift` methods, though! When we are removing items using `shift` and `pop`, the value returned by the method call is the **removed item itself**!

Finding Items

To find items inside our array, you have a handful of built-in methods: `indexOf`, `lastIndexOf`, `includes`, `find`, `findIndex`, and `filter`. For the sake of simplicity, we will focus on `indexOf` and `lastIndexOf` for now. These two methods work by scanning our array and returning the index position of the matching element.

The `indexOf` method returns the first occurrence of the item you are searching for:

```
let groceries =["Milk", "Eggs", "Frosted Flakes", "Salami",
 "Juice"];
let resultIndex = groceries.indexOf("Eggs",0);

console.log(resultIndex); // 1
```

Notice that the `resultIndex` variable stores the result of calling `indexOf` on our `groceries` array. To use `indexOf`, we pass in the element we are looking for along with the index position to start from:

```
groceries.indexOf("Eggs", 0);
```

The value returned by `indexOf` in this case will be 1.

The `lastIndexOf` method is similar to `indexOf` in how we use it, but it differs a bit on what it returns when an element is found. Whereas `indexOf` finds the first occurrence of the element we are searching for, `lastIndexOf` finds the last occurrence of the element we are searching for and returns that element's index position.

When we search for an element that does not exist in our array, both `indexOf` and `lastIndexOf` return a value of −1.

Merging Arrays

The last thing we are going to do is look at how to create a new array that is made up of two separate arrays. Let's say we have two arrays called good and bad:

```
let good = ["Mario", "Luigi", "Kirby", "Yoshi"];
let bad = ["Bowser", "Koopa Troopa", "Goomba"];
```

To combine both of these arrays into one array, we use the concat method on the array we want to make bigger and pass the array we want to merge into it as the argument. What will get returned is a new array whose contents are made up of both good and bad:

```
let goodAndBad = good.concat(bad);
console.log(goodAndBad);
```

In this example, because the concat method returns a new array, the goodAndBad variable ends up becoming an array that stores the results of our concatenation operation. The order of the elements inside goodAndBad is good first and bad second.

Mapping, Filtering, and Reducing Arrays

So far, we looked at several ways to add items, remove items, and other basic bookkeeping tasks. Some of the other things arrays bring to the table are really simple ways for you to manipulate the data contained inside them. These simple ways are brought to you via the **map**, **filter**, and **reduce** methods.

The Old School Way

Before we talk about map, filter, and reduce, and how they make accessing and manipulating data inside an array a breeze, let's look at the non-breezy approach first. This is an approach that typically involves a for loop, keeping track of where in the array you are, and you shedding a certain amount of tears.

To see this in action, let's say we have an array of names:

```
let names = ["marge", "homer", "bart", "lisa", "maggie"];
```

This aptly named names array contains a list of names that are currently lowercased. What we want to do is capitalize the first letter in each word to make these names look proper. Using the for loop approach, this can be accomplished as follows:

```
let names = ["marge", "homer", "bart", "lisa", "maggie"];
```

```
let newNames = [];

for (let i = 0; i < names.length; i++) {
  let name = names[i];
  let firstLetter = name.charAt(0).toUpperCase();

  newNames.push(firstLetter + name.slice(1));
}

console.log(newNames);
```

Notice that we go through each item, capitalize the first letter, and add the properly capitalized name to a new array called `newNames`. There is nothing magical or complicated going on here, but you'll often find yourself taking the items in your array, manipulating (or accessing) the items for some purpose, and returning a new array with the manipulated data. It's a common enough task with a lot of boilerplate code that you will keep replicating unnecessarily. In large codebases, making sense of what is going on in a loop adds unnecessary overhead. That's why `map`, `filter`, and `reduce` were introduced. You get all the flexibility of using a `for` loop without the unwanted side effects and extra code. Who wouldn't want that?

Modifying Each Array Item with map

The first of the array methods we will look at for manipulating our array data is map. We will use the `map` method to take all the items in our array and modify them into something else that is an entirely new array (see Figure 13.6).

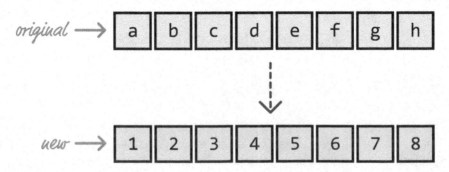

FIGURE 13.6

Our original array and new array!

How you use it looks like this:

```
let newArray = originalArray.map(someFunction);
```

This single line looks nice and friendly, but it hides a lot of complexity. Let's demystify it a bit. The way map works is as follows: You call it on the array that you wish to affect (`originalArray`), and it takes a function (`someFunction`) as the argument. This function will run on each item in the array—allowing you to write code to modify each item as you wish. The end result is a new array whose contents are the result of `someFunction` having run and potentially modified each item in the original array. Sounds simple enough, right?

Using map, let's revisit our earlier problem of taking the lowercased names from the array and capitalizing them properly. We'll look at the full code first and then focus on the interesting details next. The full code is as follows:

```
let names = ["marge", "homer", "bart", "lisa", "maggie"];

function capitalizeItUp(item) {
  let firstLetter = item.charAt(0).toUpperCase();
  return firstLetter + item.slice(1);
}

let newNames = names.map(capitalizeItUp);
console.log(newNames);
```

Take a moment to see how this code works. The interesting part is the `capitalizeItUp` function that is passed in as the argument to the map method. This function runs on each item, and notice that the array item you are currently on is passed in to this function as an argument. You can reference the current item argument via whatever name you prefer. We are referencing this argument using the boring name of `item`:

```
function capitalizeItUp(item) {
  let firstLetter = item.charAt(0).toUpperCase();
  return firstLetter + item.slice(1);
}
```

Inside this function, we can write whatever code we want to manipulate the current array item. The only thing we need to do is return the new array item value:

```
function capitalizeItUp(item) {
  let firstLetter = item.charAt(0).toUpperCase();
  return firstLetter + item.slice(1);
}
```

That's all there is to it. After all this code runs, map returns a new array with all the capitalized items in their correct locations. The original array is never modified, so keep that in mind.

 TIP Meet the Callback Functions

Our `capitalizeItUp` function is also known more generically by another name. That name is **callback function**. A callback function is a function that has two things done to it:

- It is passed in as an argument to another function.
- It is called from inside the other function.

You will see callback functions referenced all the time, such as when we look at filter and reduce next. If this is the first time you are hearing about them, you now have a better idea of what they are. If you've heard of them before, then good for you!

Filtering Items

With arrays, you'll often find yourself filtering (that is, removing) items based on a given criterion (see Figure 13.7).

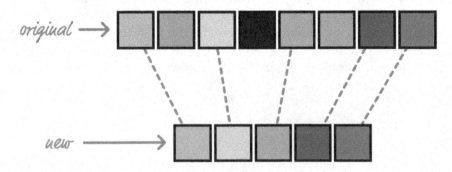

FIGURE 13.7

We start with many items but end up with fewer items.

For example, let's say we have an array of numbers:

```
let numbers = [1, 2, 3, 4, 5, 6, 7, 8, 9, 10, 11, 12];
```

Right now, our `numbers` array has both even numbers as well as odd numbers. Let's say we want to ignore all of the odd numbers and only look at the even ones. The way we can do that is by using our array's `filter` method and filtering out all the odd numbers so only the even numbers remain.

The way we use the `filter` method is similar to what we did with `map`. It takes one argument, a callback function, and this function will determine whether or not each array item will be filtered out. This will make more sense when we look at some code. Take a look at the following:

```
let numbers = [1, 2, 3, 4, 5, 6, 7, 8, 9, 10, 11, 12];

let evenNumbers = numbers.filter(function (item) {
  return (item % 2 == 0);
});

console.log(evenNumbers);
```

We create a new array called `evenNumbers` that will store the result of `filter` running on our `numbers` array. The contents of this array will be the even numbers only thanks to our callback function checking each item to see whether the result of `item % 2` is 0 (in other words, it is checking whether the remainder is 0 when you divide by 2). If the callback function returns **true**, the item is carried over to the filtered array. If the callback function returns **false**, the item is ignored.

One thing to note here is that our callback function isn't an explicitly named function like our `capitalizeItUp` function from earlier. It is simply an anonymous one, but it still gets the job done. You'll see this anonymous form commonly where a callback function needs to be specified, so become familiar with this style of defining a function.

Getting One Value from an Array of Items

The last array method we will look at is `reduce`. This is a bizarre one. With both `map` and `filter`, we went from one array with a starting set of values to another array with a different set of values. With the `reduce` method, we will still start with an array, but what we will end up with is a single value (see Figure 13.8).

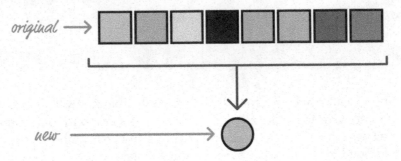

FIGURE 13.8

From many to...one!

This is definitely one of those cases where we need an example to explain what is going on.

Let's reuse our `numbers` array from earlier:

```
let numbers = [1, 2, 3, 4, 5, 6, 7, 8, 9, 10, 11, 12];
```

What we want to do is add up all the values here. This is the kind of thing the `reduce` method was built for, where we reduce all the values in our array into a single item. Take a look at the following code:

```
let total = numbers.reduce(function(total, current) {
  return total + current;
}, 0);


console.log(total);
```

We call `reduce` on our `numbers` array, and we pass it two arguments:

- The callback function

- Initial value

We start our summing at an initial value of 0, and our callback function is responsible for adding up each item in the array. Unlike earlier where our callback function took only the current array item as its argument, the callback function for `reduce` is slightly more involved. You need to deal with *two* arguments here:

- The first argument contains the total value of all the actions you've done so far.

- The second argument is the familiar current array item.

By using these two arguments, we can easily construct all sorts of scenarios involving keeping track of something. In our example, since all we want is the sum of all items in the array, we are summing up the `total` with the value of `current`. The end result will be **78**.

More on the Callback Function Arguments

For our callback functions, we've only specified one argument representing the current array item for map and `filter`. We specified two arguments representing the total value as well as the current item for `reduce`. Our callback functions have two optional arguments you can specify:

- The current index position of your current array item

- The array you are calling `map`, `filter`, or reduce on

For `map` and `filter`, these would be the second and third arguments you specify. For `reduce`, it would be the third and fourth arguments. You may go your entire life without ever having to specify these optional arguments, but if you ever run into a situation where you need them, you now know where to find them.

We are almost done here. Let's look at an example that shows the output of reduce to be something besides a number. Take a look at the following:

```
let words = ["Where", "do", "you", "want", "to", "go", "today?"];

let phrase = words.reduce(function (total, current, index) {
  if (index == 0) {
    return current;
  } else {
    return total + " " + current;
  }
}, "");

console.log(phrase);
```

In this example, we are combining the text-based content of our words array to create a single value that ends up showing **Where do you want to go today?** Notice what is going on in our callback function. Besides doing the work to combine each item into a single word, we are specifying the optional third argument that represents our current item's index position. We use this index value to special case the first word to deal with whether or not we insert a space character at the beginning.

A Short Foray into Functional Programming

As the last few sections have highlighted, the `map`, `filter`, and `reduce` methods greatly simplify how we work with arrays. There is another HUGE thing that these three methods scratch the surface of. That thing is something known as **functional programming**. Functional programming is a way of writing our code where we use functions that:

- Can work inside other functions

- Avoid sharing or changing state

- Return the same output for the same input

There are more nitpicky details that I could list here, but this is a good start. Anyway, you can see how functional programming principles apply to the various callback functions we've used so far. Our callback functions match these three criteria perfectly because they are functions that can be dropped into or out of any situation as long as the arguments still work. They definitely don't modify any state, and they work fully inside the `map`, `filter`, and `reduce` methods. Functional programming is a fun topic that needs a lot more coverage than what we've looked at in the last few sentences, so we'll leave things be for now and cover it in greater detail in future chapters.

THE ABSOLUTE MINIMUM

That is almost all there is to know about arrays...well, at least the things you will use them for most frequently. At the very least, you will have learned how to use them to create a grocery list!

Additional resources:

- ? Ask a question: **https://forum.kirupa.com**
- ✔ Practice by building real apps: **https://bit.ly/coding_exercises**
- 🎯 Errors/known issues: **https://bit.ly/javascript_errata**
- 🔭 Deeper look at arrays: **https://bit.ly/kirupaArrays**

IN THIS CHAPTER

- Understand how text is treated in JavaScript
- Learn how to perform common string operations
- Look at the various string properties

14

STRINGS

I have a hunch that you are a human being. As a human, you probably relate really well with words. You speak them. You write them. You also tend to use a lot of them in the things you program. As it turns out, JavaScript likes words a whole lot as well. The letters and funny looking symbols that make up your (and my) language have a formal name. They are known as **strings**. Strings in JavaScript are nothing more than a series of characters. Despite how boring that sounds, accessing and manipulating these characters is a skill that we must be familiar with. That's where this chapter comes in.

The Basics

When we work with strings in our code, we just need to make sure to enclose them in single or double quotes. Here are some examples:

```
let text = "this is some text";
let moreText = 'I am in single quotes!';

console.log("this is some more text");
```

Besides just listing strings, we'll often combine a couple of strings together. We can easily do that by using the + operator:

```
let initial = "hello";
console.log(initial + " world!");

console.log("I can also " + "do this!");
```

In all these examples, we are able to see the string. The only reason I point out something this obvious is that, when we can see the contents of the string as literally as we do, these strings are more appropriately known as **string literals**. That doesn't change the fact that the resulting structure is still a built-in primitive type called a **string** (you know… a simple pizza ingredient from Chapter 12, "Of Pizza, Types, Primitives, and Objects").

Figure 14.1 helps us to visualize what the `text` and `moreText` strings look like.

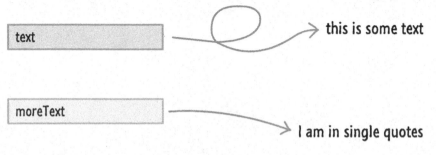

FIGURE 14.1

A visualization of strings

We just have our two variables pointing to some literal chunks of text. There isn't anything else going on. If you are wondering why I wasted this space in visualizing something so obvious, the visualizations will get more complex once we move into `Object` territory. You'll see hints of that in this chapter itself.

Anyway, all of this isn't particularly important…yet. The only important thing to keep in mind is that we need to wrap our string literals in either double quotation marks (") or single quotation marks (') to designate them as a region of text. If we don't do that, bad things happen, and our code probably won't run.

That's all there is to the basics. The fun stuff comes from using all the functionality JavaScript provides for working with strings. We'll look at that and more in the following sections.

String Properties and Methods

When we are working with strings, the underlying `String` object implementation contains a lot of properties that make working with text (usually) easier. In the following sections, instead of going over every property and boring both of us to death, I'll just focus on the important ones in the context of common tasks you and I will be doing.

Accessing Individual Characters

While a string looks like one cohesive unit, it is actually made up of a series of characters. We can access each character in several ways. The most common way is by using the array/bracket notation and passing in a number that corresponds to the index position of the character:

```
let vowels = "aeiou";
console.log(vowels[2]);
```

In this example, we will see the **i** character because it is the item at the second index position. To better visualize what just happened, take a look at Figure 14.2.

character index positions

FIGURE 14.2

Our vowels mapped with index positions

Here is something we should keep in mind when the word **index** is thrown around. Just like with arrays, index positions with strings start at 0 and move up from there. That is why our index position is 2, but the count of the element at that position is actually 3. This gets less weird the more you work with JavaScript and other languages that don't contain the words **Visual** and **Basic** where indexes start from 1.

To go one step further, we can access all characters in our string by just looping through the index positions. The start of the loop will be 0, and the end of your loop will be determined by the length of our string. The length of our string (aka the count of the number of characters) is returned by the `length` property. Yes, this is nearly identical to arrays!

Here is an example of the preceding paragraph in action:

```javascript
let vowels = "aeiou";

for (let i = 0; i < vowels.length; i++) {
  console.log(vowels[i]);
}
```

While we may not be looping through a string all the time, it is very common to use the `length` property to get a count of the number of characters in our string.

If we don't get along with the array/bracket notation, we also have the `charAt` method, which returns a character at a specified index position:

```
let vowels = "aeiou";
console.log(vowels.charAt(2));
```

The end result is identical to what we see using the array notation. I wouldn't use this method unless you care about really old browsers like Internet Explorer 7. (Do you even remember Internet Explorer 7?)

WAIT...WHAT?

If you are wondering where in the world string primitives have the ability to access properties only available to `String` objects, suspend your curiosity for a few more chapters until we get to Chapter 16, "When Primitives Behave Like Objects," where we'll look at this in much greater detail.

Combining (aka Concatenating) Strings

To combine two strings together, we can just use the + or += operator and just add the strings like we would a series of numbers:

```
let stringA = "I am a simple string.";
let stringB = "I am a simple string, too!";

console.log(stringA + " " + stringB);
```

Notice that, in the third line, we add `stringA` and `stringB` together. Between them, we specify an empty space character (" ") to ensure there is a space between each of the individual strings. We can mix and match string literals with string primitives and string objects and still get our text all combined together.

For example, this is all valid:

```
let textA = "Please";
let textB = new String("stop!");
let combined = textA + " make it " + textB;

console.log(combined);
```

Despite all the mixing going on, the type of the combined variable is simply a **string** primitive.

For combining strings, we also have the concat method. We can call this method from any string and specify a sequence of string primitives, literals, and objects that we want to combine into one megastring:

```
let foo = "I really";
let blah = "why anybody would";
let blarg = "do this";

let result = foo.concat(" don't know", " ", blah, " ", blarg);

console.log(result);
```

For the most part, just use the + and += approach for combining strings. It is faster than the `concat` approach. With everything else being equal, who wouldn't want some extra speed in their code?

One thing to point out is that there is a much more modern way to combine strings, especially if what we are trying to do is combine strings and variables together. We'll look at that in the next chapter.

Getting Substrings Out of Strings

Sometimes what we are interested in is a sequence of characters somewhere in the middle of our string. The two properties that help satisfy this interest are `slice` and `substr`. Let's say we have the following string:

```
let theBigString = "Pulp Fiction is an awesome movie!";
```

Let's mess with this string for a bit.

The slice Method

The `slice` method allows us to specify the start and end positions of the part of the string that we want to extract:

```
let theBigString = "Pulp Fiction is an awesome movie!";
console.log(theBigString.slice(5, 12));
```

In this example, we extract the characters between index positions 5 and 12. The end result is that the word **Fiction** is returned.

The start and end position values do not have to be positive. If you specify a negative value for the end position, the end position for your string is what is left when you count backwards from the end:

```
let theBigString = "Pulp Fiction is an awesome movie!";
console.log(theBigString.slice(0, -6));
```

If we specify a negative start position, our start position is the count of whatever we specify starting from the end of the string:

```
let theBigString = "Pulp Fiction is an awesome movie!";
console.log(theBigString.slice(-14, -7));
```

We just saw three variations of how the `slice` method can be used. I've never used anything but the first version with a positive start and end position, and you'll probably be in a similar boat.

The substr Method

The next approach we will look at for splitting up a string is the `substr` method. This method takes two arguments as well:

```
let newString = substr(start, length);
```

The first argument is a number that specifies our starting position, and the second argument is a number that specifies the length of our substring. This makes more sense when we look at some examples:

```
let theBigString = "Pulp Fiction is an awesome movie!";
console.log(theBigString.substr(0, 4)); // Pulp
```

We start the substring at the 0 position and count four characters up. That is why **Pulp** is returned. If we want to just extract the word **Fiction**, this is what our code would look like:

```
let theBigString = "Pulp Fiction is an awesome movie!";
console.log(theBigString.substr(5, 7)); // Fiction
```

If we don't specify the length, the substring that gets returned is the string that goes from the start position to the end:

```
let theBigString = "Pulp Fiction is an awesome movie!";
console.log(theBigString.substr(5)); // Fiction is an awesome
movie!
```

There are a few more variations of values we can pass in for substr, but these are the big ones.

Splitting a String with split

That which you can concatenate, you can also split apart. I am pretty sure a wise person once said that. Another way we can split apart a string is by using the `split` method. Calling this method on a string returns an array of substrings. These substrings are separated by a character or regular expression (aka RegEx) that we use to determine where to split apart our string.

Let's look at a simple example where this makes more sense:

```
let inspirationalQuote = "That which you can concatenate, you can
also split apart.";
```

```
let splitWords = inspirationalQuote.split(" ");

console.log(splitWords.length); // 10
```

In this example, we are splitting the `inspirationalQuote` text on the space character. Every time a space character is encountered, we break our string and make the text prior to the space an array item. This repeats until we reach the end of the string. What we see at the end is an array of strings whose contents are the individual pieces of text we had separated by a space earlier.

Here is another example:

```
let days = "Monday,Tuesday,Wednesday,Thursday,Friday,
Saturday,Sunday";
let splitWords = days.split(",");

console.log(splitWords[6]); // Sunday
```

We have the `days` variable, which stores a string of days separated only by a comma. If we wanted to separate out each day, we could use the `split` method with the separator character being the comma. The end result is an array of seven items, where each item is the day of the week from the original string.

You'll be surprised at how often you find yourself using the `split` method to break apart a sequence of characters, which can be as simple as a sentence or something more complex like data returned from a web service.

Finding Something Inside a String

If we ever need to find a character or characters inside a string, we can use the `indexOf`, `lastIndexOf`, and `match` methods. Let's look at the `indexOf` method first.

What the `indexOf` method does is take the character(s) we are looking for as its argument. If what we are looking for is found, it returns the index position in the string where the first occurrence...occurs. If no matches are found, this method gifts you with a −1. Let's look at an example:

```
let question = "I wonder what the pigs did to make these birds so
angry?";
console.log(question.indexOf("pigs")); // 18
```

We are trying to see if pigs exist in our string. Because what we are looking for does exist, the `indexOf` method lets us know that the first occurrence of this word can be found at the 18th index position. If we look for something that doesn't exist, like the letter **z** in this example, a –1 gets returned:

```
let question = "I wonder what the pigs did to make these birds so
angry?";
console.log(question.indexOf("z")); // -1
```

The `lastIndexOf` method is very similar to `indexOf`. As you can sorta maybe guess by the name, `lastIndexOf` returns the last occurrence of what you are looking for:

```
let question = "How much wood could a woodchuck chuck if a
woodchuck could chuck wood?";
console.log(question.lastIndexOf("wood")); // 65
```

There is one more argument you can specify to both `indexOf` and `lastIndexOf`. In addition to providing the characters to search for, you can also specify an index position on your string to start your search from:

```
let question = "How much wood could a woodchuck chuck if a
woodchuck could chuck wood?";
console.log(question.indexOf("wood", 30)); // 43
```

The last thing to mention about the `indexOf` and `lastIndexOf` methods is that you can match any instance of these characters appearing in your string. These functions do not differentiate between whole words and a substring of a larger set of characters. Be sure to take that into account.

Before we wrap this up, let's look at the `match` method. With the `match` method, you have a little more control. This method takes a RegEx as its argument:

```
let phrase = "There are 3 little pigs.";
let regexp = /[0-9]/;
```

```
let numbers = phrase.match(regexp);

console.log(numbers[0]); // 3
```

What gets returned is also an array of matching substrings, so you can use your array ninja skills to make working with the results a breeze. Learning how to work with regular expressions is something that goes beyond what we'll look at in this book, but the following documentation on MDN is a great starting point: https://bit.ly/kirupaRegEx

Uppercasing and Lowercasing Strings

Finally, let's end this coverage on strings with something easy that doesn't require anything complicated. To uppercase or lowercase a string, we can use the appropriately named `toUpperCase` and `toLowerCase` methods. Let's look at an example:

```
let phrase = "My name is Bond. James Bond.";

console.log(phrase.toUpperCase()); // MY NAME IS BOND. JAMES BOND.
console.log(phrase.toLowerCase()); // my name is bond. james bond.
```

See, told you this was easy!

THE ABSOLUTE MINIMUM

Strings are one of the handful of basic data types you have available in JavaScript, and you just saw a good overview of the many things you can do using them. One issue that I skirted around is where your string primitives seem to mysteriously have all these properties that are common only to objects. We'll look at that in the next chapter!

? Ask a question: **https://forum.kirupa.com**

✔ Practice by building real apps: **https://bit.ly/coding_exercises**

📛 Errors/known issues: **https://bit.ly/javascript_errata**

15

COMBINING STRINGS AND VARIABLES

Ah, yes, it's time for us to look at the ancient art of combining strings and variables, where we generate a string made up of **literal (static) text values** along with **variables** whose values are defined as a result of some JavaScript operation. This is an important topic for us to look at because we will find ourselves combining strings and variables quite often—whether it is for printing messages to the console, specifying a key to some object, generating a complex CSS property value, or trying to accomplish a boatload of other things.

In the following sections, we'll look at the two best approaches we have in JavaScript for combining strings and variables. This is going to be a hoot!

Our Setup

To help highlight the two approaches, let's work with an example. For this example, we are going to have a function called `sayGreeting`, and it will take three arguments: one argument for the greeting, one argument for whom the greeting is targeted to, and one argument for an emoji to display. This function's signature will loosely look as follows.

```
function sayGreeting(greeting, who, emoji) {
    // magic!
}
```

If we call our `sayGreeting` function with the arguments **Hello hello hello, Police Officer Panda**, and 🐼, what this function will return is a string that looks like this:

Hello hello hello, Police Officer Panda! How are you? 🐼

Notice that some of the words in the greeting are based on the arguments we passed in. Some of the words are provided by the function itself. And with this, it's time to look at what exactly goes on inside our `sayGreeting` function.

NOTE   Emojis in Code? What?!!

What you are going to see in the next few sections are examples of code where we have emojis as a part of what we type. This is totally supported, just like adding text or numbers. The easiest way to add an emoji is to copy/paste from your computer's emoji picker or from an emoji website like emojipedia (**https://emojipedia.org/**).

Using the + Operator (aka String Concatenation)

An approach as old as time for combining strings is what we looked at in the previous chapter, where we combined (concatenated) each string fragment using the + operator. Take a look at the following:

```
function sayGreeting(greeting, who, emoji) {
  let message = greeting + ", " + who + "! How are you? " + emoji;
  return message;
}


let batman = sayGreeting("Good morning", "Batman", "☺");
console.log(batman); // Good morning, Batman! How are you? ☺
```

Notice how we combine the values of the `greeting`, `who`, and `emoji` arguments with some of our predefined text to generate the final message:

```
function sayGreeting(greeting, who, emoji) {
  let message = greeting + ", " + who + "! How are you? " + emoji;
  return message;
}
```

Each literal text value is separated using quotation marks. We use the + operator to stitch together these literal text values and variables together into one final string, which is stored by message. The spaces and punctuation marks that make up our final greeting are explicitly (maybe awkwardly?) defined as well.

Now, what we have here is a fairly simple example. For more complex strings made up of a bunch of variables and literal values, the number of + operators and quotation marks can become quite large and unwieldy. If we are printing text that itself has quotation marks and special characters, we need to take extra care to escape them to ensure the final string is still valid. With this concatenation-based approach, this isn't the sort of stuff we write and have working properly on the first try...at least not for me!

Template Literals (aka String Interpolation)

A more modern approach involves using what are known as **template literals**. With template literals, instead of using the + operator to combine each string fragment, we define the full string up front and **mark the areas** where we need to substitute a value dynamically. This will make more sense with an example, so what we have here is another version of our `sayGreeting` function, this time using template literals:

```
function sayGreeting(greeting, who, emoji) {
  let message = `${greeting}, ${who}! How are you? ${emoji}`;
  return message;
}


let panda = sayGreeting("Hello hello hello", "Police Officer
anda", "🐼");
console.log(panda); // Hello hello hello, Police Officer Panda! How
are you? 🐼
```

Notice what is going on here. First, we define the full string, but we don't designate it as a string by wrapping it using quotation marks. Instead, we use the mysterious backtick character (`), which is to the left of the number 1 key on most keyboards.

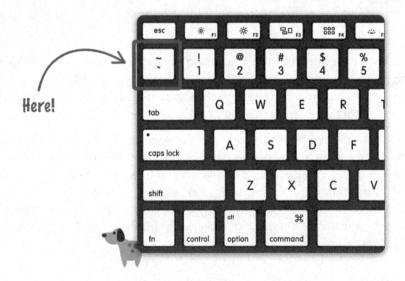

Here!

The backtick characters tell JavaScript that everything inside them should be treated as a string. Next, for the places where we need to insert or substitute a dynamic string value, we designate those placeholders by using the ${expression} syntax. At runtime, the value of ${expression} is turned into a string whose value is whatever we put inside it. Typically, what we would have for our expression are just the variables, but our expression can be any combination of JavaScript elements, like function calls, string methods, and more. We'll keep things simple and focus just on variables here, so putting this all together, our code for generating our message looks like this:

```
function sayGreeting(greeting, who, emoji) {
    let message = `${greeting}, ${who}! How are you? ${emoji}`;
    return message;
}
```

All of this is accomplished without the error-prone process of breaking up our string using + operators and inserting a series of opening and closing quotation marks around our literal string values. Because we are working with our final string output and using placeholders, this approach is also more readable. This makes substituting some text values from a large and complex string a piece of 🍰!

THE ABSOLUTE MINIMUM

We have two (good) approaches for combining literal strings with variables:

* String concatenation using the + operator
* String interpolation using template literals

The all-important question is, which one should you use? Unless you are dealing with something really trivial, I would shy away from using the string concatenation approach. It gets really error prone when you have many series of string fragments you need to deal with. Also, getting all the quotation marks and spaces right is too time consuming. Combining strings using the template literal approach is **quite good for almost any scenario** because of how readable the code is. This readability comes in quite handy for simple cases as well as more complex cases.

What we also have in JavaScript are a handful of other ways to combine strings with variables. We have the `concat` method that lives on the `String` object, we have `Array.join`, and a few more esoteric approaches. These approaches aren't very good, so I won't bore you with details about them. If you really want to know more, ask on the forums!

? Ask a question: **https://forum.kirupa.com**

✔ Practice by building real apps: **https://bit.ly/coding_exercises**

👑 Errors/known issues: **https://bit.ly/javascript_errata**

16

IN THIS CHAPTER

- Get a deeper understanding of how primitives and objects work

- Understand that even primitives have object-like traits

- Wonder how JavaScript ever got to be so popular

WHEN PRIMITIVES BEHAVE LIKE OBJECTS

In Chapter 14, "Strings," and less so in Chapter 12, "Of Pizza, Types, Primitives, and Objects," we got a sneak peek at something that is probably pretty confusing. I've stated many times that primitives are very plain and simple. Unlike objects, they don't contain properties that allow you to fiddle with their values in interesting (or boring) ways. Yet, as clearly demonstrated by all the stuff we can do with strings, our primitives seem to have a mysterious dark side to them. Look at the following example:

```
let greeting = "Hi, everybody!!!";
let shout = greeting.toUpperCase(); // where did
toUpperCase come from?
```

As we can see from this brief snippet, our `greeting` variable, which stores a primitive value in the form of text, seems to have access to the `toUpperCase` method. How is this even possible? Where did that method come from? Why are we here? Answers to confusing existential questions like this will make up the bulk of what you will see in this chapter. Also, I apologize for writing that previous sentence in passive voice. Happen again it won't.

Strings Aren't the Only Problem

Because of how fun and playful they are (kind of like a Golden Retriever), it's easy to pick on strings as the main perpetrator of this primitive/object confusion. As it turns out, many of the built-in primitive types are involved in this racket as well. Table 16.1 displays some popular built-in `Object` types with *most* of the guilty parties (`symbol` and `bigint` will be sitting this one out) that *also* exist as primitives highlighted.

TABLE 16.1   Object Types with Those That Are Primitives Highlighted

Type	What It Does
Array	Helps store, retrieve, and manipulate a collection of data.
Boolean	Acts as a wrapper around the `boolean` primitive; still very much in love with **true** and **false**.
Date	Allows you to more easily represent and work with dates.
Function	Allows you to invoke some code, among other esoteric things.
Math	The nerdy one in the group. It helps you better work with numbers.
Number	Acts as a wrapper around the `number` primitive.
RegExp	Provides a lot of functionality for matching patterns in text.
String	Acts as a wrapper around the `string` primitive.

Whenever we are working with boolean, number, or string primitives, we have access to properties their `Object` equivalent exposes. In the following sections, you'll see what exactly is going on.

Let's Pick on Strings Anyway

Just as you were taught by your parents growing up, we typically use a string in the literal form:

```
let primitiveText = "Homer Simpson";
```

As we saw in Table 16.1, strings also have the ability to be used as objects. There are several ways to create a new object, but the most common way to create an object for a built-in type like our string is to use the new keyword followed by the word String:

```
let name = new String("Batman");
```

The String in this case isn't just any normal word. It represents what is known as a **constructor function**, whose sole purpose is to be used for creating objects. Just like there are several ways to create objects, there are several ways to create String objects as well. The way I see it, knowing about one way that you really *shouldn't* be creating them with is enough.

Anyway, the main difference between the primitive and object forms of a string is the sheer amount of additional baggage the object form carries with it. Figure 16.1 helps us visualize our String object called name.

I just wanted an excuse to post this picture

FIGURE 16.1

A deeper look at what our String object looks like

We have our name variable containing a pointer to the text, **Homer Simpson**. We also have all the various properties and methods that go with the String object—things you may have used, like indexOf, toUpperCase, and so on. You'll get a massive overview of what exactly this diagram represents when we look at objects in greater detail, so don't worry too much about what you see here. Just know that the object form of any of the primitives carries with it a lot of functionality.

Why This Matters

Let's return to our earlier point of confusion. Our string is a primitive. How can a primitive type allow us to access properties on it? The answer has to do with JavaScript being really weird. Let's say we have the following string:

```
let game = "Dragon Age: Origins";
```

The `game` variable is very clearly a string primitive that is assigned to some literal text. If we wanted to access the `length` of this text, we would do something like this:

```
let game = "Dragon Age: Origins";
console.log(game.length);
```

As part of evaluating `game.length`, JavaScript will convert our primitive string into an object. For a brief moment, our lowly primitive will become a beautiful object in order to figure out what the `length` actually is. The thing to keep in mind is that all of this is temporary. Because this temporary object isn't grounded or tied to anything after it serves its purpose, it goes away, and we are left with the result of the `length` evaluation (a number) and the `game` variable still being a string primitive.

This transformation only happens for primitives. If we ever explicitly create a `String` object, then what we create is permanently kept as an object. Let's say we have the following:

```
let gameObject = new String("Dragon Age:Origins");
```

In this case, our `gameObject` variable very clearly points to something whose type is `Object`. This variable will continue to point to an `Object` type unless we modify the string or do something else that causes the reference to be changed. The primitive morphing into an object and then morphing back into a primitive is something unique to primitives. Our objects don't partake in such tomfoolery.

We can easily verify everything I've said by examining the type of our data. That is done by using the `typeof` keyword. Here is an example of me using it to confirm everything I've just told you about:

```
let game = "Dragon Age: Origins";
console.log("Length is: " + game.length);
```

```
let gameObject = new String("Dragon Age:Origins");

console.log(typeof game); // string
console.log(typeof game.length); // number
console.log(typeof gameObject); // object
```

Now, aren't you glad you learned all this?

THE ABSOLUTE MINIMUM

Hopefully this brief explanation helps you to reconcile why our primitives behave like objects when they need to. At this point, you might have a different question around why anybody would have designed a language that does something this bizarre. After all, if a primitive turns into an object when it needs to do something useful, why not just let it stay an object always? The answer has to do with memory consumption.

As we saw from our discussion on how much more baggage the object form of a primitive carries when compared to just a primitive, all of those pointers to additional functionality cost resources. The solution in JavaScript is a compromise. All literal values like text, numbers, and booleans are kept as primitives if they are declared and/or used as such. Only when they need to, are they converted to their respective Object forms. To ensure our app continues to keep a low-memory footprint, these converted objects are quickly discarded (aka **garbage collected**) once they've served their purpose.

? Ask a question: **https://forum.kirupa.com**

✔ Practice by building real apps: **https://bit.ly/coding_exercises**

🐣 Errors/known issues: **https://bit.ly/javascript_errata**

IN THIS CHAPTER

- Make sense of numbers

- Learn about the variety of numerical values you will encounter

- Meet the `Math` object and the various mathematical things you can do

NUMBERS

A large part of your time in JavaScript will be spent dealing with numbers. Even if you aren't working with numbers directly, you'll indirectly encounter them when doing even the most basic of tasks, such as keeping count of something, working with arrays, and so on.

In this chapter, I will introduce you to numbers in JavaScript by looking at how we can use them to accomplish many common tasks. Along the way, we will dive a little bit beyond the basics to broadly explore some interesting number-related things you might find useful.

Using a Number

In order to use a number, all you have to do is...well, use it. Here is a simple example of me declaring a variable called `stooges`, which is initialized to the number 3:

```
let stooges = 3;
```

That is it. There are no hoops to jump through. If you wanted to use more complex numbers, just use them as if nothing is different:

```
let pi = 3.14159;
let color = 0xFF;
let massOfEarth = 5.9742e+24;
```

In this example, I am using a decimal value, a hexadecimal value, and a really large value using exponents. In the end, your browser will automatically do the right thing. Note that the "right thing" doesn't just exist in the positive space. You can use negative numbers easily as well. To use negative numbers, just place a minus sign (−) character before the number you want to turn into a negative value:

```
let temperature = -42;
```

What you've seen in this section makes up the bulk of how you will actually use numbers. In the next couple of sections, we'll go a little bit deeper and look at some of the other interesting things you can do with numbers.

TIP Trivia: Numbers in JavaScript

If you are curious why working with numbers is so easy, the reason is because JavaScript isn't big on numerical types. You don't have to declare a number as being of type int, double, byte, float, and so on, like you may have had to do in other languages. The only exception is if you need a really large or really small number, and that is when bigint comes in. We won't talk about bigint in this book, but you can learn more about it here: https://bit.ly/kirupaBigInt

Oh, also, in JavaScript, all numbers are converted into 64-bit floating point numbers.

Operators

No introduction to numbers would be complete (or even started) without showing you how to use mathematical operators in code to implement things you learned in first-grade math class.

Let's look at the common operators in this section.

Doing Simple Math

In JavaScript, we can create simple mathematical expressions using the +, -, *, /, and % operators to add, subtract, multiply, divide, and find the remainder (modulus) of numbers, respectively. If you can use a calculator, you can do simple math in JavaScript.

Here are some examples that put these operators to use:

```
let total = 4 + 26;
let average = total / 2;
let doublePi = 2*3.14159;
let subtractItem = 50 - 25;
let remainder = total % 7;
let more = (1 + average * 10) / 5;
```

In the last line of this example, notice that I am defining a particular order of operations by using parentheses around the expression I want to evaluate as a group. Again, all of this is just calculator stuff.

JavaScript evaluates expressions in the following order:

1. Parentheses

2. Exponents

3. Multiply

4. Divide

5. Add

6. Subtract

There are various mnemonic devices out there to help you remember this. The one I grew up with since elementary school is "**P**lease **E**xcuse **M**y **D**ear **A**unt **S**ally."

Incrementing and Decrementing

A common task we will do with numbers involves incrementing or decrementing a variable by a certain amount. Here is an example of incrementing the variable i by 1:

```
let i = 4;
i = i + 1;
```

We don't have to increment or decrement by just 1. We can use any arbitrary number:

```
let i = 100;
i = i - 2;
```

All of this doesn't just have to just be addition or subtraction. We can perform other operations as well:

```
let i = 100;
i = i / 2;
```

You should start to see a pattern here. Regardless of what operator we are using, you'll notice that we are cumulatively modifying our i variable. Because of how frequently we will use this pattern, we have some operators that simplify it a bit (see Table 17.1).

TABLE 17.1 Operators for Simplifying Incrementing and Decrementing

Expression	What It Does
i++	Increments i by 1 (i = i + 1)
i--	Decrements i by 1 (i = i - 1)
i += n	Increments i by n (i = i + n)
i -= n	Decrements i by n (i = i - n)

Expression	What It Does
i *= n	Multiplies by n (i = i * n)
i /= n	Divides i by n (i = i / n)
i %= n	Finds the remainder of i when divided by n (i = i % n)
i **= n	Exponential operator, where i is raised to the power of n

If I use these operators on the three examples from earlier, the code will look as follows:

```
i++;
i -= 2;
i /= 2;
```

Before we wrap this up, there is one quirk you should be aware of. It has to do with the -- and ++ operators for incrementing or decrementing a value by 1. It matters whether the ++ and -- operators appear before or after the variable they are incrementing or decrementing

Let's look at this example:

```
let i = 4;
let j = i++;
```

After executing these two lines, the value of i will be 5, just like you would expect. The value of j will be 4. Notice that in this example, the operator appears after the variable.

If we place the operator in front of the variable, the results are a bit different:

```
let i = 4;
let j = ++i;
```

The value of i will still be 5, but here is the kicker—the value of j will also be 5.

What changed between these two examples is the position of the operator. The position of the operator determines **whether the incremented value will be returned or the pre-incremented value will be returned**. Now, aren't you glad you learned that?

Hexadecimal and Octal Values

Beyond using normal decimal values, you can use hexadecimal (base 16) and octal (base 8) values as well. When working with octal values, make sure to start your number with 0:

```
let leet = 0o2471;
```

For hexadecimal values, you need start your number with 0x:

```
let leet = 0x539;
```

In many situations, we'll find ourself dealing with octal and hexadecimal values in the form of strings. If they are strings, we cannot manipulate them as we would normal numbers. We need to convert the string to a number first.

The way we do that is by using the `parseInt` function:

```
let hexValue = parseInt('FFFFFF', 16);
let octalValue = parseInt('011', 8);
```

The `parseInt` function takes our hexadecimal or octal value followed by the base we are converting from.

Special Values—Infinity and NaN

The last thing we will look at are two global properties you will encounter that aren't numerical values. These values are `Infinity` and `NaN`.

Infinity

We can use the `Infinity` and `-Infinity` values to define infinitely large or small numbers:

```
let myLoveForYou = Infinity * 2;
```

The chances of us having to use `Infinity` are often very slim. Instead, we will probably see it returned as part of something else our code does. For example, we will see `Infinity` returned if you divide by zero.

NaN

The NaN keyword stands for "Not a Number," and it gets returned when we do some numerical operation that is invalid. For example, NaN gets returned in the following case:

```
let nope = 1920 / "blah";
```

The reason is that we cannot divide a number and a string. There are noncontrived cases where we will see this value returned, and we'll look at some later.

Going from a String to a Number

Sometimes, not often, you will have numbers that are buried inside strings. The Number method is great for this case, and the following shows it at use:

```
let calculation = "14" + 4;
console.log(calculation); // "144"


let newCalculation = Number("14") + 4;
console.log(newCalculation); // 18
```

Notice that we are adding a string version of 14 to the number 4. In the naïve case as highlighted by our calculation variable, the final answer is 144. By using the Number method and passing in our string form of 14 as an argument, the resulting value is a numerical 14. This causes the addition with 4 to result in 18, as shown by the newCalculation variable.

There are a few more quirks and co-starring appearances by parseInt and parseFloat in this gripping drama, and you can go deeper on this topic here at **https://bit.ly/stringToNumber**.

The Math Object

Numbers are used in a variety of mathematical expressions, and they often go beyond simple addition, subtraction, multiplication, and division operations. Our math classes back in the day would have been a whole lot easier if that's all there was to it. To help us more easily do complicated numerical things, we have the Math object. This object provides us with a lot of functions and constants that will come in handy, and we are going to very briefly look at some of the things this object does.

NOTE This Is Boring!

I am not going to lie to you. Looking at all the stuff the `Math` object provides is pretty boring. Unless you really want to know about all of this now, I would prefer you just very quickly skim through the following sections and refer back as needed. The `Math` object isn't going anywhere (it has no friends), so it will be waiting for you at a later time.

The Constants

To avoid you having to explicitly define mathematical constants like pi, Euler's constant, natural log, and so on, the Math object defines many common constants for you (see Table 17.2).

TABLE 17.2 Constants

Usage	What It Stands For
Math.E	Euler's constant
Math.LN2	Natural logarithm of 2
Math.LN10	Natural logarithm of 10
Math.LOG2E	Base 2 logarithm of E
Math.LOG10E	Base 10 logarithm of E
Math.PI	3.14159 (That's all I remember, and I'm too lazy to look up the rest!)
Math.SQRT1_2	Square root of 1/2
Math.SQRT2	Square root of 2

Of all of these constants, the one I've used the most is Math.PI.

You will use `Math.PI` in everything from drawing circles on your screen to specifying trigonometric expressions. In fact, I can't ever remember having used any of these other constants outside of `Math.PI`. Here is an example of a function that returns the circumference given the radius:

```
function getCircumference(radius) {
  return 2 * Math.PI * radius;
}


console.log(getCircumference(2));
```

I just wanted an excuse
to post this picture

You would use `Math.PI` or any other constant just as you would any named variable.

Rounding Numbers

Your numbers will often end up containing a ridiculous amount of precision:

```
let position = getPositionFromCursor(); // 159.3634493939
```

To help you round these numbers up to a reasonable integer value, you have the `Math.round()`, `Math.ceil()`, and `Math.floor()` functions, which take a number as an argument (see Table 17.3).

TABLE 17.3 Rounding Functions

Function	What It Does
`Math.round()`	Returns a number that is rounded to the nearest integer. You round up if your argument is greater than or equal to .5. You stay at your current integer if your argument is less than .5.
`Math.ceil()`	Returns a number that is greater than or equal to your argument.
`Math.floor()`	Returns a number that is less than or equal to your argument.

The easiest way to make sense of Table 17.3 is to see these three functions in action:

```
Math.floor(.5); // 0
Math.ceil(.5); // 1
Math.round(.5); // 1

Math.floor(3.14); // 3
Math.round(3.14); // 3
Math.ceil(3.14); // 4

Math.floor(5.9); // 5
Math.round(5.9); // 6
Math.ceil(5.9); // 6
```

These three functions always round you to an integer. If you want to round to a precise set of digits, we can call the toFixed method on a number and provide the number of digits of precision we want to round to:

```
let pi = 3.14159;

console.log(pi.toFixed(2)); // 3.14
console.log(pi.toFixed(3)); // 3.142
console.log(pi.toFixed(4)); // 3.1416
```

If you try to provide more digits of precision than the number you are trying to round can handle, that's all good. The number is returned as-is.

Trigonometric Functions

My favorite of the functions, the Math object gives you handy access to almost all of the trigonometric functions you will need, as shown in Table 17.4.

TABLE 17.4 Trigonometric Functions

Function	What It Does
`Math.cos()`	Gives you the cosine for a given argument
`Math.sin()`	Gives you the sine for a given argument
`Math.tan()`	Gives you the tan for a given argument
`Math.acos()`	Gives you the arccosine (isn't that such a cool name?) for a given argument
`Math.asin()`	Gives you the arcsine for a given argument
`Math.atan()`	Gives you the arctan for a given argument

To use any of these, just pass in a number as the argument:

```
Math.cos(0); // 1
Math.sin(0); // 0
Math.tan(Math.PI / 4); // 1
Math.cos(Math.PI); // 1
Math.cos(4 * Math.PI); // 1
```

These trigonometric functions take arguments in the form of radian values. If your numbers are in the form of degrees, be sure to convert them to radians first.

Powers and Square Roots

Continuing down the path of defining the `Math` object functions, you have `Math.pow()`, `Math.exp()`, and `Math.sqrt()`, as explained in Table 17.5.

TABLE 17.5 Functions for Powers and Square Roots

Function	What It Does
`Math.pow()`	Raises a number to a specified power
`Math.exp()`	Raises the Euler's constant to a specified number
`Math.sqrt()`	Returns the square root of a given argument

Let's look at some examples:

```
Math.pow(2, 4); //equivalent of 2^4 (or 2 * 2 * 2 * 2)
Math.exp(3); //equivalent of Math.E^3
Math.sqrt(16); //4
```

Note that `Math.pow()` takes two arguments. This might be the first built-in function we've looked at that takes two arguments. This little detail is somehow mildly exciting.

Getting the Absolute Value

If you want the absolute value of a number, simply use the `Math.abs()` function:

```
Math.abs(37); //37
Math.abs(-6); //6
```

That's all I got for this.

Random Numbers

To generate a somewhat random number between 0 and a smidgen less than 1, you have the `Math.random()` function. This function doesn't take any arguments, but you can simply use it as part of a mathematical expression:

```
let randomNumber = Math.random() * 100;
```

Each time your `Math.random` function is called, you will see a different number returned. A general approach for calculating a random number is as follows:

```
Math.floor(Math.random() * (1 + High - Low)) + Low
```

The value for **High** is the largest random number you would like to generate. The value for **Low** is the smallest random number you would like to generate instead. When you run this code, you will get a number that randomly falls somewhere between the bounds specified by **High** and **Low**.

Here are some examples:

```javascript
// Random number between 0 and 10 (inclusive)
let foo = Math.floor(Math.random() * 11);
console.log(foo);

// Random number between 0 and 100 (inclusive)
let bar = Math.floor(Math.random() * 101);
console.log(bar);

// Random number between 5 and 25 (inclusive)
let zorb = Math.floor(Math.random() * 21) + 5;
console.log(zorb);
```

To make things simple, here is a function you can use instead:

```javascript
function getRandomNumber(low, high) {
  let r = Math.floor(Math.random() * (high - low + 1)) + low;
  return r;
}
```

Just call getRandomNumber and pass in the lower and upper bounds as arguments:

```javascript
// Random number between 0 and 10 (inclusive)
let foo = getRandomNumber(0, 10);
console.log(foo);

// Random number between 0 and 100 (inclusive)
let bar = getRandomNumber(0, 100);
console.log(bar);

// Random number between 5 and 25 (inclusive)
let zorb = getRandomNumber(5, 25);
console.log(zorb);
```

That's all there is to generating a random number that falls within a range that you specify. Now, here is something that you may find interesting. When using **Math. random**, the number that gets returned isn't cryptographically secure. That isn't a concern most of the time, but it does matter if you are doing something that requires generating a random number where extra security is a requirement. To learn a bit more about this, visit: **https://bit.ly/cryptoRandom**

NOTE Visualizing Frequency of Random Numbers

One of the more difficult parts of random numbers is wrapping our heads around the idea that a range of numbers gets chosen randomly *and* nearly equally after enough tries. To help us visualize this, take a look at the handy dandy Random Number Frequency Visualizer at **https://bit.ly/randomNumberVisualizer**.

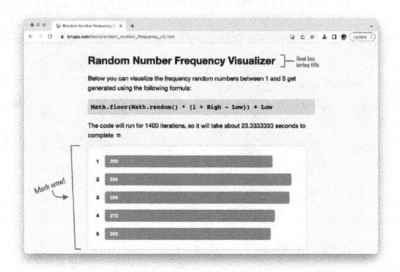

We are picking a random number between 1 and 5 inclusively. This visualizer plots the frequency that each of these numbers get hits across 1400 runs. Unless something is really off, you will see all of the numbers being hit fairly evenly.

THE ABSOLUTE MINIMUM

That's all there is to it for this introductory chapter on numbers and the `Math` object in JavaScript. As you can see, it doesn't get much easier than this. JavaScript provides a very no-frills approach to working with them, and this chapter gave you a slight peek at the edges in case you need to go there.

? Ask a question: **https://forum.kirupa.com**

✔ Practice by building real apps: **https://bit.ly/coding_exercises**

🖋 Errors/known issues: **https://bit.ly/javascript_errata**

18

GETTERS AND SETTERS

The properties we have been working with so far are known as **data properties**. We give these properties a name and assign a value to them:

```
let foo = {
  a: "Hello",
  b: "Monday";
}
```

To read back the value, all we do is just access it directly:

```
console.log(foo.a);
```

Writing a value to this property is sorta what we would expect as well:

```
foo.a = "Manic";
```

Outside of setting and reading a value, there really isn't much more we can do. That is the sad tale of a data property. Now, as part of reading and writing properties, what if we had the ability to do the following?

- Maintain our existing syntax for reading and writing property values

- Gain the ability to run some custom code behind the scenes

That would be pretty cool, right? As it turns out, we have the ability to do all of this. It is brought to you by another friendly and hardworking property variant known as an **accessor property**! In the following sections, we'll learn all about them and run into the real stars of this show—the mysterious getters and setters.

A Tale of Two Properties

On the surface, accessor properties and data properties look very similar. With a data property, you can read and write to a property:

```
theObj.storedValue = "Unique snowflake!"; // setting
console.log(theObj.storedValue); // reading
```

With an accessor property, you can pretty much do the exact same thing:

```
myObj.storedValue = "Also a unique snowflake!"; // setting
console.log(myObj.storedValue); // reading
```

We can't tell by looking at how a property is used whether it is a data property or an accessor property. To tell the difference, we have to go where the property is actually defined. Take a look at the following code, where we have a few properties defined inside our zorb object:

```
let zorb = {
  message: "Blah",

  get greeting() {
    return this.message;
  },

  set greeting(value) {
    this.message = value;
  }
};
```

First up is message, a regular old data property:

```
let zorb = {
  message: "Blah",

  get greeting() {
    return this.message;
  },

  set greeting(value) {
    this.message = value;
  }
};
```

We know this is a data property because it is just a property name and a value. There isn't anything else going on here. Now, here is where things get a little exciting. The next property we have is greeting, and it doesn't look like any property we've seen in the past:

```
let zorb = {
  message: "Blah",

  get greeting() {
```

```
    return this.message;
  },

  set greeting(value) {
    this.message = value;
  }
};
```

Instead of a simple name and value arrangement like we saw with `message`, the `greeting` property is broken up into two *functions* preceded by either a `get` or `set` keyword:

```
let zorb = {
  message: "Blah",

  get greeting() {
    return this.message;
  },

  set greeting(value) {
    this.message = value;
  }
};
```

These keyword and function pairs are commonly known as **getters** and **setters**, respectively. What makes them special is that we don't access `greeting` as a function. We access it just like we would any old property:

```
zorb.greeting = "Hola!";
console.log(zorb.greeting);
```

The real interesting stuff happens at the getter and setter level, so we will dive deeper into them next.

Meet Getters and Setters

Based on what we know so far, *getter* and *setter* are just fancy names for functions that behave like properties. When we try to read an accessor property (zorb. greeting), the getter function gets called:

```
let zorb = {
  message: "Blah",

  get greeting() {
    return this.message;
  },

  set greeting(value) {
    this.message = value;
  }
};
```

Similarly, when we set a new value to our accessor property (zorb.greeting = "Hola!"), the setter function gets called:

```
let zorb = {
  message: "Blah",

  get greeting() {
    return this.message;
  },

  set greeting(value) {
    this.message = value;
  }
};
```

The full power of getters and setters lies in the code we can execute when reading or writing a property. **Because we are dealing with functions under the covers, we can run any code we want**. In our zorb example, we used our greeting getter and setter to closely mimic what a data property would do. We can set a value, and we can read back the value we just set. Pretty boring, right? It doesn't have to be that way, though, and the following examples kick up the interesting-ness of our getters and setters a bunch of notches.

Shout Generator

Here is an example where whatever message we specify gets turned into all caps:

```
var shout = {
  _message: "HELLO!",

  get message() {
    return this._message;
  },

  set message(value) {
    this._message = value.toUpperCase();
  }
};

shout.message = "This is sparta!";
console.log(shout.message);
```

Notice that, as part of setting the value for the message property, we store the entered value in all caps thanks to the toUpperCase method all String objects carry around. All this ensures that, when we try to read back the message we had stored, we see the fully capitalized version of whatever we entered.

Logging Activity

In our next example, we have our superSecureTerminal object, which logs all usernames:

```
var superSecureTerminal = {
  allUserNames: [],
  _username: "",

  showHistory() {
    console.log(this.allUserNames);
```

```
  },

  get username() {
    return this._username;
  },

  set username(name) {
    this._username = name;
    this.allUserNames.push(name);
  }
}
```

This logging is handled inside the `username` setter, where each username we provide gets stored in the `allUserNames` array, and the `showHistory` function displays the stored usernames to the screen. Before we move on, let's actually put this code to the test. We are going to access `superSecureTerminal` differently from what we have done in the past. We are going to take some of our **object-creation knowledge** and do the following:

```
var myTerminal = Object.create(superSecureTerminal);
myTerminal.username = "Michael Gary Scott";
myTerminal.username = "Dwight K. Schrute";
myTerminal.username = "Creed Bratton";
myTerminal.username = "Pam Beasley";

myTerminal.showHistory();
```

We are creating a new object called `myTerminal` that is based on the `superSecureTerminal` object. From here, we can do everything with the `myTerminal` object and call it business as usual.

Property Value Validation

The last example we will look at is one where our setters do some validation on the values sent to them:

```
let person = {
  _name: "",
```

```javascript
  _age: "",

  get name() {
    return this._name;
  },

  set name(value) {
    if (value.length > 2) {
      this._name = value;
    } else {
      console.log("Name is too short!");
    }
  },

  get age() {
    return this._age;
  },

  set age(value) {
    if (value < 5) {
      console.log("Too young!");
    } else {
      this._age = value;
    }
  },

  get details() {
    return "Name: " + this.name + ", Age: " + this.age;
  }
}
```

Notice that we check for an acceptable input in both our name and age properties. If the name we provide is fewer than two characters, we show an alert. If the age is less than five, we show an alert as well. Being able to check whether a value we assign to a property is good or not is probably one of the best features that getters and setters bring to the table.

THE ABSOLUTE MINIMUM

Should we all stop creating regular data properties and go with the fancier accessor properties? Not really. It depends on your current needs and potential future needs. If a property you know will never really need the extra flexibility that getters and setters provide, you can just keep them as data properties. If you ever need to revisit that, going from a data property to an accessor property is something that happens entirely behind the scenes. You and I have the ability to change that without altering how the property itself will be used. Cool, right?

Additional resources:

? Ask a question: **https://forum.kirupa.com**

✔ Practice by building real apps: **https://bit.ly/coding_exercises**

🖋 Errors/known issues: **https://bit.ly/javascript_errata**

IN THIS CHAPTER

- Understand at a deeper level how objects work
- Learn to create custom objects
- Demystify the prototype property
- Do some inheriting

A DEEPER LOOK AT OBJECTS

In the "What Are Objects?" section of Chapter 12, "Of Pizzas, Types, Primitives, and Objects," you received a very high-level overview of what objects in JavaScript are and how to think about them. That was good enough to cover the basics and some of the built-in types, but we need to go a little deeper. This chapter will make that earlier chapter seem like the tip of a ginormous iceberg.

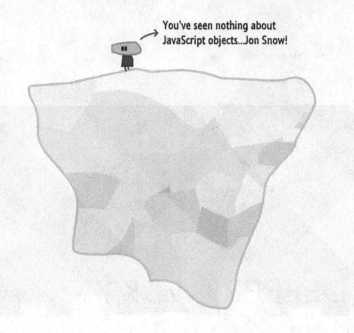

You've seen nothing about JavaScript objects...Jon Snow!

In this chapter, we are going look at objects again, but in greater detail, and touch on some more advanced topics such as using the `Object` object, creating our own custom objects, inheritance, prototypes, and the `this` keyword. If all that I've listed so far makes no sense, it will after we've reached the end of this chapter. I guarantee it.

Meet the Object

At the very bottom of the food chain, we have the `Object` type, which lays the groundwork for custom objects as well as built-in types like `Function`, `Array`, and `RegExp`. Pretty much everything except `null` and `undefined` is directly related to an `Object` or can become one, as needed.

As we saw from the introduction to objects forever ago, the functionality that `Object` brings to the table is pretty minimal. It allows us to specify a bunch of named key and value pairs that we lovingly call **properties**. This isn't all that different from what we see in other languages with data structures like hash tables, associative arrays, and dictionaries.

Anyway, all of this is pretty boring. Instead, let's learn more about objects by getting our hands dirty working with them directly.

Creating Objects

The first thing we will look at is how to create an object. There are several ways to go about this, but all the cool kids are creating objects these days by using the funny-looking (yet compact) **object literal syntax**:

```
let funnyGuy = {};
```

That's right. Instead of typing in `new Object()` like our great-grandparents did, we can just initialize our object by typing **{}**. When this line gets executed, we will have created an object called `funnyGuy` whose type is `Object`.

funnyGuy

One funny dude!

There is a little more to creating objects than what we've just seen with the object literal syntax, but we'll cover all that in due time.

Adding Properties

Once we have an object, there are several paths we can take to add properties to it. The path we will take is a simple and effective one that uses the array-like bracket notation with our new property name acting as the index.

Let's continue with where we left off with our `funnyGuy` object:

```
let funnyGuy = {};
```

Let's say we want to add a new property called `firstName` and give it a value of **Conan**. The way we would add this property is by using **dot notation syntax**, as follows:

```
funnyGuy.firstName = "Conan";
```

That's all there is to it. Once we have added this property, we can access it using the same syntax:

```
let funnyFirstName = funnyGuy.firstName;
```

Now, before we move on, since we are already here (and probably paid for a few more hours of parking), let's add another property called `lastName` and give it the value of **O'Brien**:

```
funnyGuy.lastName = "O'Brien";
```

NOTE There Is Also a Bracket Notation

For setting and reading properties, we used what is known as the dot notation approach. There is an alternate approach for setting and reading properties that uses brackets instead of the dot:

```
let funnyGuy = {};

funnyGuy["firstName"] = "Conan";
funnyGuy["lastName"] = "O'Brien";
```

Whether you prefer dots or brackets is up to you (or your team if you are working with a bunch of people), but there is one area for which brackets are uniquely qualified: dealing with properties whose names we need to generate dynamically. In the case of `firstName` and `lastName`, we hardcoded these property names. Take a look at the following snippet:

```
let myObject = {};
```

```
for (let i = 0; i < 5; i++) {
  let propertyName = "data" + i;

  myObject[propertyName] = Math.random() * 100;
}
```

We have an object called `myObject`. Notice how we are setting properties on it. We don't have a hardcoded list of property names, Instead, we create the property name by relying on the index values from our array. Once we have figured out the property name, we then use that data to create a property for `myObject`. The property names we will generate are **data0**, **data1**, **data2**, **data3**, and **data4**. This ability to dynamically specify a property name as part of setting or reading from an object is something the bracket syntax easily makes possible.

At this point, we are in good shape. Our complete `funnyGuy` code will look like this:

```
let funnyGuy = {};

funnyGuy.firstName = "Conan";
funnyGuy.lastName = "O'Brien";
```

When this code runs, we will have created our `funnyGuy` object and set two properties on it called `firstName` and `lastName`.

What we have just seen is how to create an object and set properties on it in **separate** steps. If we know what properties we want to set from the beginning, we can combine some steps together:

```
let funnyGuy = {
  firstName: "Conan",
  lastName: "O'Brien"
};
```

The end result of this code is identical to what we saw earlier where we created our `funnyGuy` object first and set the properties afterwards.

There is yet another detail about adding properties we should look at. By now, we have looked at a variety of different objects that have properties whose values are made of up numbers, strings, and so on. Did you know that a property value can be another object itself? That's right! Take a look at the following `colors` object whose `content` property stores an object:

```
let colors = {
  header: "blue",
  footer: "gray",
  content: {
    title: "black",
    body: "darkgray",
    signature: "light blue"
  }
};
```

The way you specify an object inside an object is as direct as specifying a property and using the bracket syntax for setting the property value to an object. If we want to add a property to a nested object, we can combine everything we've seen so far to do this.

Let's say we want to add a property called **frame** to the nested `content` object. Here's how we would do this:

```
colors.content.frame = "yellow";
```

We start with our `colors` object, move to our `content` object, and then specify the property and value we want. If you prefer to use the bracket notation for accessing the `content` property, you can do this instead:

```
colors["content"]["frame"] = "yellow";
```

If you want to mix things up between the dot and bracket notations, this also works:

```
colors.content["frame"] = "yellow";
```

Before we wrap this up, I mentioned at the beginning that you have several paths you can take to add properties to an object. We looked at one such path. A more complex path you could take involves the `Object.defineProperty` and `Object.defineProperties` methods. These methods allow you to set a property and its value, but they also allow you to specify whether a property can be enumerated, whether a property can be customized, and much more. It's definitely overkill for what we will want to do 99 percent of the time, but know this: if overkill is what you want, then these two methods deliver. **The MDN documentation** at **https://mzl.la/3AIOVBN** does a good job providing examples of how you can use these methods to add one or more properties to an object.

Removing Properties

If you thought adding properties to an object was fun, removing properties from an object is a bit boring. It is also simpler. Let's continue to work with our `colors` object:

```
let colors = {
  header: "blue",
  footer: "gray",
  content: {
    title: "black",
    body: "darkgray",
    signature: "light blue"
  }
};
```

What we want to do is remove the `footer` property. We have two ways of doing this, depending on whether we want to access the `footer` property using the bracket notation or whether we want to access it using the dot notation:

```
delete colors.footer;


// or


delete colors["footer"];
```

The key to making all this work is the delete keyword. Simply use the delete keyword and follow it up with the property you'd like to remove. That's all there is to it.

Now, this wouldn't be JavaScript if I didn't mention a caveat. This one has to do with performance. If you will be deleting a lot of properties on a frequent basis across a large number of objects, delete is much slower than just setting the value of the property to something like **undefined**:

```
colors.footer = undefined;

// or

colors["footer"] = undefined;
```

The flipside is that setting a property to **undefined** means the property still exists in memory. You'll need to calculate the tradeoffs (speed versus memory) in your situation and optimize for the one that makes the most sense for you.

What Is Going on Behind the Scenes?

We saw how to create objects and make some typical modifications to them. Because objects really are the core of what makes JavaScript do all the things it does, it is important for us to have a deeper understanding of what is happening. This isn't just for the sake of trivial knowledge, though it will be fun to impress your friends and family over dinner with what you have learned. A large part of working with JavaScript is building objects based on other objects and doing other traditional object-oriented things. All of those things will make more sense when we have a better idea of what really goes on when we are working with objects.

Let's start with our funnyGuy object again:

```
let funnyGuy = {};
```

Now, what can we do with an empty object? We have no properties defined on it. Is our funnyGuy object truly alone and isolated with nothing at all going for it? As it turns out, the answer is a resounding **nope**. The reason has to do with how objects we create in JavaScript are automatically interlinked with the bigger Object and all the functionality it brings to the table. The best way to make sense of this interlinking is to visualize it. Take a really, REALLY deep breath and look at Figure 19.1.

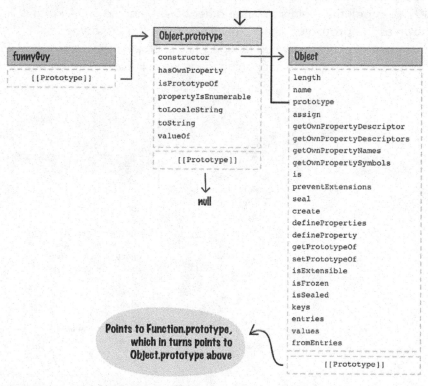

FIGURE 19.1

What our seemingly simple funnyGuy object actually has going on!

This diagram maps out what really happens behind the scenes when we create our empty funnyGuy object.

In this view, we still start off with our funnyGuy object. That part is still the same. What is different is everything else. See, our funnyGuy is simply an empty object. It has no properties that we defined for it. It does have properties that come defined out of the box, and these properties link our funnyGuy object to the underlying Object type without us having to do any work. This link allows us to call traditional Object properties on funnyGuy like the following:

```
let funnyGuy = {};
funnyGuy.toString();  // [object Object]
```

To hammer the point home, this link is what allows `toString` to work when called on our seemingly empty `funnyGuy` object. Now, calling this link a *link* isn't accurate. Our link is actually known as a prototype (and often represented as [[Proto-type]]) that ends up pointing to another object. *Another* object can have its own [[Prototype]] that points to yet another object, and so on. All of this linking is known as the **prototype chain**. Traveling across the prototype chain is a big part of what JavaScript does when trying to find a property you are calling. Figure 19.2 shows us what is actually happening when we call `toString` on our `funnyGuy` object.

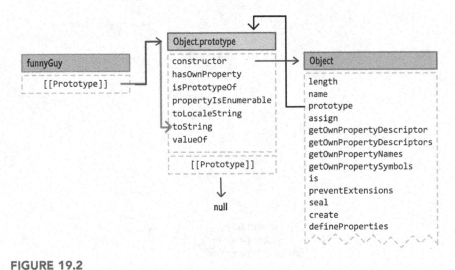

FIGURE 19.2

Walking the prototype chain to find the property we are looking for

With the prototype chain, even if our object doesn't have a particular property that we are looking for defined, JavaScript will walk through the chain and see if every stop along the way has that property defined instead. Now, our `funnyGuy` object's prototype chain includes just itself and `Object.prototype`. It isn't a complex chain at all. As we work with more complex objects, the prototype chain will get very long and more complex. We'll dip our toes into this complexity shortly.

NOTE   Object Isn't a Part of the Prototype Chain

In our previous visualizations, we see our `Object` having a dedicated entry with lines going between properties on it and the `Object.prototype`. The thing to note is that `Object` is not a part of the prototype chain. It plays a role in how objects implement the relationship between their `constructor` and a poorly named prototype property (not related to our [[Prototype]]), and we'll touch on the Object's role later. For completeness, I will continue to show `Object`'s role in future visualizations of our objects, but do note that it doesn't play a role in our prototype chain traversal.

Next, as we can see, our funnyGuy object right now is very basic. Let's add the firstName and lastName properties from earlier to make things a bit more interesting:

```
let funnyGuy = {
    firstName: "Conan",
    lastName: "O'Brien"
};
```

With these two properties thrown into the mix, our earlier visualization will now look as shown in Figure 19.3.

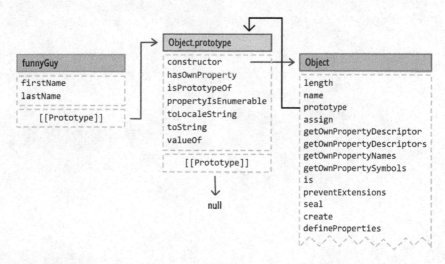

FIGURE 19.3

Say hello to the firstName and lastName properties.

The firstName and lastName properties are a part of the funnyGuy object and visualized as such as well. With this initial coverage of the object out of the way, it's time for us to go into a bit more detail.

Creating Custom Objects

Working with the generic `Object` and putting properties on it serves a useful purpose, but its awesomeness fades away really quickly when we are creating many objects that are basically the same thing. Take a look at the following snippet:

```
let funnyGuy = {
  firstName: "Conan",
  lastName: "O'Brien",

  getName: function () {
    return "Name is: " + this.firstName + " " + this.lastName;
  }
};

let theDude = {
  firstName: "Jeffrey",
  lastName: "Lebowski",

  getName: function () {
    return "Name is: " + this.firstName + " " + this.lastName;
  }
};

let detective = {
  firstName: "Adrian",
  lastName: "Monk",

  getName: function () {
    return "Name is: " + this.firstName + " " + this.lastName;
  }
};
```

This snippet builds on our `funnyGuy` object and introduces two new objects that are very similar to it: `theDude` and `detective`. Our visualization of all this will now look as shown in Figure 19.4.

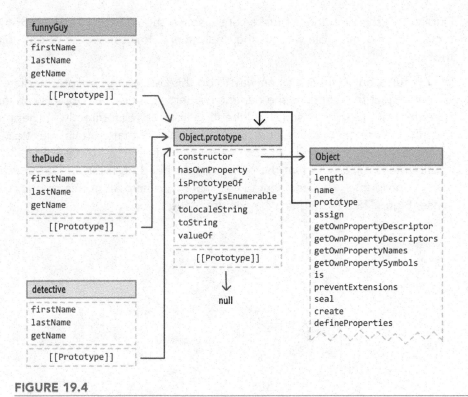

FIGURE 19.4

Each new object we created extends from `Object.prototype`.

At first glance, there seems to be quite a bit of duplication going on. Each of our new objects carries with it its own copy of the `firstName`, `lastName`, and `get-Name` properties. Now, not all duplication is bad. Yes, that does go against what I had stated earlier, but hear me out. In the case of objects, we need to figure out what properties make sense to be duplicated and which ones don't. From our example, the `firstName` and `lastName` properties will typically have a unique value per object. Keeping these duplicated on each object makes sense. The `getName` property, though, acts as a helper and doesn't contain anything one particular object will want to uniquely customize:

```
getName: function () {
  return "Name is: " + this.firstName + " " + this.lastName;
}
```

Duplicating this one doesn't make sense, so we should look at making `getName` more generally available without the duplication. How can we go about doing this?

Well, it turns out there is a clean way to do this by creating an intermediate **parent** object that contains the generic properties. Our **child** objects can inherit from this parent object instead of inheriting from `Object` directly. To get more specific, we are going to create a new person object that contains `getName`. Our `funnyGuy`, `theDude`, and `detective` objects will inherit from `person`. This arrangement will ensure that the properties we need duplicated get duplicated and the properties we need shared get shared. To help all of this cryptic text make sense, Figure 19.5 highlights what we are trying to do.

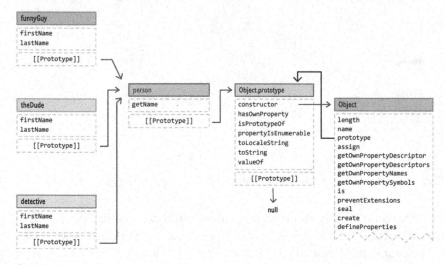

FIGURE 19.5

Adding an intermediate `person` object with our (now shared) `getName` property

Notice that `person` is now a part of the prototype chain, happily nestled between `Object.prototype` and our child objects. How do we go about doing this? One approach we saw earlier is to rely on `Object.create`. When using `Object.create`, we can specify an object to create our object from. Here's an example:

```
let myObject = Object.create(fooObject);
```

When we do this, what happens behind the scenes is the following: our `myObject` object's **prototype** will be `fooObject`. It becomes a part of the prototype chain. Now that we have taken a detour and expanded our understanding of `Object`.

create with what we've seen in this chapter, let's go back to our original problem of how we get funnyGuy, theDude, and detective to inherit from our person object.

Here's the code for doing all this:

```
let person = {
  getName: function () {
    return "The name is " + this.firstName + " " + this.lastName;
  }
};


let funnyGuy = Object.create(person);
funnyGuy.firstName = "Conan";
funnyGuy.lastName = "O'Brien";


let theDude = Object.create(person);
theDude.firstName = "Jeffrey";
theDude.lastName = "Lebowski";


let detective = Object.create(person);
detective.firstName = "Adrian";
detective.lastName = "Monk";
```

Because of how the prototype chain works, we can call getName on any of our funnyGuy, theDude, and detective objects, and the right things would happen:

```
detective.getName(); // The name is Adrian Monk
```

If we decide to enhance our person object, we can do so just once and have any objects that inherit from it benefit from our enhancement without any repetition. Let's say that we add a getInitials method that returns the first letter of the first name and last name:

```
let person = {
  getName: function () {
```

```
    return "The name is " + this.firstName + " " + this.lastName;
  },
  getInitials: function () {
    if (this.firstName && this.lastName) {
      return this.firstName[0] + this.lastName[0];
    }
  }
};
```

We add this `getInitials` method to our `person` object. To use this method, we can call it on any object that extends `person`, like our `funnyGuy`:

```
funnyGuy.getInitials(); // CO
```

This ability to create intermediate objects to help divide up the functionality in our code is a powerful thing. It allows us to be more efficient in how we create objects and what functionality we provide on each one. Neat, right?

The this Keyword

One thing you may have noticed in our previous snippets is the use of the `this` keyword, especially when we used it in our `person` object to refer to properties created on its children instead. Let's go back to our person object and, more specifically, the `getName` property:

```
let person = {
  getName: function () {
    return "The name is " + this.firstName + " " + this.lastName;
  },
  getInitials: function () {
    if (this.firstName && this.lastName) {
      return this.firstName[0] + this.lastName[0];
    }
  }
};
```

When we call getName, depending on which object we called it from, we'll see the appropriate name returned. For example, let's say we do the following:

```
let spaceGuy = Object.create(person);
spaceGuy.firstName = "Buzz";
spaceGuy.lastName = "Lightyear";


console.log(spaceGuy.getName()); // Buzz Lightyear
```

When we run this, we'll see **Buzz Lightyear** printed to our console. If we look at the getName property again, there is absolutely no existence of the firstName and lastName properties on the person object. When a property doesn't exist, we walk down the prototype chain from parent to parent, as shown in Figure 19.6.

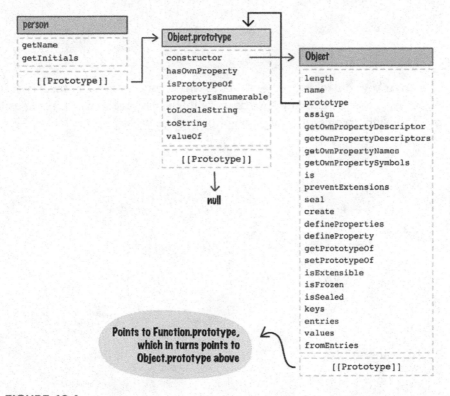

FIGURE 19.6

The prototype chain for our person object

In our case, the only stop on the chain would be `Object.prototype`. There are no `firstName` and `lastName` properties on `Object.prototype` either. How is it that this `getName` method happens to work and return the right values?

The answer has to do with the `this` keyword that precedes `firstName` and `lastName` as part of the `return` statement in `getName`:

```
let person = {
  getName: function () {
    return "The name is " + this.firstName + " " + this.lastName;
  },
  getInitials: function () {
    if (this.firstName && this.lastName) {
      return this.firstName[0] + this.lastName[0];
    }
  }
};
```

The `this` keyword refers to the object to which our `getName` method is bound. That object is, in this case, `spaceGuy`, because that is the object we are using as the entry point to all this prototype navigation goodness, as highlighted in Figure 19.7.

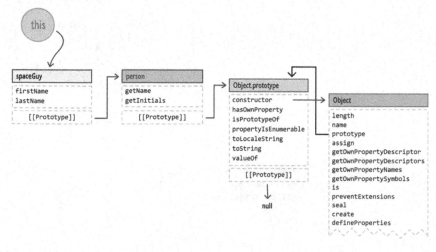

FIGURE 19.7

The `this` keyword refers to `spaceGuy`!

At the point where the getName method is evaluated and the `firstName` and `lastName` properties have to be resolved, the lookup starts at whatever the `this` keyword is pointing to. This means our lookup starts with the `spaceGuy` object—an object that, as it turns out, actually contains the `firstName` and `lastName` properties! That is why we get the correct result when the code for `getName` (and `getInitials` as well) is called.

Knowing what the `this` keyword refers to is something barrels of ink have been spilled on, and covering it fully goes a bit beyond what we want to talk about. The good thing is that what you've seen here will you get you pretty far.

THE ABSOLUTE MINIMUM

Because so much fuss is made about JavaScript's object-oriented-ness, it is only natural that a topic that covers it would be as wide and deep as what you've seen here. A bulk of what you saw here dealt with inheritance directly or indirectly, where objects are derived and based on other objects. Unlike other, more classical languages that use classes as templates for objects, JavaScript has no such concept of a class in a strict sense. JavaScript uses what is known as a **prototypical inheritance model**. You don't instantiate objects from a template. Instead, you create objects either from scratch or, more commonly, by copying/cloning another object. JavaScript sits in this gray area where it doesn't fit the mold of a class-ical language like Java or C#, but it does have many class-like constructs. This fuzziness gives JavaScript just enough credibility to comfortably sit at a table where other class-ical languages may congregate while still allowing it to rub shoulders with non-classical languages at the same time.

In this chapter, I tried to reinforce JavaScript's new functionality for working with objects and extending them for your own needs. There is still more to cover, so take a break and we'll touch upon some more interesting topics starting with the next chapter that extend what you've seen in more powerful, expressive, and awesome ways.

? Ask a question: **https://forum.kirupa.com**

✔ Practice by building real apps: **https://bit.ly/coding_exercises**

☛ Errors/known issues: **https://bit.ly/javascript_errata**

IN THIS CHAPTER

- Learn what classes in the JavaScript world are
- Create objects more easily by using the class syntax
- Understand the role the constructor and related class constructs play

20

USING CLASSES

When it comes to working with objects, we have covered a lot of ground so far. We saw how to create them, we learned about prototypical inheritance, and we even looked at the dark art of extending objects. In doing all of this, we worked at a very low level and were exposed to how the object-flavored sausage is made. That's great for really understanding what is going on. That's not so great when making sense of complex object happenings in your app. To simplify all of this, with the ES6 version of JavaScript, you have support for these things called **classes**.

If you have a background in other object-oriented programming languages, you are probably familiar with that term. Don't worry if you are not. In the world of JavaScript, classes are nothing special. They are nothing more than just a handful of new keywords and conventions that *simplify what we have to type* when working with objects. In the following sections, we'll get a taste of what all that means.

The Class Syntax and Object Creation

We are going to learn about the class syntax the same way our grandparents did—by writing code. Because there is a lot of ground to cover, we won't try to bite off everything at once. We'll start by focusing on how to use the class syntax when creating objects. As you'll see, there is a lot going on there that will keep us plenty busy!

Creating an Object

You can think of a class as a template that objects refer to when they are being created. Let's say that we want to create a new class called **Planet**. The most basic version of that class will look as follows:

```
class Planet {

}
```

We use a keyword called `class` followed by the name we want to give our class. The body of our class will live inside curly brackets—that is, { and }. As you can see, our class is currently empty. That's not very exciting, but it is okay for now. We want to start off simple.

To create an object based on this class, all you need to do is the following:

```
let myPlanet = new Planet();
```

We declare the name of our object and use the `new` keyword to create (aka instantiate) our object based on the `Planet` class. If we had to visualize what is happening under the hood, Figure 20.1 shows what you would see.

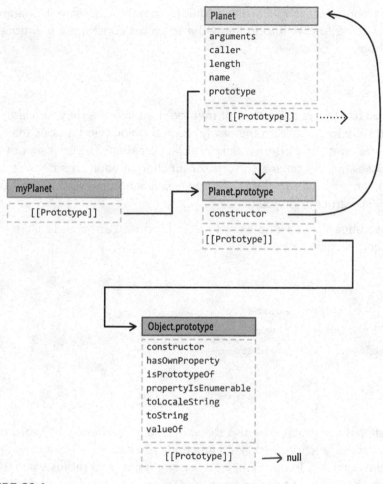

FIGURE 20.1

What myPlanet is made up of behind the scenes

This looks a bit different from what we saw when creating objects using `Object.create()`. The difference has to do with us creating our `myPlanet` object by using the `new` keyword. When we create objects with the `new` keyword, the following things happen:

1. Our new object is simply of type **Planet**.

2. Our new object's `[[Prototype]]` is our *new* function or class's `prototype` property.

3. A constructor function gets executed that deals with initializing our newly created object.

I won't bore you too much with additional details, but there is one important item we are going to dive into further—the so-called constructor mentioned in the third item.

Meet the Constructor

The **constructor** is a function (or method) that lives inside your class's body. It is responsible for initializing the newly created object, and it does that by running any code contained inside it during object creation. This isn't an optional detail. All classes must contain a constructor function. If your class doesn't contain one (kinda like our `Planet` class right now), JavaScript will automatically create an empty constructor for you.

Let's go ahead and define a constructor for our `Planet` class. Take a look at the following modification:

```
class Planet {
  constructor(name, radius) {
    this.name = name;
    this.radius = radius;
  }
}
```

To define a constructor, we use the special `constructor` keyword to create what is basically a function. Just like a function, you can also specify any arguments you would like to use. In our case, we specify a **name** and **radius** value as arguments and use them to set the `name` and `radius` properties on our object:

```
class Planet {
  constructor(name, radius) {
    this.name = name;
    this.radius = radius;
  }
}
```

You can definitely do a lot more (or a lot less!) interesting things from inside your constructor, but the main thing to keep in mind is that this code will run every single time we are creating a new object using our `Planet` class. Speaking of which, here is how you call our `Planet` class to create an object:

```
let myPlanet = new Planet("Earth", 6378);
console.log(myPlanet.name); // Earth
```

Notice that the two arguments we need to set on our constructor are actually set directly on the `Planet` class itself. When our `myPlanet` object gets created, the constructor is run and the **name** and **radius** values we passed in get set on our object. Figure 20.2 shows what this looks like.

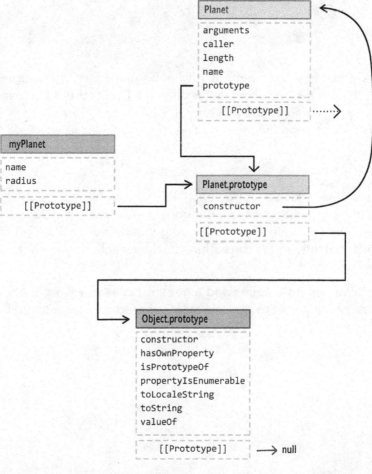

FIGURE 20.2

We can see our `myPlanet` object containing the `name` and `radius` properties.

While we are learning about the `class` syntax and the details surrounding it, never forget that all of this is just frosting—delicious syntactic sugar designed to make your life easy. If we didn't use the `class` syntax, we could have done something like this instead:

```
function Planet(name, radius) {
  this.name = name;
  this.radius = radius;
};


let myPlanet = new Planet("Earth", 6378);
console.log(myPlanet.name); // Earth
```

The end result is almost identical to what we gained with the `class` syntax. How we got there is the only thing that is different. Don't let this comparison give you the wrong impression, though. Other helpful uses of the `class` syntax won't be as easy to convert using the more traditional approaches, as we've seen here.

What Goes Inside the Class

Our class objects look a lot like functions, but they have some quirks. We saw that one of the things that goes into the body of our class is this special constructor function. The only other things that can go inside our class are other **functions/ methods**, **getters**, and **setters**. That's it. No variable declarations and initializations are welcome.

To see all of this at work, let's add a `getSurfaceArea` function that prints the surface area of our planet to the console. Go ahead and make the following change:

```
class Planet {
  constructor(name, radius) {
    this.name = name;
    this.radius = radius;
  }

  getSurfaceArea() {
    let surfaceArea = 4 * Math.PI * Math.pow(this.radius, 2);
    console.log(surfaceArea + " square km!");
    return surfaceArea;
  }
}
```

You call `getSurfaceArea` off our created object to see it in action:

```
let earth = new Planet("Earth", 6378);
earth.getSurfaceArea();
```

When this code runs, you'll see something like 511 million square kilometers printed out. That's good. Since we mentioned the other things that can go inside our class body are getters and setters, let's throw those in as well. We'll use them to help us represent our planet's gravity:

```
class Planet {
  constructor(name, radius) {
    this.name = name;
    this.radius = radius;
  }

  getSurfaceArea() {
    let surfaceArea = 4 * Math.PI * Math.pow(this.radius, 2);
    console.log(surfaceArea + " square km!");
    return surfaceArea;
  }

  set gravity(value) {
    console.log("Setting value!");
    this._gravity = value;
  }

  get gravity() {
    console.log("Getting value!");
    return this._gravity;
  }
}

let earth = new Planet("Earth", 6378);
earth.gravity = 9.81;
```

```
earth.getSurfaceArea();

console.log(earth.gravity) // 9.81
```

That's all there is to it. One cool thing about adding these things to our class body is that they all **will not live on the created object**. They will live on the prototype (`Planet.prototype`) instead, as shown by Figure 20.3.

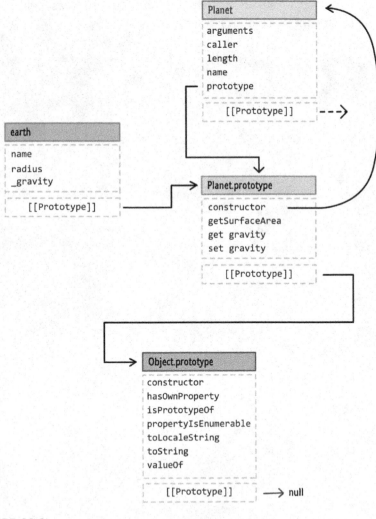

FIGURE 20.3

We don't have to do anything special to target the prototype object.

That is a good thing because we don't want every object to unnecessarily carry around a copy of the class's internals when a shared instance would work just fine! Given that, you can see this represented in the diagram in Figure 20.3. Our `gravity` getter and setter, along with our `getSurfaceArea` function, live entirely on our prototype!

WHY DO THE FUNCTIONS INSIDE OUR CLASS LOOK WEIRD?

One thing you may have noticed is that the appearance of our functions inside the class body looks a bit odd. They are missing the function keyword, for example. That weirdness (for once) is actually not related to classes. When defining functions inside an object, you have a shorthand syntax you can use.

For example, instead of writing something like

```
let blah = {
  zorb: function() {
    // something interesting
  }
};
```

you can abbreviate the `zorb` function definition as follows:

```
let blah = {
  zorb() {
    // something interesting
  }
};
```

It is this abbreviated form you will see and use when specifying functions inside your class body.

Extending Objects

The last thing we will look at has to do with extending objects in this class-based world. To help with this, we are going to be working with a whole new type of planet known as the **Potato Planet**.

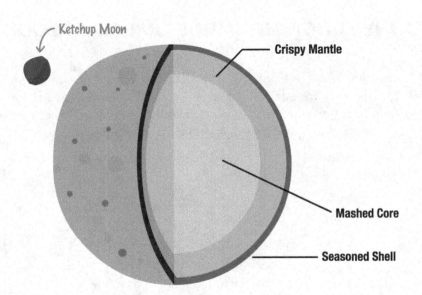

The Potato Planet contains everything a regular planet brings to the table, but it is made up entirely of potatoes...as opposed to the silly molten rocks and gas that the other planets are made up of. What we are going to do is define our Potato Planet as a class. Its functionality will largely mirror that of the `Planet` class, but we will have some additional doodads like a `potatoType` argument in the constructor and the `getPotatoType` method that prints to the console the value of `potatoType`.

A not-so-good approach would be to define our Potato Planet class as follows:

```
class PotatoPlanet {
  constructor(name, radius, potatoType) {
    this.name = name;
    this.radius = radius;
```

```
    this.potatoType = potatoType;
  }


  getSurfaceArea() {
    let surfaceArea = 4 * Math.PI * Math.pow(this.radius, 2);
    console.log(surfaceArea + " square km!");
    return surfaceArea;
  }
  getPotatoType() {
    var thePotato = this.potatoType.toUpperCase() + "!!1!!!";
    console.log(thePotato);
    return thePotato;
  }


  set gravity(value) {
    console.log("Setting value!");
    this._gravity = value;
  }

  get gravity() {
    return this._gravity;
  }
}
```

We now have our `PotatoPlanet` class, and it contains not just the new potato-related things but also all the functionality of our `Planet` class as well. This approach isn't great because we are duplicating code. Now, instead of duplicating our code, what if we had a way of extending the functionality our `Planet` class provides with the few additional pieces of functionality that our `PotatoPlanet` would need? Wouldn't that be a better approach? Well, as luck would have it, we do have such a way via the `extends` keyword. By having our `PotatoPlanet` class extend our `Planet` class, we can do something like the following:

```
class Planet {
  constructor(name, radius) {
    this.name = name;
```

```javascript
    this.radius = radius;
  }

  getSurfaceArea() {
    let surfaceArea = 4 * Math.PI * Math.pow(this.radius, 2);
    console.log(surfaceArea + " square km!");
    return surfaceArea;
  }

  set gravity(value) {
    console.log("Setting value!");
    this._gravity = value;
  }

  get gravity() {
    return this._gravity;
  }
}

class PotatoPlanet extends Planet {
  constructor(name, width, potatoType) {
    super(name, width);

    this.potatoType = potatoType;
  }

  getPotatoType() {
    let thePotato = this.potatoType.toUpperCase() + "!!!1!!!";
    console.log(thePotato);
    return thePotato;
  }
}
```

Notice how we are declaring our `PotatoPlanet` class. We are using the extends keyword and specifying the class we will be extending from, which is `Planet`:

```
class PotatoPlanet extends Planet {
  .

  .

  .

  .

}
```

From there, the other thing to keep in mind has to do with the `constructor`. If we are going to be extending a class without needing to modify the constructor, we can totally skip specifying the constructor inside our class:

```
class PotatoPlanet extends Planet {
  sayHello() {
    console.log("Hello!");
  }
}
```

In our case, since we are modifying what the constructor does by adding a property for the type of potato, we define our constructor again with one important addition:

```
class PotatoPlanet extends Planet {
  constructor(name, width) {
    super(name, width);

    this.potatoType = potatoType;
  }

  getPotatoType() {
```

```
    var thePotato = this.potatoType.toUpperCase() + "!!1!!!";
    console.log(thePotato);
    return thePotato;
  }
}
```

We make an explicit call to the parent (`Planet`) constructor by using the `super` keyword and passing in the relevant arguments needed. This `super` call ensures that whatever the `Planet` part of our object needs as part of its functioning is triggered.

To use our `PotatoPlanet`, we would create our object and populate its properties or call methods on it just like we would for any plain, non-extended object. Here is an example of us creating an object of type PotatoPlanet appropriately called spudnik:

```
let spudnik = new PotatoPlanet("Spudnik", 12411, "Russet");
spudnik.gravity = 42.1;
spudnik.getPotatoType();
```

The cool thing is that `spudnik` has access not only to functionality we defined as part of our `PotatoPlanet` class; all of the functionality provided by the `Planet` class we are extending is also available as well. We can see why that is the case by revisiting a more complex version of our prototype/object relationship diagram, as seen in Figure 20.4.

If we follow the prototype chain, we go from our `spudnik` object to the `Potato-Planet.prototype` to `Planet.prototype` to, finally, `Object.prototype`. Our `spudnik` object has access to any property or method defined at any of these prototype stops, which is why it can call things on `Object` or on `Planet` without skipping a beat, even though `PotatoPlanet` doesn't define a whole lot on its own. This is the powerful awesomeness of extending objects.

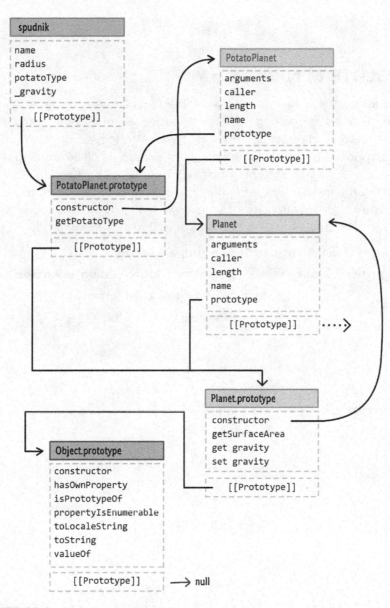

FIGURE 20.4

What extending an object looks like

THE ABSOLUTE MINIMUM

The class syntax makes working with objects really easy. You may have caught some glimpses of that here, but you'll start to see more of it later in the book. The thing about the class syntax is that it allows us to focus more on what we want to do as opposed to fiddling with how exactly to do it. While working with `Object.create` and the `prototype` properties gives us a lot of control, that control has often been unnecessary for the majority of our cases. By working with classes, we trade complexity in favor of simplicity. That's not a bad thing when the simple solution also turns out to be the right one...most of the time!

? Ask a question: **https://forum.kirupa.com**

✔ Practice by building real apps: **https://bit.ly/coding_exercises**

🐾 Errors/known issues: **https://bit.ly/javascript_errata**

EXTENDING BUILT-IN OBJECTS

As you know very well by now, JavaScript comes from the factory with a good supply of built-in objects. These objects provide some of the core functionality for working with text, numbers, collections of data, dates, and a whole lot more. As you become more familiar with JavaScript and start doing more interesting and clever things, you'll often find that you want to go further than what the built-in objects allow.

Let's take a look at an example of when something like this might occur. Here is an example of how we can shuffle the contents of an array:

```
function shuffle(input) {
  for (let i = input.length - 1; i >= 0; i--) {

    let randomIndex = Math.floor(Math.random() *
(i + 1));
    let itemAtIndex = input[randomIndex];

    input[randomIndex] = input[i];
    input[i] = itemAtIndex;
  }
  return input;
}
```

We use this `shuffle` function by simply calling it and passing in the array whose contents we want shuffled:

```
let shuffleArray = [1, 2, 3, 4, 5, 6, 7, 8, 9, 10];
shuffle(shuffleArray);

// and the result is...
console.log(shuffleArray);
```

After this code has run, the end result is that the contents of our array are now rearranged. Now, this functionality is pretty useful. In fact, I would say this shuffling ability is so useful that it should be a part of the `Array` object and be as easily accessible as `push`, `pop`, `slice`, and the other doodads the `Array` object offers.

If the `shuffle` function were a part of the `Array` object, we could simply use it as follows:

```
let shuffleArray = [1, 2, 3, 4, 5, 6, 7, 8, 9, 10];
shuffleArray.shuffle();
```

This is an example of us extending a built-in object (`Array`) with some functionality that we defined (`shuffle`). In this chapter, we are going to look at how exactly to accomplish this, why it all works, and why extending built-in objects is pretty controversial.

Say Hello to prototype Again, Sort Of!

Extending a built-in object with new functionality sounds complicated, but it is really simple once you understand what needs to be done. To help with this, we are going to look at a combination of sample code and diagrams all involving the very friendly `Array` object:

```
let tempArray = [1, 2, 3, 4, 5, 6, 7, 8, 9, 10];
```

If we were to diagram the full hierarchy of the `tempArray` object, it would look as shown in Figure 21.1.

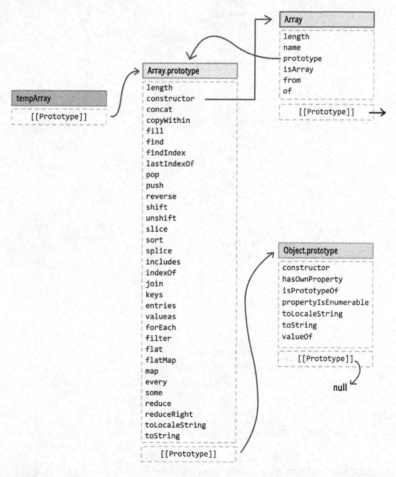

FIGURE 21.1

The tangled web of objects (and possibly lies!) that live just beneath the surface

On the left, we have our `tempArray` object that is an instance of `Array.prototype`, which in turn is an instance of the basic `Object.prototype`. Now we want to extend what our array is capable of with our `shuffle` function. This means we need to figure out a way to get our `shuffle` function inserted into our `Array.prototype`, as shown in Figure 21.2.

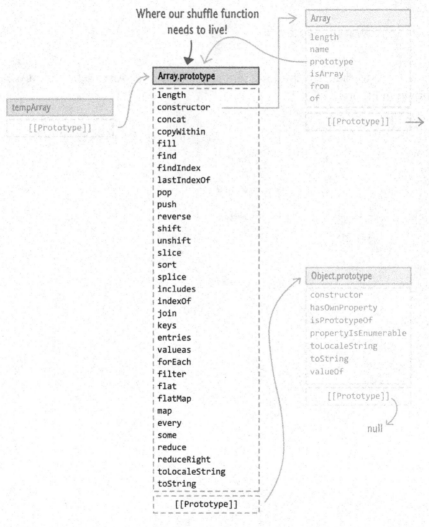

FIGURE 21.2

Where we want our shuffle function to live!

Here is the part where the quirkiness of JavaScript shines through. We don't have access to the code that makes up all of the array functionality. We can't find the function or object that makes up the `Array` and insert our `shuffle` function into it like we might for a custom object that we defined. Our built-in objects, such as the `Array`, are defined deep inside our browser's volcanic underbelly where no human being can go. We need to take another approach.

That other approach involves casually sneaking in and attaching our functionality to the `Array` object's `prototype` property. That would look something like this:

```
Array.prototype.shuffle = function () {
  let input = this;

  for (let i = input.length - 1; i >= 0; i--) {

    let randomIndex = Math.floor(Math.random() * (i + 1));
    let itemAtIndex = input[randomIndex];

    input[randomIndex] = input[i];
    input[i] = itemAtIndex;
  }
  return input;
}
```

Notice that our `shuffle` function is declared on `Array.prototype`! As part of this attachment, we made a minor change to how the function works. The function no longer takes an argument for referencing the array we need shuffled:

```
function shuffle(input) {
  .
  .
  .
  .
  .
}
```

Instead, because this function is now a part of the `Array`, the `this` keyword inside the function body points to the array that needs shuffling:

```
Array.prototype.shuffle = function () {
  let input = this;
```

```
    •
    •
    •
    •
}
```

Taking a step back, once we run this code, our `shuffle` function will find itself shoulder to shoulder with all the other built-in methods the `Array` object exposes through `Array.prototype`, as highlighted in Figure 21.3.

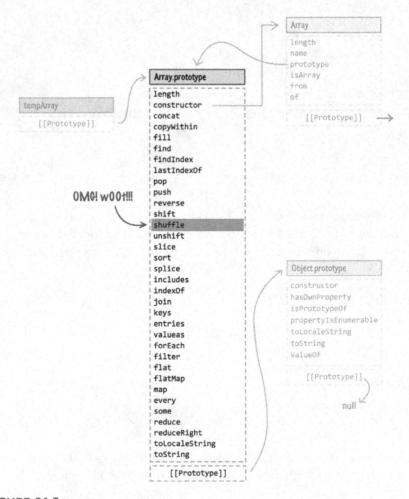

FIGURE 21.3

Great success! The `shuffle` function is now where it belongs.

If we wanted to access the `shuffle` capabilities, we can now do so using the approach we initially desired:

```
let numbers = [1, 2, 3, 4, 5, 6, 7, 8, 9, 10];
numbers.shuffle();
```

Best of all, any new arrays we create will also have access to the `shuffle` functionality by default thanks to how prototype inheritance works.

Using a Subclassing Approach

Instead of adding more capabilities directly to our object's prototype, we have a more modern approach, building on what we saw in the previous chapter, where we can create a new object that extends the behavior of another object. This is something known as **subclassing**, where our custom object has any custom methods/properties we define in addition to everything the base object provides. The behavior that works for extending custom objects works almost identically for built-in objects as well.

Continuing our look at extending our `Array` from the previous section, take a look at the following example of some sweet subclassing in action:

```
class AwesomeArray extends Array {
  swap(index_A, index_B) {
    let input = this;

    let temp = input[index_A];
    input[index_A] = input[index_B];
    input[index_B] = temp;
  }
}
```

We are defining a class called `AwesomeArray` that subclasses our `Array` by using the `extends` keyword. Inside `AwesomeArray`, we define our `swap` method that, as its name implies, swaps the value of two items in the array. We can use this swap method by creating an `AwesomeArray` object and then just calling swap on it, like so:

```
class AwesomeArray extends Array {
  swap(index_A, index_B) {
    let input = this;

    let temp = input[index_A];
    input[index_A] = input[index_B];
    input[index_B] = temp;
  }
}


let myData = new AwesomeArray("a", "b", "c", "d", "e", "f", "g");
myData.swap(0, 1);
console.log(myData); // ["b", "a", "c", "d", "e", "f", "g"]
```

In the above code, notice how we create our `AwesomeArray` object called `myData`. We create it by using the `new` keyword and calling the `AwesomeArray` constructor. Because `AwesomeArray` is still an `Array` behind the scenes, we can perform our usual array-like operations. For example, to initialize our array with some default values, we pass in our initial values as arguments to our `AwesomeArray` constructor:

```
let myData = new AwesomeArray("a", "b", "c", "d", "e", "f", "g");
```

This is just like what we can do with regular arrays. Now, what we can't do is use the bracket syntax that we have been using a bunch of times. We can't do this and expect our `myData` object to be an `AwesomeArray`:

```
let myData = ["a", "b", "c", "d", "e", "f", "g"];
```

The reason is that this syntax is designed to work only with the built-in `Array` type. If we were to use the bracket-based approach for creating our array, we would end up creating a traditional `Array` instead of an `AwesomeArray` with the swap method we defined. Using the explicit constructor-based approach for creating an object is our best solution for ensuring our array is awesome—an `AwesomeArray`. Overloading the bracket operator is sorta kinda possible using some cutting-edge JavaScript features like proxies, but that's a rabbit hole I won't take you down today.

There is one more thing to cover when it comes to subclassing our array. A handful of array methods (map, filter, and so on) return an array as part of their regular operation. The array that gets returned respects the type of the array it was invoked from. This means calling map on our AwesomeArray type will return an array that is also an AwesomeArray:

```
class AwesomeArray extends Array {
    swap(index_A, index_B) {
      let input = this;

      let temp = input[index_A];
      input[index_A] = input[index_B];
      input[index_B] = temp;
    }
  }

let myData = new AwesomeArray("a", "b", "c", "d", "e", "f", "g");

let newData = myData.map((letter) => letter.toUpperCase());
console.log(newData); // ["A", "B", "C", "D", "E", "F", "G"]

console.log(newData.constructor.name) // AwesomeArray
```

We can verify this by checking the value of newData.constructor (where new-Data.constructor === AwesomeArray will be **true**) or by just printing its name to our console like we did in the preceding snippet. This ability for our subclassed array to still maintain its subclassiness when dealing with methods that return arrays is very desirable. It means we can still party in our subclassed world while still taking advantage of powerful methods that exist in the base Array object at the same time.

Extending Built-in Objects Is Controversial

Given how easy it is to extend a built-in object's functionality by declaring methods and properties using the prototype property, it's easy to think that everybody loves the ability to do all of this. As it turns out, extending built-in objects is a bit controversial. The reasons for this controversy revolve around the topics discussed in the following sections.

You Don't Control the Built-in Object's Future

There is nothing preventing a future implementation of JavaScript from including its own version of shuffle that applies to Array objects. At this point, you have a collision where your version of shuffle and the browser's version of shuffle are in conflict with each other—especially if their behavior or performance characteristics differ wildly. Ruh-roh!

Some Functionality Should Not Be Extended or Overridden

Nothing prevents you from using what you've learned here to modify the behavior of existing methods and properties. For example, this is me changing how the slice behavior works:

```
Array.prototype.slice = function () {
  let input = this;
  input[0] = "This is an awesome example!";

. return input;
}

let tempArray = [1, 2, 3, 4, 5, 6, 7, 8, 9, 10]
tempArray.slice();

// and the result is...
console.log(tempArray);
```

While this is a terrible example, it does show how easy it was for me to break existing functionality.

FURTHER READING

To see a more comprehensive discussion and for further reading around this controversy, check out this StackOverflow thread: **http://stackoverflow.com/ questions/8859828/.**

THE ABSOLUTE MINIMUM: WHAT SHOULD YOU DO?

My answer to what you need to do is simple: **Use your best judgment!** The two cases I outlined are only a few of the numerous issues that people raise when extending built-in objects is discussed. For the most part, all of the objections are valid. The question you need to ask is, "Are these objections valid for my particular scenario?" My guess is that they probably won't be.

From personal experience, I have never had any issues extending built-in objects with my own functionality. I wrote this `shuffle` function years ago, and no browser as of now has even hinted at implementing its own version. I am certainly not complaining! What's more, for any functionality I do add, I test to make sure that it works well across the browsers I am currently targeting. As long as your testing is somewhat comprehensive (probably the latest one or two versions of the major browsers), you should be good to go.

If you are worried about future-proofing your app, name any properties or methods in such a way that only your app would use them. For example, the chances of `Array.prototype.kirupaShuffle` or `AwesomeArray` being introduced by any future browser release is pretty close to zero.

Anyway, now that we've sufficiently covered some detailed topics around objects in this and the previous chapters, let's go back to looking at some of the other types you will run into before we move on to some really exciting stuff.

? Ask a question: **https://forum.kirupa.com**

✔ Practice by building real apps: **https://bit.ly/coding_exercises**

🎯 Errors/known issues: **https://bit.ly/javascript_errata**

IN THIS CHAPTER

- Learn about arrow functions and their abbreviated syntax
- Learn when arrow functions make a whole lot of sense to use

22

ARROW FUNCTIONS

Before we move on, let's address the elephant in the room. **Arrow function** is probably the coolest name for some technical thing ever. It makes the names for all the other JavaScript concepts we've seen so far (and will see in the future) seem downright dreadful. With this important observation out of the way, let's get down to business and learn about what arrow functions are and what makes them an upgrade over the traditional functions we have seen.

What Are Arrow Functions?

The best way to understand arrow functions is to dive right in, start looking at examples, and observe their behavior. On the surface, arrow functions are nothing more than an abbreviated syntax on a typical function expression. There is a whole lot more to arrow functions than just that, but we'll start there and gradually go deeper.

Starting with the Basics

Let's say we have a traditional function like the following:

```
let laugh = function () {
  return "Hahahaha!";
}
console.log(laugh()); // "Hahahaha!"
```

This function is called laugh, and it returns the text **Hahahaha!** when called. If we turn this into an arrow function, it will take on this more concise form:

```
let laugh = () => "Hahahaha!";
console.log(laugh()); // "Hahahaha!"
```

Notice what just happened:

1. We got rid of the function keyword.

2. We specified an arrow (=>) that lives between the parentheses and the function body.

3. We removed the curvy brackets because we don't need them if our arrow function is just a single statement. Going further, if our single statement is an expression that returns a value (which is what we have), we can remove the return keyword as well.

Summarizing what just happened, we went from three lines of function-related code to just a single line. The behavior between our more verbose traditional function and the more concise arrow function is identical, where calling laugh prints **Hahahaha!** to the console in both cases.

Of Arguments and Parenthesis

Building on what we just saw, if our function takes a single argument, we can remove the opening/closing parentheses when defining our arrow function:

```
let laugh = name => "Hahahaha! " + name + "!";
console.log(laugh("Zoidberg")); // "Hahahaha! Zoidberg!"
```

Notice that our `laugh` function takes the argument `name`, and it returns the combination of name and **Hahahaha!**. This is the most concise form of an arrow function, where we remove all of the syntactical fluff when we have just a single argument. If we add more arguments to our function, the parentheses around the arguments will come back:

```
let laugh = (first, last) => "Hahahaha! " + first + " " + last +
"!";
console.log(laugh("John", "Zoidberg")); // "Hahahaha! John
Zoidberg!"
```

The main thing to keep in mind is that the way the parentheses behave is identical to how you would treat them with traditional functions. We can specify as many arguments as we want with a comma separating each individual argument. We can even specify default values for the arguments.

To Curly Bracket or Not to Curly Bracket

I mentioned earlier that we can omit the curly brackets if our function has only a single statement. If our function specifies multiple statements, the curly brackets have to be back:

```
let anotherExample = () => {
  console.log("Hello");
  console.log("Everybody");
}
anotherExample();
```

If our function with multiple statements is returning a value, we have to ensure the `return` keyword is used as well:

```
let anotherExample = () => {
  let a = "Hello ";
  let b = "Everybody");

  return a + b;
}
anotherExample();
```

When we think about it, this makes a whole lot of sense. If we have multiple statements, it is hard to know which statement contains the value we want to return. Having an explicit `return` avoids that confusion.

NOTE Preferences May Vary!

Here's the thing: You or your team may not particularly enjoy toggling between showing brackets and using `return` or not based on what exactly the function is doing or how many statements are in it. There is nothing wrong with always displaying curly brackets and using a `return`:

```
let laugh = () => {
  return "Hahahaha!";
}
laugh();
```

Here is an example of our `laugh` function from earlier where we display both the curly brackets and the `return` keyword despite the function body having just a single expression that returns a value. This function totally works and isn't wrong at all.

Putting It All Together

Just for good measure, let's review what we have just seen and explore one last example:

```
let calculateDiameter = (radius = 1) => {
  let pi = 3.14159;
  let diameter = 2 * pi * radius;

  return diameter;
};
console.log(calculateDiameter(4)); // 25.13272
console.log(calculateDiameter()); // 6.28318
```

We have a function called `calculateDiameter`, and it takes a single argument called `radius` (which has a default value of 1 that is used when we don't specify an argument). Calling the `calculateDiameter` function with (or without) a `radius` argument returns the correct value.

The biggest takeaway for us with arrow functions is this: *almost* anything you can do with traditional functions, you can do with arrow functions as well. Now, there are a few big differences, hence the emphasis on *almost*. Arrow functions and traditional functions have different scoping behavior, and arrow functions have a few limitations we should be aware of. We'll get to the bottom of what's up with all this in the next chapter when looking at some quirks involving the `this` keyword.

THE ABSOLUTE MINIMUM: WHAT SHOULD YOU DO?

It is time to answer the inflation-adjusted million-dollar question: When should we use arrow functions? There are several answers here. If you enjoy the abbreviated syntax arrow functions have compared to traditional functions, use them as much as you want. If you are someone who finds this abbreviated arrow functions syntax to lack the clarity of the more verbose traditional functions, you don't ever have to use it. My personal take is to be somewhere in the middle, like Malcolm!

Arrow functions are great for situations where we need to provide an anonymous function as part of an event handler, timer, and so on:

```
let myButton = document.querySelector("#myButton");
myButton.addEventListener("click", () => console.log("Click!"));
```

The reason is partly for the abbreviated syntax, but the other reason is mostly because of the more sensible treatment of `this`. What's that? Well, we'll cover that topic in the next chapter, so stay tuned.

- ? Ask a question: **https://forum.kirupa.com**
- ✔ Practice by building real apps: **https://bit.ly/coding_exercises**
- Errors/known issues: **https://bit.ly/javascript_errata**

IN THIS CHAPTER

- Get a broader overview of the `this` keyword
- Explore solutions for ensuring `this` points to the right object by looking at approaches that involve arrow functions, redefining `this`, and using the bind method

23

MAKING SENSE OF THIS AND MORE

In English, there are many situations where you need to refer to yourself:

> I am hungry.
>
> This teleportation device belongs to me.
>
> I don't know who microwaved the mustard.
>
> I digress.

In JavaScript, things aren't too different. We will write or encounter code where we need to refer to the **current object** in a very general way. The way we get a reference to this object is by the appropriately named `this` keyword. We've seen this keyword a few times already, but now it's time for us to look deeper into what `this` actually is and how to work around some quirks where what we think our current object should be and what `this` actually references don't match.

The this Keyword 101

When our JavaScript code runs, it always runs inside some context. We saw a bit of this when we looked at variable scopes earlier in the book. Depending on where our code is defined, it could run fully localized inside a function. It could run globally at the `Window` scope. Our code could also be constrained to a particular object, such as inside a class or object definition. We can figure out in which context our code is operating by referring to the `this` keyword.

For example, let's say we print the value of `this` from our global context:

```
console.log(this); // Window
```

What we will see printed to our console is our `Window` object. Now, let's say we are inside an `Object` and print the value of `this` from inside a property:

```
let myObject = {
  whatIsThis: function () {
    console.log(this);
  }
};
myObject.whatIsThis(); // Object
```

The value of `this` references the `myObject` object it is contained inside. If we didn't have a way to use this, there are many things we simply couldn't do. For example, let's say we want to reference a property within our object, as shown here:

```
let myObject = {
  name: "Iron Man",
  whatIsThis: function () {
    console.log(name); // won't work!
  }
};
myObject.whatIsThis(); // undefined
```

We can't do that. However, if we rely on this, we can totally pull it off:

```
let myObject = {
  name: "Iron Man",
  whatIsThis: function () {
    console.log(this.name); // yay!
  }
};
myObject.whatIsThis(); // "Iron Man"
```

Most recently, we saw the this keyword being used extensively when working with classes. Take a look at the following example:

```
class Fruit {
  constructor(name) {
    this.name = name;
  }
  getName() {
    return this.name;
  }
}

let apple = new Fruit("Apple");
console.log(apple.getName()); // "Apple"


let orange = new Fruit("Orange");
console.log(orange.getName()); // "Orange"
```

When we use the this keyword as part of creating objects using the class syntax, this references the object instance it is bound to, such as Apple or Orange. Because this behaves this way inside our class definition, the appropriate name value gets returned.

When this Just Ain't Right

Now that we have looked at cases where this behaves exactly like we would expect, brace yourself. This is going to be a sordid tale involving **variable scopes** and the value of this. These are two topics that, on the best of days, can make anyone's head spin. The best way to understand the quirks of how this behaves is to look at an example:

```
let counter = {
  initial: 100,
  interval: 1000,
  startCounting: function () {
    setInterval(function () {
      this.initial++;
      console.log(this.initial);
    }, this.interval);
  }
}
counter.startCounting();
```

We have an object called counter, and it has the initial, interval, and startCounting properties. The property that we want to focus on is startCounting, and it represents a function whose body is a setInterval function:

```
let counter = {
  initial: 100,
  interval: 1000,
  startCounting: function () {
    setInterval(function () {
      this.initial++;
      console.log(this.initial);
    }, this.interval);
  }
}
counter.startCounting();
```

When someone calls `startCounting`, the idea is for us to increment the value of `initial` at a rate specified by the interval property.

Thinking out loud, when we call `counter.startCounting()`, the value of initial is initially (ha!) **100**. After 1000 milliseconds (as specified by the `interval` property) elapses, the value of `initial` is incremented by 1 to be **101**. After another 1000 milliseconds, the value of initial becomes **102**. You get the picture.

Now, if we test this code, what do you think we are going to see? What will the `console.log` statement inside our `interval` loop show when it prints the value of `initial` every 1000 milliseconds? As it turns out, what we will see is *not* a nice set of numbers increasing by 1, starting from 100. Instead, what we will see is **NaN** being printed over and over again, as shown in Figure 23.1.

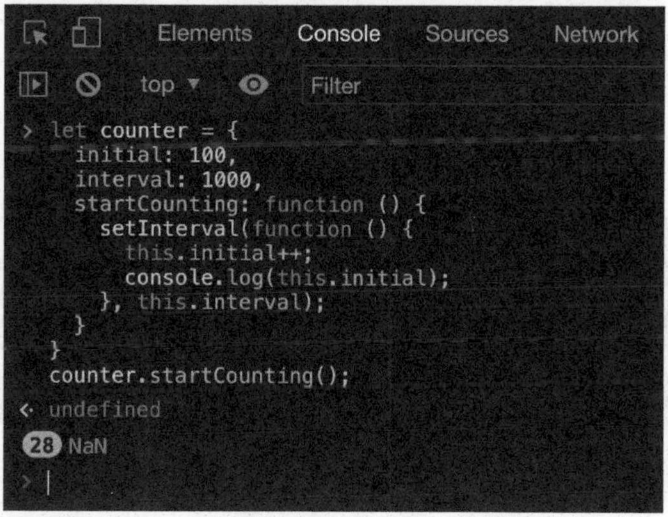

FIGURE 23.1

The value of our call to `this.initial` doesn't look right!

Why is this the case? We can see more details if we add a few more `console.log` statements to see what the value of `this` is inside the `startCounting` and `setInterval` functions:

```
let counter = {
  initial: 100,
  interval: 1000,
```

```
  startCounting: function () {
    console.log("startCounting:");
    console.log(this);
    setInterval(function () {
      console.log("setTimeout:");
      console.log(this);
      this.initial++;
      console.log(this.initial);
    }, this.interval);
  }
}
counter.startCounting();
```

If we run this code, we'll see our additional information being printed to the console. The value of this under startCounting will refer to the counter object, as shown in Figure 23.2.

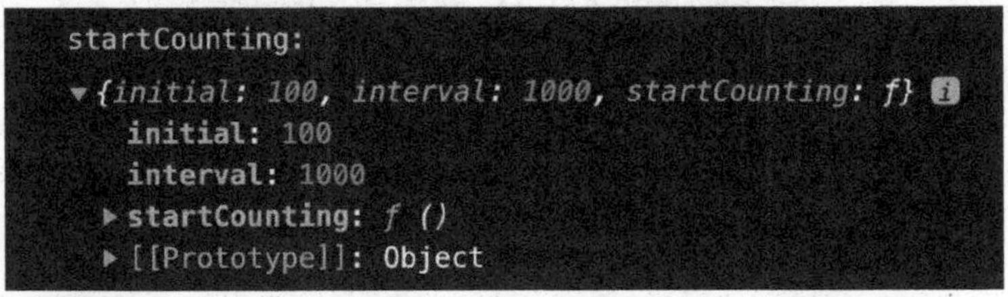

FIGURE 23.2

Our first call to this refers to the startCounting function

The value of this inside our setTimeout function will refer to the Window object, as shown in Figure 23.3.

FIGURE 23.3

The value of this inside setTimeout refers to Window. That doesn't look right, does it?

Here is where things are problematic. You may think that `setInterval` would inherit the value of `this` from its outer environment, as defined by `startCounting`, but that isn't the case. The reason is that traditional functions don't behave in this seemingly logical way. They define their own value for `this`, and that is always going to refer to the context in which they are being used.

Our anonymous function inside our `setTimeout` doesn't get created when our `counter` object is initialized. It gets created only when we call the `startCounting` method:

```
counter.startCounting();
```

This call lives in the context of the `Window` object. When `startCounting` is invoked and the anonymous function is created, the `this.initial` call is looking for the value of `initial` on the `Window` object. That property doesn't exist there, and that is why trying to increment this nonexistent variable gives us a **NaN**.

Using a Redefined Version of the this Keyword

One approach to get us out of this gully is to store the value of `this` and pass the stored `this` value into our anonymous function. Take a look at the following:

```
let counter = {
  initial: 100,
  interval: 1000,
  startCounting: function () {
    let that = this;
    setInterval(function () {
      that.initial++;
      console.log(that.initial); // works
    }, this.interval);
  }
}
counter.startCounting();
```

Notice that we introduced a `that` variable in the `startCounting` context to store a local reference to `this`. Inside our anonymous function, we use `that` where we earlier used `this`. Because `that` is properly storing a version of `this` that is tied to our `counter` object, our use of `that.initial` properly resolves to the correct value. If we run this code, we'll see the output of `initial` properly incrementing when we examine our console, as shown in Figure 23.4.

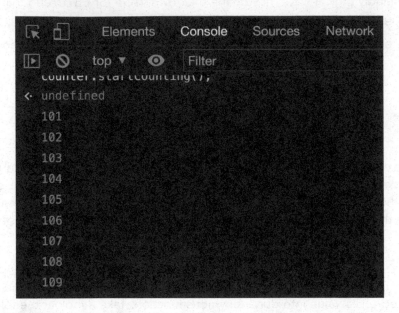

FIGURE 23.4

The value increments correctly! Yay.

All of these mentions of `this` and `that` in this explanation can be a bit confusing, but we are just redefining the value of `this` into a local variable. You don't have to use the variable name `that` either. You can call it anything you want:

```
let counter = {
  initial: 100,
  interval: 1000,
  startCounting: function () {
    let baconAndEggs = this;
    setInterval(function () {
      baconAndEggs.initial++;
      console.log(baconAndEggs.initial); // undefined
    }, this.interval);
```

```
    }
  }
counter.startCounting();
```

I won't say that this variable name for the redefined `this` makes our code run better, but it certainly does make it run as part of a complete breakfast!

Arrow Functions and Their Lexical Scope

We just saw one approach of addressing this problem by storing the value of `this` and using this stored value in place of the actual `this`. There is an arguably better approach. Let's say we replace our anonymous function inside our `setInterval` with an arrow function:

```
let counter2 = {
  initial: 100,
  interval: 1000,
  startCounting: function () {
    setInterval(() => {
      this.initial++;
      console.log(this.initial); // works
    }, this.interval);
  }
}
counter2.startCounting();
```

When we run this code, what gets printed this time around is 100, 101, 102, and so on, just like we want. No mess. No fuss. No this and that confusion. Why does an arrow function work here while traditional functions require extra gymnastics?

The reason is that arrow functions *do not* define their own `this` value. Instead, they inherit the value of `this` from where their code is *defined* in the document. Another way of saying this is that the `this` value inside arrow functions is determined by its surrounding scope, more formally called the **lexical scope**. This is in contrast to traditional functions whose `this` value comes from the context in which they are used. This is a subtle difference with a huge (and beneficial) change in behavior.

NOTE Some Other Things Arrow Functions Don't Have

Beyond not having their own `this` value (which they inherit from their surroundings), arrow functions have no constructor or prototype properties. They also don't support the `bind`, `call`, and `apply` methods. If you have existing code that relies on these properties and methods, your best bet is to stay with traditional functions or learn how to use arrow functions and adapt your code accordingly.

One Method to Bind Them All

We have seen several cases so far where the value of `this` inside a function isn't quite what it needs to be. Instead of letting the environment dictate the `this` value, what if we had a magical way to just tell a function (very sternly, yet kindly) what its value of `this` should be? That magical way happens to be something the `bind` method provides. The way `bind` works is a bit mysterious, but what we need are just two things to use it:

- A function whose value of `this` we want to set

- The star of this section, the `bind` method itself

If we had to illustrate this, we would see something that looks as follows in Figure 23.5.

FIGURE 23.5

*Meet the **function** and the **bind** method, the two key pieces of our solution here!*

What we do next is where the magic part comes in: We take our regular function, call `bind` from it, and provide the value of `this` that we want our regular function to use. The syntax looks a bit like the following:

```
let boundFunction = myRegularFunction.bind(valueOfThis);
boundFunction();
```

When called, `bind` creates a new function known as a **bound** (or **exotic**) **function**, where it wraps our regular function and injects the value of `this` that it needs to have to behave correctly:

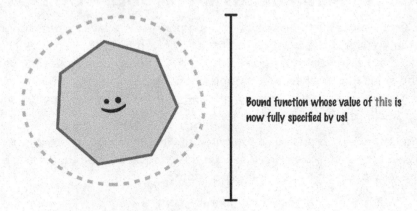

Bound function whose value of this is now fully specified by us!

Getting back to our example from earlier, here is how we use `bind` to ensure our `setInterval` gets the correct value for `this`:

```
let counter3 = {
  initial: 100,
  interval: 1000,
  startCounting: function () {
    setInterval(function() {
      this.initial++;
      console.log(this.initial); // works
    }.bind(this), this.interval);
  }
}
counter3.startCounting();
```

When we run this code, we'll see our console printing 100, 101, 102, and so on, just like we expect. As the highlighted line shows, we have our anonymous function tagged with the `bind` method, and the argument we pass to `bind` is the value of `this` from the same context our `setInterval` is defined in. This ensures that any code inside our anonymous function that references `this` (such as `this.initial++`) gets the value of `this` from what we passed in via `bind`, as opposed to inferring the `Window` object from its environment...which we don't want!

THE ABSOLUTE MINIMUM: WHAT SHOULD YOU DO?

One of the most frustrating parts of writing or reading JavaScript is figuring out what in the world this is referring to at any given time. Unlike other JavaScript quirks that have managed to be replaced by better solutions over the years, there are no signs that we'll ever stop using this. The best we can do is take the time to better understand how this works and prepare ourselves for what surprises this will have in store in the future!

Using console.log helps us to figure out what the value of this is at any given time, and the techniques we've seen in this chapter will help us make this be whatever we want it to be! Really cool, right?

? Ask a question: **https://forum.kirupa.com**

✔ Practice by building real apps: **https://bit.ly/coding_exercises**

Errors/known issues: **https://bit.ly/javascript_errata**

24

BOOLEANS AND THE STRICTER === AND !== OPERATORS

While it's polite to say that all types are interesting and fun to be around, you and I both know that is a lie. Some types are just boring. The boolean type is one such example. Here is the reason why: Whenever we initialize a variable using either **true** or **false**, we create a boolean:

```
let sunny = false;
let traffic = true;
```

Congratulations. If you just know this, you are 80 percent of the way there in fully understanding how booleans operate. Of course, 80 percent isn't really adequate when you think about it. It's like eating a hot dog without any condiments. It's like watching a live concert and leaving before the encore set. It's like leaving a sentence mid....

In this chapter, we are going to cover the other 20 percent, which is made up of various boolean quirks, the boolean object, the `Boolean` function, and the important === and !== operators.

The Boolean Object

Booleans are meant to be used as primitives. I'm going to be extra lazy and just reuse the example you saw a few moments earlier to show you what a boolean primitive would look like:

```
let sunny = false;
let traffic = true;
```

Like you've seen so many times already, behind every primitive there is an `Object`-based representation lurking in the shadows. The way you create a new boolean object is by using the `new` keyword, the `Boolean` constructor name, and an initial value:

```
let boolObject = new Boolean(false);
let anotherBool = new Boolean(true);
```

The initial value you can pass in to the `Boolean` constructor is commonly **true** and **false**, but you can pretty much pass anything in there that will result in the final evaluation being **true** or **false**. I will detail what kinds of values will predictably result in a **true** or **false** outcome in a little bit, but here is the obligatory warning from the Surgeon General about this approach: *Unless you really, REALLY want a boolean object, you should stick with primitives.*

The Boolean Function

There is one major advantage the `Boolean` constructor provides, and that advantage revolves around being able to pass in any arbitrary value or expression as part of creating your boolean object:

```
let boolObject = new Boolean(< arbitrary expression >);
```

This is really advantageous because you may find yourself wanting to evaluate a boolean expression where the data you end up with isn't a clean **true** or **false**. This is especially common when you are dealing with external data or code, and you have no control over which of the various **false**-y or **true**-y values you get. Here is a contrived example:

```
let isMovieAvailable = getMovieData()[4];
```

The value for `isMovieAvailable` is probably a **true** or **false**. When it comes to processing data, you often have no guarantee that something at some point will break or change what gets returned. Just like in real life, simply hoping that things will work is never adequate without you taking some actionable steps. The `Boolean` function is one such step.

Now, creating your own function to deal with the ambiguity may be overkill, but the downside with the `Boolean` constructor is that you are obviously left with a boolean object—which isn't desirable. Fortunately, there is a way to get the flexibility of the `Boolean` constructor with the lightweight nature of a boolean primitive extremely easily. That way is led by the `Boolean` function:

```
let  bool = Boolean(true);
```

The `Boolean` function allows you to pass in arbitrary values and expressions while still returning a **primitive boolean value** of **true** or **false**. The main difference in how you use it compared to the constructor approach is that you don't have the new keyword. W00t! Anyway, let's take a few moments and look at the variety of things you can pass in to the `Boolean` function, and note that all of this will also apply to what you can pass in to the `Boolean` constructor you saw in the previous section as well.

The values you can pass in to return **false** are **null**, **undefined**, empty/nothing, **0**, an empty string, and (of course) **false**:

```
let bool;

bool = Boolean(null);
bool = Boolean(undefined);
bool = Boolean();
```

```
bool = Boolean(0);
bool = Boolean("");
bool = Boolean(false);
```

In all of these examples, the `bool` variable will return **false**. To return **true**, we can pass in a value of **true** or ANYTHING that results in something other than the various **false** values we saw earlier:

```
let bool;

bool = Boolean(true);
bool = Boolean("hello");
bool = Boolean(new Boolean()); // Inception!!!
bool = Boolean("false"); // "false" is a string
bool = Boolean({});
bool = Boolean(3.14);
bool = Boolean(["a", "b", "c"]);
```

In these examples, the `bool` variable will return a **true**. That may seem bizarre given some of the statements, so let's look at a few of the subtle things in play here. If what we are evaluating is an object, such as `new Boolean(new Boolean())`, the evaluation will always be **true**. The reason is that the mere existence of an object will trigger the **true** switch, and calling `new Boolean()` results in a new object. Extending this logic a bit, it means the following `if` statement actually results in a **true** as well:

```
let boolObject = new Boolean(false);

if (boolObject) {
  console.log("Bool, you so crazy!!!");
}
```

It doesn't matter that the object we are evaluating is secretly a **false** in disguise... or a `String` object, an `Array`, and so on. The rules for primitives are simpler. If we are passing in a primitive (or something that evaluates to a primitive), anything other than **null**, **undefined**, **0**, an empty string, **NaN**, or **false** will result in a result of **true**.

Strict Equality and Inequality Operators

The last thing we are going to look at is combining what we know about types and booleans to add a twist to the various conditional operators we saw earlier. So, we know about == and != and have probably seen them in use a few times. These are the equality and inequality operators that let us know if two things are either equal or unequal. Here is the plot twist: They exhibit a subtle and deviant behavior we may not be aware of.

Here is an example:

```
function theSolution(answer) {

  if (answer == 42) {

    console.log("You have nothing more to learn!");

  }

}


theSolution("42"); //42 is passed in as a string
```

In this example, the expression answer == 42 will evaluate to **true**. This works despite the 42 we passed in being a string and the 42 we are checking against being a number. What is going on here? In what kind of a world is a string and a number equal? With the == and != operators, this is expected behavior. The value for the two things we are comparing is **42**. To make this work, JavaScript forces the two different yet similar values to be the same under the hood. This is formally known as **type coercion.**

The problem is that this behavior can be undesirable—especially when this is happening without us knowing about it. To avoid situations like this, we have stricter versions of the equality and inequality operators, and they are === and !==, respectively. These operators check for **both value and type** and do not perform any type coercion. They basically force us to write code where the burden on ensuring true equality or inequality falls squarely on us. That is a good thing.

Let's fix our earlier example by replacing the == operator with the === operator:

```
function theSolution(answer) {
  if (answer === 42) {
    console.log("You have nothing more to learn!");
  }
}
```

```
theSolution("42"); //42 is passed in as a string
```

This time around, the conditional expression will evaluate to **false**. In this stricter world, a string and number are of different types despite the values being similar. Because no type coercion takes place, the final result is **false**.

The general word on the street is to *always use the stricter forms of the equality and inequality operators*. If anything, using them will help us to spot errors in our code—errors that might otherwise turn out very difficult to identify.

 CAUTION   If we are comparing two *different* objects, the strict equality operator (and the not-so-strict equality operator) won't work as we might expect. For example, all of the following cases will be false:

```
console.log(new String("A") == new String("A"));
console.log([1, 2, 3] == [1, 2, 3]);
console.log({ a: 1 } == { a: 1 });
```

Keep that in mind when you are comparing the equality or inequality of two separate, individual objects.

THE ABSOLUTE MINIMUM

Booleans make up one of the most frequently used types in our code. They play a key role in allowing our code to branch out into different directions despite the simplicity they exhibit on the surface. While I can count on one hand the number of times I had to use the Boolean function or even the stricter equality and inequality operators, there aren't enough hands with fingers for me to count the number of times I've encountered these strange things in the wild.

? Ask a question: **https://forum.kirupa.com**

✔ Practice by building real apps: **https://bit.ly/coding_exercises**

🐦 Errors/known issues: **https://bit.ly/javascript_errata**

25

NULL AND UNDEFINED

One of the great mysteries of the world revolves around making sense of `null` and `undefined`. Most code you see is littered with them, and you've probably run into them yourself a few times. As mysteries go, making sense of `null` and `undefined` isn't particularly bizarre. It is just dreadfully boring...like the most boring (yet important) thing about JavaScript you'll ever have to learn.

Null

Let's start with `null`. The `null` keyword is a primitive that fills a special role in the world of JavaScript. It is an explicit definition that stands for **no value**. If you've ever browsed through code others have written, you'll probably see `null` appear a number of times. It is quite popular because the advantage of `null` lies in its definitiveness. Instead of having variables contain stale values or mysterious undefined values, setting it to `null` is a clear indication that you **want the value to not exist**.

This advantage is important when you are writing code and want to initialize or clear a variable to something that represents nothing.

Here is an example:

```
let name = null;

if (name === null) {
    name = "Peter Griffin";
} else {
    name = "No name";
}
```

The `null` primitive isn't a naturally occurring resource. It is something you consciously assign, so you will often see it used as part of variable declarations or passed in as arguments to function calls. Using `null` is easy. Checking for its existence is pretty easy as well:

```
if (name === null) {
   // do something interesting...or not
}
```

The only thing to note is that you should use the === operator instead of the lowly == one. While the world won't end if you use ==, it's good practice to check for both type and value when working with `null`.

Undefined

Here is where things get a little interesting. To represent something that isn't defined, you have the `undefined` primitive. You see `undefined` in a few cases. The most common ones are when you try to access a variable that hasn't been initialized or when accessing the value of a function that doesn't actually return anything.

Here is a code snippet that points out `undefined` in a few of its natural habitats:

```
let myVariable;
console.log(myVariable); // undefined


function doNothing() {
   // watch paint dry
   return;
}


let weekendPlans = doNothing();
console.log(weekendPlans); // undefined


let person = {
   firstName: "Isaac",
   lastName: "Newton"
}
console.log(person.title); // undefined
```

In your code, you probably won't be assigning `undefined` to anything. Instead, you will spend time checking to see if the value of something is `undefined`. You have several ways to perform this check. The first is a naive way that usually (almost always) works:

```
if (myVariable === undefined) {
   // do something
}
```

The downside of this approach has to do with what `undefined` actually is. Brace yourself—`undefined` is a global variable that happens to be automatically defined for us, and this means we can potentially overwrite it to something like **true** or whatever else we want to set it to. If `undefined` ever gets overwritten, it would break our code if we just check with === or even ==. To avoid any shenanigans around this, the safest way to perform a check for undefined involves typeof and the === operator:

```
let myVariable;

if (typeof myVariable === "undefined") {
    console.log("Define me!!!");
}
```

This ensures that you will perform a check for undefined and always return the correct answer.

NOTE Null == Undefined, But Null !== Undefined

Continuing the == and === weirdness, if you ever check for null == undefined, the answer will be **true**. If you use === and have null === undefined, the answer in this case will be **false**.

The reason is that == does type coercion, where it arm-twists types to conform to what JavaScript thinks the value should be. Using ===, you check for both type and value. This is a more comprehensive check that detects that undefined and null are indeed two different things.

A hat tip to senocular (aka Trevor McCauley) for pointing this out!

THE ABSOLUTE MINIMUM

There is a reason why I saved these built-in types for last. Both null and undefined are the least exciting of the bunch, but they are also often misunderstood. Knowing how to use null and detecting for it and undefined are very important skills to get right. Not getting them right will lead to very subtle errors that are going to be hard to pinpoint.

? Ask a question: **https://forum.kirupa.com**

✔ Practice by building real apps: **https://bit.ly/coding_exercises**

🖋 Errors/known issues: **https://bit.ly/javascript_errata**

26

ALL ABOUT JSON (JAVASCRIPT OBJECT NOTATION)

When it comes to storing, retrieving, or transmitting data, you can use a bunch of file formats and data structures. You've probably used text files, Word documents, Excel spreadsheets, ZIP files, and so on to deal with the various kinds of data you handle. On the web front, one format reigns supreme over all others. It runs faster. It jumps higher. It has a shinier (and furrier) coat of fur. That format is known as **JSON**—short for **JavaScript Object Notation**.

In this chapter, you are going to learn all about what makes JSON objects awesome. We'll look in detail at what goes inside them and how you can read values from them as part of your own implementations.

What Is JSON?

In JavaScript, you have a way of defining objects using the object literal syntax:

```javascript
let funnyGuy = {
  firstName: "Conan",
  lastName: "O'Brien",

  getName: function () {
    return "Name is: " + this.firstName + " " + this.lastName;
  }
};

let theDude = {
  firstName: "Jeffrey",
  lastName: "Lebowski",

  getName: function () {
    return "Name is: " + this.firstName + " " + this.lastName;
  }
};

let detective = {
  firstName: "Adrian",
  lastName: "Monk",

  getName: function () {
    return "Name is: " + this.firstName + " " + this.lastName;
  }
};
```

If you aren't familiar with this syntax, I highly recommend you read more about it in Chapter 19, "A Deeper Look at Objects." It will make understanding and working with JSON objects significantly easier!

On the surface, the object literal syntax looks like a bunch of brackets and colons and weird curly braces that define your object's properties and values. Despite how weird it looks, under the covers, it is fairly descriptive. Many of the common data types you would want to use are available. You can neatly represent their properties and values as key and value pairs separated by a colon. Equally as important as all the other stuff I just mentioned, this syntax allows you to have structure and nested values. Overall, it is a pretty sweet way of representing JavaScript objects...in a literal representation!

The JSON format borrows heavily from this object literal syntax. Here is an example of some honest-to-goodness real JSON data returned by the WeatherUnderground API for displaying the weather in my hometown of Seattle:

```json
{
  "response": {
    "version": "0.1",
    "termsofService": "http://www.wunderground.com/weather/api/d/
erms.html",
    "features": {
      "conditions": 1
    }
  },
  "current_observation": {
    "image": {
      "url": "http://icons.wxug.com/graphics/wu2/logo_130x80.png",
      "title": "Weather Underground",
      "link": "http://www.wunderground.com"
    },
    "display_location": {
      "full": "Seattle, WA",
      "city": "Seattle",
      "state": "WA",
      "state_name": "Washington",
      "country": "US",
```

```
          "country_iso3166": "US",
          "zip": "98101",
          "magic": "1",
          "wmo": "99999",
          "latitude": "47.61167908",
          "longitude": "-122.33325958",
          "elevation": "63.00000000"
     },
     "observation_location": {
          "full": "Herrera, Inc., Seattle, Washington",
          "city": "Herrera, Inc., Seattle",
          "state": "Washington",
          "country": "US",
          "country_iso3166": "US",
          "latitude": "47.616558",
          "longitude": "-122.341240",
          "elevation": "121 ft"
     },
     "estimated": {},
     "station_id": "KWASEATT187",
     "observation_time": "Last Updated on August 28, 9:28 PM PDT",
     "observation_time_rfc822": "Fri, 28 Aug 2015 21:28:12 -0700",
     "observation_epoch": "1440822492",
     "local_time_rfc822": "Fri, 28 Aug 2015 21:28:45 -0700",
     "local_epoch": "1440822525",
     "local_tz_short": "PDT",
     "local_tz_long": "America/Los_Angeles",
     "local_tz_offset": "-0700",
     "weather": "Overcast",
     "temperature_string": "68.0 F (20.0 C)",
     "temp_f": 68.0,
     "temp_c": 20.0,
     "relative_humidity": "71%",
     "wind_string": "Calm",
     "wind_dir": "NNW",
```

```
    "wind_degrees": 331,
    "wind_mph": 0.0,
    "wind_gust_mph": "10.0",
    "wind_kph": 0,
    "wind_gust_kph": "16.1",
    "pressure_mb": "1008",
    "pressure_in": "29.78",
    "pressure_trend": "-",
    "dewpoint_string": "58 F (15 C)",
    "dewpoint_f": 58,
    "dewpoint_c": 15,
    "heat_index_string": "NA",
    "heat_index_f": "NA",
    "heat_index_c": "NA",
    "windchill_string": "NA",
    "windchill_f": "NA",
    "windchill_c": "NA",
    "feelslike_string": "68.0 F (20.0 C)",
    "feelslike_f": "68.0",
    "feelslike_c": "20.0",
    "visibility_mi": "10.0",
    "visibility_km": "16.1",
    "solarradiation": "--",
    "UV": "0",
    "precip_1hr_string": "0.00 in ( 0 mm)",
    "precip_1hr_in": "0.00",
    "precip_1hr_metric": " 0",
    "precip_today_string": "0.00 in (0 mm)",
    "precip_today_in": "0.00",
    "precip_today_metric": "0",
    "icon": "cloudy",
    "icon_url": "http://icons.wxug.com/i/c/k/nt_cloudy.gif",
    "nowcast": ""
  }
}
```

Ignoring the size of the data returned, you can see a lot of similarities between the JSON data here and the object literal syntax you saw earlier. There are some major differences you need to be aware of as well, but we'll look at all that boring stuff later. First, let's take a deeper look at what exactly makes up a JSON object.

Looking Inside a JSON Object

A JSON object is nothing more than a combination of property names and their values. That seems pretty simple, but there are some important details we need to go over in this section.

Property Names

Property names are the identifiers you will use to access a value. Visually, they are the items to the left of the colon character:

```
{
  "firstName": "Kirupa",
  "lastName": "Chinnathambi",
  "special": {
    "admin": true,
    "userID": 203
  },
  "devices": [
    {
      "type": "laptop",
      "model": "Macbook Pro 2015"
    },
    {
      "type": "phone",
      "model": "iPhone 6"
    }
  ]
}
```

In this JSON snippet, the property names are **firstName**, **lastName**, **special**, **admin**, **userID**, **devices**, **type**, and **model**. Notice how the property names are defined. They are string values wrapped in quotation marks. The quotation mark is an important detail that you don't have to specify in the object literal case for property names, so don't forget to include them when working in the JSON world!

The Values

Each property name maps to a value, and the types of values you can have are as follows:

- Numbers
- Strings
- Booleans (**true** or **false**)
- Objects
- Arrays
- Null

Let's map these various types to the example we just looked at.

Strings

The string values are the following highlighted lines:

```
{
  "firstName": "Kirupa",
  "lastName": "Chinnathambi",
  "special": {
    "admin": true,
    "userID": 203
  },
  "devices": [
    {
      "type": "laptop",
      "model": "Macbook Pro"
    },
    {
      "type": "phone",
      "model": "iPhone XS"
```

```
        }
    ]
}
```

The double quotation marks are a dead giveaway that these values are strings. Besides your usual letters and numbers and symbols, you can also include **escape characters** like \', \", \\, V, and so on to define characters in your string that would otherwise get parsed as some JSON operation.

Numbers

Our lone representative of the number family is the value for the `userID` property:

```
{
    "firstName": "Kirupa",
    "lastName": "Chinnathambi",
    "special": {
        "admin": true,
        "userID": 203
    },
    "devices": [
        {
            "type": "laptop",
            "model": "Macbook Pro"
        },
        {
            "type": "phone",
            "model": "iPhone XS"
        }
    ]
}
```

You can specify both decimal values (for example, **0.204**, **1200.23**, **45**) as well as exponential values (for example, **2e16**, **3e+4**, **1.5e-2**). There are some quirks you need to be aware of, though. You can't prefix your number with a 0 followed by another number. For example, a value of **03.14** isn't allowed.

Booleans

Boolean values are easy:

```
{
  "firstName": "Kirupa",
  "lastName": "Chinnathambi",
  "special": {
    "admin": true,
    "userID": 203
  },
  "devices": [
    {
      "type": "laptop",
      "model": "Macbook Pro"
    },
    {
      "type": "phone",
      "model": "iPhone XS"
    }
  ]
}
```

The values can either be **true** or **false**. One thing to note—the capitalization is important. Both **true** and **false** have to be lowercase. Using sentence casing (**True** or **False**) or going with all caps (**TRUE** or **FALSE**) is forbidden.

Objects

This is where things get a little interesting:

```
{
  "firstName": "Kirupa",
  "lastName": "Chinnathambi",
  "special": {
    "admin": true,
```

```
    "userID": 203
  },
  "devices": [
    {
      "type": "laptop",
      "model": "Macbook Pro"
    },
    {
      "type": "phone",
      "model": "iPhone XS"
    }
  ]
}
```

Objects contain a collection of property names and values, and they are separated from the rest of your content with curly brackets. See? Wasn't that a *little* interesting?

Arrays

Our `devices` property represents an array:

```
{
  "firstName": "Kirupa",
  "lastName": "Chinnathambi",
  "special": {
    "admin": true,
    "userID": 203
  },
  "devices": [
    {
      "type": "laptop",
      "model": "Macbook Pro"
    },
    {
      "type": "phone",
```

```
        "model": "iPhone XS"
    }
  ]
}
```

Arrays store an ordered collection of zero or more values that you can iterate through, and they are separated by the bracket notation. Inside an array, you can use any of the JSON types we've seen so far, including other arrays!

Null

The last data type is also the most boring one:

```
{
  "foo": null
}
```

Your JSON values can be **null**. This represents an empty value.

Reading JSON Data

I admit it. The previous section was extremely dull, but there is some good news! Given how boring what you just saw was, this section is by comparison going to seem a whole lot more exciting than it really is. Yay!

Anyway, almost all your interactions with JSON will revolve around reading data. When it comes to reading JSON data, the main thing to keep in mind is that it is very similar to reading values stored inside a typical JavaScript object. You can either dot into the value you want (property.propertyFoo) or you can use the array approach (property["propertyFoo"]) and access the value that way.

To help explain all this, let's use the following example:

```
let exampleJSON = {
  "firstName": "Kirupa",
  "lastName": "Chinnathambi",
  "special": {
    "admin": true,
```

```
    "userID": 203
  },
  "devices": [
    {
      "type": "laptop",
      "model": "Macbook Pro"
    },
    {
      "type": "phone",
      "model": "iPhone XS"
    }
  ]
};
```

To read the value stored by firstName, you can do either of the following:

```
exampleJSON.firstName;
exampleJSON["firstName"];
```

Both lines will return a value of **Kirupa**. There is no right or wrong answer to whether you want to use the dot notation approach or the array approach to access the value you are interested in. Use whatever you are comfortable with, but my personal preference is to use dot notation. Passing in property names as strings makes me queasy, so I will only use the dot notation approach in the code snippets that you will be seeing.

Similar to what you saw earlier, to access the value stored by lastName, you can do this:

```
exampleJSON.lastName;
```

For simple properties that store simple values, life is pretty simple. The only very, VERY minor complication you'll run into is when working with more complex values made up of objects and arrays. To read a value stored inside an object, just keep dotting into each property until you reach the property that stores the value you are interested in.

Here is what trying to access the value stored by the `userID` property will look like:

```
exampleJSON.special.userID;
```

Arrays are no different, but you will eventually have to switch into array notation once you get to the property that stores your array values. If we wanted to access the `model` value of the first device in the `devices` array, we can type something that looks as follows:

```
exampleJSON.devices[0].model;
```

Because the `devices` property refers to an array, you can also perform stereotypical array-like operations, such as the following:

```
let devicesArray = exampleJSON.devices;

for (let i = 0; i < devicesArray.length; i++) {
  let type = devicesArray[i].type;
  let model = devicesArray[i].model;

  // do something interesting with this data!
}
```

To reiterate what you saw in the previous section, your JSON values can be either strings, numbers, objects, arrays, booleans, or nulls. Everything that JavaScript supports for a given data type that you encounter inside your JSON object, you can easily take advantage of.

Parsing JSON-Looking Data into Actual JSON

In our example, we had our JSON data defined neatly inside the `exampleJSON` variable. There is no doubt in anybody's mind that what we're dealing with is a real JS object that is represented using JSON semantics.

With real-world scenarios, that won't always be the case. Your JSON data could be coming from a variety of different sources, and not all of them will return the JSON data into this workable format we just saw. Many will return JSON data as **raw text**. You will have something that looks like a JSON object, but you can't interact with the data like you would when you are working with a real JSON object.

To deal with this, you have the `JSON.parse` method that takes your "fake" JSON data as its argument:

```
function processRequest(e) {
  if (xhr.readyState == 4 && xhr.status == 200) {
    let response = JSON.parse(xhr.responseText);
    selectInitialState(response.region);
  }
}
```

As you can see from our highlighted line, this method takes whatever JSON-looking data you end up with and converts it into a real JSON object that you can work with more easily. Whenever I am working with JSON data from an external source, I always use `JSON.parse` just to be safe.

Writing JSON Data?

We just had a section devoted entirely to reading values from JSON data. It would seem logical to also have a section that is focused on writing JSON data. As it turns out, writing JSON data just isn't all that popular unless you are saving JSON data to a file or doing something with web services. If you are doing either of these tasks, statistically you are doing development on Node or writing code in a programming language other than JavaScript.

For frontend development, I can't think of too many cases where information on writing JSON would be useful. If you run into the rare situation where you need to do something other than reading JSON data, my recommendation is for you to use Google!

THE ABSOLUTE MINIMUM

At one point in time, this chapter would have been focused on XML. Even today, XML is still widely popular as a file format for storing or communicating information. Only in a world where the web browser is king (in other words, the world we live in) is JSON extremely popular. Outside of websites, web applications, and REST-based web services, dealing with data in the JSON format isn't all that popular. You should keep that in mind when running into older, less-web-centric situations!

? Ask a question: **https://forum.kirupa.com**

✔ Practice by building real apps: **https://bit.ly/coding_exercises**

📝 Errors/known issues: **https://bit.ly/javascript_errata**

IN THIS CHAPTER

- Learn how JavaScript and the rest of your page interact
- Understand what the fuss about the Document Object Model (DOM) is all about
- Figure out the fuzzy boundaries between HTML, CSS, and JavaScript

27

JS, THE BROWSER, AND THE DOM

So far, we've looked at JavaScript in isolation. We learned a lot about its basic functionality, but we did so with little to no connection with how it ties to the real world—a world that is represented by your browser, swimming with little HTML tags and CSS styles. This chapter will serve as an introduction to this world, and subsequent chapters will dive in much deeper.

In the following sections, you will learn about the mysterious data structure and programming interface known as the **Document Object Model (DOM)**. You'll learn what it is, why it is useful, and how it ties in to everything you'll be doing in the future.

What HTML, CSS, and JavaScript Do

Before we dive in and start answering the meaning of life...err, the DOM, let's quickly look at some things you probably already know. For starters, the stuff you put into your HTML documents revolves around Hypertext Markup Language (HTML), Cascading Style Sheets (CSS), and JavaScript. We treat these three things as equal partners in building up what you see in your browser (Figure 27.1).

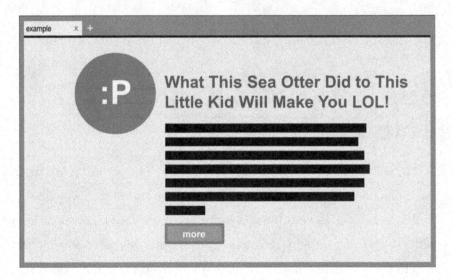

FIGURE 27.1

A typical web page is made up of HTML, CSS, and JavaScript.

Each partner has an important role to play, and the role each one plays is very different.

HTML Defines the Structure

Your HTML defines the structure of your page and typically contains the content you see:

```
<!DOCTYPE html>
<html>
```

```html
<head>
  <meta content="sea otter, kid, stuff" name="keywords">
  <meta content="Sometimes, sea otters are awesome!"
name="description">
  <title>Example</title>

  <link href="foo.css" rel="stylesheet" />
</head>

<body>
  <div id="container">
    <img src="seaOtter.png" />

    <h1>What This Sea Otter Did to This Little Kid Will Make You
LOL!</h1>

    <p class="bodyText">
      Nulla tristique, justo eget semper viverra,
      massa arcu congue tortor, ut vehicula urna mi
      in lorem. Quisque aliquam molestie dui, at tempor
      turpis porttitor nec. Aenean id interdum urna.
      Curabitur mi ligula, hendrerit at semper sed,
      feugiat a nisi.
    </p>

    <div class="submitButton">
      more
    </div>
  </div>
  <script src="stuff.js"></script>
</body>

</html>
```

HTML by itself, kinda like Meg Griffin in *Family Guy*, is pretty boring. If you don't know who Meg is and are too lazy to google her, Figure 27.2 is an approximation of what she looks like.

A non-copyright-infringing interpretation of Meg Griffin!

FIGURE 27.2

An artistic interpretation of Meg Griffin

Anyway, you don't want your HTML documents to be boring. To transform your content from something plain and drab to something appealing, you have CSS.

Prettify My World, CSS!

CSS is your primary styling language. It allows you to give your HTML elements some much-needed aesthetic and layout appeal:

```
body {
  font-family: "Arial";
  background-color: #CCCFFF;
}
#container {
  margin-left: 30%;
}
```

```
#container img {
  padding: 20px;
}
#container h1 {
  font-size: 56px;
  font-weight: 500;
}
#container p.bodyText {
  font-size: 16px;
  line-height: 24px;
}
.submitButton {
  display: inline-block;
  border: 5px solid #669900;
  background-color: #7BB700;
  padding: 10px;
  width: 150px;
  font-weight: 800;
}
```

For the longest time, between HTML and CSS, you had everything you needed to create an awesome-looking and functioning page. You had structure and layout. You had navigation. You even had simple interactions such as mouseovers. Life was good.

It's JavaScript Time!

For all the great things HTML and CSS had going for them, they were both limited in how much interactivity they provided. People wanted to do more on a web document than just passively sit back and observe what is going on. They wanted their web documents to do more. They wanted their documents to help them play with media; remember where they left off; do things with their mouse clicks, keyboard taps, and finger presses; use fancy navigation menus; see spiffy (yes, I used the word *spiffy*) programmatic animations; interact with their webcams/microphones; not require a page reload/navigation for any kind of action; and a whole lot more.

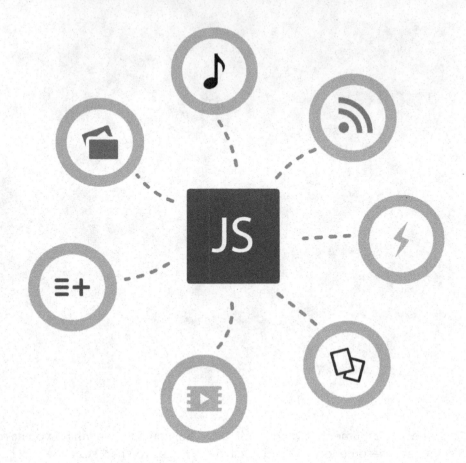

It certainly helped that web developers and designers (that is, you and me) were itching for a way to help create these kinds of things as well.

To fill in this gap between what HTML and CSS provided and what people wanted, you had third-party components like Java and Flash that thrived for many years. It wasn't until recently that this trend changed. There were many technical and political reasons for this shift, but one reason was that JavaScript for many years just wasn't ready. It didn't have what it took either in the core language or in what browsers supported to be effective.

That's no longer the case today. JavaScript is now a perfectly capable language that allows you to add the kinds of interactive things people are looking for. All of these capabilities are accessed by the real star of all this, the DOM.

Meet the Document Object Model

What your browser displays is a web document. More specifically, to summarize the entirety of the previous sections, what you see is a collision of HTML, CSS, and JavaScript working together to create what gets shown. Digging one step deeper, under the covers, there is a hierarchical structure that your browser uses to make sense of everything going on.

This structure is known (again) as the Document Object Model. Friends just call it the DOM. Figure 27.3 shows a very simplified view of what the DOM for our earlier example would look like.

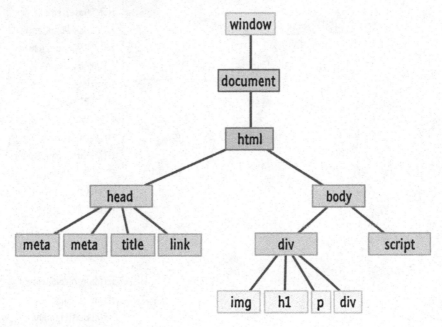

FIGURE 27.3

Our DOM for all the HTML you saw earlier looks sorta like this!

Despite the simplicity, there are several things to drill in on that apply to all DOM structures in general. Your DOM is actually made up many kinds of things beyond just HTML elements. All of those things that make up your DOM are more generically known as **nodes**.

These nodes can be elements (which shouldn't surprise you), attributes, text content, comments, document-related stuff, and various other things you simply never think about. That detail is important to someone, but that "someone" shouldn't be you and me. Almost always, the only kind of node we will care about is the element kind because that is what we will be dealing with 99 percent of the time. At the boring/technical level, nodes still play a role in our element-centric view.

Every HTML element you want to access has a particular type associated with it, and all of these types extend from the Node base that makes up all nodes, as shown in Figure 27.4.

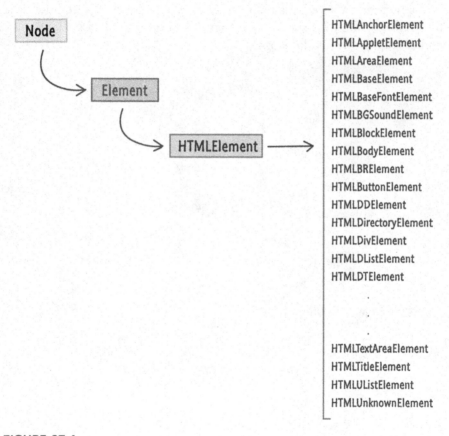

FIGURE 27.4

The arrangement of how the elements we typically see are structured

Your HTML elements are at the end of a chain that starts with Node and continues with Element and HTMLElement, before ending with a type (HTMLDivElement, HTMLHeadingElement, and so on) that matches the HTML element itself. The properties and methods you will see for manipulating HTML elements are introduced at some part of this chain.

Now, before we run toward using the DOM to modify HTML elements, let's first talk about two special objects that get in the way before the road clears up for what we want to do.

The window Object

In the browser, the root of your hierarchy is the `window` object, which contains many properties and methods that help you work with your browser (see Figure 27.5).

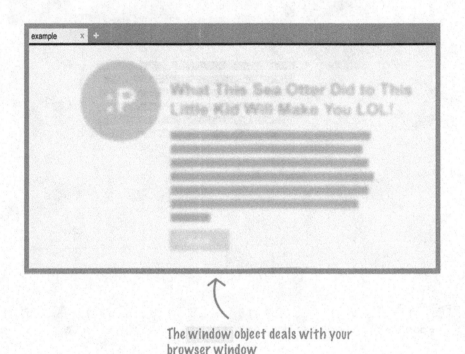

The window object deals with your browser window

FIGURE 27.5

The `window` is a pretty big deal up in these here parts.

Some of the things you can do with the help of the `window` object include accessing the current URL, getting information about any frames in the page, using local storage, seeing information about your screen, fiddling with the scroll bar, setting the status bar text, and all sorts of things that are applicable to the container your web page is displayed in.

The Document Object

Now, we get to the `document` object highlighted in Figure 27.6. Here is where things get interesting, and it is also where you and I will be focusing a lot of our time.

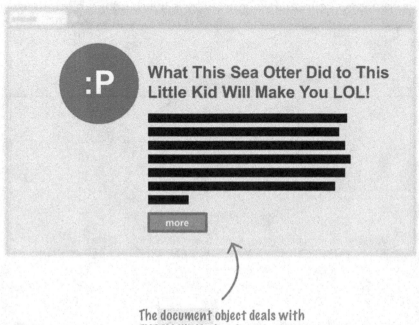

The document object deals with
EVERYTHING that lives in your document

FIGURE 27.6

The document object is also kinda sorta a big deal.

The `document` object is the gateway to all the HTML elements that make up what gets shown. The thing to keep in mind (and one that makes more sense as we look at future chapters) is that the `document` object does not simply represent a read-only version of the HTML document. It is a two-way street, where you can read as well as manipulate your document at will.

Any change you make to the DOM via JavaScript is reflected in what gets shown in the browser. This means you can dynamically add elements, remove them, move them around, modify attributes on them, set inline CSS styles, and per-form all sorts of other shenanigans. Outside of the very basic HTML needed via a `<script>` tag to get some JavaScript to run in an HTML document, you can construct a fully functioning page using nothing but JavaScript if you feel like it. Used properly, this is a pretty powerful feature.

Another import aspect of the document object has to do with events. I will go into more detail on this topic shortly, but if you want to react to a mouse click/hover, check a check box, detect when a key was pressed, and so on, you will be relying on functionality the document object provides for listening to and reacting to events.

There are a few more big buckets of functionality the DOM provides, but I'll highlight them as we get to them in the coming chapters.

THE ABSOLUTE MINIMUM

The DOM is the single most important piece of functionality you have for working with your HTML documents. It provides the missing link that ties your HTML and CSS with JavaScript. It also provides access one level up to your browser.

Now, knowing about the DOM is just part of the fun. Actually using its functionality to interact with your web document is the much larger and *funner* other part. When you are ready, turn (or flip) to the next chapter, where we will go further into the DOM.

? Ask a question: **https://forum.kirupa.com**

✔ Practice by building real apps: **https://bit.ly/coding_exercises**

🖎 Errors/known issues: **https://bit.ly/javascript_errata**

FINDING ELEMENTS IN THE DOM

As we saw in the previous chapter, our DOM is nothing more than a tree-like structure made up of all the elements that exist in our HTML document (see Figure 28.1).

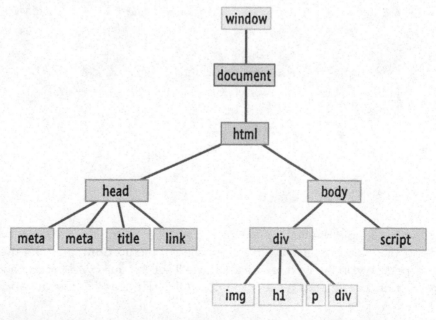

FIGURE 28.1

Yep. Looks like a tree-like structure alright!

That detail is only sort of important. What is important is that you have all of these HTML elements floating around that you want to access and read data from or modify. There are many ways to find these HTML elements. After all, these elements are arranged in a tree-like structure, and if there is one thing computer scientists like to do, it is figuring out crazy ways to run up and down a tree to find something.

I won't subject you to that torture...just yet. In this chapter, you are going to learn how to use two built-in functions called `querySelector` and `querySelectorAll` to solve a good chunk of all your DOM searching needs.

Meet the querySelector Family

To help explain the awesomeness that `querySelector` and `querySelectorAll` bring to the table, take a look at the following HTML:

```
<div id="main">
  <div class="pictureContainer">
    <img class="theImage" src="smiley.png" height="300"
width="150" />
  </div>
  <div class="pictureContainer">
    <img class="theImage" src="tongue.png" height="300" width="150"
/>
  </div>
  <div class="pictureContainer">
    <img class="theImage" src="meh.png" height="300" width="150" />
  </div>
  <div class="pictureContainer">
    <img class="theImage" src="sad.png" height="300" width="150" />
  </div>
</div>
```

In this example, we have one `div` with an `id` of **main**, and then we have four `div` and `img` elements, each with a class value of **pictureContainer** and **theImage**, respectively. In the next few sections, we'll set the `querySelector` and `querySelectorAll` functions loose on this HTML and see what happens.

querySelector

The `querySelector` function basically works as follows:

```
let element = document.querySelector("CSS selector");
```

The `querySelector` function takes an argument, and this argument is a string that represents the CSS selector for the element we wish to find. What gets returned by `querySelector` is the first element it finds—even if other elements exist—that could get targeted by the selector. This function is pretty stubborn like that.

Taking the HTML from our earlier example, if we wanted to access the `div` whose id is **main**, we would write the following:

```
let element = document.querySelector("#main");
```

Because **main** is the `id`, the selector syntax for targeting it would be #main. Similarly, let's specify the selector for the **pictureContainer** class:

```
let element = document.querySelector(".pictureContainer");
```

What gets returned is the first `div` whose class value is **pictureContainer**. The other `div` elements with the class value of **pictureContainer** will simply be ignored.

The selector syntax is not modified or made special because you are in JavaScript. The exact syntax you would use for selectors in your stylesheet or style region can be used!

querySelectorAll

The `querySelectorAll` function returns all elements it finds that match whatever selector you provide:

```
let elements = document.querySelectorAll("CSS selector");
```

With the exception of the number of elements returned, everything I've described about `querySelector` applies to `querySelectorAll` as well. That important detail changes how you end up actually using the `querySelectorAll` function. What gets returned is not a single element. Instead, what gets returned is an array-like container of elements!

Continuing to use the HTML from earlier, here is what our JavaScript would look like if we wanted to use `querySelectorAll` to help us display the `src` attribute of all the `img` elements that contain the class value **theImage**:

```
let images = document.querySelectorAll(".theImage");

for (let i = 0; i < images.length; i++) {
  let image = images[i];
  console.log(image.getAttribute("src"));
}
```

See? This is pretty straightforward. The main thing you need to do is remember how to work with arrays, which you should be a pro at by now. The other (slightly weirder) thing is the mysterious `getAttribute` function. If you aren't familiar with `getAttribute` and how to read values from elements, that's totally okay. We'll look at all that in Chapter 29, "Modifying DOM Elements." For now, just know that it allows you to read the value of any HTML attribute the HTML element in question may be sporting.

It Really Is the CSS Selector Syntax

The thing that surprised me when I first used `querySelector` and `querySelectorAll` is that it actually takes the full range of CSS selector syntax variations as its argument. You don't have to keep it simple like I've shown you so far.

If you wanted to target all the `img` elements without having to specify the class value, here is what our `querySelectorAll` call could look like:

```
let images = document.querySelectorAll("img");
```

If you wanted to target only the image whose `src` attribute is set to **meh.png**, you can do the following:

```
let images = document.querySelectorAll("img[src='meh.png']");
```

Note that I just specified an **attribute selector** as my argument to `querySelectorAll`. Pretty much any complex expression you can specify for a selector in your CSS document is fair game for specifying as an argument to either `querySelector` or `querySelectorAll`.

There are some caveats that you should be aware of, however. First, not all pseudo-class selectors are allowed. A selector made up of `:visited`, `:link`, `::before`, and `::after` is ignored and no elements are found.

Second, how crazy you can get with the selectors you provide depends on the browser's CSS support. Internet Explorer 8 supports `querySelector` and `querySelectorAll`. It doesn't support CSS3. Given that situation, using anything more recent than the selectors defined in CSS2 will not work when used with `querySelector` and `querySelectorAll` on IE8. Chances are, this doesn't apply to you because you are probably supporting more recent versions of browsers where this IE8 issue isn't even on the radar.

Finally, the selector you specify only applies to the descendants of the starting element you are beginning your search from. The starting element itself is not included. Not all `querySelector` and `querySelectorAll` calls need to be made from a `document`.

THE ABSOLUTE MINIMUM

The `querySelector` and `querySelectorAll` functions are extremely useful in complex documents where targeting a particular element is often not straightforward. By relying on the well-established CSS selector syntax, we can cast as small or as wide a net over the elements we want. If I want all image elements, I can use `querySelectorAll("img")`. If I only want the immediate img element contained inside its parent div, I can use the following:

```
querySelector("div + img")
```

Now, that's pretty awesome!

Before we wrap up, there is one more thing I'd like to chat with you about. Missing in all of this element-finding excitement were the `getElementById`, `getElementsByTagName`, and `getElementsByClassName` functions. Back in the day, these were the functions you would have used to find elements in your DOM. These functions still exist today, but our reasons for using them are very, VERY limited. One good reason is if you are looking for a list of DOM nodes that are live as opposed to static. To go into detail on what this means, check out **https://bit.ly/dom_live_nodes** for a tip from Trevor McCauley, the technical editor for this book!

? Ask a question: **https://forum.kirupa.com**

✔ Practice by building real apps: **https://bit.ly/coding_exercises**

🏗 Errors/known issues: **https://bit.ly/javascript_errata**

🍃 Tutorial on CSS attribute selectors: **http://bit.ly/kirupaAttribute**

29

MODIFYING DOM ELEMENTS

At this point, you kinda sorta know what the DOM is. You also saw how to find elements using querySelector and querySelectorAll. What's next is for you to learn how to modify the DOM elements you found:

✓ **1. Get a vague overview of the DOM**

✓ **2. Learn to find elements**

→ **3. Modify elements**

We are here!

4. ???

5. Profit!!!

I have no idea why there is a pizza here.

After all, what's the fun in having a giant lump of clay (or cookie dough) if we can't put our hands on it and make a giant mess? Anyway, besides it being fun and all, we will find ourselves modifying the DOM all the time. Whether we are using JavaScript to change some element's text, swap out an image with a different one, move an element from one part of a document to another, set an inline style, or perform any of the bazillion other changes we will want to do, **we will be modifying the DOM.** This chapter will teach you the basics of how to go about doing that.

DOM Elements Are Objects, Sort Of!

Our ability to use JavaScript to modify what gets shown by the browser is made possible because of one major detail. That detail is that every HTML tag, style rule, or any other thing that goes into your page has some sort of a representation in the DOM.

To visualize what I just said, let's say we have an image element defined in markup:

```
<img src="images/lol_panda.png" alt="Sneezing Panda!" width="250"
height="100"/>
```

When our browser parses the document and hits this image element, it creates a node in the DOM that represents it as shown in Figure 29.1.

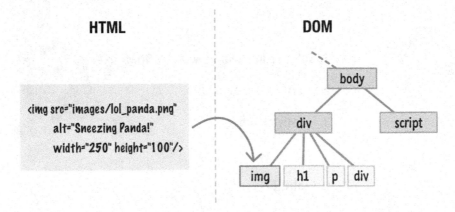

FIGURE 29.1

All of our HTML elements will eventually end up having a DOM representation.

This DOM representation provides us with the ability to do everything we could have done in markup. As it turns out, this DOM representation actually ends up allowing **us to do more with our HTML elements** than we could have done using just plain-old markup itself. This is something we'll see a little bit of here and a whole lot of in the future. The reason why our HTML elements are so versatile when viewed via the DOM is because they share a lot of similarities with plain JavaScript objects. Our DOM elements contain properties that allow us to get/set values and call methods. They have a form of inheritance that we saw a little bit about earlier, where the functionality each DOM element provides is spread out across the `Node`, `Element`, and `HTMLElement` base types, as shown again in Figure 29.2.

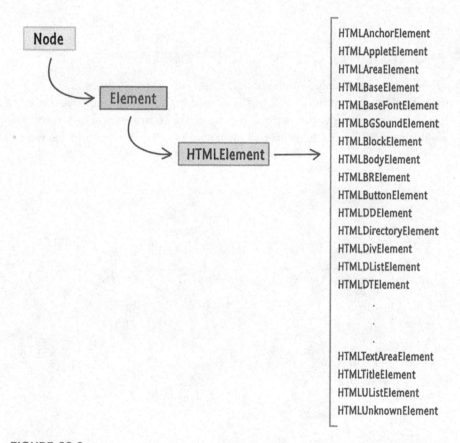

FIGURE 29.2

The hierarchy of the visual elements we'll typically encounter in the HTML

DOM elements probably even smell like an object when they run inside the house after rolling around in the rain for a bit.

Despite all of the similarities, for legal and possibly health reasons, I need to provide the following disclaimer: **the DOM was never designed to mimic the way objects work.** Many of the things we can do with objects we can certainly do with the DOM, but that is because the browser vendors help ensure that. The W3C specifications don't state that our DOM should behave identically to how we may expect things to behave with plain-old objects. While I wouldn't lose any sleep worrying about this, if you ever decide to extend DOM elements or perform more advanced object-related gymnastics, be sure to test across all browsers just to make sure everything works the way you intended.

Now that we got this awkward conversation out of the way, let's start to actually modify the DOM.

Let's Actually Modify DOM Elements

While we can certainly lean back and passively learn all there is about how to modify elements in the DOM, this is one of those cases where you may have more fun following along with a simple example. If you are interested in following along, we'll be using the following HTML as a sandbox for the techniques we will be covering:

```
<!DOCTYPE html>
<html>

<head>
  <title>Hello...</title>

  <style>
    .highlight {
      font-family: "Arial";
      padding: 30px;
    }


    .summer {
      font-size: 64px;
      color: #0099FF;
    }
  </style>
```

```
</head>

<body>

  <h1 id="bigMessage" class="highlight summer">What's happening?
</h1>

  <script>

  </script>
</body>

</html>
```

Just put all of that into an HTML document and follow along. If you preview this HTML in the browser, you will see something that looks like Figure 29.3.

FIGURE 29.3

What's happening?

There isn't really a whole lot going on here. The main piece of content is the `h1` tag that displays the **What's happening?** text:

```
<h1 id="bigMessage" class="highlight summer">What's happening?</h1>
```

Now, switching over to the DOM side of things, Figure 29.4 illustrates what this example looks like with all the HTML elements and nodes like `document` and `window` mapped.

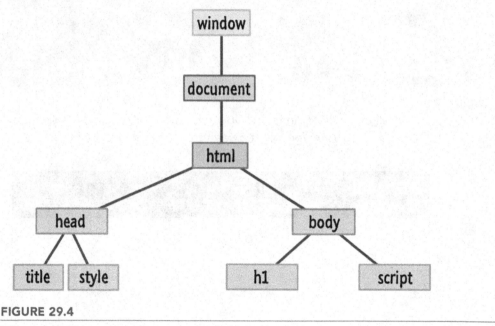

FIGURE 29.4

What our DOM structure for our example looks like

In the following sections, we'll look at some of the common things you can do in terms of modifying a DOM element.

Changing an Element's Text Value

Let's start off with an easy one. Many HTML elements have the ability to display some text. Examples of such elements are our headings, paragraphs, sections, inputs, buttons, and many more. There is one thing they all have in common. The way you modify the text value is by setting the `textContent` property.

Let's say we want to change the text that appears in the h1 element from our example. The following snippet shows what that would look like:

```
<body>
  <h1 id="bigMessage" class="highlight summer">What's happening?
</h1>

  <script>
    let headingElement = document.querySelector("#bigMessage");
    headingElement.textContent = "Oppa Gangnam Style!";
  </script>
</body>
```

If you make this change and preview it in the browser, you will see what is shown in Figure 29.5.

FIGURE 29.5

Changing a heading's text value.

Let's look at what exactly we did to cause this change. The first step to modifying any HTML element in JavaScript is to first get a reference to it:

```
let headingElement = document.querySelector("#bigMessage");
```

Here is where our old friends `querySelector` and `querySelectorAll` come in. As we will see later, we also have indirect ways of referencing an element. The direct approach shown here, though, is what you will use when you have a very specific idea of what element or elements you wish to target.

Once we have the reference to the element, we can just set the `textContent` property on it:

```
headingElement.textContent = "Oppa Gangnam Style!";
```

The `textContent` property can be read like any variable to show the current value. We can also set the property like we are here to change the value that is stored currently. After this line has run, our markup's original value of **What's happening?** will be replaced in the DOM by what we specified in JavaScript.

Attribute Values

An important part of HTML elements are the attributes they carry with them. Common attributes we see all the time include the `id` attribute, `class` attribute, and then a boatload of element-specific ones like `src` for `img` elements, `autoplay` for video elements, and so on. When something is important in HTML, you know it is important for us to know how to handle it via JavaScript. That's what the following sets of sections are all about.

Basics of Attribute Access

Before we jump ahead and look at custom attributes, let's take a quick moment and discuss how to access attributes in general. Let's say that we have an HTML element that looks as follows:

```
<img id="tv" src="foo.png">
```

The two attributes on this element are `id` and `src`. In fine JavaScript tradition, we have a multitude of ways to perform the same tasks. We are going to explore some of those ways in this section.

Reading Attributes

The first thing we are going to do is look at how we can access these attributes in JavaScript. The most popular way is by using `getAttribute` and providing the attribute name as the argument:

```
let imgElement = document.querySelector("#tv");


let idValue = imgElement.getAttribute("id");
let srcValue = imgElement.getAttribute("src");


console.log(idValue) // tv
console.log(srcValue) // foo.png
```

For built-in attributes such as the `id` and `src` attributes on an image element, we can access them directly by just dotting into it:

```
let imgElement = document.querySelector("#tv");


let idValue = imgElement.id;
let srcValue = imgElement.src;


console.log(idValue); // tv
console.log(srcValue); // <full-path>/foo.png
```

Another approach is to use the `attributes` property on the DOM element and iterate through the attributes, but that is one we can table for later.

Setting Attributes

Reading attributes is one thing. Setting attributes is a whole other thing that is handled by the `setAttribute` method, which takes the attribute name and the new value as its arguments:

```
let imgElement = document.querySelector("#tv");
imgElement.setAttribute("src", "bar.png");

console.log(imgElement.getAttribute("src")); // bar.png
```

Notice that we use `setAttribute` to change the value of the `src` attribute to be **bar.png**.

Removing Attributes

The last **basic** attribute-related activity we will look at is how to remove attributes. This task is handled by the `removeAttribute` method:

```
let imgElement = document.querySelector("#tv");
imgElement.removeAttribute("src");


console.log(imgElement.getAttribute("src")); // undefined
```

To use the `removeAttribute` method, we need to provide the name of the attribute to remove, as shown in the preceding example. Notice we are removing the `src` attribute from our image element, and when we try to access the removed attribute, we can see that it returns a value of **undefined**.

Custom Attributes

Moving beyond the standard, built-in attributes our elements carry with them, we have the fun world of custom attributes. In the past, if we ever wanted to mark or tag our elements for any sort of programmatic access later, we didn't have too many good choices. The most common thing we did was add or remove class values from an element:

```
<img class=``"ufo friendly healthy" src=``"spaceship.png"``>
<img class=``"ufo enemy destroyed" src=``"spaceship.png"``>
```

That was fine if what we were doing resulted in our element visually changing. There are many times when we just want to store some data in an element—data that we wouldn't want to surface to the user. Overloading the more CSS-oriented class attribute seemed a bit distasteful. Also distasteful was abusing the `rel` tag, declaring custom namespaces, and doing other things to make up for the lack of a standardized way to embed data into our page.

Fortunately, something sweeter was on the horizon. We have the ability to specify **custom data attributes** (aka _data dash or data- attributes_*) whose sole job is to allow us to tag elements with data that we can programmatically access later. Let's say that we have a list of images:

```
<img src="foo.png"/>
<img src="bar.png"/>
<img src="zorb.png"/>
<img src="blarg.png"/>
```

What we want to do is store the name of the photographer as part of each image. The way we are going to do this is by using a custom data attribute called **photographer**:

```
<img src="foo.png" data-photographer="Bart"/>
<img src="bar.png" data-photographer="Lisa"/>
<img src="zorb.png" data-photographer="Ralph"/>
<img src="blarg.png" data-photographer="Milhouse"/>
```

Notice how the custom data attribute is defined. Whatever attribute name you are interested in using, simply prefix **data-** in front of it. You can have as many custom data attributes as you want. In case you were wondering, simply adding a custom data attribute has no bearing on the appearance or layout of an application.

Working with Custom Data Attributes in JS

With custom data attributes, the two most common things we will do is to retrieve the value stored by such an attribute and to set the value stored by such an attribute. What we saw with `getAttribute`, `setAttribute`, and `removeAttribute` work identically here.

To retrieve the value stored by a **data-*** attribute, use the trusty `getAttribute` method on the HTML element the attribute lives on:

```
<img id="tv" src="foo.png" data-photographer="Krusty the Clown">

<script>
let tvImg = document.getElementById("tv");
let name = tvImg.getAttribute("data-photographer");
</script>
```

To set the value, we use `getAttribute`'s mortal enemy, the `setAttribute` method:

```
tvImg.setAttribute("data-photographer", "Sideshow Bob");
```

You get the picture. The helpful thing to note is that our **data-*** attributes are nothing more than just plain, boring attributes. Everything we could do in JavaScript before with attributes, we can still do now. These attributes are just named a little bit differently. That's all.

The dataset Property

Okay, there is one thing that custom data attributes have that regular attributes don't. That is the handy `dataset` property. It makes sense when we look at an example of it in action:

```
<img id="tv" src="foo.png" data-size="large" data-name="Picasso">

<script>
  let imgElement = document.querySelector("#tv");
  let imgSize = imgElement.dataset.size;
  let imgName = imgElement.dataset.name;

  console.log(imgSize); // large
  console.log(imgName); // Picasso
</script>
```

Notice that we have **data-size** and **data-name** as custom attributes. The way we access these attributes is directly via the `dataset` property and omitting the **data-** prefix. This handy way of reading custom data properties applies to setting them as well, where we can just assign the new attribute value just like we would any variable:

```
<img id="tv" src="foo.png" data-size="large" data-name="Picasso">

<script>
  let imgElement = document.querySelector("#tv");
```

```
    let imgSize = imgElement.dataset.size;


    imgElement.dataset.name = "Van Gogh";

    let imgName = imgElement.dataset.name;


    console.log(imgSize); // large

    console.log(imgName); // Van Gogh

</script>
```

We set the value for our data-name attribute to **Van Gogh** via JavaScript. We can see the new value being set, but we can go one level deeper and inspect the element to see for certain that the new value is what we see:

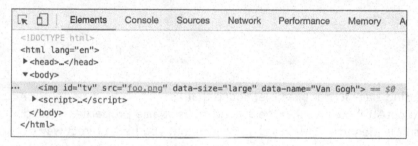

Pretty neat, right?

When to use Data-* Attributes

Now that you've seen all of this, a worthy next question to ask is, when should you use these **data-*** attributes in your HTML or set them on the DOM via JavaScript? There are some mixed opinions on this, but here is how I would summarize when you should or shouldn't use custom data attributes:

- Use **data-*** attributes for storing nonvisual data that also makes working with your JavaScript easier.

- Don't use **data-*** attributes for storing data that is better represented by another element.

- Using `getAttribute` and `setAttribute` is an expensive operation relative to just working with in-memory JavaScript objects. For performance-intensive operations, avoid using **data-*** attributes.

If you must use them, read the data from your custom attributes, but do all further processing in memory. Don't write the data back to the attribute via `setAttribute` unless you really have a good reason to do so.

There is something I need to clarify before we move on. In the examples for how to use `setAttribute` and `getAttribute`, I picked on `id` and `class`. For these two attributes, we do have another way of setting them. Because of how common setting `id` and `class` attributes is, our HTML elements expose the `id` and `className` properties directly:

```
<body>

  <h1 id="bigMessage" class="highlight summer">What's happening?</h1>

  <script>

    let headingElement = document.querySelector("h1");
    console.log(headingElement.id); // bigMessage

    headingElement.className = "bar foo";

  </script>
</body>
```

Getting back to our example, notice that I switched from using `getAttribute` and `setAttribute` to using the `id` and `className` properties instead. The end result is identical. The only difference is that you had a direct way of setting these attribute values without having to use `getAttribute` or `setAttribute`. Now, before we go further, I have to point out something strange: yes, we can't use `class` in JavaScript for referring to the class attribute because *class* has a whole different meaning that has to do with dealing with objects. That's why we are using `className` instead.

 TIP There is a much better way of setting class values besides using `className`. That way is via the much more awesome `classList` property, which you will learn all about in the next chapter.

THE ABSOLUTE MINIMUM

It may seem a bit odd to end our discussion around modifying DOM elements at this point. While changing an element's text and attribute values is very popular, these are by no means the only major kinds of modifications you will perform. The reason for ending at this cliffhanger is because manipulating the DOM and using an element's properties and methods to accomplish our task are central to everything you are going to be learning. In subsequent chapters, you are going to see a whole lot more of what you've seen here.

Your main takeaway from this chapter is that the DOM changes you perform will almost always take one of the following two forms:

- Setting a property
- Calling a method

The `textContent`, `setAttribute`, and `getAttribute` methods you saw here cover both of those approaches, and you'll see a lot more of them and their friends shortly.

? Ask a question: **https://forum.kirupa.com**

✔ Practice by building real apps: **https://bit.ly/coding_exercises**

🐾 Errors/known issues: **https://bit.ly/javascript_errata**

STYLING OUR CONTENT

In the previous chapter, we looked at how to modify our DOM's content using JavaScript. The other part of what makes our HTML elements stand out is their appearance, their styling. When it comes to styling some content, the most common way is by creating a style rule and having its selector target an element or elements. A style rule would look as follows:

```css
.batman {
  width: 100px;
  height: 100px;
  background-color: #333;
}
```

An element that would be affected by this style rule could look like this:

```
<div class="batman"></div>
```

On any given web page, we'll see anywhere from just a few to many, MANY style rules, each beautifully stepping over each other to style everything we see. This isn't the only approach we can use to style content using CSS, though. It wouldn't be HTML if there weren't multiple ways to accomplish the same task!

Ignoring inline styles, the other approach we can use to introduce elements to the goodness that is CSS styling involves JavaScript. We can use JavaScript to **directly set a style on an element**, and we can also use JavaScript to **add or remove class values on elements**, which will alter which style rules get applied.

In this chapter, we're going to learn about both of these approaches.

Why Would We Set Styles Using JavaScript?

Before we go further, it is probably useful to explain why we would ever want to use JavaScript to affect the style of an element in the first place. In the common cases where we use style rules or inline styles to affect how an element looks, the styling kicks in when the page is loaded. That's awesome, and that's probably what we want most of the time.

There are many cases, especially as our content gets more interactive, where we want styles to dynamically kick in based on user input, some code having run in the background, and more. In these sorts of scenarios, the CSS model involving style rules or inline styles won't help us. While pseudoselectors like `hover` provide some support, we are still greatly limited in what we can do.

The solution we will need to employ for all of them is one that involves JavaScript. JavaScript not only lets us style the element we are interacting with; more importantly, it allows us to style elements all over the page. This freedom is very powerful and goes well beyond CSS's limited ability to style content inside (or very close to) itself.

A Tale of Two Styling Approaches

Like we saw in the introduction, we have two ways to alter the style of an element using JavaScript. One way is by setting a CSS property directly on the element. The other way is by adding or removing class values from an element, which may result in certain style rules getting applied or ignored. Let's look at both of these cases in greater detail.

Setting the Style Directly

Every HTML element you access via JavaScript has a style object. This object allows you to specify a CSS property and set its value. For example, this is what setting the background color of an HTML element whose id value is **superman** looks like:

```
let myElement = document.querySelector("#superman");
myElement.style.backgroundColor = "#D93600";
```

To affect many elements, you can do something like the following:

```
let myElements = document.querySelectorAll(".bar");

for (let i = 0; i < myElements.length; i++) {
  myElements[i].style.opacity = 0;
}
```

In a nutshell, to style elements directly using JavaScript, the first step is to access the element. Our handy querySelector method from earlier is quite helpful here. The second step is just to find the CSS property you care about and give it a value. Remember, many values in CSS are actually strings. Also remember that many values require a unit of measurement, such as **px** or **em**, to actually get recognized. Also remember...actually, I forgot.

Lastly, some CSS properties require a more complex value to be provided with a bunch of random text followed by the value you care about. One of the more popular ones in this bucket is the transform property. One approach for setting a complex value is to use good old-fashioned string concatenation:

```
myElement.style.transform = "translate3d(" + xPos + ", " + yPos +
"px, 0)";
```

That can get really irritating, because keeping track of the quotation marks and so on is something tedious and error-prone. One less-irritating solution is to use the template literal syntax:

```
myElement.style.transform = `translate3d(${xPos}px, ${yPos}px, 0)`;
```

Notice how this approach allows you to still provide custom values while avoiding all of the string concatenation complexity. We'll look at this syntax in greater detail a bit later!

 TIP   Special Casing Some Names of CSS Properties

JavaScript is very picky about what makes up a valid property name. Most names in CSS would get JavaScript's seal of approval, so you can just use them straight out of the carton. There are a few things to keep in mind, though.

To specify a CSS property in JavaScript that contains a dash, simply remove the dash. For example, `background-color` becomes `backgroundColor`, the `border-radius` property transforms into `borderRadius`, and so on.

Also, certain words in JavaScript are reserved and can't be used directly. One example of a CSS property that falls into this special category is `float`. In CSS, it is a layout property. In JavaScript, it stands for something else. To use a property whose name is entirely reserved, prefix the property with `css`, where `float` becomes `cssFloat`.

Adding and Removing Classes Using JavaScript

The second approach involves adding and removing class values that, in turn, change which style rules get applied. For example, let's say we have a style rule that looks as follows:

```
.disableMenu {
  display: none;
}
```

In HTML, we have a menu whose `id` is **dropDown**:

```
<ul id="dropDown">
    <li>One</li>
    <li>Two</li>
    <li>Three</li>
    <li>Four</li>
    <li>Five</li>
    <li>Six</li>
</ul>
```

Now, if we wanted to apply our `.disableMenu` style rule to this element, all we would need to do is add **disableMenu** as a `class` value to the **dropDown** element:

```
<ul class="disableMenu" id="dropDown">
    <li>One</li>
    <li>Two</li>
    <li>Three</li>
    <li>Four</li>
    <li>Five</li>
    <li>Six</li>
</ul>
```

One way to accomplish this involves setting an element's `className` property, an approach we saw earlier. The trouble with `className` is that we are responsible for maintaining the current list of class values applied. Worse, the list of class values is returned to us as a string. If we have multiple class values we want to add, remove, or just toggle on/off, we have to do a bunch of error-prone string-related trickery that just isn't fun.

To help alleviate some of the inconvenience, we now have a much nicer API that makes adding and removing class values from an element ridiculously easy. This new API is affectionately known as `classList`, and it provides a handful of methods that will make working with class values a piece of cake:

- `add`
- `remove`
- `toggle`
- `contains`

What these four methods do may be pretty self-explanatory from their names, but let's look at them in further detail.

Adding Class Values

To add a class value to an element, get a reference to the element and call the add method on it via `classList`:

```
let divElement = document.querySelector("#myDiv");
divElement.classList.add("bar");
divElement.classList.add("foo");
divElement.classList.add("zorb");
divElement.classList.add("baz");


console.log(divElement.classList);
```

After this code runs, our `div` element will have the following class values: **bar**, **foo**, **zorb**, and **baz**. The `classList` API takes care of ensuring spaces are added between class values. If we specify an invalid class value, the `classList` API will complain and not `add` it. If we tell the `add` method to add a class that already exists on the element, our code will still run, but the duplicate class value will not get added.

Removing Class Values

To remove a class value, we can call the `remove` method on `classList`:

```
let divElement = document.querySelector("#myDiv");
divElement.classList.remove("foo");

console.log(divElement.classList);
```

After this code executes, the **foo** class value will be removed. What we will be left with is just **bar, zorb, and baz**. Pretty simple, right?

Toggling Class Values

For many styling scenarios, there is one very common workflow. First, we check if a class value on an element exists. If the value exists, we remove it from the element. If the value does not exist, we add that class value to the element. To simplify this very common toggling pattern, the `classList` API provides you with the `toggle` method:

```
let divElement = document.querySelector("#myDiv");
divElement.classList.toggle("foo"); // remove foo
divElement.classList.toggle("foo"); // add foo
divElement.classList.toggle("foo"); // remove foo

console.log(divElement.classList);
```

The `toggle` method, as its name implies, adds or removes the specified class value on the element each time it is called. In our case, the **foo** class is removed the first time the `toggle` method is called. The second time, the **foo** class is added. The third time, the **foo** class is removed. You get the picture.

Checking Whether a Class Value Exists

The last thing we are going to look at is the `contains` method:

```
let divElement = document.querySelector("#myDiv");

if (divElement.classList.contains("bar") == true) {
  // do something
}
```

This method checks to see if the specified class value exists on the element. If the value exists, you get **true**. If the value doesn't exist, you get **false**.

Going Further

As you can see, the `classList` API provides you with almost everything you need to add, remove, or inspect class values on an element very easily—the emphasis being on the word *almost*. For the few things the API doesn't provide by default, you can go online and read my full article on many more things you can do with `classList` at **http://bit.ly/kClassList**.

THE ABSOLUTE MINIMUM

So, there you have it—two perfectly fine JavaScript-based approaches you can use for styling your elements. Of these two choices, if you have the ability to modify your CSS, I would prefer you go style elements by adding and removing classes. The simple reason is that this approach is far more maintainable. It is much easier to add and remove style properties from a style rule in CSS as opposed to adding and removing lines of JavaScript.

? Ask a question: **https://forum.kirupa.com**

✔ Practice by building real apps: **https://bit.ly/coding_exercises**

Errors/known issues: **https://bit.ly/javascript_errata**

USING CSS CUSTOM PROPERTIES

When setting CSS properties with JavaScript, especially the really complex ones, you will often find yourself wrestling with strings:

```
var myCircle = document.querySelector("#myCircle");
setTranslate(50, 75, myCircle);

// Old approach
function setTranslate(xPos, yPos, el) {
  el.style.transform = "translate3d(" + xPos + ", " + yPos +
"px, 0)";
}

// Slightly better ES6-based old approach
function setTranslate(xPos, yPos, el) {
  el.style.transform = `translate3d(${xPos}px, ${yPos}px,
0)`;
}
```

Don't get me wrong. I love a good string manipulation here and there, but you have to admit that something like the preceding is a bit frustrating to generate and prone to all sorts of errors if you aren't careful. The more complex the value you are trying to set, the worse everything is. Besides, there is also something just really odd-looking about having giant strings of CSS embedded inside your JavaScript.

In this chapter, we are going to look at something known as **CSS custom properties** (aka **CSS variables**) that will greatly simplify how we specify a complex value by getting us out of the string-generation business. Let's see how we can do that!

What Are CSS Custom Properties/Variables?

One of the big recent additions to the CSS language is this thing known as **CSS custom properties**, commonly also referred to as **CSS variables**. What CSS custom properties allow you to do is pretty neat. Inside a style rule, you can specify a custom property name and initialize it to whatever value you want:

```css
#container {
  --myAlign: center;

  width: 100%;
  height: 350px;
  background-color: #0099FF;
  display: flex;
  align-items: var(--myAlign);
  justify-content: var(--myAlign);
}
```

This custom property can then be used elsewhere in your CSS, where you can specify it instead of specifying the inline value directly:

```css
#container {
  --myAlign: center;

  width: 100%;
  height: 350px;
  background-color: #0099FF;
  display: flex;
```

```
    align-items: var(--myAlign);
    justify-content: var(--myAlign);
}
```

Notice in this example that the value for the `align-items` and `justify-content` properties isn't specified directly. It is inferred from the custom `--myAlign` property name instead.

Just like with variables you would use in JavaScript, you now have a single location where the value is being specified. If you change the value of our custom `myAlign` property, any uses of it will use the new value instead. This is all pretty consistent with how variables work. The CSS-specific behavior has to do with scope. The custom property you define **follows typical CSS cascading rules**, so where you specify the property is important to determine whether the property's value can be used. If you wish to declare some custom CSS properties globally, you can specify them in the body selector or go one level higher with the root selector instead:

```
:root {
    --logoColor: "#333";
    --headerColor: "green";
    --avatarWidth: 150px;
}
```

If you aren't familiar with the root selector, it roughly translates to styles being applied at the `<html>` tag level.

Now, to modify the values of a custom CSS property using JavaScript, there isn't anything special you have to do. The tried and tested `setProperty` method you have used in the past will still work:

```
myLogo.style.setProperty("--logoColor", "#505168");
```

In the preceding code, we are setting our `--logoColor` custom property to a dark shade of purple. Because we are setting this value inline on our `myLogo` element, it will have a higher specificity and override whatever value we had earlier in the root style rule. It goes without saying that any CSS property values that rely on the value of `--logoColor` will automatically update to reflect the new value.

If you are wishing to read a custom CSS property value, there are a few minor extra steps you need to follow. Let's say you have a custom property called `themeColor` set on the body selector:

```css
body {
  --themeColor: "blue";
}
```

The way you would read this property and its value is by using `getComputedStyle`, like so:

```javascript
var bodyStyle = getComputedStyle(document.body);
var theme = bodyStyle.getPropertyValue("--themeColor");
alert(theme);
```

This seems pretty easy, right? Well, you probably know that whenever a question like that is asked, the answer is never a straightforward *yes*. You would think the value we would ultimately get is **"blue"**. What we would actually get is **" blue"**. Ignore the quotation marks, but notice the leading space. This is because the *original* behavior as defined by the W3C (only for custom properties) is to read the space value between `--themeColor: "blue"` as a valid entry. That behavior is due to change in the near future, and the leading space will be ignored. This means that if you are using a conditional to check for the custom property value, you need to account for both cases, with and without a leading space:

```javascript
if ((theme == "blue") || (theme == " blue")) {
  // do something
}
```

You can read more about this strange behavior in the following discussion: https://bit.ly/css_custom_prop_quirk

Setting Complex Values Easily

This ability for us to modify a custom CSS property value via JavaScript and have all uses of that property update is a massive win. We no longer have to specify our values using string manipulation logic like we saw at the beginning of this chapter.

Continuing our transform example, in the CSS variable-based world, we can specify the values for the horizontal and vertical values as follows:

```
#myCircle {
  --xPos: 0px;
  --yPos: 0px;

  width: 100px;
  height: 100px;
  transform: translate3d(var(--xPos), var(--yPos), 0);
}
```

To update these values, our JavaScript can just be the following:

```
var myCircle = document.querySelector("#myCircle");
setTranslate(50, 75, myCircle);

function setTranslate(xPos, yPos, el) {
  el.style.setProperty("--xPos", xPos + "px");
  el.style.setProperty("--yPos", yPos + "px");
}
```

Notice that we no longer have to generate a massive string, worry about escaping the characters at the right places, and so on. We just update the value of the custom CSS properties directly, and that updating takes care of everything else! Another benefit we get from this approach is that if we ever wanted to get even more complex with our transform property, we can totally do so without having to make changes in JavaScript:

```
#myCircle {
  --xPos: 0px;
  --yPos: 0px;

  width: 100px;
  height: 100px;
```

```css
background-color: #FFF;
border: 10px solid #0066CC;
border-radius: 50%;
transform: translate3d(var(--xPos), var(--yPos), 0)
            rotate(30deg)
            scale3d(1.5, 1.5, 0);
}
```

We added the `rotate` and `scale3d` functions, but it doesn't modify what our
JS does. Now, you may feel the `transform` property is an easy one that doesn't
effectively highlight the benefits. If so, feast your eyes on the following:

```css
#container {
  --stripeColor: #1F505B;


  width: 100%;
  height: 400px;
  background-color: #3891A6;
}
#container.stripes {
  background-image:
    repeating-linear-gradient(
      -45deg,
      var(--stripeColor),
      var(--stripeColor) 20px,
      #3891A6 20px,
      #3891A6 40px
    );
  background-size: 200% 200%;
  animation: slide 5s linear infinite;
}
```

What we have here is a fairly *simple* linear-gradient function for our `background-image` property. Despite being simple, it is already six lines. Imagine having to set the stripe color without being able to rely on the `--stripeColor` custom property. Would you really want to generate that full string inside some JavaScript in this case?

CSS custom properties make setting complex values via JavaScript extremely simple. As long as we don't modify our custom CSS property name or the kind of value it expects, we can do whatever we want inside the style rule without having to ensure our JavaScript is in sync with the changes. This is something we couldn't do in the old world, where we had to generate the *full* complex value in JavaScript, even if we only needed to modify one small part of it—or, worst case, change the shape of the value entirely, like going from a linear gradient to a radial gradient!

THE ABSOLUTE MINIMUM

Before we had CSS custom properties (aka CSS variables), we still had the ability to set and modify complex CSS property values. It just wasn't fun or easy, especially for really complex values like the kind you commonly run into with layout, animation/transition, backgrounds (especially involving gradients), transforms, and more. While the motivation for creating CSS custom properties may not have been to make our lives easier when setting values via JavaScript, it indirectly did end up having that effect, where the `setProperty` function makes all of this a breeze.

? Ask a question: **https://forum.kirupa.com**

✔ Practice by building real apps: **https://bit.ly/coding_exercises**

🗲 Errors/known issues: **https://bit.ly/javascript_errata**

IN THIS CHAPTER

- Learn how to navigate the DOM tree
- Use the various APIs you have for moving and re-parenting elements
- Find an element's sibling, parent, children, and more

32

TRAVERSING THE DOM

As you may have realized by now, our DOM looks like a giant tree—a giant tree with elements dangerously hanging on to branches and trying to avoid the pointy things that litter the place. To get a little more technical, elements in our DOM are arranged in a hierarchy, as illustrated in Figure 32.1, that defines what we will eventually see in the browser.

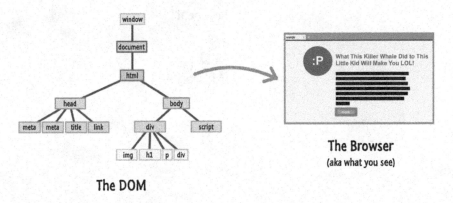

FIGURE 32.1

The DOM and the browser are like two peas in a pod.

This hierarchy is used to help organize our HTML elements. It is also used to help our CSS style rules make sense of what styles to apply on which things. From the JavaScript angle, this hierarchy does add a bit of complexity. We will spend a fair amount of time trying to figure out where in the DOM we are right now and where we need to be. This is something that will become more apparent when we look into creating new elements or moving elements around. This complexity is something that we need to be comfortable with.

That's where this chapter comes in. To help you understand how to easily navigate from branch to branch (basically, like a monkey), the DOM provides you with a handful of properties you can combine with techniques you already know. This chapter will give you an overview of all that and more.

Finding Your Way Around

Before we can find elements and do awesome things with them, we need to first get to where the elements are. The easiest way to tackle this topic is to just start from the top and slide all the way down. That's exactly what we are going to do.

The view from the top of our DOM is made up of our window, document, and html elements, as shown in Figure 32.2.

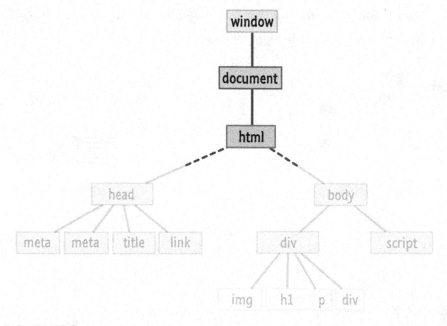

FIGURE 32.2

The view from the top of this tree never changes.

Because of how important these three things are, the DOM provides us with easy access to them via window, document, and document.documentElement:

```
let windowObject = window; // um....
let documentObject = document;  // this is probably unnecessary
let htmlElement = document.documentElement;
```

One thing to note is that both window and document are global properties. We don't have to explicitly declare them like I did. Just shake and use them straight out of the container.

Once we go below the HTML element level, our DOM will start to branch out and get more interesting. At this point, we have several ways of navigating around. One way that we've seen plenty of is by using querySelector and querySelectorAll to precisely get at the elements we are interested in. For many practical cases, these two methods are too limiting.

Sometimes, we don't know where we want to go. The querySelector and querySelectorAll methods won't help us here. We just want to get in the car and drive...and hope we find what we are looking for. When it comes to navigating the DOM, we'll find ourselves in this position all the time. That's where the various built-in properties the DOM provides will help us out, and we are going to look at those properties next.

The thing that will help us out is knowing that all our elements in the DOM have at least one combination of **parents**, **siblings**, and **children** to rely on. To visualize this, take a look at the row containing the div and script elements in Figure 32.3.

Both the div and script elements are siblings. The reason they are siblings is because they share the body element as their parent. The script element has no children, but the div element does. The img, h1, p, and div are children of the div element, and all children of the same parent are siblings as well. Just like in real life, the parent, child, and sibling relationship is based on where in the tree we are focusing. Almost every element, depending on the angle at which we look at them, can play multiple familial roles.

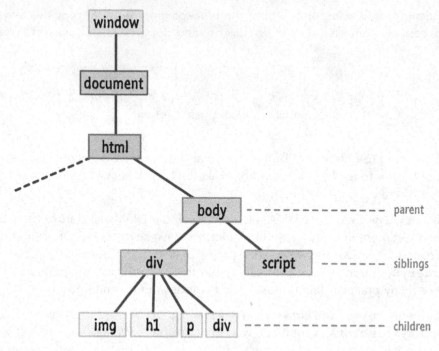

FIGURE 32.3

An example of our tree with some parents, siblings, and children

To help us through all this, we have a handful of properties on which we will rely. These properties are `firstChild`, `lastChild`, `parentNode`, `children`, `previousSibling`, and `nextSibling`. From just looking at their names, you should be able to infer what role these properties play. The guy in red with the pointed pitchfork is in the details, so we'll look at this topic in greater detail next.

Dealing with Siblings and Parents

Of these properties, the easiest ones to deal with are the parents and siblings. The relevant properties are `parentNode`, `previousSibling`, and `nextSibling`. Figure 32.4 gives you an idea of how these three properties work.

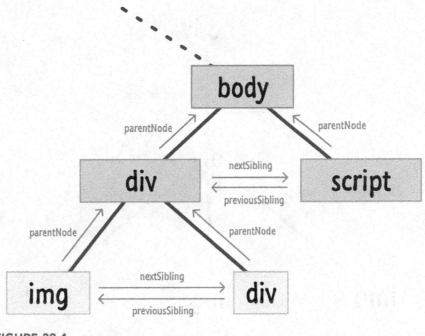

FIGURE 32.4

The relationship between siblings and parents from our DOM's point of view

This diagram is a little busy, but you can sort of make out what is going on here. The parentNode property points you to the element's parent. The previousSibling and nextSibling properties allow an element to find its previous or next sibling. You can see this visualized in the diagram by just moving in the direction of the arrow. In the last line, our img's nextSibling is the div. Our div's previousSibling is the img. Accessing parentNode on either of these elements will take you to the parent div in the second row. It's all pretty straightforward.

Let's Have Some Kids!

What is a little less straightforward is how the children fit into all of this, so let's take a look at the firstChild, lastChild, and children properties, shown in Figure 32.5.

The firstChild and lastChild properties refer to a parent's first and last child elements. If the parent only has one child, as is the case with the body element in our example, then both firstChild and lastChild point to the same thing. If an element has no children, these properties return **null**.

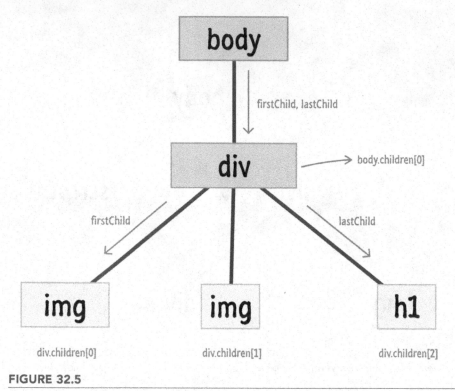

FIGURE 32.5

A view of children and more children!

The tricky one compared to the other properties we've looked at is the `children` property. When you access the `children` property on a parent, you basically get a collection of the child elements the parent has. This collection is not an `Array`, but it does have some `Array`-like powers. Just like with `Array`, you can iterate through this collection or access the children individually, kind of like what you see in the figure. This collection also has a `length` property that tells you the count of how many children the parent is dealing with. If your head is spinning from this, don't worry. The snippets in the next section will help clarify the vagueness in my explanation.

Putting It All Together

Now that we have a good idea of all the important properties we have for traversing the DOM, let's look at some code snippets that tie in all the diagrams and words into some sweet lines of JavaScript.

Checking If a Child Exists

To check if an element has a child, we can do something like the following:

```
let bodyElement = document.querySelector("body");


if (bodyElement.firstChild) {
  // do something interesting
}
```

This `if` statement will return **null** if there are no children. We could also have used `bodyElement.lastChild` or `bodyElement.children.count` if you enjoy typing, but I prefer to just keep things simple.

Accessing All the Child Elements

If we want to access all of a parent's children, we can always rely on good-old uncle `for` loop:

```
let bodyElement = document.body;


for (let i = 0; i < bodyElement.children.length; i++) {
  let childElement = bodyElement.children[i];


  document.writeln(childElement.tagName);
}
```

Notice that we are using the `children` and `length` properties, just like we would an `Array`. The thing to note is that this collection is actually not an `Array`. Almost all of the `Array` methods we may want to use will not be available in this collection returned by the `children` property.

Walking the DOM

Our last snippet touches upon a little bit of everything we've seen so far. This snippet recursively walks the DOM and touches every HTML element it can find:

```
function theDOMElementWalker(node) {
  if (node.nodeType == Node.ELEMENT_NODE) {

    console.log(node.tagName);

    node = node.firstChild;

    while (node) {
      theDOMElementWalker(node);
      node = node.nextSibling;
    }
  }
}
```

To see this function in action, we just call it by passing in a node that we want to start our walk from:

```
let texasRanger = document.querySelector("#texas");
theDOMElementWalker(texasRanger);
```

In this example, we are calling theDOMElementWalker function on an element referenced by the texasRanger variable. If you want to run some code on the element that this script found, replace the commented-out line with whatever you want to do.

THE ABSOLUTE MINIMUM

Finding your way around the DOM is one of those skills that every JavaScript developer should be familiar with. This tutorial provided you an overview of what is technically possible. Applying this in more practical ways falls entirely onto you...or a cool friend who helps you out with these things. With that said, in subsequent chapters, we will expand on what we've seen here as part of continuing our deep dive into everything we can do with the DOM. Doesn't that sound exciting?

? Ask a question: **https://forum.kirupa.com**

✔ Practice by building real apps: **https://bit.ly/coding_exercises**

🖆 Errors/known issues: **https://bit.ly/javascript_errata**

33

CREATING AND REMOVING DOM ELEMENTS

This part may blow you away. For the following sentences, I suggest you hold onto something sturdy:

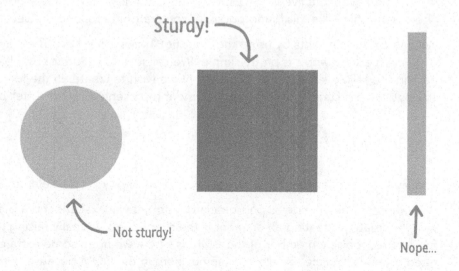

Sturdy!

Not sturdy!

Nope...

Despite what our earlier discussions about the DOM may have led you to believe, our DOM does not have to be made up of HTML elements that exist in markup. We have the ability to create HTML elements out of thin air and add them to our DOM using just a few lines of JavaScript. We also have the ability to move elements around, remove them, and do all sorts of god-like things. Let's pause for a bit while we let all of that sink in. This is pretty big.

Besides the initial coolness of all this, the ability to dynamically create and modify elements in our DOM is an important detail that makes a lot of our favorite websites and applications tick. When you think about this, this makes sense. Having everything predefined in our HTML is very limiting. We want our content to change and adapt when new data is pulled in, when we interact with the page, when we scroll further, or when we do a billion other things.

In this chapter, we are going to cover the basics of what makes all this work. We are going to look at how to create elements, remove elements, re-parent elements, and clone elements. This is also the last of our chapters looking directly at DOM-related shenanigans, so call your friends and get the balloons ready!

Creating Elements

It is very common for interactive sites and apps to dynamically create HTML elements and have them live in the DOM. If this is the first time you are hearing about something like this being possible, you are going to love this section!

We can create elements by using the `createElement` method. The way `createElement` works is pretty simple. We call it via our `document` object and pass in the HTML tag name of the element we wish to create. In the following snippet, we are creating a paragraph element represented by the letter *p*:

```
let myElement = document.createElement("p");
```

The `myElement` variable holds a reference to our newly created element.

If we run this line of code as part of a larger app, it will execute and a p element will get created. Creating an element is the simple part. Actually raising it to be a fun and responsible member of the DOM is where we need some extra effort. We need to actually place this element somewhere in the DOM because our dynamically created p element is just floating around aimlessly right now:

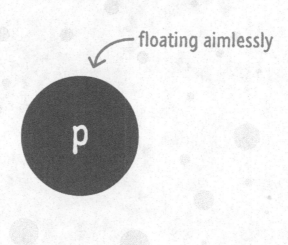

floating aimlessly

The reason for this aimlessness is because our DOM has no real knowledge that this element exists. In order for an element to be a part of the DOM, we need to do two things:

1. Find an element that will act as the parent.

2. Use `appendChild` and add the element we want into that parent element.

The best way to make sense of all this is to look at an example that ties this all together. If you want to follow along, create a new HTML document and add the following HTML, CSS, and JS into it:

```
<!DOCTYPE html>
<html>

<head>
  <title>Creating Elements</title>

  <style>
    body {
      background-color: #0E454C;
      padding: 30px;
```

```
    }

  h1 {
    color: #14FFF7;
    font-size: 72px;
    font-family: sans-serif;
    text-decoration: underline;
  }

  p {
    color: #14FFF7;
    font-family: sans-serif;
    font-size: 36px;
    font-weight: bold;
  }
  </style>
</head>

<body>
  <h1>Am I real?</h1>
  <script>
    let newElement = document.createElement("p");
    let bodyElement = document.querySelector("body");

    newElement.textContent = "Or do I exist entirely in your
imagination?";

    bodyElement.appendChild(newElement);
  </script>
</body>

</html>
```

Save this file and preview it in your browser. If everything worked out, you should see something that resembles the following screenshot:

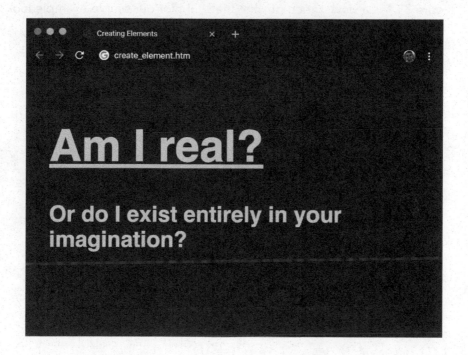

Now, we are going to take a step back and look at what exactly is going on in our example. If we look at our JavaScript, everything we need for creating an element and adding it to our DOM is located in between the `<script>` tags:

```
let newElement = document.createElement("p");
let bodyElement = document.querySelector("body");

newElement.textContent = "Or do I exist entirely in your
imagination?";

bodyElement.appendChild(newElement);
```

With `newElement`, we are storing a reference to our newly created p tag. With `bodyElement`, we are storing a reference to our `body` element. On our newly created element (`newElement`), we set the `textContent` property to what we ultimately end up displaying. The last thing we do is take our aimlessly floating `newElement` and make it a child of our `body` element by relying on good-old `appendChild`.

Figure 33.1 is a visualization of what the DOM for our simple example looks like.

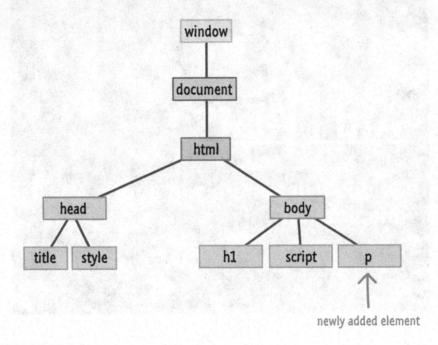

FIGURE 33.1

What the DOM looks like after our code has run

Now, a detail about the `appendChild` function is that it always adds the element to the end of whatever children a parent may have. In our case, our body element already has the `h1` and `script` elements as its children. The p element gets appended after them as the youngest child. With that said, we do have control over the exact order where under a parent a particular element will live.

If we want to insert `newElement` directly after our `h1` tag, we can do so by calling the `insertBefore` function on the parent. The `insertBefore` function takes two arguments. The first argument is the element you want to insert. The second argument is a reference to the sibling (aka the child of a parent) you want to precede. Here is our example modified to have our `newElement` live after our `h1` element (and before our `script` element):

```
let newElement = document.createElement("p");
let bodyElement = document.querySelector("body");
```

```
let scriptElement = document.querySelector("script");

newElement.textContent = "I exist entirely in your imagination.";

bodyElement.insertBefore(newElement, scriptElement);
```

Notice that we call insertBefore on the bodyElement and specify that newElement should be inserted before our script element. Our DOM in this case would look as shown in Figure 33.2.

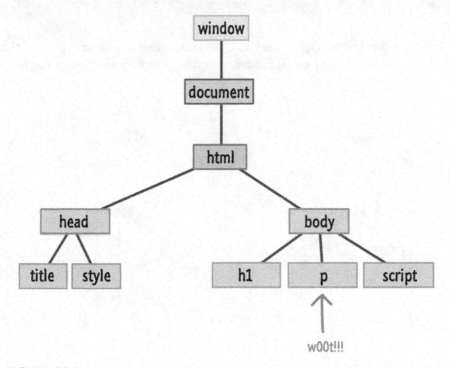

FIGURE 33.2

The newly inserted element is in between the h1 and script elements.

You might think that if there is an insertBefore method, there must be an insertAfter method as well. As it turns out, that isn't the case. There isn't a widely supported built-in way of inserting an element *after* an element instead of before it. What we can do is trick the insertBefore function by telling it to insert an element **an extra element ahead**. That probably makes no sense, so let me show you the code first and explain later:

```
let newElement = document.createElement("p");
let bodyElement = document.querySelector("body");
let h1Element = document.querySelector("h1");


newElement.textContent = "I exist entirely in your imagination.";


bodyElement.insertBefore(newElement, h1Element.nextSibling);
```

Pay attention to the highlighted lines and then take a look at Figure 33.3, which illustrates what is happening before our code runs and after our code runs.

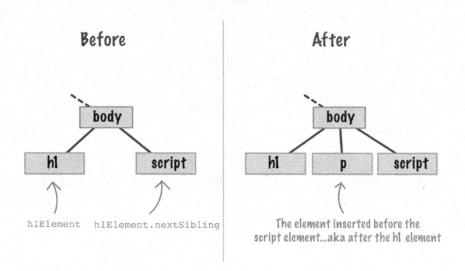

FIGURE 33.3

A trick we can use to simulate an `insertAfter` *behavior*

The `h1Element.nextSibling` call finds the `script` element. Inserting our `newElement` before our `script` element accomplishes our goal of inserting our element after the `h1` element. What if there is no sibling element to target? Well, the `insertBefore` function in that case is pretty clever and just appends the element you want to the end automatically.

HANDY DANDY FUNCTION

If for some reason you find yourself wanting to insert elements after another sibling all the time, you may want to use this function to simplify your life a bit:

```
function insertAfter(target, newElement) {
  target.parentNode.insertBefore(newElement, target.nextSibling);
}
```

Yes, I do realize this is a roundabout way of doing this, but it works really well. Here is an example of this function at work:

```
let newElement = document.createElement("p");
let bodyElement = document.querySelector("body");
let h1Element = document.querySelector("h1");

newElement.textContent = "I exist entirely in your imagination.";

function insertAfter(target, element) {
  target.parentNode.insertBefore(element, target.nextSibling);
}

insertAfter(bodyElement, newElement);
```

You can even go all out and extend `HTMLElement` with this function to provide this functionality more conveniently to all your HTML elements. Chapter 21, "Extending Built-in Objects," covers how to do something like that in greater detail. Note that extending your DOM is frowned upon by some people, so make sure to have some witty banter on the ready to lighten the mood if you ever are accosted by these people.

A more generic way of adding children to a parent is by realizing that parent elements treat `children` like entries in an array. To access this array of children, we have the `children` and `childNodes` properties. The `children` property only returns HTML elements, and the `childNodes` property returns the more generic nodes that represent a lot of things we don't care about. Yes, I realize I am repeating myself, but you can check out Chapter 32, "Traversing the DOM," for details on more ways you have for pinpointing an element.

Removing Elements

I think somebody smart once said the following: "That which has the ability to create, also has the ability to remove." In the previous section, we saw how we can use the `createElement` method to create an element. In this section, we are going to look at `removeChild`, which, given its slightly unsavory name, is all about removing elements.

Take a look at the following snippet of code that can be made to work with the example we have been looking at for some time:

```
let newElement = document.createElement("p");
let bodyElement = document.querySelector("body");
let h1Element = document.querySelector("h1");


newElement.textContent = "I exist entirely in your imagination.";


bodyElement.appendChild(newElement);


bodyElement.removeChild(newElement);
```

The p element stored by newElement is being added to our body element by the appendChild method. We saw that earlier. To remove this element, we call removeChild on the body element and pass in a pointer to the element we wish to remove. That element is, of course, newElement. Once removeChild has run, it will be as if your DOM never knew that newElement existed.

The main thing to note is that we need to call removeChild from the parent of the child we wish to remove. This method isn't going to traverse up and down our DOM trying to find the element we want to remove. Now, let's say that we don't have direct access to an element's parent and don't want to waste time finding it. We can still remove that element very easily by using the parentNode property, as follows:

```
let newElement = document.createElement("p");
let bodyElement = document.querySelector("body");
```

```
let h1Element = document.querySelector("h1");
newElement.textContent = "I exist entirely in your imagination.";


bodyElement.appendChild(newElement);


newElement.parentNode.removeChild(newElement);
```

In this variation, we remove newElement by calling removeChild on its parent by specifying newElement.parentNode. This looks roundabout, but it gets the job done.

Now, there is a newer, shinier, and better way to remove an element. In this way, we just call the remove method on the element we wish to remove directly. This example looks as follows:

```
let newElement = document.createElement("p");
let bodyElement = document.querySelector("body");
let h1Element = document.querySelector("h1");


newElement.textContent = "I exist entirely in your imagination.";


bodyElement.appendChild(newElement);


newElement.remove();
```

Now, why am I not beginning and ending this conversation around removing elements with the remove method? It has to do with browser support. This approach is still fairly new, so older browsers like Internet Explorer don't have support for it. If supporting Internet Explorer is important for you, the other approaches we've looked at will work.

If you are looking for a universally accepted approach for removing elements, despite some minor quirks, the removeChild function is quite merciless in its efficiency. If you want something direct, remove is your friend. Both of these approaches have the ability to remove any DOM element—including ones that were created in markup originally. We aren't limited to removing DOM elements we dynamically added. If the DOM element we are removing has many levels of children and grandchildren, all of them will be removed as well.

Cloning Elements

This chapter just keeps taking a turn for the weirder the further we go into it, but fortunately we are at the last section. The one remaining DOM manipulation technique we need to be aware of is one that revolves around cloning elements, where we start with one element and create identical replicas of it:

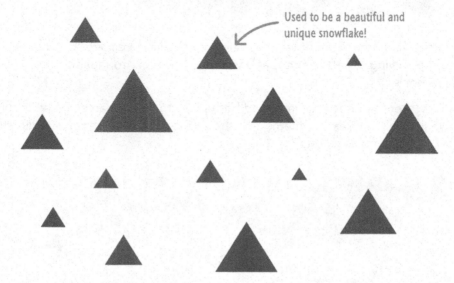

Used to be a beautiful and unique snowflake!

We clone an element by calling the `cloneNode` function on the element we wish to clone, along with providing a **true** or **false** argument to specify whether we want to clone just the element or the element and all of its children. Here is what the snippet of code for cloning an element (and adding it to the DOM) will look like:

```
let bodyElement = document.querySelector("body");
let item = document.querySelector("h1");

let clonedItem = item.cloneNode(false);

// add cloned element to the DOM
bodyElement.appendChild(clonedItem);
```

Once our cloned elements have been added to the DOM, we can then use all the tricks we've learned to modify them. Cloning elements is such an important thing for us to get familiar with, let's go beyond this snippet and look at a fuller example:

```html
<!DOCTYPE html>
<html>

<head>
  <title>Cloning Elements</title>

  <style>
    body {
      background-color: #60543A;
      padding: 30px;
    }

    h1 {
      color: #F2D492;
      font-size: 72px;
      font-family: sans-serif;
      text-decoration: underline;
    }

    p {
      color: #F2D492;
      font-family: sans-serif;
      font-size: 36px;
      font-weight: bold;
    }
  </style>
</head>

<body>
  <h1>Am I real?</h1>
  <p class="message">I exist entirely in your imagination.</p>

  <script>
```

```
    let bodyElement = document.querySelector("body");
    let textElement = document.querySelector(".message");

    setInterval(sayWhat, 1000);

    function sayWhat() {
      let clonedText = textElement.cloneNode(true);
      bodyElement.appendChild(clonedText);
    }
  </script>
</body>

</html>
```

If you put all of this code into an HTML document and preview it in your browser, you'll see something that resembles our earlier example:

After a few seconds, though, you'll notice that this example is quite a bit different. The message keeps duplicating:

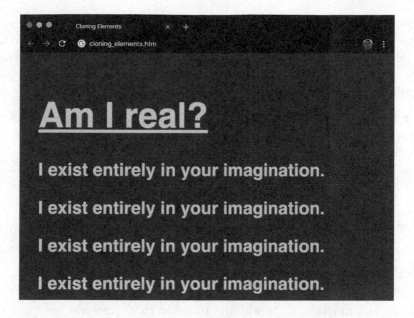

The secret to what is going on here lies in our code. Let's jump back to the code inside the `<script>` tags and take a moment to understand what is going on:

```
let bodyElement = document.querySelector("body");
let textElement = document.querySelector(".message");
```

At the top, we have our `bodyElement` variable that references the `body` element in our HTML. Similarly, we have our `textElement` variable that references our `p` element with a class value of **message**. Nothing too special here.

Now, here is where things get a little interesting. We have our `setInterval` timer function that calls the `sayWhat` function every 1000 milliseconds (1 second):

```
setInterval(sayWhat, 1000);
```

It is inside this `sayWhat` function where the actual cloning takes place:

```
function sayWhat() {
    let clonedText = textElement.cloneNode(true);
    bodyElement.appendChild(clonedText);
}
```

We call `cloneNode` on our `textElement`. The result of us doing this is that a copy of our `textElement` is now created and stored as part of the `clonedText` variable. The last step is for us to add our newly cloned element to the DOM so that it shows up. Thanks to our `setInterval`, all of the code under `sayWhat` repeats to keep adding our cloned element to the page.

One thing you may have noticed is that what we are cloning is the following paragraph element:

```
<p class="message">I exist entirely in your imagination.</p>
```

What we specified in our code is the following:

```
let clonedText = textElement.cloneNode(true);
```

We are calling `cloneNode` with the **true** flag to indicate we want to clone all of the children as well. Why? Our paragraph element doesn't seem to have any children, right? Well, this is where the distinction between *elements* and *nodes* comes into play. Our paragraph tag doesn't have any child *elements*, but the text wrapped by the p tag is a child *node*. This detail is important to keep in mind when you find yourself cloning something and finding that you don't exactly get what you want when you specify that children shouldn't get cloned.

THE ABSOLUTE MINIMUM

If there is anything you walk away with after reading all this, I hope you walk away with the knowledge that our DOM is something you can touch and extensively modify. We sort of talked about how everything in the DOM can be altered earlier, but it is here where we saw firsthand the depth and breadth of the alterations we can easily make using methods like `createElement`, `removeElement`, `remove`, and `cloneNode`.

With everything you've learned here, there is nothing preventing you from starting off with a completely empty page and using just a few lines of JavaScript to populate everything inside it:

```
<!DOCTYPE html>

<html>
```

```
<head>
  <title>Look what I did, ma!</title>
</head>
<body>
  <script>
    let bodyElement = document.querySelector("body");

    let h1Element = document.createElement("h1");
    h1Element.textContent = "Do they speak English in 'What'?";

    bodyElement.appendChild(h1Element);

    let pElement = document.createElement("p");
    pElement.textContent = "I am adding some text here...like a
boss!";

    bodyElement.appendChild(pElement);
  </script>
</body>

</html>
```

Just because you can do something like this doesn't mean you always should. The main problem with dynamically creating content is that search engines, screen readers, and other accessibility tools often have difficulty knowing what to do. They are more familiar with content specified in markup than they are with things created using JavaScript. Just be aware of that limitation if you ever decide to get overenthusiastic with dynamically modifying your DOM.

? Ask a question: **https://forum.kirupa.com**

✔ Practice by building real apps: **https://bit.ly/coding_exercises**

🖋 Errors/known issues: **https://bit.ly/javascript_errata**

34

QUICKLY ADDING MANY ELEMENTS INTO THE DOM

An important part of working with the DOM is learning how to take a bunch of data and turning it into visuals we see onscreen. This general approach of having data drive what we see is a common pattern, especially as our apps get increasingly more dynamic. Let's take Netflix for example, as shown in Figure 34.1.

FIGURE 34.1

Netflix is one of those web apps with a lot of content.

As we navigate through the Netflix app, we see a bunch of thumbnails for the videos we can watch. All of these thumbnails and related content such as the headings and descriptions aren't predefined or hardcoded. The visuals are dynamically generated based on the data the server returns for each category we are navigating through.

A far less interesting example is what happens when we use the search form on the **KIRUPA.com** website, as shown in Figure 34.2.

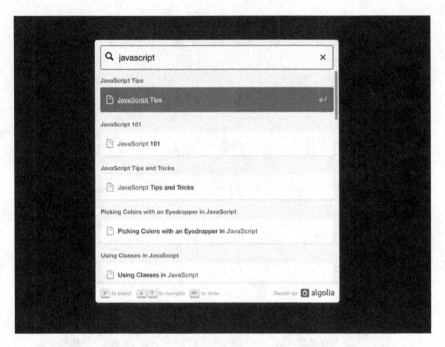

FIGURE 34.2

Search results appear as we type in search terms.

As we type into the search box, we see inline results appear that we can click. These results are generated by the search service, and we have no idea what they are until we start typing into the search box. Behind the scenes, there is a step where our search terms return some data from the server. This data is then mapped to the appropriate HTML elements and then added to our DOM, where we can see and interact with the results.

In this chapter, we'll go deep into learning how to take a bunch of boring old data and turn it into HTML elements that we can see and interact with. We'll look at several approaches for being able to do this while keeping an eye on performance. It's going to be a hoot!

General Approach

In the previous chapter, we learned how to create and display HTML elements using JavaScript. A lot of those techniques will apply here as well, but the twist is that we are optimizing for creating and displaying a really large (think hundreds or thousands!) number of elements. There is just one extra detail to keep in mind when dealing with such a large quantity of elements: **for maximum performance, whether you are adding one element or a million elements, make all of your DOM updates at once**. And with this nugget of wisdom imparted, it's time to learn how exactly to pull all of this off.

Example

Before we start diving into the fun technical details, take a look at an example that nicely captures what we are trying to do: **https://bit.ly/addManyElements**.

Now, if you do visit that page, you'll see something that looks as follows:

Quickly Add Elements

Click the **Generate** button below to display *ten thousand* elements that are created entirely in code! Neat, huh?

Generate

Find the **Generate** button and click it. When you click it, we have some code that dynamically creates 1000 elements and adds them to the DOM:

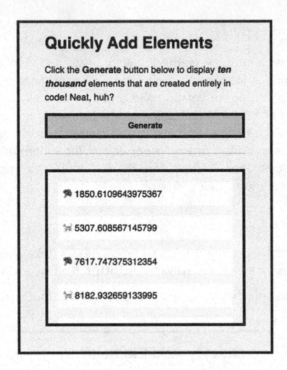

We can see the newly added items in the scrollable region below, and we can even scroll through them with our fingers/mouse to see that all these dynamically created items are real. We'll take this example and riff on it a bit as part of learning how to generate a bunch of elements and display them in our DOM.

Getting Started

In the following sections, we'll look at the techniques we can use to get a lot of elements dynamically added to the DOM, just like in the preceding example. If you want to follow along, create a new document and add the following content into it:

```
<!DOCTYPE html>
<html lang="en">
<head>
```

```html
<meta charset="UTF-8">
<meta http-equiv="X-UA-Compatible" content="IE=edge">
<meta name="viewport" content="width=device-width,
initial-scale=1.0">
<title>Add Element</title>

<style>
  body {
    display: grid;
    place-content: center;
    background-color: #e8ffe7;
  }
  .topContent {
    width: 400px;
    border-bottom: 2px solid #CCC;
    padding-bottom: 30px;
  }
  h1 {
    font-family: sans-serif;
    font-size: 32px;
    font-weight: bold;
  }
  p {
    font-family: sans-serif;
    font-size: 18px;
    line-height: 1.5;
  }
  #container {
    min-height: 300px;
    height: 300px;
    border: 5px solid black;
    margin-top: 30px;
    overflow: auto;
    background-color: #f4f4f4;
  }
```

```css
.item {
  margin: 20px;
  background-color: #FFF;
}
.item p {
  padding: 10px;
}


#generateItems {
  border: 5px solid black;
  padding: 10px;
  font-size: 16px;
  font-weight: bold;
  background-color: #ffd91e;
  width: 100%;
}
#generateItems:hover {
  background-color: #1bf1f9;
}

</style>
</head>
<body>
  <div class="topContent">
    <h1>Quickly Add Elements</h1>
    <p>Click the <b>Generate</b> button below to display <i><b>ten
thousand</b></i> elements that are created entirely in code! Neat,
huh?</p>
    <button id="generateItems">Generate</button>
  </div>
  <div id="container">

  </div>

  <script>
    let container = document.querySelector("#container");
```

```
    let generateButton =  document.querySelector("#generateItems");

    // Visit emojipedia.org to copy/paste emojis if needed!
    let emojis = ["😀", "😃", "😄", "😁", "🐵", "🐶",
"🐱", "🐭", "🐹", "🐰", "🦊", "🐻"];

    generateButton.addEventListener("click", generateContent,
false);

    function generateContent(e) {
      // code goes here!
    }
  </script>
</body>
</html>
```

Take a moment to look at what all of this HTML, CSS, and JS does. There is some basic HTML for displaying the heading text, description, and our **Generate** button. Nothing too fancy here. To make the HTML elements look the way they do, we have a bunch of CSS style rules.

While the HTML and CSS are very important, they aren't going to be the focus of our attention. That honor is reserved for our JavaScript:

```
let container = document.querySelector("#container");
let generateButton =  document.querySelector("#generateItems");

let emojis = ["😀", "😃", "😄", "😁", "🐵", "🐶", "🐱", "🐭", "🐹", "🐰",
"🦊", "🐻"];

generateButton.addEventListener("click", generateContent, false);

function generateContent(e) {
  // code goes here!
}
```

The JavaScript we have currently doesn't do a whole lot. It declares a few variables, references a few DOM elements, and contains the event handler (`generateContent`) that gets called each time our **Generate** button is clicked. A lot of the work we'll be doing will go inside and around the `generateContent` function to create the many HTML elements we will be adding to our DOM, so we'll be seeing a lot of this code in the following sections.

The innerHTML Approach

Let's start with one of the easiest and fastest approaches for adding a bunch of elements into our DOM. This approach works by setting a DOM element's `innerHTML` property with *all* of the content we want to add in the form of a string. If you are actively following along, replace the contents of `generate-Content` with the following:

```javascript
function generateContent(e) {
  let htmlToAdd = "";
  let numberOfItems = 1000;


  for (let i = 0; i < numberOfItems; i++) {
    let num = Math.random() * 10000;
    let emoji = emojis[Math.floor(Math.random() * emojis.length)];


    htmlToAdd += `<div class="item"><p>${emoji} ${num}</p></div>`;
  }

  container.innerHTML = htmlToAdd;
}
```

Take a moment to look at what we are doing. We have a loop that runs 1000 times, corresponding to the number of elements we want to add. Inside this loop, we are generating the HTML we want to add to our DOM. We do this by treating the HTML we want to add as a string and concatenating it to the `htmlToAdd` variable:

```javascript
function generateContent(e) {
  let htmlToAdd = "";
  let numberOfItems = 1000;


  for (let i = 0; i < numberOfItems; i++) {
```

```
    let num = Math.random() * 10000;

    let emoji = emojis[Math.floor(Math.random() * emojis.length)];


    htmlToAdd += `<div class="item"><p>${emoji} ${num}</p></div>`;
}


    container.innerHTML = htmlToAdd;
}
```

Each time our loop runs, a new chunk of HTML in string form containing a `div` and `p` element are added to the `htmlToAdd` variable. By the end of our loop running, this variable will be quite large since it will contain the HTML for every element we want to add to our DOM. Here is a console view of what the `htmlToAdd` variable contains:

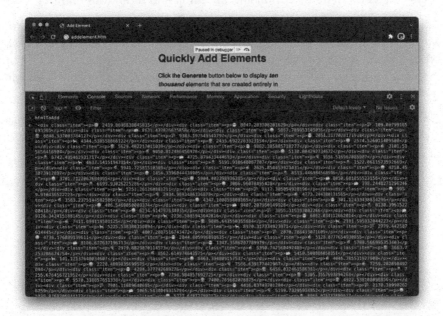

All of this HTML in string form doesn't do much until it is actually added to a DOM element. The DOM element that will host all of this HTML is our `container` element, and our last step is to set its `innerHTML` property to `htmlToAdd`:

```
function generateContent(e) {
    let htmlToAdd = "";
```

```
let numberOfItems = 1000;

for (let i = 0; i < numberOfItems; i++) {
  let num = Math.random() * 10000;
  let emoji = emojis[Math.floor(Math.random() * emojis.length)];

  htmlToAdd += `<div class="item"><p>${emoji} ${num}</p></div>`;
}


container.innerHTML = htmlToAdd;
}
```

When that last line runs, all of our HTML stored in string form is turned into actual HTML and assigned as the content to our container element. The end result is the large collection of items containing an emoji and a random number that we see.

What makes this approach awesome is the fact that it is very simple. We just deal with strings and concatenating them, and the template literal syntax makes this a breeze. Also, this approach is extremely fast. We make only one DOM update at the very end when we set the `innerHTML` to the giant blob of HTML elements we generated.

On the downside, if we want more fine-grained control over the HTML we generate beyond doing string replacement, then working with strings can involve a lot of conditional statements, which can get a bit unwieldy

 NOTE Don't Forget to Design the HTML for Your Data

An important detail when visualizing our data is actually figuring out what HTML elements will be used to get our data to display. For example, the HTML we generate for displaying our emoji and random number looks like this:

```
<div class="item"><p>🦄 1093.9706792591553</p></div>
```

How did we come up with this structure? There are several ways to make this work, but my recommended approach is to ignore the JavaScript for a moment and add the proposed HTML to the relevant part of our document directly:

```
<div class="topContent">
  <h1>Quickly Add Elements</h1>
  <p>Click the <b>Generate</b> button below to display
<i><b>ten thousand</b></i> elements that are created
entirely in code! Neat, huh?</p>
  <button id="generateItems">Generate</button>
</div>
<div id="container">
  <div class="item"><p> 7488.253603325752</p></div>
  <div class="item"><p> 6694.840973924077</p></div>
  <div class="item"><p> 610.9320877589108</p></div>
  <div class="item"><p> 3368.3944750666337</p></div>
  <div class="item"><p> 5051.139001335616</p></div>
</div>
```

By using this temporary HTML structure, we can make changes and see the results quickly. We can even use the in-browser DOM tools to make edits to the HTML and CSS in real time. Once we are happy with the final result, we can then translate this HTML into a less fungible JavaScript-friendly approach to make it come alive with our actual data.

In the previous section, the approach we used to map our data to real HTML elements was to turn the relevant HTML into a string. In the next section, we'll look at a more traditional DOM-oriented way of going from data to HTML.

The DocumentFragment Approach

The next approach we will look at is where we create a virtual DOM element, make all of our DOM changes on it, and then assign that virtual DOM element to our real DOM once we are ready to commit. Working with a virtual DOM element is made possible thanks to the DocumentFragment object, and the following is how our generateContent method can be modified to use it:

```
function generateContent(e) {
  let fragment = new DocumentFragment();
```

```
let numberOfItems = 1000;

for (let i = 0; i < numberOfItems; i++) {
  let num = Math.random() * 10000;
  let emoji = emojis[Math.floor(Math.random() * emojis.length)];

  let divElement = document.createElement("div");
  divElement.classList.add("item");

  let pElement = document.createElement("p");
  pElement.innerText = `${emoji} ${num}`;

  divElement.appendChild(pElement);
  fragment.appendChild(divElement);
}

container.appendChild(fragment);
}
```

Our `fragment` variable stores a reference to our `DocumentFragment` object, and we treat this like we would any other DOM element. Remember, our goal is to generate HTML that looks as follows for each item:

```
<div class="item"><p>😊 47.5121104</p></div>
```

Because we are dealing with DOM elements here, we use the tried-and-true DOM methods like `createElement`, `appendChild`, and `classListto` to generate our HTML structure and build out our DOM subtree.

Now, earlier I mentioned that the way to ensure we add our DOM elements quickly is to make all of our DOM updates just once. What we are seeing in this example seems counter to that because we are creating and appending DOM elements at each iteration of our loop:

```
function generateContent(e) {
  let fragment = new DocumentFragment();
  let numberOfItems = 1000;
```

```
  for (let i = 0; i < numberOfItems; i++) {
    let num = Math.random() * 10000;
    let emoji = emojis[Math.floor(Math.random() * emojis.length)];

    let divElement = document.createElement("div");
    divElement.classList.add("item");

    let pElement = document.createElement("p");
    pElement.innerText = `${emoji} ${num}`;

    divElement.appendChild(pElement);
    fragment.appendChild(divElement);
  }

  container.appendChild(fragment);
}
```

The detail to note is that our DocumentFragment is not your typical DOM element. It isn't parented to any visual onscreen, so it is a virtual element where no styles or layout get modified as a result of us changing its structure. We can't even see it! Think of a DocumentFragment as an invisible, virtual container that gives us all the handy helper methods and capabilities that regular DOM elements provide **without actually creating** a new DOM element. All of the DOM manipulation we are doing that would typically be expensive when done on our live DOM tree doesn't apply here.

Once we have finished building our DOM subtree, it's time to commit our changes to the DOM and visualize the result of all this data being mapped to HTML elements. This step we do **exactly once** after our loop has finished, and the gigantic DOM subtree stored by our fragment is appended to our container element:

```
function generateContent(e) {
  let fragment = new DocumentFragment();
  let numberOfItems = 1000;

  for (let i = 0; i < numberOfItems; i++) {
    let num = Math.random() * 10000;
```

```javascript
        let emoji = emojis[Math.floor(Math.random() * emojis.length)];

        let divElement = document.createElement("div");
        divElement.classList.add("item");

        let pElement = document.createElement("p");
        pElement.innerText = `${emoji} ${num}`;

        divElement.appendChild(pElement);
        fragment.appendChild(divElement);
    }

    container.appendChild(fragment);
}
```

Driving home the invisible and virtual nature of our DocumentFragment, when we append our DocumentFragment to another DOM element, the Document-Fragment disappears. Because it acted like a temporary container to help us build the DOM subtree, only the **contents** of the DocumentFragment survived and became a part of the parent element. If we inspect the contents of our container element, we won't see any evidence of our DocumentFragment having played a key role in helping us visualize all of this data:

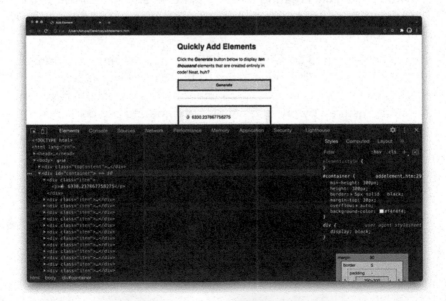

This approach is awesome for three reasons. First, it's powerful. By having access to all of the DOM methods, we can build our DOM subtree without having to deal with raw strings. Second, it's fast. Our `DocumentFragment` isn't a real DOM element with all of the performance overhead that comes along with it, so we can performantly build our DOM subtree and assign it once to our DOM when we are ready to commit the changes. Finally, the `DocumentFragment` disappears once it's parented under a DOM element, so we aren't inserting an additional HTML element that we'll need to keep around.

The downside of this approach, however, is that it's verbose. Working with the DOM methods does mean that we have to write additional code to create an element, make any attribute changes on the element, append it to any intermediate elements, and do other bookkeeping tasks to get our DOM subtree just right.

Removing Elements (Emptying an Entire Subtree)

We spent all this time looking at how to add a bunch of elements to our DOM. What about the opposite, where we want to remove a bunch of elements instead? Removing elements is far less glamourous because what we are looking to do is just clear out an entire DOM subtree of content. The easiest way to do this is by relying on the `replaceChildren` method.

If we wanted to clear out all of the contents of our container element, here is what we would do:

```
container.replaceChildren();
```

That's all there is to it. A practical use for this is actually in our current example. Each time we click the **Generate** button, we don't want to keep adding a thousand elements each time. We want to clear out the current DOM elements before adding new ones. The change would be to add the preceding line to the top of our `generateContent` function, like so:

```
function generateContent(e) {
  container.replaceChildren();

  let htmlToAdd = "";
  let numberOfItems = 1000;

  for (let i = 0; i < numberOfItems; i++) {
```

```
    let num = Math.random() * 10000;
    let emoji = emojis[Math.floor(Math.random() * emojis.length)];


    htmlToAdd += `<div class="item"><p>${emoji} ${num}</p></div>`;
  }


  container.innerHTML = htmlToAdd;
}
```

With this change, each time `generateContent` is called, we ensure that we are dealing with an empty container element before adding any new elements to it.

THE ABSOLUTE MINIMUM

In this chapter, we looked at two approaches for being able to dynamically generate a bunch of elements using JavaScript and add them to the DOM. One approach had us treating all of our HTML as strings and setting the `innerHTML` property. Another approach had us creating a virtual DOM element using DocumentFragment and creating our DOM subtree using the usual DOM manipulation methods. Both of these approaches are quite good. In my testing, the performance characteristics for both are really good, with the `innerHTML` approach being slightly faster. Your mileage may vary, so definitely double-check which happens to be faster for your situation.

? Ask a question: **https://forum.kirupa.com**

✔ Practice by building real apps: **https://bit.ly/coding_exercises**

Errors/known issues: **https://bit.ly/javascript_errata**

35

IN-BROWSER DEVELOPER TOOLS

All of the major browsers—Google Chrome, Apple Safari, Mozilla Firefox, and Microsoft Edge (formerly Internet Explorer)—do more than just display web pages. For developers, they provide access to a lot of cool functionality for figuring out what is actually going on with the web page being displayed. They do all of this via what I'll generically just call the **developer tools**. These are tools that are built in to the browser, and they give you the ability to fiddle with your HTML, CSS, and JavaScript in a lot of neat and interesting ways.

In this chapter, let's look at these developer tools and learn how we can use them to make our lives easier.

I'LL BE USING GOOGLE CHROME

For all of the examples you are about to see, I'll be using Google's Chrome browser. While each browser provides similar functionality for what I'll be describing, the exact user interface (UI) and steps to get there will vary. Just be aware of that, and also note that the version of Chrome you may be using might be more recent than the one used in this chapter.

Meet the Developer Tools

Let's start at the very beginning. When you navigate to a web page, your browser will load whatever document it was told to load:

This should all be very familiar for you, as this part of the browser functionality really hasn't changed much since the very first browser was released in the 1800s...or thereabouts. While using Chrome, press **command+option+I** on the Mac or the **F12** key (or **Ctrl+Shift+I**) in Windows.

Notice what happens. While you may not hear heavenly music followed by the earth rumbling and laser beams shooting across the sky, you will see your browser's layout change to show something mysterious (usually) toward the bottom or right of the screen, as shown in Figure 35.1.

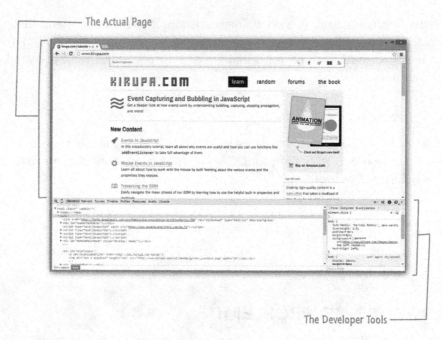

The Actual Page

The Developer Tools

FIGURE 35.1

Your browser with its developer tools displayed right below it

Your browser will split into two parts. One part is where your browser deals with displaying your web pages. We like this guy and have known him for quite some time. The other part, the new guy whom we eye suspiciously from a distance, provides you with access to information about the currently displayed page that only a developer such as yourself would appreciate. This guy is better known as the developer tools.

The developer tools provide you with the ability to do the following:

- Inspect the DOM

- Debug JavaScript

- Inspect objects and view messages via the console

- Figure out performance and memory issues

- See the network traffic

- ...and a whole lot more!

In the interest of time (*Game of Thrones* is about to start soon, and this is the episode where I believe Ned Stark comes back to life as a dire wolf), I'm going to focus on the first three items that are directly related to what you are learning about in this book.

Inspecting the DOM

The first developer tool feature we will look at is how you can inspect and even manipulate the contents of your DOM. With Chrome launched, navigate to **http://bit.ly/kirupaDevTool**.

NO BROWSER? NO PROBLEM!

Now, if you don't have a browser handy or simply can't access that link, don't worry. I'll explain what is going on at each step of the way so that you aren't left out of all the fun.

When you load this page, you will see a colorful background with some text displayed:

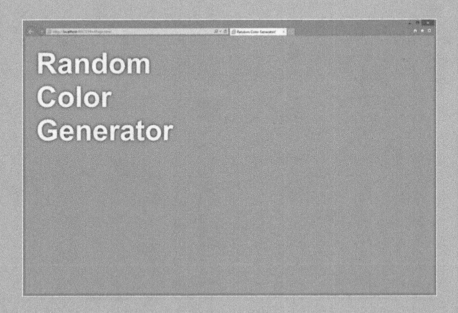

If you reload this page, you'll see it showing up with a different background color. As you can guess, each page reload will result in a different background color getting generated:

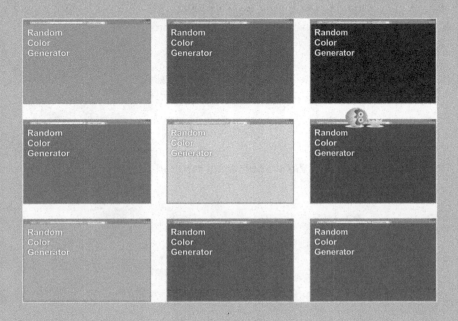

The first thing we'll do with this example is examine the DOM to see what is going on. Make sure your developer tools are visible and ensure the **Elements** tab is selected:

```
Q  □  | Elements | Network  Sources  Timeline  Profiles  Resources  Audits  Console
▼ <html>
  ▼ <head>
      <title>Random Color Generator!</title>
    ▼ <style>
              h2 {
                  font-family: Arial, Helvetica;
                  font-size: 100px;
                  color: #FFF;
                  text-shadow: 0px 0px 11px #333333;
                  margin: 0;
                  padding: 30px;
              }

      </style>
    </head>
  ▼ <body style="background-color: rgb(153, 177, 66);">
      ▼ <h2>
<!DOCTYPE>
```

What you will see is a view of your *live* markup from the page that is currently shown. To be more specific, this is a **view of your DOM**. The importance of this distinction is that this view provides you with a live version of what your page looks like. Any shenanigans JavaScript or your browser may have pulled on the DOM will be shown in this view.

For our example, using **View Source** will result in something like the following:

```
<!DOCTYPE html>

<html>


<head>

  <title>Random Color Generator!</title>
```

```
  <style>
    h2 {
        font-family: Arial, Helvetica;
        font-size: 100px;
        color: #FFF;
        text-shadow: 0px 0px 11px #333333;
        margin: 0;
        padding: 30px;
    }
  </style>
</head>

<body>
  <h2>Random
    <br />Color
    <br />Generator</h2>
  <script src="js/randomColor.js"> </script>
  <script>
    let bodyElement = document.querySelector("body");
    bodyElement.style.backgroundColor = getRandomColor();
  </script>
</body>

</html>
```

The **View Source** command simply gives us a view of the markup as stored in the HTML page. Another way of saying this is that **View Source** gives us a (stale) version of the markup as it lives on the server and not a version of the DOM.

If you use the developer tools' DOM view, you will see a *DOM-based representation* of our document based on the *live version of the page*:

```
<!DOCTYPE html>
<html>

<head>
```

```html
<title>Random Color Generator!</title>
<style>
  h2 {
    font-family: Arial, Helvetica;
    font-size: 100px;
    color: #FFF;
    text-shadow: 0px 0px 11px #333333;
    margin: 0;
    padding: 30px;
  }
</style>

<body style="background-color: rgb(75, 63, 101);">
  <h2>Random
    <br>Color
    <br>Generator</h2>
  <script src="js/randomColor.js"> </script>
  <script>
    let bodyElement = document.querySelector("body");
    bodyElement.style.backgroundColor = getRandomColor();
  </script>

</body>

</html>
```

If you pay close attention, you'll notice some subtle differences in how some elements look. The biggest difference is the highlighted inline `background-color` style on the `body` element that exists in the DOM view but not in the traditional View Source view. The reason is that we have some JavaScript that dynamically sets an inline style on the `body` element. The following note expands on why this happens!

NOTE The Difference Between the DOM View and View Source

The reason for the discrepancy between the two code views goes back to what the DOM represents. To repeat this one more time, your DOM is the result of your browser and JavaScript having run to completion. It provides you with a fresh-from-the-oven look that mimics what your browser sees.

View Source is just a static representation of your document as it was on the server (or your computer). It doesn't contain any of the liveliness of your running page that the DOM view highlights. If you look at our JavaScript, you'll see that I specified that our body element get its `backgroundColor` set dynamically:

```
let bodyElement = document.querySelector("body");
bodyElement.style.backgroundColor = getRandomColor();
```

When this code runs, it modifies the DOM to set the back-groundColor property on the body element. You would never see this using View Source. Ever. That's why the DOM view the developer tools provide is your bestest friend in the whole wide world.

As examples highlighting the differences between the source and DOM go, our example was quite simple. To see the real benefit of the DOM view, you should experiment with some element re-parentings, creations, and deletions to really see the divergence between viewing the source and examining the DOM. Some of the examples you saw in the previous chapters around DOM manipulation would be good things to inspect as well.

Debugging JavaScript

Moving along, the other big thing that the developer tools bring to the table is **debuggability**. I don't know if that's really a word, but the developer tools allow you to poke and prod at your code to figure out what is going wrong (or not wrong). The general catchall phrase for all this is known as **debugging**.

In your developer tools, click the **Sources** tab:

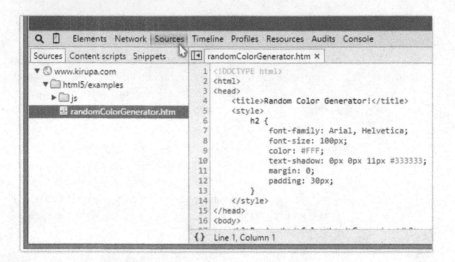

The **Sources** tab gives you access to all the files currently being used by your document. As the name implies, you are looking at the raw contents of these files—not the DOM-generated version from earlier that is your *bestest* friend.

From the tree view on the left, ensure the **randomColorGenerator.htm** file is selected. This will ensure that the contents of this file are displayed for you to examine on the right. In the displayed file, scroll all the way down until you see the `<script>` tag with the two lines of code you saw earlier. Based on the line counts shown in the left gutter, our lines of JavaScript should be lines 20 and 21.

What we want to do is examine what happens when the code in line 21 is about to execute. To do this, we need to tell the browser to stop when line 21 is about to get executed. We do that by setting what is known as a **breakpoint**. To set a breakpoint, click directly on the 21 label in the left gutter.

Once you've done that, you'll see the **21** highlighted:

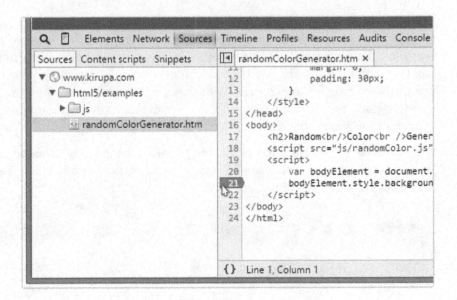

At this point, a breakpoint has been set. The next step is to actually have your browser run into this breakpoint. This is more peacefully known as "hitting the breakpoint." The way a breakpoint is hit is by ensuring your code runs into it. In our case, all we need to do is just hit **F5** to refresh the page, as line 21 will just execute as part your page loading and executing everything inside the `<script>` tags.

If everything worked as expected, you'll see your page load and suddenly pause, with line 21 getting highlighted:

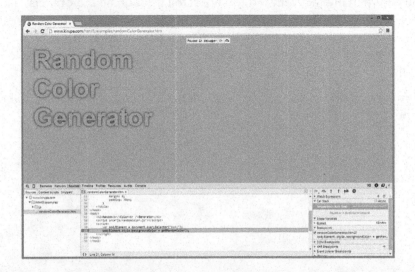

You are currently in **debugging mode**. The breakpoint you set on line 21 has been hit. This means your entire page ground to a screeching halt the moment the browser hit the breakpoint. At this point, with your browser being in suspended animation, you have the ability to fiddle with everything going on in your page. Think of this as time having stopped with only you having the ability to move around, inspect, and alter the surroundings. If a movie hasn't been made about this, somebody should get on it!

While in this mode, go back to line 21 and hover over the bodyElement variable. When you hover over it, you'll see a tooltip indicating the various properties and values that this particular object contains:

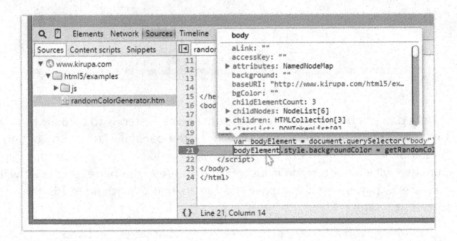

You can then interact with the tooltip, scroll through all the objects, and even dig deeper into complex objects that have more objects inside them. Because body-Element is basically the JavaScript/DOM representation of the body element, we'll see a lot of properties that we encountered indirectly from our look at HTMLElement a few chapters ago.

On the right side of the source view, we have more angles through which we can inspect our code:

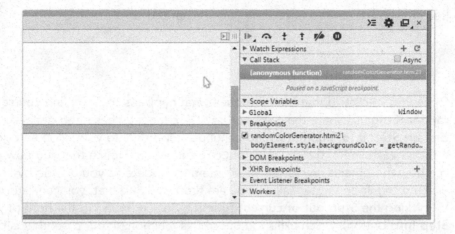

I won't be explaining what all of those categories do, but I am pointing that area out just so you know that you have the ability to examine the current state of all your JavaScript variables and objects in much greater detail if you wanted to.

The other big advantage a breakpoint provides is the ability for you to step through your code just like your browser would. Right now, we are stuck on line 21. To step through the code, click the **Step into function call** button found on the right side of the screen:

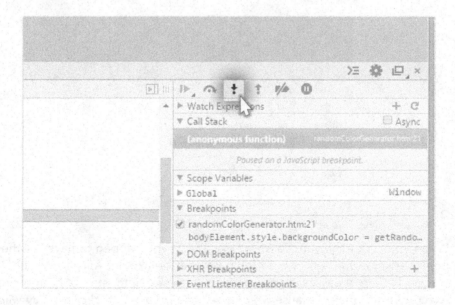

Remember, this is the line of code you are currently broken at:

```
bodyElement.style.backgroundColor = getRandomColor();
```

Once you've clicked that button, notice what happens. You will find yourself inside **randomColor.js**, where the `getRandomColor` function has been defined. Keep clicking **Step into function call** to continue stepping into your code and going through each line of the `getRandomColor` function. Notice that you now get to see how the objects in your browser's memory update as you go line-by-line and execute the code sequentially. If you are tired of doing that, you can "step back" by clicking the **Step out of current function** button (found to the right of your **Step into** button), which exits you out of this function. In our case, that is back to line 21 in **randomColorGenerator.htm**.

If you just want to execute your app without stepping through any more of the code, click the **Play** button found a few pixels to the left of **Step into**:

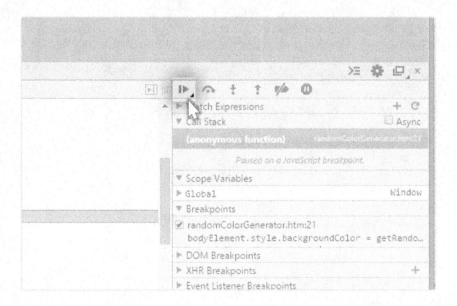

When you click **Play**, your code will execute. If you happen to have another breakpoint set somewhere in your code's path, that breakpoint will also get hit. When stopped at any breakpoint, you can choose to step into, step out, or just resume execution with **Play**. Because we only set one breakpoint, clicking **Play** will just run the code to completion and have your random color appear as the background for your body element:

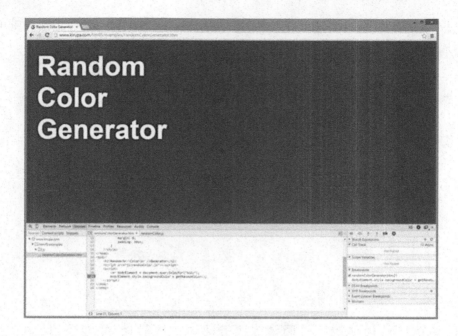

To remove a breakpoint, just click the line number you set the breakpoint on. If you click the 21 label again, the breakpoint will toggle itself off and you can just run your application without getting into debugging mode.

So, there you have it. A whirlwind tour of how to use some of the debugging functionality you and I have at our disposal. To reiterate something I mentioned at the beginning of this chapter, I am only scratching the surface of what is possible.

Meet the Console

The other, OTHER big debugging tool functionality we will look at is using what is known as the **Console**. We've seen the Console in action quite a bit when we looked at it earlier, so I am just repeating some of the information here for the sake of completeness, but going a bit further as well. As we know, the Console provides us with the ability to do several things. It allows us to see messages logged by our code. It also allows us to pass commands and inspect any object that is currently in scope.

To show the Console, navigate to the **Console** tab by clicking (or tapping) it:

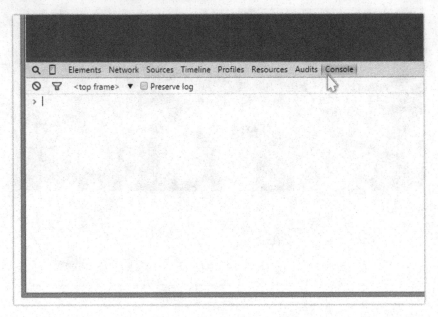

Don't be afraid of the vast emptiness you see in front of you. Instead, embrace the freedom and fresh air.

Anyway, the Console provides us with the ability to inspect or call any object that exists in whatever scope our application is currently running in. With no break-points set, launching the Console puts us in the global state.

Inspecting Objects

Where your cursor is right now, type in **window** and press **Enter**:

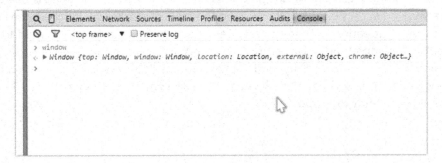

What you will see is an interactive listing of all the things that live in your `window` object. You can start to type in any valid object or property, and if it is in scope, you will be able to access it, inspect its value, or even execute it:

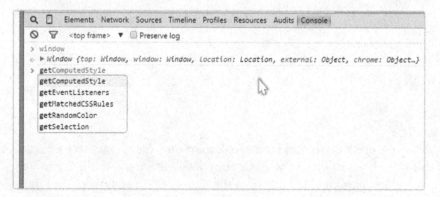

This is by no means a read-only playground. We can cause all sorts of mayhem. For example, if you type in **document.body.remove()** and press **Enter**, your entire document will just disappear. If you did end up deleting the body, just refresh the page to get back to your earlier state. Developer tools primarily work with the in-memory representation of our page and don't write back to source. Your experimentations will safely stay in the transient realm.

REFRESHER ON THE SCOPE/STATE

On several occasions, I mentioned that your console allows you to inspect the world at whatever scope you are currently in. This is basically just applying what you learned about variable scope in Chapter 8, "Variable Scope," to the Console's behavior.

Let's say we have a breakpoint set at the following highlighted line:

```
let oddNumber = false;

function calculateOdd(num) {
  if (num % 2 == 0) {
```

```
      oddNumber = false;
   } else {
      oddNumber = true;
   }
}
calculateOdd(3);
```

When we run the code and the breakpoint gets hit, the value of oddNumber is still **false**. Our breakpointed line hasn't been executed yet, and we can verify this by testing the value of oddNumber in the Console. Next, let's say we run this code, hit this breakpoint, and step through to the next line.

At this point, our oddNumber value is set to **true**. Our Console will now reflect the new value because that is what the in-memory representation of oddNumber states. The main takeaway is that your Console's view of the world is directly tied to where in the code you are currently focusing. This is especially made obvious when you are stepping through code and the scope you are in changes frequently.

Logging Messages

We are almost done with all of this "developer tools" business. The last thing we will look at is the Console's ability to log messages from your code. This is something we looked at in detail earlier in Chapter 11, so we'll keep it brief. Remember all those times in the earlier chapters where we did something like this?

```
function doesThisWork() {
  alert("It works!!!");
}
```

Here we are using an `alert` statement to print some value or prove that the code is being executed. Well, we can stop doing that now. By using the Console, we have a far less annoying way of printing messages without interrupting everything with a modal dialog. You can use the `console.log` function to pass in whatever you want to print to the Console:

```
function doesThisWork() {
  console.log("It works!!!")
}
```

When this code executes, you'll see whatever you logged get printed in your Console when you bring it up:

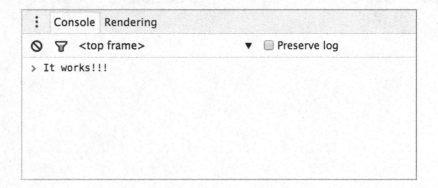

Using the Console is, in almost every way, superior to using `alert` for debugging purposes.

THE ABSOLUTE MINIMUM

If you have never used a developer tool before, I really, REALLY think you should take some time to get familiar with one. JavaScript is one of those languages where things can go wrong even when everything looks right. In the very simple examples you'll encounter in this book, it's easy to spot mistakes. When you start working on larger and more complex applications, having the right tools to diagnose issues will save you many hours of effort.

? Ask a question: **https://forum.kirupa.com**

✔ Practice by building real apps: **https://bit.ly/coding_exercises**

Errors/known issues: **https://bit.ly/javascript_errata**

36

IN THIS CHAPTER

- Understand how communication happens between you and your app

- Learn about events

- Use event arguments to better handle event-related scenarios

EVENTS

In case you haven't noticed, most applications and websites are pretty boring when left alone. They launch with great fanfare and gusto, but the excitement they bring to the table goes away very quickly if we don't start interacting with them:

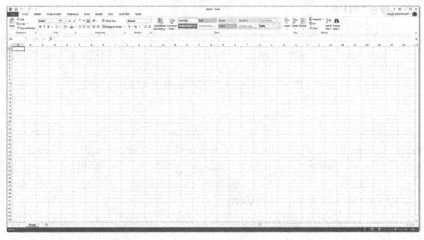

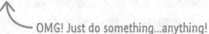
OMG! Just do something...anything!

The reason for this is simple: Our applications exist to react to things we do to them. They have some built-in motivation when we launch them to get themselves out of bed and ready for the day. Everything else that they do afterward depends largely on what we tell them to do. This is where things get really interesting.

We tell our applications what to do by having them react to what are known as **events**. In this chapter, we will take an introductory look at what events are and how we can use them.

What Are Events?

At a high level, everything we create can be modeled by the following statement:

When _____ happens, do _____ .

We can fill in the blanks in this statement in a bajillion different ways. The first blank calls out something that happens. The second blank describes the reaction to that. Here are some examples of this statement filled out:

When <u>a page load</u> happens, do <u>play the video of a cat sliding into cardboard</u>.

When <u>a click</u> happens, do <u>submit my online purchase</u>.

When <u>a mouse release</u> happens, do <u>hurl the giant/not-so-happy bird</u>.

When <u>a delete key press</u> happens, do <u>send this file to the Recycle Bin</u>.

When <u>a touch gesture</u> happens, do <u>apply this old timey filter to this photo</u>.

When <u>a file download</u> happens, do <u>update the progress bar</u>.

This generic model applies to all the code we've written together. This model also applies to all the code our favorite developer/designer friends wrote for their applications. There is no way of escaping this model, so there is no point in resisting. Instead, we need to learn to embrace the star of this model—the very talented critter known as the **event**.

An event is nothing more than a signal. It communicates that something has just happened. This something could be a mouse click. It could be a key press on our keyboard. It could be our window getting resized. It could just be our document simply getting loaded. The thing to take away is that our signal could be any one of hundreds of somethings that are built in to the JavaScript language—or custom somethings that we created just for our app alone.

Getting back to our model, events make up the first half:

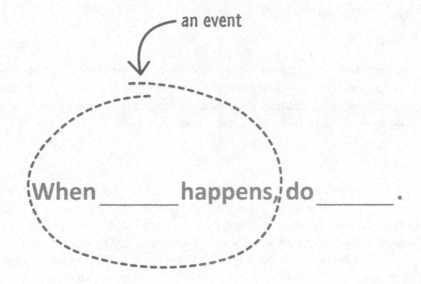

an event

When _____ happens, do _____.

An event defines the thing that happens. **It fires the signal**. The second part of the model is defined by the reaction to the event:

When _____ happens, do _____.

react to the event

After all, what good is a signal if there isn't someone somewhere who is waiting for it and then takes the appropriate action?! Okay, now that we have a high-level overview of what events are, let's dive into how events live in the nature reserve known as JavaScript.

Events and JavaScript

Given the importance of events, it should be no surprise to you that JavaScript provides us with a lot of great support for working with them. To work with events, there are two things we need to do:

1. Listen for events.

2. React to events.

These two steps seem pretty simple, but never forget that we are dealing with JavaScript here. The simplicity is just a smokescreen for the depth of the trauma JavaScript will inflict upon us if we take a wrong step. Maybe I am being overly dramatic here, but we'll find out soon enough.

Listening for Events

To more bluntly state what I danced around earlier, almost everything we do inside an application results in an event getting fired. Sometimes, our application will fire events automatically, such as when it loads. Sometimes, our application will fire events as a reaction to us actually interacting with it. The thing to note is that our application is bombarded by events constantly, regardless of whether we intended to have them get fired. Our task is to tell our application to listen only to the events we care about.

The thankless job of listening to the right event is handled entirely by a function called `addEventListener`. This function is responsible for being eternally vigilant so that it can notify another part of our application when an interesting event gets fired.

The way we use this function looks as follows:

```
source.addEventListener(eventName, eventHandler, false);
```

That's probably not very helpful, so let's dissect what each part of this function means.

The Source

We call `addEventListener` via an element or object that we want to listen for events on. Typically, that will be a DOM element, but it can also be our `document`, `window`, or any object specially designed to fire events.

The Event Name

The first argument we specify to the `addEventListener` function is the name of the event we are interested in listening to. The full list of events we have at our disposal is simply too large to show here (go to the following page instead: **https://bit.ly/kirupaEventsList**), but some of the most common events you will encounter are shown in Table 36.1.

TABLE 36.1 Common Events

Event	When the Event Is Fired
`click`	When you press down and release the primary mouse button, track-pad, and so on.
`mousemove`	Whenever you move the mouse cursor.
`mouseover`	When you move the mouse cursor over an element. This is the event you would use for detecting a hover!
`mouseout`	When your mouse cursor moves outside the boundaries of an element.
`dblclick`	When you quickly click twice.
`DOMContent-Loaded`	When your document's DOM has fully loaded. We'll look into this event in more detail in Chapter 40.
`load`	When your entire document (DOM, external stuff like images, scripts, and so on) has fully loaded.
`keydown`	When you press down on a key on your keyboard.
`keyup`	When you stop pressing down on a key on your keyboard.
`scroll`	When an element is scrolled around.
`wheel` and `DOMMouseScroll`	Every time you use your mouse wheel to scroll up or down.

In subsequent chapters, we will look at a lot of these events in greater detail. For now, just take a quick glance at the `click` event. We will be using that one in a few moments.

The Event Handler

The second argument requires us to specify a function that will get called when the event is overheard. This function is very affectionately known as the **event handler** by friends and family. We'll learn a whole lot more about this function (and occasionally an object) in a few moments.

To Capture or Not to Capture? That Is the Question!

The last argument is made up of either a **true** or a **false**. To fully help us understand the implications of specifying either value, we are going to have to wait until Chapter 37, "Event Bubbling and Capturing in JavaScript," which happens to be the next chapter, so we won't be waiting long.

Putting It All Together

Now that we've seen the `addEventListener` function and what it looks like, let's tie it all up with an example of this function fully decked out:

```
document.addEventListener("click", changeColor, false);
```

Our `addEventListener` in this example is attached to the `document` object. When a `click` event is overheard, it calls the `changeColor` function (aka the event handler) to react to the event. This sets us up nicely for the next section, which is all about reacting to events.

Reacting to Events

As we saw in the previous section, listening to events is handled by `addEventListener`. What to do after an event is overheard is handled by the event handler. I wasn't joking when I mentioned earlier that an event handler is nothing more than a function or object:

```
function normalAndBoring() {
  // I like hiking and puppies and other stuff!
}
```

The only distinction between a typical function and one that is designated as the event handler is that our event handler function is specifically called out by name in an `addEventListener` call (and receives an `Event` object as its argument):

```
document.addEventListener("click", changeColor, false);

function changeColor(event) {
  // I am important!!!
}
```

Any code we place inside our event handler will execute when the event our `addEventListener` function cares about gets overheard.

A Simple Example

The best way to make sense of what we've learned so far is to see all of this fully working. To play along, add the following markup and code to an HTML document:

```
<!DOCTYPE html>
<html>

<head>
  <title>Click Anywhere!</title>
</head>

<body>
  <script>
    document.addEventListener("click", changeColor, false);

    function changeColor() {
      document.body.style.backgroundColor = "#FFC926";
    }
  </script>
</body>

</html>
```

If we preview our document in the browser, we will initially just see a blank page, as shown in Figure 36.1.

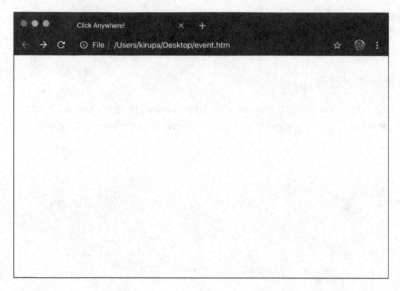

FIGURE 36.1

A blank page is all we see!

Things will change when you click anywhere on the page, though. Once you've completed your click (that is, released the mouse press), your page's background will change from being white to a yellowish color (or a different shade of gray if you are in the paperback edition of this book!), as seen in Figure 36.2.

FIGURE 36.2

Our blank page turns yellow when clicked!

The reason why this example does what it does lies in our code:

```
document.addEventListener("click", changeColor, false);

function changeColor() {
  document.body.style.backgroundColor = "#FFC926";
}
```

The addEventListener call is identical to what we saw earlier, so let's skip that one. Instead, let's pay attention to the changeColor event handler:

```
document.addEventListener("click", changeColor, false);

function changeColor() {
  document.body.style.backgroundColor = "#FFC926";
}
```

This function gets called when the click event on the document is overheard. When this function gets called, it sets the background color of the body element to a shade of yellow. Tying this back to the very beginning where we generalized how applications work, here is what this example looks like:

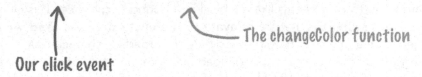

When **a click** happens, do **change the background color.**

↑ The changeColor function

Our click event

If all of this makes complete sense to you, that's great! You just learned about one of the most important concepts you'll encounter. We aren't done just yet. We let the event handler off the hook a little too easily, so let's pay it one more visit.

The Event Arguments and the Event Type

Our event handler does more than just get called when an event is overheard by an event listener. It also provides access to the underlying event object as part of its arguments. To access this event object easily, we need to modify our event handler signature to support this argument.

Here is an example where we specify the `event` name to refer to our event arguments:

```
function myEventHandler(event) {
   // event handlery stuff
}
```

At this point, our event handler is still a plain-old boring function. It just happens to be a function that takes one argument—the event argument! We can go with any valid identifier for the argument, but I tend to go with `event` or just `e` because that is what all the cool kids do. There is nothing technically wrong with identifying our event as follows:

```
function myEventHandler(isNyanCatReal) {
   // event handlery stuff
}
```

The important detail is that the event argument points to an event object, and this object is passed in as part of the event firing. There is a reason why we are paying attention to what seems like a typical and boring occurrence. This event object contains properties that are **relevant to the event that was fired**. An event triggered by a mouse click will have different properties when compared to an event triggered by a key press, a page load, an animation, and so on. Most events will have their own specialized behavior we will rely on, and the event object is our window into all of that uniqueness.

Despite the variety of events and resulting event objects we can get, there are certain properties that are common. This commonality is made possible because all event objects are derived from a base `Event` type (technically, an `Interface`). Some of the popular properties from the `Event` type we will use are:

- `currentTarget`
- `target`
- `preventDefault`

- `stopPropagation`

- `type`

To fully understand what these properties do, we need to go a little deeper in our understanding of events. We aren't there yet, so just know that these properties exist. We'll be seeing them real soon in subsequent chapters.

REMOVING AN EVENT LISTENER

Sometimes, we will need to remove an event listener from an element. The way we do that is by using `addEventListener`'s archnemesis, the `removeEventListener` function:

```
something.removeEventListener(eventName, eventHandler, false);
```

As we can see, this function takes the exact type of arguments as an `addEventListener` function. The reason for that is simple. When we are listening for an event on an element or object, JavaScript uses the `eventName`, the `eventHandler`, and the **true/false** value to uniquely identify that event listener. To remove this event listener, we need to specify the exact same arguments.

Here is an example:

```
document.addEventListener("click", changeColor, false);
document.removeEventListener("click", changeColor, false);

function changeColor() {
  document.body.style.backgroundColor = "#FFC926";
}
```

The event listener we added in the first line is completely neutralized by the `removeEventListener` call in the highlighted second line. If the `removeEventListener` call used any argument that was different from what was specified with the corresponding `addEventListener` call, its impact would be ignored and the event listening will continue.

THE ABSOLUTE MINIMUM

Well, that's all there is to getting an introduction to events. Just remember that you have your addEventListener function, which allows you to register an event handler function. This event handler function will get called when the event your event listener is listening for gets fired. Although we touched on a few other topics, they will make more sense when we view them in the context of the more advanced event-related examples you will see in the following chapters!

? Ask a question: **https://forum.kirupa.com**

✔ Practice by building real apps: **https://bit.ly/coding_exercises**

🖋 Errors/known issues: **https://bit.ly/javascript_errata**

EVENT BUBBLING AND CAPTURING

In the previous chapter, you learned how to use the `addEventListener` function to listen for events that you want to react to. That chapter covered the basics, but it glossed over an important detail about how events actually get fired. An event isn't an isolated disturbance. Like a butterfly flapping its wings, an earthquake, a meteor strike, or a Godzilla visit, many events ripple and affect a bunch of elements that lie in their path.

In this chapter, I will put on my investigative glasses, a top hat, and a serious British accent to explain what exactly happens when an event gets fired. You will learn about the two phases events live in, why all of this is relevant, and a few other tricks to help you better take control of events.

Event Goes Down, Event Goes Up

To better help us understand events and their lifestyle, let's frame all of this in the context of a simple example. Here is some HTML we'll refer to:

```html
<!DOCTYPE html>
<html>

<head>
  <title>Events!</title>
</head>

<body id="theBody" class="item">
  <div id="one_a" class="item">
    <div id="two" class="item">
      <div id="three_a" class="item">
        <button id="buttonOne" class="item">one</button>
      </div>
      <div id="three_b" class="item">
        <button id="buttonTwo" class="item">two</button>
        <button id="buttonThree" class="item">three</button>
      </div>
    </div>
  </div>
  <div id="one_b" class="item">

  </div>
  <script>

  </script>
</body>

</html>
```

As you can see, there is nothing really exciting going on here. The HTML should look pretty straightforward (as opposed to being shifty and constantly staring at its phone), and its DOM representation is shown in Figure 37.1.

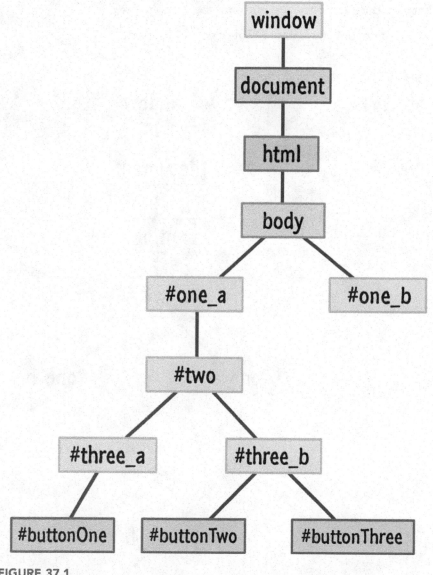

FIGURE 37.1

What the DOM for the markup looks like

Here is where our investigation is going to begin. Let's say that we click the **buttonOne** element. From what we saw previously, you know that a `click` event is going to be fired. The interesting part that I omitted is where exactly the `click` event is going to get fired from. Your `click` event (just like almost every other JavaScript event) does not actually originate at the element you interacted with. That would be too easy and make far too much sense.

Instead, an event starts at the root of your document:

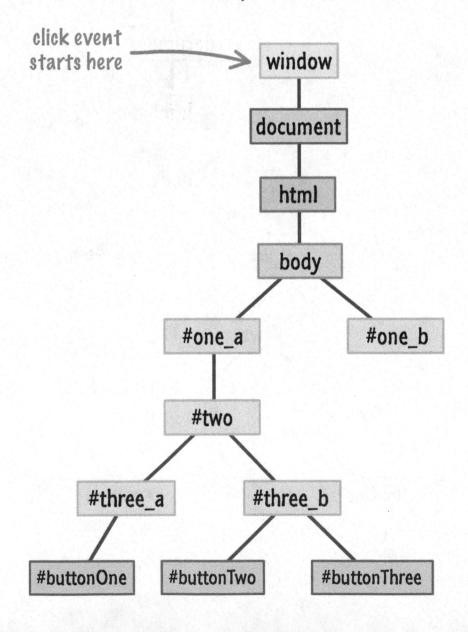

From the root, the event makes its way through the narrow pathways of the DOM and stops at the element that triggered the event, **buttonOne** (also more formally known as the **event target**):

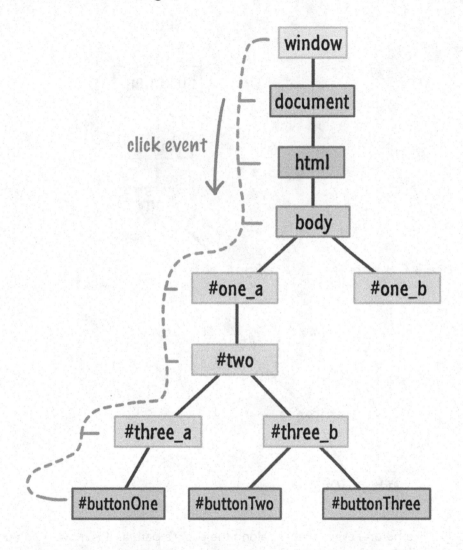

As shown in the diagram, the path our event takes is direct, but it does obnoxiously notify every element along that path. This means that if we were to listen for a `click` event on **body**, **one_a**, **two**, or **three_a**, the associated event handler will get fired. This is an important detail that we will revisit in a little bit.

Now, once our event reaches its target, it doesn't stop. Like some sort of an energetic bunny for a battery company whose trademarked name I probably can't mention here, the event keeps going by retracing its steps and returning back to the root:

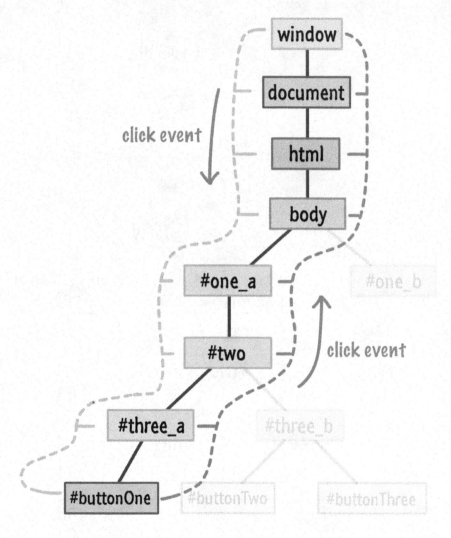

Just like before, every element along the event's path as it is moving on up gets notified about its existence.

Meet the Phases

One of the main things to note is that it doesn't matter where in your DOM you initiate an event. The event always starts at the root, goes down until it hits the target, and then goes back up to the root. This entire journey is very formally defined, so let's look at all of this formalness.

The part where you initiate the event and the event barrels down the DOM from the root is known as the **event capturing phase**:

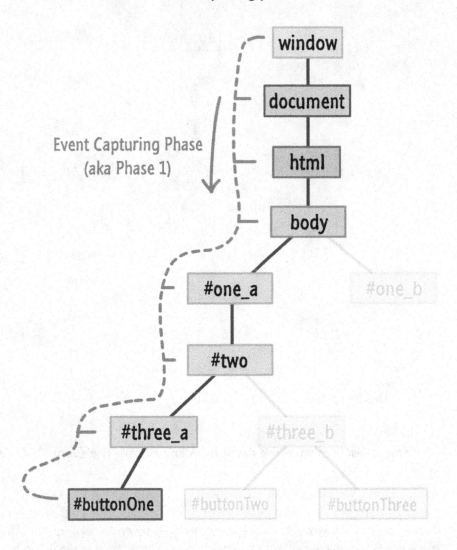

The less learned in the world may just call it **Phase 1**, so be aware that you'll see the proper name and the phase name used interchangeably in event-related content you may encounter in real life. Up next is **Phase 2**, where our event bubbles back up to the root:

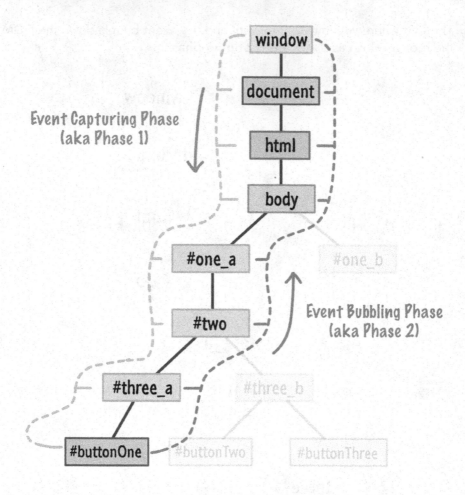

This phase is also known as the **event bubbling phase**. The event "bubbles" back to the top!

Anyway, all the elements in an event's path are pretty lucky. They have the good fortune of getting notified twice when an event is fired. This kinda sorta maybe affects the code we write, because every time we listen for events, we make a choice on which phase we want to listen for our event on. Do we listen for our event as it is fumbling down in the capture phase? Do we listen for our event as it climbs back up in the bubbling phase?

Choosing the phase is a very subtle detail that we specify with a **true** or **false** as part of our addEventListener call:

```
item.addEventListener("click", doSomething, true);
```

If you remember, I glossed over the third argument to `addEventListener` in the previous chapter. This third argument specifies whether you want to listen for this event during the capture phase. An argument of **true** means that you want to listen to the event during the capture phase. If you specify **false**, this means you want to listen for the event during the bubbling phase.

To listen to an event across both the capturing and bubbling phases, you can simply do the following:

```
item.addEventListener("click", doSomething, true);
item.addEventListener("click", doSomething, false);
```

I don't know why you would ever want to do this, but if you ever do, you now know what needs to be done.

NOT SPECIFYING A PHASE

Now, you can be rebellious and choose to not specify this third argument for the phase altogether:

```
item.addEventListener("click", doSomething);
```

When you don't specify the third argument, the default behavior is to listen to your event during the bubbling phase. It's equivalent to passing in a **false** value as the argument.

Who Cares?

At this point, you are probably wondering why all of this matters. This is doubly true if you have been happily working with events for a really long time and this is the first time you've ever heard about all this. Your choice of listening to an event in the capturing or bubbling phase is mostly irrelevant to what you will be doing. Very rarely will you find yourself scratching your head because your event listening and handling code isn't doing the right thing because you accidentally specified **true** instead of **false** in your addEventListener call.

With all this said, there will come a time in your life when you need to know and deal with a capturing or bubbling situation. This time will sneak up on your code and cause you many hours of painful head scratching. Over the years, these are the situations where I've had to consciously be aware of which phase of my event's life I am watching for:

- Dragging an element around the screen and ensuring the drag still happens, even if the element I am dragging slips out from under the cursor.

- Nested menus that reveal submenus when I hover over them.

- I have multiple event handlers on both phases, and I want to focus only on the capturing or bubbling phase event handlers exclusively.

- A third-party component/control library has its own eventing logic, and I want to circumvent it for my own custom behavior.

- I want to override some built-in/default browser behavior such as when I click the scrollbar or give focus to a text field.

In my nearly 105 years of working with JavaScript, these five things were all I was able to come up with. Even this is a bit skewed toward the last few years, since various browsers didn't work well with the various phases at all.

Event, Interrupted

The last thing I am going to talk about before re-watching *Godzilla* is how to prevent our event from propagating. An event isn't guaranteed to live a fulfilling life, where it starts and ends at the root. Sometimes, it is actually desirable to prevent our event from growing old and happy.

To end the life of an event, we have the stopPropagation method on the Event object:

```
function handleClick(e) {
  e.stopPropagation();

  // do something
}
```

As its name implies, the stopPropagation method prevents our event from continuing through the phases. Continuing with our earlier example, let's say that we are listening for the `click` event on the **three_a** element and wish to stop the event from propagating. The code for preventing the propagation will look as follows:

```
let theElement = document.querySelector("#three_a");
theElement.addEventListener("click", doSomething, true);

function doSomething(e) {
  e.stopPropagation();
}
```

When you click **buttonOne**, here is what our event's path will look like:

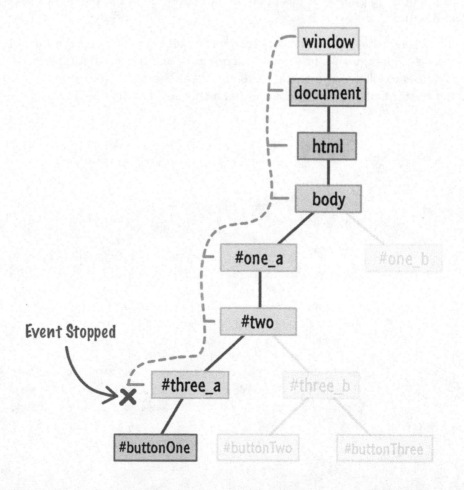

Our `click` event will steadfastly start moving down the DOM tree, notifying every element on the path to **buttonOne**. Because the **three_a** element is listening for the `click` event during the capture phase, the event handler associated with it will get called:

```
function doSomething(e) {
  e.stopPropagation();
}
```

In general, events will not continue to propagate until an event handler that gets activated is fully dealt with. Because **three_a** has an event listener specified to react on a `click` event, the `doSomething` event handler gets called. Our event is in a holding pattern at this point until the `doSomething` event handler executes and returns.

In this case, the event will not propagate further. The `doSomething` event handler is its last client, thanks to the `stopPropagation` function that is hiding in the shadows to kill the event right there and then. The `click` event will never reach the **buttonOne** element, nor will it get a chance to bubble back up. So tragically sad.

 TIP   Another function that lives on your event object that you may awkwardly run into is `preventDefault`:

```
function overrideScrollBehavior(e) {
  e.preventDefault();

  // do something
}
```

What this function does is a little mysterious. Many HTML elements exhibit a default behavior when you interact with them. For example, clicking in a text box gives that text box focus with a little blinking text cursor appearing. Using your mouse wheel in a scrollable area will scroll in the direction you are scrolling. Clicking a check box will toggle the checked state on or off. All of these are examples of built-in reactions to events your browser instinctively knows how to handle.

If you want to turn off this default behavior, you can call the `preventDefault` function. This function needs to be called when reacting to an event on the element whose default reaction you want to ignore. You can see an example of me using this function in the "Smooth Parallax Scrolling" tutorial online at http://bit.ly/kirupaParallax.

THE ABSOLUTE MINIMUM

So, yeah! How about those events and their bubbling and capturing phases? One of the best ways to learn more about how event capturing and bubbling works is to just write some code and see how your event makes its way around the DOM.

We are done with the technical part of this topic, but if you have a few more minutes to spare, I encourage you to watch the somewhat related episode of *Comedians in Cars Getting Coffee* aptly titled "It's Bubbly Time, Jerry." In what is probably the series' *bestest* episode, Michael Richards and Jerry Seinfeld just chat over coffee about events, the bubbling phase, and other very important topics. I think.

? Ask a question: **https://forum.kirupa.com**

✔ Practice by building real apps: **https://bit.ly/coding_exercises**

🎬 Errors/known issues: **https://bit.ly/javascript_errata**

38

IN THIS CHAPTER

- Learn how to listen to the mouse using the various mouse events

- Understand the `MouseEvent` object

- Deal with the mouse wheel

MOUSE EVENTS

One of the most common ways people (and possibly cats) interact with their computers is by using a pointing device known as a **mouse** (see Figure 38.1).

⌐ Aww! Looks sooo cute. Can we keep him?!

FIGURE 38.1

Cats probably like them, too.

This magical device allows you to accomplish great things by moving it around with your hands and clicking around with your fingers. Using a mouse as a user is one thing. As a developer, trying to make your code work with a mouse is something else. That's where this chapter comes in.

Meet the Mouse Events

In JavaScript, our primary way of dealing with the mouse is through events. There are a boatload of events that deal with the mouse, but we won't be looking at all of them here. Instead, we'll focus on just the cool and popular ones, such as the following:

- `click`
- `dblclick`
- `mouseover`
- `mouseout`
- `mouseenter`
- `mouseleave`
- `mousedown`
- `mouseup`
- `mousemove`
- `contextmenu`
- `mousewheel` and `DOMMouseScroll`

The names of these events should give you a good idea of what they do, but we'll take nothing for granted and look at each of these events in some level of greater detail in the following sections. I should warn you that some events are just more interesting than others!

Clicking Once and Clicking Twice

Let's start with probably the most popular of all the mouse events you will use—the `click` event. This event is fired when you **click** an element. To state this differently in a way that doesn't involve mentioning the thing I am describing as part of my description, the `click` event is fired when you use your mouse to press down on an element and then release the press while still over that same element.

Here is a totally unnecessary visualization of what I am talking about:

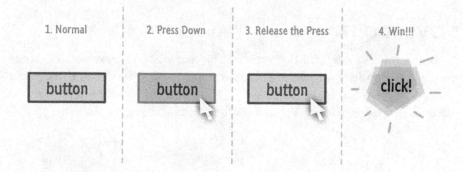

You've seen the code for working with the click event a few times already, but you can never really get enough of it. Here is another example:

```
let button = document.querySelector("#myButton");
button.addEventListener("click", doSomething, false);

function doSomething(e) {
  console.log("Mouse clicked on something!");
}
```

The way you listen for the click event is just like almost any other event you'll encounter, so I won't unnecessarily bore you with that detail and our old friend addEventListener. Instead, I will bore you with details about the somewhat related dblclick event.

The dblclick event is fired when you quickly repeat a click action a double number of times, and the code for using it looks as follows:

```
let button = document.querySelector("#myButton");
button.addEventListener("dblclick", doSomething, false);

function doSomething(e) {
  console.log("Mouse clicked on something...twice!");
}
```

The amount of time between each click that ends up resulting in a dblclick event is based on the OS you are running the code in. It's neither browser specific nor something you can define (or read) using JavaScript.

DON'T OVERDO IT

If you happen to listen for both the `click` and `dblclick` events on an element, your event handlers will get called three times when the element is double-clicked. You will get two `click` events to correspond to each time the element is clicked. After the second click, you will also get a `dblclick` event.

Mousing Over and Mousing Out

The classic hover over and hover out scenarios are handled by the appropriately titled `mouseover` and `mouseout` events, respectively:

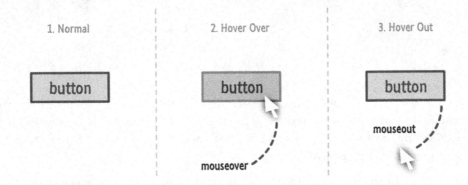

Here is a snippet of these two events in action:

```
let button = document.querySelector("#myButton");
button.addEventListener("mouseover", hovered, false);
button.addEventListener("mouseout", hoveredOut, false);

function hovered(e) {
  console.log("Hovered!");
}
```

```
function hoveredOut(e) {
  console.log("Hovered Away!");
}
```

That's all there is to these two events. They are pretty boring overall, which, as you've probably found out by now, is actually a good thing when it comes to programming concepts.

WHAT ABOUT THE OTHER TWO SIMILAR-LOOKING EVENTS?

We just looked at two events (mouseover and mouseout), which are all about hovering over something and hovering away from something. As it turns out, you have two more events that pretty much do the exact same thing. These are your mouseenter and mouseleave events. There is one important detail to know about these events that makes them unique. The mouseenter and mouseleave events do not bubble.

This detail only matters if the element you are interested in hovering over or out from has child elements. All four of these events behave identically when there are no child elements at play. If there are child elements at play, then keep the following points in mind:

- The mouseover and mouseout events will get fired each time you move the mouse over and around a child element. This means you could be seeing many unnecessary events fire, even though it seems like you are moving your mouse within a single region.

- The mouseenter and mouseleave events will get fired only once. It doesn't matter how many child elements your mouse moves through.

For 90 percent of what you will do, mouseover and mouseout will be good enough. For the other times, often involving slightly more complex user interface (UI) scenarios, you'll be happy the non-bubbling mouseenter and mouseleave events are available.

The Very Click-Like Mousing Down and Mousing Up Events

Two events that are almost subcomponents of the `click` event are the mousedown and mouseup events. From the following diagram, you'll see why:

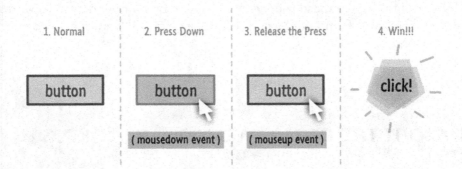

When you press down with your mouse, the mousedown event is fired. When you release the press, the mouseup event is fired. If you pressed down on and released from the same element, the click event will also fire.

You can see all of this from the following snippet:

```
let button = document.querySelector("#myButton");
button.addEventListener("mousedown", mousePressed, false);
button.addEventListener("mouseup", mouseReleased, false);
button.addEventListener("click", mouseClicked, false);

function mousePressed(e) {
  console.log("Mouse is down!");
}

function mouseReleased(e) {
  console.log("Mouse is up!");
}

function mouseClicked(e) {
  console.log("Mouse is clicked!");
}
```

You may be wondering why you would bother with these two events, given that the click event seems perfectly suited for most cases where you may want to use mousedown and mouseup. If you are spending sleepless nights wondering about this, the answer is...**yes, you are correct!** A more helpful (and sensible) answer is that the mousedown and mouseup events simply give you more control in case you need it. Some interactions (such as drags, or awesome moves in video games where you press and hold to charge a lightning bolt of doom!) need you to act only when the mousedown event has happened but the mouseup event hasn't.

The Event Heard Again...and Again...and Again!

One of the most chatty events you'll ever encounter is the very friendly mousemove event. This event fires a whole lotta times as your mouse moves over the element you are listening for the mousemove event on:

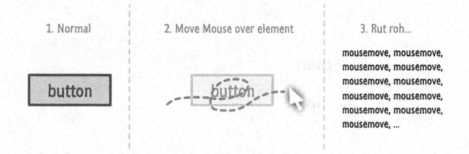

What follows is an example of the mousemove event in code:

```
let button = document.querySelector("#myButton");
button.addEventListener("mousemove", mouseIsMoving, false);


function mouseIsMoving(e) {
  console.log("Mouse is on the run!");
}
```

Your browser controls the rate at which the mousemove event gets fired, and this event gets fired if your mouse moves even a single pixel. This event is great for many interactive scenarios where your mouse's current position is relevant to keep track of, for example.

The Context Menu

The last mouse-related event we are going to look at is affectionately called `con-textmenu`. As you probably know very well, when you right-click in various applications, you will commonly see a menu:

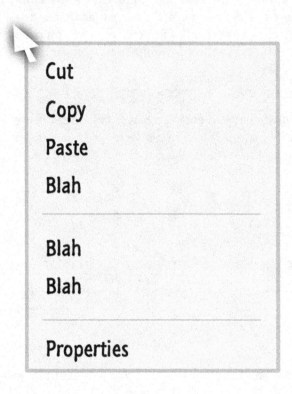

This menu is known as the **context menu**. The `contextmenu` event is fired just before this menu appears.

Now, you may be wondering why anybody would want an event for this situation. To be completely honest with you (as opposed to all the other times when I've been lying), there is only one primary reason to listen for this event. That reason has to do with preventing this menu from appearing when you right-click or use a context menu keyboard button or shortcut.

Here is an example of how you can **prevent** the **default** behavior where the context menu appears:

```
document.addEventListener("contextmenu", hideMenu, false);

function hideMenu(e) {
```

```
    e.preventDefault();
}
```

The `preventDefault` method on any type of `Event` stops whatever the default behavior is from actually happening. Because the `contextmenu` event is fired before the menu appears, calling `preventDefault` on it ensures the context menu never shows up. The default behavior has been prevented from running. Yes, this is also the second time I'm mentioning this property. As you know, I am being paid by the word (ha, ha).

With all of that said, I can think of a billion other ways you could prevent the context menu from appearing without using an event for dealing with all of this, but that's the way things are...for now!

The MouseEvent Properties

Let's get a little bit more specific. All of the mouse events we've seen so far are based around `MouseEvent`. Normally, this is the kind of factoid you keep under your hat for trivia night and ignore. This time around, though, this detail is important because `MouseEvent` brings with it a number of properties that make working with the mouse easier. Let's look at some of them.

The Global Mouse Position

The `screenX` and `screenY` properties return the distance your mouse cursor is from the top-left location of your primary monitor:

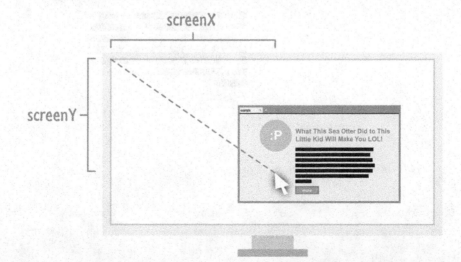

Here is a very simple example of the `screenX` and `screenY` properties at work:

```
document.addEventListener("mousemove", mouseMoving, false);

function mouseMoving(e) {
  console.log(e.screenX + " " + e.screenY);
}
```

It doesn't matter what other margin/padding/offset/layout craziness you may have going on in your page. The values returned are always going to be the distance between where your mouse is now and where the top-left corner of your primary monitor is.

The Mouse Position Inside the Browser

The `clientX` and `clientY` properties return the x and y position of the mouse relative to your browser's (technically, the browser viewport's) top-left corner:

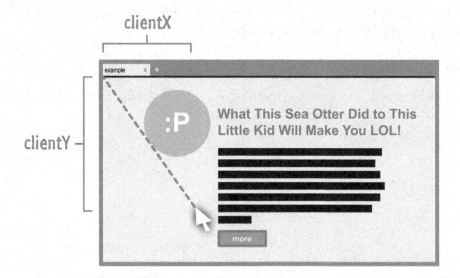

The code for this is nothing exciting:

```
let button = document.querySelector("#myButton");
document.addEventListener("mousemove", mouseMoving, false);
```

```
function mouseMoving(e) {
  console.log(e.clientX + " " + e.clientY);
}
```

You just call the `clientX` and `clientY` properties of the event argument that got passed in to the event handler to get the values.

Detecting Which Button Was Clicked

Mice often have multiple buttons or ways to simulate multiple buttons. The most common button configuration involves a left button, a right button, and a middle button (often a click on your mouse wheel). To figure out which mouse button was pressed, you have the `button` property. This property returns a **0** if the left mouse button was pressed, a **1** if the middle button was pressed, and a **2** if the right mouse button was pressed:

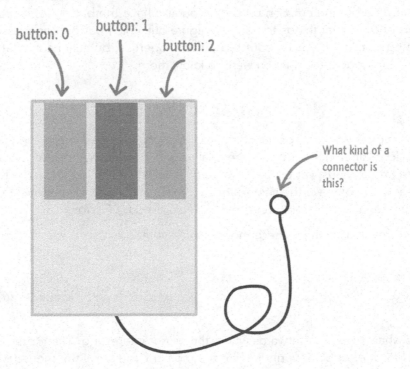

The code for using the `button` property to check for which button was pressed looks exactly as you would expect:

```
document.addEventListener("mousedown", buttonPress, false);

function buttonPress(e) {
  if (e.button == 0) {
    console.log("Left mouse button pressed!");
  } else if (e.button == 1) {
    console.log("Middle mouse button pressed!");
  } else if (e.button == 2) {
    console.log("Right mouse button pressed!");
  } else {
    console.log("Things be crazy up in here!!!");
  }
}
```

In addition to the button property, you also have the buttons and properties that sort of do similar things to help you figure out which button was pressed. I'm not going to talk too much about those two properties, but just know that they exist. You can google them if you want to know more.

Dealing with the Mouse Wheel

The mouse wheel is special compared to everything else we've seen so far. The obvious difference is that we are dealing with a wheel as opposed to a button. The less obvious, yet probably more relevant, detail is that you have two events to deal with. You have the mousewheel event that is used by Internet Explorer and Chrome, and the DOMMouseScroll event used by Firefox.

The way you listen for these mouse wheel-related events is just the usual:

```
document.addEventListener("mousewheel", mouseWheeling, false);
document.addEventListener("DOMMouseScroll", mouseWheeling, false);
```

It's what happens afterwards where things get interesting. The mousewheel and DOMMouseScroll events will fire the moment you scroll the mouse wheel in any direction. For all practical purposes, the direction you are scrolling the mouse wheel is important. To get that information, we'll need to go spelunking in the event handler to find the event argument.

The event arguments for a `mousewheel` event contain a property known as `wheelDelta`. For the `DOMMouseScroll` event, you have the `detail` property on the event argument. Both of these properties are similar in that their values change from positive or negative depending on what direction you scroll the mouse wheel. The thing to note is that they are inconsistent in what sign they go with. The `wheelDelta` property associated with the `mousewheel` event is positive when you scroll up on the mouse wheel, and it is negative when you scroll down. The exact opposite holds true for `DOMMouseScroll`'s `detail` property. This property is negative when you scroll up, and it is positive when you scroll down.

Handling this `wheelDelta` and `detail` inconsistency is pretty simple, as you can see in the following snippet:

```
function mouseWheeling(e) {
  let scrollDirection;
  let wheelData = e.wheelDelta;

  if (wheelData) {
    scrollDirection = wheelData;
  } else {
    scrollDirection = -1 * e.detail;
  }

  if (scrollDirection > 0) {
    console.log("Scrolling up! " + scrollDirection);
  } else {
    console.log("Scrolling down! " + scrollDirection);
  }
}
```

The `scrollDirection` variable stores the value contained by the `wheelData` property or the `detail` property. Depending on whether this value is positive or negative, you can adjust your code to react to the scroll direction accordingly.

THE ABSOLUTE MINIMUM

Generally, it is true that if you know how to just work with one event, you pretty much know how to work with all other events. The only thing you need to know is which event corresponds to what you are trying to do. The mouse events are a good introduction to working with events because they are very easy to play with. They aren't very fussy, and the things you learn about them you will use in almost all apps you build.

? Ask a question: **https://forum.kirupa.com**

✔ Practice by building real apps: **https://bit.ly/coding_exercises**

Errors/known issues: **https://bit.ly/javascript_errata**

39

KEYBOARD EVENTS

We spend a lot of time in various applications tapping away at our keyboards. In case you are wondering what a keyboard looks like, Figure 39.1 features a sweet one from I think about a hundred years ago.

This is a keyboard!

FIGURE 39.1

What a keyboard might look like...in a museum probably

Anyway, our computers (more specifically, the applications that run on them) just know how to deal with our board of plastic depressible keys. You never really think about it. Sometimes, however, depending on what you are doing, you will have to think about them. In fact, you'll have to deal with them and make them work properly. Better cancel any plans you have because this chapter is going to be pretty intense!

By the end of this chapter, you will learn all about how to listen to the keyboard events, what each of those events do, and you'll see a handful of examples that highlight some handy tricks that may come in, um, *handy*.

Meet the Keyboard Events

To work with keyboards in an HTML document, you will need to familiarize yourself with three events:

- `keydown`
- `keypress`
- `keyup`

Given what these events are called, you probably already have a vague idea of what each event does. The `keydown` event is fired when you press down on a key on your keyboard. The `keyup` event is fired when you release a key you just pressed. Both of these events work on any key you interact with.

The `keypress` event is a special bird. At first glance, it seems like this event is fired when you press down on any key. Despite what the name claims, the `keypress` event is fired only when you press down on a key that displays a character (letter, number, and the like). What this means is somewhat confusing, but it makes sense in its own twisted way.

If you press and release a character key such as the **Y** key, you will see the `keydown`, `keypress`, and `keyup` events fired in order. The `keydown` and `keyup` events fire because the **Y** key is simply a key to them. The `keypress` event is fired because the **Y** key is a character key. If you press and release a key that doesn't display anything on the screen (such as the spacebar, arrow keys, or function keys), all you will see are the `keydown` and `keyup` events fired.

This difference is subtle but very important when you want to ensure your key presses are actually overheard by your application.

SAY WHAT?

It is weird that an event called `keypress` doesn't fire when any key is pressed. Maybe this event should be called something else like `characterkeypress`, but that is probably a moo point. (What is a "moo point"? Well...**http://bit.ly/kirupaMoo**.)

Using These Events

The way you listen for the `keydown`, `keypress`, and `keyup` events is similar to any other event you may want to listen for and react to. You call `addEventListener` on the element that will be dealing with these events, specify the event you want to listen for, specify the event-handling function that gets called when the event is overheard, and provide a **true/false** value indicating whether you want this event to bubble.

Here is an example of me listening to our three keyboard events on the `window` object:

```
window.addEventListener("keydown", dealWithKeyboard, false);
window.addEventListener("keypress", dealWithKeyboard, false);
window.addEventListener("keyup", dealWithKeyboard, false);


function dealWithKeyboard(e) {
  // gets called when any of the keyboard events are overheard
}
```

If any of these events are overheard, the `dealWithKeyboard` event handler gets called. In fact, this event handler will get called three times if you happen to press down on a character key. This is all pretty straightforward, so let's kick everything up a few notches and go beyond the basics in the next few sections.

The Keyboard Event Properties

When an event handler that reacts to a keyboard event is called, a Keyboard event argument is passed in. Let's revisit our dealWithKeyboard event handler you saw earlier. In that event handler, the keyboard event is represented by the e argument that is passed in:

```
function dealWithKeyboard(e) {
    // gets called when any of the keyboard events are overheard
}
```

This argument contains a handful of properties:

- **KeyCode**: Every key you press on your keyboard has a number associated with it. This read-only property returns that number.

- **CharCode**: This property only exists on event arguments returned by the keypress event, and it contains the ASCII code for whatever character key you pressed.

- **ctrlKey, altKey, shiftKey**: These three properties return a **true** if the **Ctrl** key, **Alt** key, or **Shift** key is pressed.

- **MetaKey**: The metaKey property is similar to the ctrlKey, altKey, and shiftKey properties in that it returns a **true** if the meta key is pressed. The meta key is the **Windows** key on Windows keyboards and the **command** key on Apple keyboards.

The Keyboard event contains a few other properties, but the ones in the preceding list are the most interesting ones. With these properties, you can check for which key was pressed and react accordingly. In the next few sections, you'll see some examples of this.

 CAUTION   The charCode and keyCode properties are currently marked as deprecated by the web standards people at the W3C. Their replacement might be the mostly unsupported code property. Just be aware of this and be ready to update your code in the future when whichever successor to charCode and keyCode has taken its rightful place on the throne.

Some Examples

Now that you've seen the horribly boring basics of how to work with keyboard events, let's look at some examples that clarify (or potentially confuse!) everything you've seen so far.

Checking That a Particular Key Was Pressed

The following example shows how to use the keyCode property to check if a particular key was pressed:

```
window.addEventListener("keydown", checkKeyPressed, false);


function checkKeyPressed(e) {
  if (e.keyCode == 65) {
    console.log("The 'a' key is pressed.");
  }
}
```

The particular key I check is the **A** key. Internally, this key is mapped to the keyCode value of **65**. In case you never memorized all of them in school, you can find a handy list of all key and character codes at **http://bit.ly/kirupaKeyCode**. Please do not memorize every single code from that list. There are far more interesting things to memorize instead.

Note that the charCode and keyCode values for a particular key are not the same. Also, the charCode is only returned if the event that triggered your event handler was a keypress. In our example, the keydown event would not contain anything useful for the charCode property.

If you wanted to check the charCode and use the keypress event, here is what the preceding example would look like:

```
window.addEventListener("keypress", checkKeyPressed, false);


function checkKeyPressed(e) {
  if (e.charCode == 97) {
    console.log("The 'a' key is pressed.");
  }
}
```

The `charCode` for the **A** key is **97**. Again, refer to the table of key and character codes I referenced earlier for such details.

Doing Something When the Arrow Keys Are Pressed

We see this most often in games where pressing the arrow keys does something interesting. The following snippet of code shows how that is done:

```
window.addEventListener("keydown", moveSomething, false);

function moveSomething(e) {
  switch (e.keyCode) {
    case 37:
      // left key pressed
      break;
    case 38:
      // up key pressed
      break;
    case 39:
      // right key pressed
      break;
    case 40:
      // down key pressed
      break;
  }
}
```

Again, this should be pretty straightforward. And, would you believe it—it's an actual use for the `switch` statement you learned about forever ago in Chapter 4, "Conditional Statements: if, else, and switch."

Detecting Multiple Key Presses

Now, this is going to be epic! An interesting case revolves around detecting when we need to react to multiple key presses. What follows is an example of how to do that:

```
window.addEventListener("keydown", keysPressed, false);
window.addEventListener("keyup", keysReleased, false);
```

```javascript
let keys = [];

function keysPressed(e) {
  // store an entry for every key pressed
  keys[e.keyCode] = true;

  // Ctrl + Shift + 5
  if (keys[17] && keys[16] && keys[53]) {
    // do something
  }

  // Ctrl + f
  if (keys[17] && keys[70]) {
    // do something

    // prevent default browser behavior
    e.preventDefault();
  }
}

function keysReleased(e) {
  // mark keys that were released
  keys[e.keyCode] = false;
}
```

Going into great detail about this will require another chapter by itself, but let's just look at how this works very briefly.

First, we have a keys array that stores every single key you press:

```javascript
let keys = [];
```

As keys get pressed, the keysPressed event handler gets called:

```javascript
function keysPressed(e) {
  // store an entry for every key pressed
```

```
  keys[e.keyCode] = true;

  // Ctrl + Shift + 5
  if (keys[17] && keys[16] && keys[53]) {
    // do something
  }

  // Ctrl + f
  if (keys[17] && keys[70]) {
    // do something

    // prevent default browser behavior
    e.preventDefault();
  }
}
```

When a key gets released, the `keysReleased` event handler gets called:

```
function keysReleased(e) {
  // mark keys that were released
  keys[e.keyCode] = false;
}
```

Notice how these two event handlers work with each other. As keys get pressed, an entry gets created for them in the `keys` array with a value of **true**. When keys get released, those same keys are marked with a value of **false**. The existence of the keys you press in the array is superficial. It is the values they store that is actually important.

As long as nothing interrupts your event handlers from getting called properly, such as an alert window, you will get a one-to-one mapping between keys pressed and keys released as viewed through the lens of the `keys` array. With all of this said, the checks for seeing which combination of keys has been pressed are handled in the `keysPressed` event handler. The following highlighted lines show how this works:

```
function keysPressed(e) {
  // store an entry for every key pressed
```

```
  keys[e.keyCode] = true;

  // Ctrl + Shift + 5
  if (keys[17] && keys[16] && keys[53]) {
    // do something
  }


  // Ctrl + f
  if (keys[17] && keys[70]) {
    // do something


    // prevent default browser behavior
    e.preventDefault();
  }
}
```

There is one thing you need to keep in mind. Some key combinations result in your browser doing something. To avoid your browser from doing its own thing, use the `preventDefault` method, as indicated here, when checking to see if **Ctrl+F** is being used:

```
function keysPressed(e) {
  // store an entry for every key pressed
  keys[e.keyCode] = true;

  // Ctrl + Shift + 5
  if (keys[17] && keys[16] && keys[53]) {
    // do something
  }


  // Ctrl + f
  if (keys[17] && keys[70]) {
    // do something


    // prevent default browser behavior
```

```
        e.preventDefault();
    }
}
```

The `preventDefault` method prevents an event from triggering a default behavior. In this case, it was preventing the browser from showing the Find dialog. Different key combinations will trigger different reactions by the browser, so keep this method handy to put a stop to those reactions.

Anyway, looking at the code in aggregate, you have a basic blueprint for how to check for multiple key presses easily.

THE ABSOLUTE MINIMUM

The keyboard is pretty important when it comes to how people interact with their computer-like devices. Despite the keyboard's importance, you often won't have to deal with one directly. Your browser, the various text-related controls/elements, and everything in-between just handle it as you would expect, by default. There are certain kinds of applications where you may want to deal with a keyboard, though, which is why I wrote this chapter.

This chapter started off in the most boring way possible, by explaining how to work with the `Keyboard` events and their event arguments. Along the way, things (hopefully) got more interesting as you saw several examples that addressed common things you would do when dealing with the keyboard in code.

- ? Ask a question: **https://forum.kirupa.com**
- ✔ Practice by building real apps: **https://bit.ly/coding_exercises**
- 📖 Errors/known issues: **https://bit.ly/javascript_errata**

IN THIS CHAPTER

- Learn about all the events that fire as your page is getting loaded
- Understand what happens behind the scenes during a page load
- Fiddle with the various script element attributes that control exactly when your code runs

40

PAGE LOAD EVENTS AND OTHER STUFF

An important part of working with JavaScript is ensuring that your code runs at the right time. Things aren't always as simple as putting your code at the bottom of your page and expecting everything to work once your page has loaded. Yes, we are going to revisit some things we looked at in Chapter 10, "Where Should Your Code Live?" Every now and then, you may have to add some extra code to ensure your code doesn't run before the page is ready. Sometimes, you may even have to put your code at the top of your page...like an animal!

There are many factors that affect what the "right time" really is to run your code, and in this chapter, we're going to look at those factors and narrow down what you should do to a handful of guidelines.

The Things That Happen During Page Load

Let's start at the very beginning. You click a link or press **Enter** after typing in a URL and, if the stars are aligned properly, your page loads. All of that seems pretty simple and takes up a very tiny sliver of time to complete from beginning to end:

In that short period of time between you wanting to load a page and your page loading, a lot of relevant and interesting stuff happens that you need to know more about. One example of the relevant and interesting stuff that happens is that any code specified on the page will run. When exactly the code runs depends on a combination of the following things that all come alive at some point while your page is getting loaded:

- The `DOMContentLoaded` event
- The `load` Event
- The `async` attribute for script elements
- The `defer` attribute for script elements
- The location your scripts live in the DOM

Don't worry if you don't know what these things are. You'll learn (or re-learn) what all of these things do and the effect they have when your code runs really soon. Before we get there, though, let's take a quick detour and look at the three stages of a page load.

Stage Numero Uno

The first stage is when your browser is about to start loading a new page:

Stage #1: Nothing Much Going On

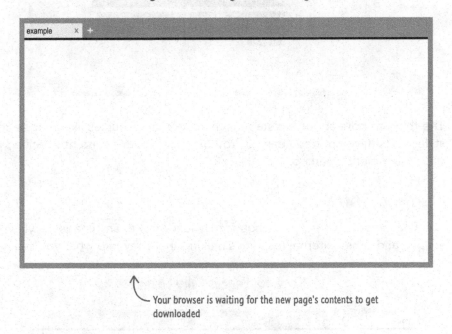

Your browser is waiting for the new page's contents to get downloaded

At this stage, there isn't anything interesting going on. A request has been made to load a page, but nothing has been downloaded yet.

Stage Numero Dos

Things get a bit more exciting with the second stage, where the raw markup and DOM of your page has been loaded and parsed:

Stage #2: The DOM Is Ready

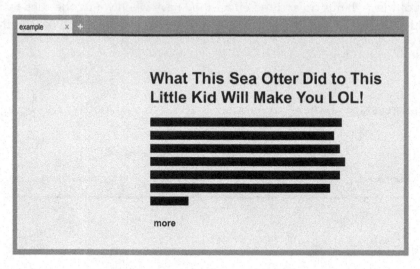

The thing to note about this stage is that external resources like images and linked stylesheets have not been parsed. You only see the raw content specified by your page/document's markup.

Stage Numero Three

The final stage is where your page is fully loaded with any images, stylesheets, scripts, and other external resources making their way into what you see:

Stage #3: Page Is Fully Loaded

This is the stage where your browser's loading indicators stop animating, and this is also the stage you almost always find yourself in when interacting with your HTML document. That said, sometimes you'll find yourself in an in-between state where 99 percent of your page has loaded, with only some random thing taking forever to load. If you've been to one of those viral/buzz/feedy sites, you'll totally know what I am talking about.

Now that you have a basic idea of the three stages your document goes through when loading content, let's move forward to the more interesting stuff. Keep these three stages at the tip of your fingers (or under your hat if you are wearing one while reading this), as we'll refer back to these stages a few times in the following sections.

The DOMContentLoaded and load Events

Two events represent the two important milestones while your page loads: DOM-ContentLoaded and load. The DOMContentLoaded event fires at the end of Stage #2 when your page's DOM is fully parsed. The load event fires at the end of Stage #3 once your page has fully loaded. You can use these events to time when exactly you want your code to run.

The following is a snippet of these events in action:

```
document.addEventListener("DOMContentLoaded", theDomHasLoaded,
false);
window.addEventListener("load", pageFullyLoaded, false);


function theDomHasLoaded(e) {
  // do something
}


function pageFullyLoaded(e) {
  // do something again
}
```

You use these events just like you would any other event, but the main thing to note about them is that you need to listen to DOMContentLoaded from the document element and load from the window element.

Now that we've got the boring technical details out of the way, why are these events important? Simple. If you have any code that relies on working with the DOM, such as anything that uses the `querySelector` or `querySelectorAll` functions, you want to ensure your code runs only after your DOM has been fully loaded. If you try to access your DOM before it has fully loaded, you may get incomplete results or no results at all.

Here is an awesome, extreme example from Kyle Murray (https://twitter.com/krilnon) that should help explain this:

```html
<!DOCTYPE html>
<html>

<head>
  <script>
      // try to analyze the book's meaning here
  </script>
</head>

<body>
  [INSERT ENTIRE COPY OF /WAR AND PEACE/ HERE]
</body>

</html>
```

War and Peace is a massively large novel. If all of its contents were pasted into the body element as shown above, it will take our browser some time to fully make sense of it. If we happen to have any script preceding it that tries to process the contents inside our body element, that script would run far sooner than our browser would have gotten to the end of *War and Peace*.

A surefire way to ensure you never get into a situation where your code runs before your DOM is ready is to listen for the `DOMContentLoaded` event and let all of the code that relies on the DOM to run only after that event is overheard:

```js
document.addEventListener("DOMContentLoaded", theDomHasLoaded,
false);
```

```
function theDomHasLoaded(e) {
  let headings = document.querySelectorAll("h2");


  // do something with the images
}
```

For cases where you want your code to run only after your page has fully loaded, use the `load` event. In my years of doing things in JavaScript, I never had too much use for the `load` event at the document level, outside of checking the final dimensions of a loaded image or creating a crude progress bar to indicate progress. Your mileage may vary, but I doubt it.

Scripts and Their Location in the DOM

In Chapter 8, "Variable Scope," we looked at the various ways in which you can have scripts appear in your document. You saw that the position of your script elements in the DOM affects when they run. In this section, we again emphasize that simple truth and go a few steps further.

To review, a simple script element can be some code stuck inline somewhere:

```
<script>
  let number = Math.random() * 100;
  console.log("A random number is: " + number);
</script>
```

A simple script element can also be something that references some code from an external file:

```
<script src="/foo/something.js"></script>
```

Now, here is the important detail about these elements. Your browser parses your DOM sequentially from the top to the bottom. Any script elements that are found along the way will get parsed in the order they appear in the DOM.

Here is a very simple example where you have many script elements:

```html
<!DOCTYPE html>
<html>

<body>
  <h1>Example</h1>
  <script>
    console.log("inline 1");
  </script>
  <script src="external1.js"></script>
  <script>
    console.log("inline 2");
  </script>
  <script src="external2.js"></script>
  <script>
    console.log("inline 3");
  </script>
</body>

</html>
```

It doesn't matter if the script contains inline code or references something external. All scripts are treated the same and run in the order in which they appear in your document. Using the preceding example, the order in which the scripts will run is as follows: **inline 1**, **external 1**, **inline 2**, **external 2**, and **inline 3**.

Now, here is a really, REALLY important detail to be aware of. Because your DOM gets parsed from top to bottom, your script element has access to all of the DOM elements that were already parsed. Your script has no access to any DOM elements that have not yet been parsed. Say, what?!

Let's say you have a script element that is at the bottom of your page just above the closing body element:

```html
<!DOCTYPE html>
<html>
```

```
<body>
  <h1>Example</h1>


  <p>

    Quisque faucibus, quam sollicitudin pulvinar dignissim, nunc
velit sodales leo, vel vehicula odio lectus vitae
    mauris. Sed sed magna augue. Vestibulum tristique cursus orci,
accumsan posuere nunc congue sed. Ut pretium sit amet
    eros non consectetur. Quisque tincidunt eleifend justo, quis
molestie tellus venenatis non. Vivamus interdum urna ut
    augue rhoncus, eu scelerisque orci dignissim. In commodo purus
id purus tempus commodo.
  </p>


  <button>Click Me</button>


  <script src="something.js"></script>
</body>

</html>
```

When **something.js** runs, it has the ability to access all the DOM elements that appear just above it, such as the h1, p, and button elements. If your script element was at the very top of your document, it wouldn't have any knowledge of the DOM elements that appear below it:

```
<!DOCTYPE html>
<html>


<body>
  <script src="something.js"></script>


  <h1>Example</h1>


  <p>
```

```
        Quisque faucibus, quam sollicitudin pulvinar dignissim, nunc
velit sodales leo, vel vehicula odio lectus vitae
      mauris. Sed sed magna augue. Vestibulum tristique cursus orci,
accumsan posuere nunc congue sed. Ut pretium sit amet
      eros non consectetur. Quisque tincidunt eleifend justo, quis
molestie tellus venenatis non. Vivamus interdum urna ut
      augue rhoncus, eu scelerisque orci dignissim. In commodo purus
id purus tempus commodo.
   </p>


   <button>Click Me</button>


</body>

</html>
```

By putting your script element at the bottom of your page, as shown earlier, the end behavior is identical to what you would get if you had code that explicitly listened for the DOMContentLoaded event. If you can guarantee that your scripts will appear toward the end of your document after your DOM elements, you can avoid following the whole DOMContentLoaded approach described in the previous section. Now, if you really want to have your script elements at the top of your DOM, ensure that all of the code that relies on the DOM runs after the DOMContentLoaded event gets fired.

Here is the thing. I'm a huge fan of putting script elements at the bottom of the DOM. There is another reason besides easy DOM access why I recommend having your scripts live toward the bottom of the page. When a script element is being parsed, your browser stops everything else on the page from running while the code is executing. If you have a really long-running script or your external script takes its sweet time in getting downloaded, your HTML page will appear frozen. If your DOM is only partially parsed at this point, your page will also look incomplete in addition to being frozen. Unless you are Facebook, you probably want to avoid having your page look frozen for no reason.

Script Elements: async and defer

In the previous section, I explained how a script element's position in the DOM determines when it runs. All of that only applies to what I call **simple** script elements. To be part of the non-simple world, script elements that point to external scripts can have the `defer` and `async` attributes set on them:

```
<script async src="myScript.js"></script>
<script defer src="somethingSomethingDarkSide.js"></script>
```

These attributes alter when your script runs independent of where in the DOM they actually show up, so let's look at how they end up altering your script.

async

The `async` attribute allows a script to run asynchronously:

```
<script async src="someRandomScript.js"></script>
```

If you recall from the previous section, if a script element is being parsed, it could block your browser from being responsive and usable. By setting the `async` attribute on your script element, you avoid that problem altogether. Your script will run whenever it is able to, but it won't block the rest of your browser from doing its thing.

This casualness in running your code is pretty awesome, but you must realize that your scripts marked as `async` will not always run in order. You could have a case where several scripts marked as `async` will run in an order different from what was specified in your markup. The only guarantee you have is that your scripts marked with `async` will start running at some mysterious point before the `load` event gets fired.

defer

The `defer` attribute is a bit different from `async`:

```
<script defer src="someRandomScript.js"></script>
```

Scripts marked with `defer` run in the order in which they were defined, but they only get executed at the end, just a few moments before the `DOMContent-Loaded` event gets fired. Take a look at the following example:

```
<!DOCTYPE html>
<html>

<body>
  <h1>Example</h1>
  <script defer src="external1.js"></script>
  <script>
    console.log("inline 1");
  </script>
  <script src="external2.js"></script>
  <script>
    console.log("inline 2");
  </script>
  <script defer src="external3.js"></script>
  <script>
    console.log("inline 3");
  </script>
</body>

</html>
```

Take a second and tell the nearest human/pet the order in which these scripts will run. It's okay if you don't provide them with any context. If they love you, they'll understand.

Anyway, your scripts will execute in the following order: **inline 1**, **external 1**, **inline 2**, **inline 3**, **external 3**, and **external 2**. The **external 3** and **external 2** scripts are marked as `defer`, and that's why they appear at the very end, despite being declared in different locations in your markup.

THE ABSOLUTE MINIMUM

In the previous sections, we looked at all sorts of factors that influence when your code will execute. The following diagram summarizes everything you saw into a series of lines and rectangles:

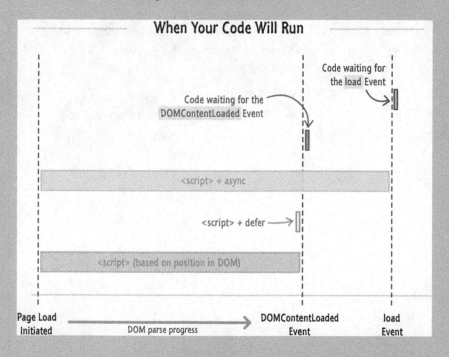

Now, here is probably what you are looking for. When is the right time to load your JavaScript? The answer is as follows:

1. Place your script references below your DOM directly above your closing body element.

2. Unless you are creating a library that others will use, don't complicate your code by listening to the DOMContentLoaded or load events. Instead, see the previous point.

3. Mark your scripts referencing external files with the `defer` attribute.

4. If you have code that doesn't rely on your DOM being loaded and runs as part of teeing things off for other scripts in your document, you can place this script at the top of your page with the `async` attribute set on it.

That's it. I think those four steps will cover almost 90 percent of all your cases to ensure your code runs at the right time. For more advanced scenarios, you should definitely take a look at a third-party library like **require.js**, which gives you greater control over when your code will run.

? Ask a question: **https://forum.kirupa.com**

✔ Practice by building real apps: **https://bit.ly/coding_exercises**

🐣 Errors/known issues: **https://bit.ly/javascript_errata**

IN THIS CHAPTER

- Learn how to load script files efficiently
- Learn how to use the appropriate script load events to customize when your code runs

41

LOADING SCRIPT FILES DYNAMICALLY

In the previous Chapter 40, "Page Load Events and Other Stuff," a part of what we looked at were the various ways we have to load and run external JavaScript files in our pages. All of these various ways assumed we knew exactly what script file we wanted to load with the `src` attribute already pointing to our file:

```
<script src="https://www.example.com/foo.js">
</script>
```

Now, what if you were in the situation where you didn't know what script file you wanted to load at the time your page is loading? What if you had to choose between loading **foo.js** or **bar.js** depending on what actions the user took? Having a hardcoded script element doesn't really work well in this case. What does work well is having a way to load our script file dynamically! In this short chapter, we will go into greater detail about it.

The Basic Technique

For loading a script file dynamically using JavaScript, the basic steps are as follows:

1. Create the script element.

2. Set the `src` attribute on the script element to point to the file we want to load.

3. Add the script element to the DOM.

This numbered list turned into code looks like the following three lines:

```
let myScript = document.createElement("script");
myScript.setAttribute("src", "https://www.example.com/foo.js");
document.body.appendChild(myScript);
```

The `myScript` variable stores a reference to our newly created script element. The `setAttribute` method allows us to set the `src` value for the script we'd like to load. We seal the deal by adding our script element to the bottom of our body element via `appendChild`. If some of these steps seem a bit outlandish, Chapter 33, "Creating and Removing DOM Elements," will get you familiarized (or re-familiarized!) with the fun world of DOM manipulation.

To see this code in action as part of a fully working example, create a new HTML document and add/copy/paste the following content into it:

```
<!DOCTYPE html>
<html>

<head>
```

```html
  <title>Dynamic Script Loading</title>
  <style>
    body {
      padding: 50px;
      background-color: #EAC5D8;
    }

    h1 {
      font-family: sans-serif;
      font-size: 128px;
      margin: 0;
      line-height: 1em;
      font-weight: bold;
      color: #D68FB5;
    }
  </style>
</head>

<body>
  <h1>I am <br>in your<br> code!</h1>

  <script>
    let myCoolCode = document.createElement("script");
    myCoolCode.setAttribute("src",
"https://www.kirupa.com/js/easing.js");
    document.body.appendChild(myCoolCode);
  </script>

</body>

</html>
```

Take a moment to look at all that is contained here. We have some HTML and CSS, and by now that isn't anything exciting to write home about. Mainly, we have a script element that contains some code to dynamically load a file called **easing. js** and append it to the bottom of our body element. To see all of this in action, save your HTML document and preview it in your favorite browser.

What you will see in your favorite browser will look something like the following:

What we visually see doesn't really tell us much. What we need to do is go undercover and inspect the live version of our DOM! For that, we need to bring up the browser developer tools and inspect the page to see exactly what the browser sees. When we do this, notice that our dynamically created script element shows up in the DOM:

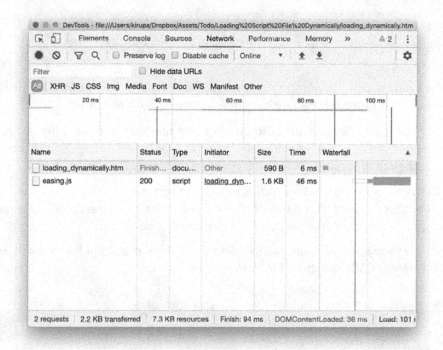

```
Elements    Console    Sources    Network    Performance

<!doctype html>
<html>
  ▶ <head>…</head>
  ▼ <body>
    ▶ <h1>…</h1>
    ▼ <script>
          var myCoolCode = document.createElement("script");
          myCoolCode.setAttribute("src",
      "https://www.kirupa.com/js/easing.js");
          document.body.appendChild(myCoolCode);

      </script>
...   <script src="https://www.kirupa.com/js/easing.js"></script>
    </body>
</html>
```

html   body   **script**

To go even further, we can inspect the network traffic and see that the **easing.js** script file referenced by our script element gets loaded as well:

If **easing.js** isn't showing up for you, refresh the page with the **Network** tab open. That will ensure you can see the external script file being requested and then loaded.

At this point, we have looked at the basics of how to load an external script file using just a few lines of JavaScript. This doesn't mean we have to be done, though. There are some quirks and edge cases that might bite us if we aren't careful, so the next couple of sections will prepare us to not get bitten...or bite back!

Running Our Dynamically Loaded Script First

Adding a script element to the bottom of the body element means that our page will render first without being blocked by our JavaScript from loading and executing. That is usually the correct behavior we want. Now, there will be cases when you want the JavaScript to run first ahead of anything else your page might do. To handle those cases, we need to adjust our code.

Take a look at what we are now doing:

```
let myScript = document.createElement("script");
myScript.setAttribute("src", "https://www.example.com/foo.js");
myScript.setAttribute("async", "false");


let head = document.head;
head.insertBefore(myScript, head.firstElementChild);
```

Two new things are going on in the code that ensure our external script file is loaded and runs before anything else on the page is rendered:

1. We set the `async` attribute on our script element to **false**. Why do we do that? It is because dynamically loaded script files are loaded asynchronously by default. We want to explicitly override that default behavior.

2. We ensure we load our script before the rest of the page loads. Adding our script element at the top of the head element is the best place to ensure it runs ahead of anything else the page might be up to.

If we modify our full example to load our external script file first, here is what the full HTML, CSS, and JS will look like:

```
<!DOCTYPE html>
<html>
```

```html
<head>
  <title>Dynamic Script Loading</title>
  <style>
    body {
      padding: 50px;
      background-color: #EAC5D8;
    }

    h1 {
      font-family: sans-serif;
      font-size: 128px;
      margin: 0;
      line-height: 1em;
      font-weight: bold;
      color: #D68FB5;
    }
  </style>

  <script>
    let myCoolCode = document.createElement("script");
    myCoolCode.setAttribute("src",
"https://www.kirupa.com/js/easing.js");
    myCoolCode.setAttribute("async", "false");

    let head = document.head;
    head.insertBefore(myCoolCode, head.firstElementChild);
  </script>
</head>

<body>
  <h1>I am <br>in your<br> code!</h1>
</body>

</html>
```

One additional change the larger example calls out is relevant here. The code for actually loading our external script file **needs to be inside the head element** as well. If we kept this code at the bottom of the page like we saw earlier, our page will still render and load everything as usual before even realizing it needs to handle loading an external script file. At that point, it doesn't matter if our external script file is loaded from the top of the page or the bottom of the page. The page's DOM has already loaded.

Running Dependent Code After Our Script File Has Loaded

Before wrapping things up, we just have one last tidbit for dealing with dynamic script files. It is common to load an external script file and then call a function (or rely on something from the loaded script) immediately afterward. Here is one such example of what this traditionally looks like:

```
 8    <script src="https://cdn.jsdelivr.net/npm/docsearch.min.js"></script>
 9
10    <script>
11      docsearch({
12        apiKey: 'e59d8b56a7ba3ed403538ca3c82fe533',
13        indexName: 'kirupa',
14        inputSelector: '#sbi',
15        debug: false
16      })
17    </script>
```

The first script element loads **docsearch.min.js**. The second script element calls something dependent on **docsearch.min.js** loaded by the earlier script element. All of this just works because the browser handles this scenario naturally. Best of all, we get this behavior for free.

For dynamically loaded script files, if we want to ensure similar behavior, we have a small amount of extra work to do. This extra work involves listening to our script element's `load` event and, once this event is overheard, calling any dependent code afterward. This will make more sense when we look at the code:

```
let myScript = document.createElement("script");
myScript.setAttribute("src", "https://www.example.com/foo.js");
document.body.appendChild(myScript);
```

```
myScript.addEventListener("load", scriptLoaded, false);


function scriptLoaded() {
  console.log("Script is ready to rock and roll!");
}
```

Let's take a moment to walk through what is going on:

1. Our trusty old `myScript` element is loading **foo.js**.

2. Once **foo.js** fully loads and executes, `myScript` will fire the `load` event.

3. The `addEventListener` call that is listening for the `load` event will overhear it and, in turn, call the `scriptLoaded` event handler.

4. Any code that lives inside `scriptLoaded` can call and access any method or property that comes from **foo.js** and its contents.

If you need a fun refresher on how to work with events and event handlers, check out Chapter 36, "Events in JavaScript."

THE ABSOLUTE MINIMUM

As you and I build websites and apps that get increasingly more dynamic, we wouldn't want to overwhelm our users by loading every possible script file they may need up front. The techniques we looked at in this chapter highlight one way to break up when our script files load by, essentially, loading them on demand.

? Ask a question: **https://forum.kirupa.com**

✔ Practice by building real apps: **https://bit.ly/coding_exercises**

🖋 Errors/known issues: **https://bit.ly/javascript_errata**

IN THIS CHAPTER

- Learn to efficiently react to multiple events
- Revisit how events work for one last time

42

HANDLING EVENTS FOR MULTIPLE ELEMENTS

In its most basic case, an event listener deals with events fired from a single element:

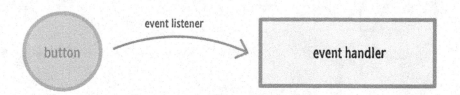

As you build more complicated things, the "one event handler for one element" mapping starts to show its limitation. The most common reason revolves around you creating elements dynamically using JavaScript. These elements you are creating can fire events that you may want to listen for and react to, and you can have anywhere from a handful of elements that need eventing support to many, MANY elements that need to have their events dealt with.

What you don't want to do is this:

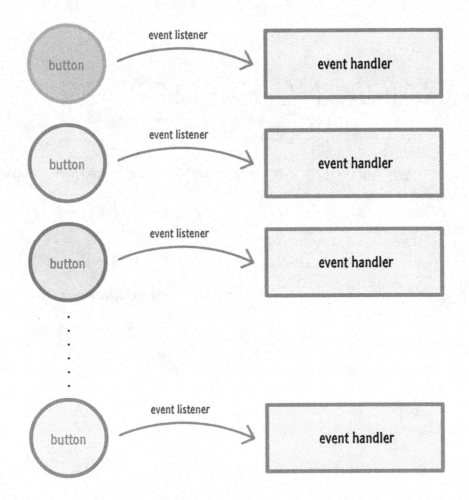

You don't want to create an event listener for each element **if the event listener is the same for all of them**. One reason is because your parents told you so. The other reason is because it is inefficient. Each of these elements carries around data about the same event listener and its properties, which can really start adding up the memory usage when you have a lot of content. Instead, what you want is a clean and fast way of handling events on multiple elements with minimal duplication and unnecessary things. What you want will look a little bit like this:

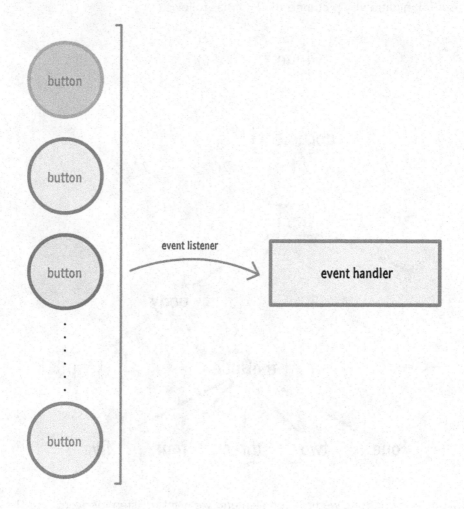

All of this sounds a bit crazy, right? Well, in this chapter, you will learn all about how non-crazy this is and how to implement it using just a few lines of JavaScript.

How to Do All This

Okay, at this point, you know how simple event handling works, where you have one element, one event listener, and one event handler. Despite how different the case with multiple elements may seem, by taking advantage of the disruptiveness of events, solving it is actually quite easy.

Imagine we have a case where we want to listen for the `click` event on any of the sibling elements whose `id` values are **one**, **two**, **three**, **four**, and **five**. Let's use our imagination by picturing the DOM as follows:

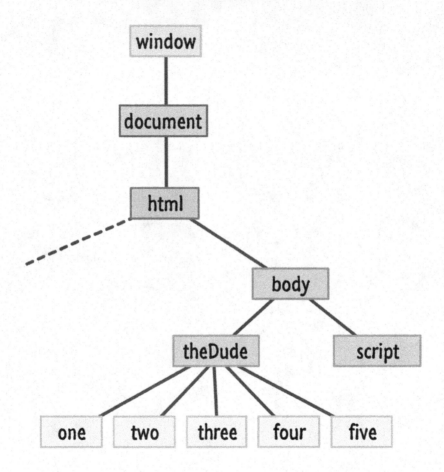

At the very bottom, we have the elements we want to listen for events on. They all share a common parent with an element whose `id` value is **theDude**. To solve our event-handling problems, let's look at a terrible solution followed by a good solution.

A Terrible Solution

Here is what we don't want to do. We don't want to have five event listeners for each of these buttons:

```
let oneElement = document.querySelector("#one");
let twoElement = document.querySelector("#two");
```

```
let threeElement = document.querySelector("#three");
let fourElement = document.querySelector("#four");
let fiveElement = document.querySelector("#five");

oneElement.addEventListener("click", doSomething, false);
twoElement.addEventListener("click", doSomething, false);
threeElement.addEventListener("click", doSomething, false);
fourElement.addEventListener("click", doSomething, false);
fiveElement.addEventListener("click", doSomething, false);

function doSomething(e) {
  let clickedItem = e.target.id;
  console.log("Hello " + clickedItem);
}
```

To echo what I mentioned in the chapter intro, the obvious reason is that you don't want to duplicate code. The other reason is that each of these elements now has its addEventListener property set. This is not a big deal for five elements. It starts to become a big deal when you have dozens or hundreds of elements, each taking up a small amount of memory. The other, OTHER reason is that your number of elements, depending on how adaptive or dynamic your user interface (UI) really is, can vary. Your app may add or remove elements depending on what the user is doing, so it would be difficult to keep track of all the individual event listeners that each object may or may not need. Having one overarching event handler makes this situation much more fun.

A Good Solution

The good solution for this mimics the figure you saw much earlier where we have just one event listener. I am going to confuse you first by describing how this works. Then I'll hopefully unconfuse you by showing the code and explaining in detail what exactly is going on. Here is the simple and confusing solution to this:

1. Create a single event listener on the parent element (**theDude**).

2. When any of the **one**, **two**, **three**, **four**, or **five** elements is clicked, rely on the propagation behavior that events possess and intercept the click event when they hit the parent **theDude** element.

3. (Optional) Stop the event propagation at the parent element just to avoid having to deal with the event obnoxiously running up and down the DOM tree.

I don't know about you, but I'm certainly confused after having read those three steps! Let's begin to unconfuse ourselves by starting with a figure that explains those steps visually:

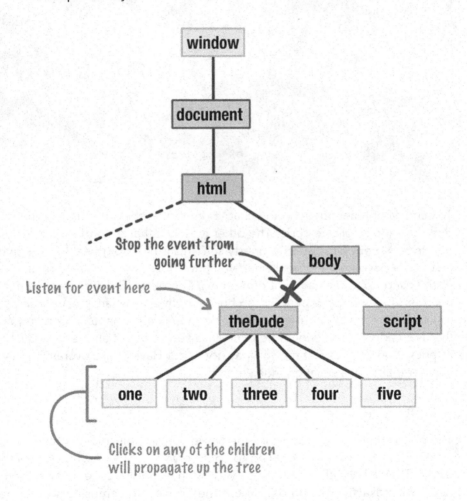

The last step in our quest for complete unconfusedness is the code that translates what the figure and the three steps represent:

```
let theParent = document.querySelector("#theDude");
theParent.addEventListener("click", doSomething, false);
```

```
function doSomething(e) {
  if (e.target != e.currentTarget) {
    let clickedItem = e.target.id;
    console.log("Hello " + clickedItem);
  }
  e.stopPropagation();
}
```

Take a moment to read and understand the code you see here. After seeing our initial goals and the figure, we will listen for the event on the parent **theDude** element:

```
let theParent = document.querySelector("#theDude");
theParent.addEventListener("click", doSomething, false);
```

There is only one event listener to handle this event, and that lonely creature is called doSomething:

```
function doSomething(e) {
  if (e.target != e.currentTarget) {
    let clickedItem = e.target.id;
    console.log("Hello " + clickedItem);
  }
  e.stopPropagation();
}
```

This event listener will get called each time **theDude** element is clicked, along with any children that get clicked as well. We only care about click events relating to the children, and the proper way to ignore clicks on this parent element is to simply avoid running any code if the element the click is from (aka the event target) is the same as the event listener target (that is, **theDude** element):

```
function doSomething(e) {
  if (e.target != e.currentTarget) {
    let clickedItem = e.target.id;
    console.log("Hello " + clickedItem);
```

```
    }
    e.stopPropagation();
}
```

The target of the event is represented by e.target, and the target element the event listener is attached to is represented by e.currentTarget. By simply checking that these values are not equal, you can ensure that the event handler doesn't react to events fired from the parent element that you don't care about.

To stop the event's propagation, we simply call the stopPropagation method:

```
function doSomething(e) {
  if (e.target != e.currentTarget) {
    let clickedItem = e.target.id;
    console.log("Hello " + clickedItem);
  }
  e.stopPropagation();
}
```

Notice that this code is actually outside of our if statement. This is because we want the event to stop traversing the DOM under all situations once it is overheard.

Putting It All Together

The end result of all of this code running is that you can click any of **theDude**'s children and listen for the event as it propagates up:

Because all of the event arguments are still unique to the element we are interacting with (that is, the source of the event), we are able to identify and special case the clicked element from inside the event handler despite the addEventListener being active only on the parent. The main thing to call out about this solution is that it satisfies the problems we set out to avoid. We only created one event listener. It doesn't matter how many children **theDude** ends up having. This approach is generic enough to accommodate all of them without any extra modification to our code. This also means that we should do some strict filtering if our **theDude** element ends up having children besides buttons and other elements we care about.

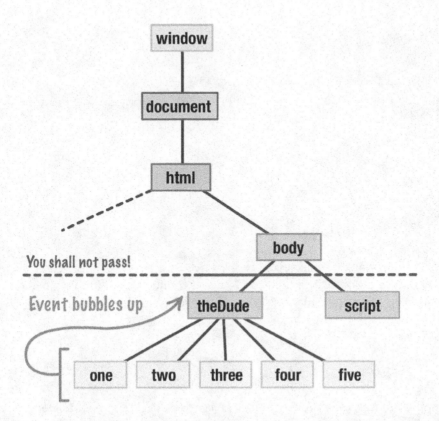

THE ABSOLUTE MINIMUM

For some time, I actually proposed a solution for our Multiple Element Eventing Conundrum (or **MEEC**, as the cool kids call it!) that was inefficient but didn't require you to duplicate many lines of code. Before many people pointed out the inefficiencies of it, I thought it was a valid solution.

This solution used a `for` loop to attach event listeners to all the children of a parent (or an array containing HTML elements). Here is what that code looked like:

```
let theParent = document.querySelector("#theDude");


for (let i = 0; i < theParent.children.length; i++) {
```

```
    let childElement = theParent.children[i];
    childElement.addEventListener('click', doSomething, false);
}

function doSomething(e) {
  let clickedItem = e.target.id;
  console.log("Hello " + clickedItem);
}
```

The end result was that this approach allowed us to listen for the `click` event directly on the children. The only code I wrote manually was this single event listener call that was parameterized to the appropriate child element based on where in the loop the code was:

```
childElement.addEventListener('click', doSomething, false);
```

The approach isn't great because each child element has an event listener associated with it. This goes back to our efficiency argument, where this approach unnecessarily wastes memory.

Now, if you do have a situation where your elements are spread throughout the DOM with no nearby common parent, using this approach on an array of HTML elements is not a bad way of solving the MEEC problem.

Anyway, as you start working with larger quantities of UI elements for games, data-visualization apps, and other HTML element-rich things, you'll end up having to use everything you saw here at least once...I hope. If all else fails, this chapter still served an important purpose. All of the stuff about event tunneling and capturing you saw earlier in the book clearly came in handy here. That's something!

?   Ask a question: **https://forum.kirupa.com**

✔   Practice by building real apps: **https://bit.ly/coding_exercises**

🖋   Errors/known issues: **https://bit.ly/javascript_errata**

43

USING EMOJIS IN HTML, CSS, AND JAVASCRIPT

From their humble beginnings in 1999, emojis are all the rage these days. They're no longer something only people half our age use to communicate. You and I use them all the time, and almost every chat or messaging-related app under the sun provides great support for them:

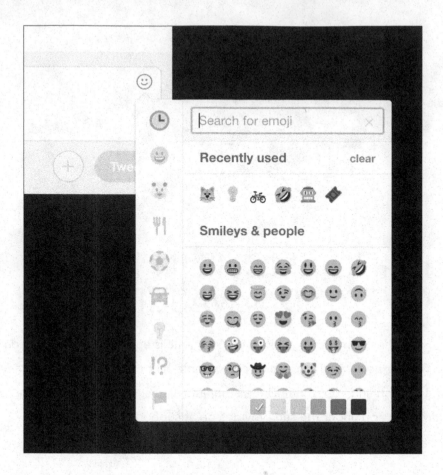

For everyday users, emojis are great. They are fun and easy to use. For us web developers wanting to use emojis in our HTML, CSS, and JavaScript, the story is a bit different. There are a few hoops we need to learn how to jump through, but don't worry. This chapter will help you master all of this hoop jumping like a pro!

What Are Emojis Exactly?

We already know that emojis are these tiny colorful icons. While this may give you the impression that they are images in the traditional sense, they aren't. They are more like the letters, numbers, punctuation marks, and weird symbols we tend to bucket with text:

Towards the end of this chapter, I go into much greater detail on what emojis are and some of the details under the covers that make them work. For now, just know the following:

- They are just characters.

- You can select them, copy them, paste them, adjust their size, and so on.

- They have a more primitive numerical representation you can use to get them to display.

To say we just scratched the surface in understanding emojis is an overstatement, but this is enough for us to get started. It's time to see emojis in action inside our web documents!

Emojis in HTML

To use emojis in HTML, the first thing we need to do is set the document's character encoding to UTF-8. This ensures our emojis display consistently across the variety of browsers and devices our users may be running. Doing this is simple. Inside your `<head>` tag, be sure to specify the following `<meta>` tag:

```
<meta charset="UTF-8">
```

Once you've done this, now comes the fun part of actually getting an emoji to display. You have two ways of being able to do this, each with a varying degree of funness. One way is by using the emoji directly in your HTML. The other way is by specifying the emoji via its *primitive numerical representation*. We'll look at both of these cases.

Using the Emoji Directly

The easiest way to display an emoji involves simply copying and pasting. You just need an app or website that allows you to copy emojis in their native, character form. One great place for doing that is Emojipedia (**https://emojipedia.org**). You can use Emojipedia to search or browse for whatever emoji you are looking for. Once you've found your emoji, there is a section where you can easily see and copy it:

Once you have copied it, just paste it in its intended destination in your markup:

```
<p>🍔</p>
```

Because emojis are treated as text-based content, you can paste them almost any-where in your document where text is supported. Now, if this is your first time see-ing emojis randomly appearing inside your text-based code or your code editor, it will look a bit strange:

```
<body>
    <div id="container">
        <h1>My favorite emoji!</h1>
        <p>🍔</p>
    </div>
    <script type="text/babel">
        class Counter extends React.Component {
```

Your traditional text-only environment where you've written your markup all these years will suddenly have something visual in it. Don't worry. It's cool. When you preview your HTML document in your browser, everything will still work.

Before we wrap up our look at emojis in HTML, let's talk about accessibility. Emo-jis are ultimately visual artifacts, but they are represented as text under the cov-ers using elements like p and span that are semantically ambiguous in this case. Screen readers and related tools may not interpret what the emoji is trying to signify properly, but the solution is simple. To use emojis in an accessibility-friendly way (**a11y**, as the cool kids call it!), set the role and aria-label attributes on the element you are using to represent your emoji:

```
<p role="img" aria-label="hamburger">🍔</p>
```

With this change, you still get to use emojis in HTML and make them accessible at the same time. That's a win, win, win!

Specifying the Emoji Codepoint

If specifying the emoji directly doesn't work, there is a less fun path you can take. You can use the emoji's numerical representation and specify it in your markup instead. If you scroll down in Emojipedia for any emoji, you'll see the numerical representation (more formally known as a **codepoint**) displayed:

For the hamburger emoji, the codepoint is **U+1F354**. To specify this emoji in HTML using the codepoint, we have to modify the value a bit. Add the **&#x** characters, remove the **U+1** from the beginning of the codepoint, and just add the remaining digits from the codepoint as part of any text element.

Here is the hamburger emoji in codepoint form:

```
<p>&#x1F354</p>
```

When you preview your document in your browser, you'll still see the hamburger emoji displayed correctly, despite it looking strange in our markup compared to the copy/paste solution we looked at earlier.

Emojis in CSS

You can totally use emojis in CSS. The same tricks we saw for emojis in HTML will work with only some slight modifications. You can specify the emoji directly:

```
h1::before  {
  content: "🍔";
}
```

You can also specify the emoji by setting the codepoint:

```
h1::before  {
  content: "\01F354";
}
```

How you specify the codepoint is a bit different from what we saw for HTML. All you have to do is remove the **U+** from the Unicode endpoint and add the **\0** (slash zero) characters just before it.

Emojis in JavaScript

The last thing we will look at is how to use emojis in JavaScript. The approach of using them directly will work here as well. Just make sure to treat the emoji as text:

```
document.body.innerText = "😀";
```

To use an emoji via its codepoint value instead, we have to pass it through the `String.fromCodePoint` method. This method takes a codepoint value as its argument:

```
document.body.innerText = String.fromCodePoint(0x1F354);
```

What gets returned is the character at that codepoint location. How you specify the codepoint is different from both HTML and CSS. If the codepoint is **U+1F354**, replace the **U+** with **0x** (zero and **x**) before passing it in. That's it. If you want to go further, since you are in JavaScript, you can do all sorts of JavaScript-y things. You can have an array of emojis, you can dynamically generate them, and so on:

```
let emojis = [0x1F600, 0x1F604, 0x1F34A, 0x1F344, 0x1F37F, 0x1F363,
   0x1F370, 0x1F355, 0x1F354, 0x1F35F, 0x1F6C0, 0x1F48E, 0x1F5FA,
   0x23F0, 0x1F579, 0x1F4DA, 0x1F431, 0x1F42A, 0x1F439, 0x1F424];
```

If you are curious to see a working example that uses emojis defined in JavaScript, check out my Koncentration game (**https://www.kirupa.com/react/ koncentration/index.html**). The GitHub repo (**https://github.com/kirupa/kirupa/ tree/master/reactjs/koncentration/src**, especially **Board.js**) contains everything you need to see how the game is tied together.

Some Emoji Details

We've glossed over what emojis really are and what purpose codepoints serve. To start from what I said earlier, emojis are just characters like all of the text we type.

That is often a confusing thing to understand. A part of the reason for this confusion is because we tend to think of characters as just what our keyboards support. Here is the problem: **What our keyboards allow us to represent is a very tiny percentage of the overall set of characters available to us.**

If you want to see this for yourself, you can view all the characters your operating system supports by using Character Map on Windows or the Character Viewer on Mac:

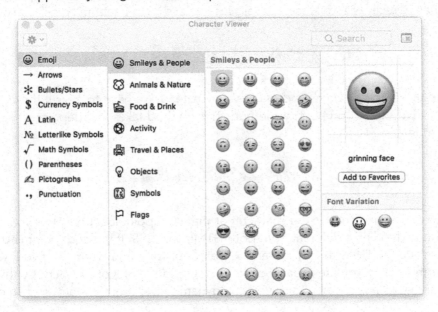

Notice that you have many categories of characters that go beyond just the usual things we see on a typical keyboard. If we had to have a keyboard to support every character our operating system supports, it would need to be *at least...three times bigger* than the usual keyboard (**https://www.youtube.com/watch?v=NQ-8luUkJJc&t=60s**).

Okay, let's go one level deeper. We saw that the emojis we wanted to use had a bizarre numerical representation. As it turns out, *all* characters we use have the same bizarre representation under the covers as well. On our screens, we may see letter characters like **A**, **B**, **C**, **D**, **E**, **F**, and **G**. Under the covers, these characters look like the following: **U+0041, U+0042, U+0043, U+0044, U+0045, U+0046, and U+0047**. I already said that this representation is known as a codepoint, but the more precise term is **Unicode codepoint**. This detail is important to know about because Unicode is an industry standard for ensuring the text you see on your screen is the same on another screen somewhere else—regardless of language, locale, system capabilities, operating system, and so on. A codepoint is the most basic unit of representing information in Unicode. A series of codepoints represents characters and text. Phew!

THE ABSOLUTE MINIMUM

If you can get away with it, copying and pasting emojis is the easiest thing you can do across HTML, CSS, and JavaScript. There will be situations where you can't do that, so you need the fallback approach involving codepoints. There is one last thing that may be important to you. Because emojis are native to the app or platform you are on, they can look different for different users:

Also Known As
🐈 Domestic Cat
🐈 Feline
🐈 Housecat

Apple

Google

Microsoft

Samsung

The Unicode standard ensures that the appropriate codepoints represent, in this case, a cat. Each implementer has full creative freedom in interpreting that as they wish. For some developers, this inconsistency isn't desirable. What they have done instead is re-create the emojis in SVG or PNG format so that they can ensure consistency. An example of someone who does that is Twitter! I used a screenshot of their emoji picker to start this chapter off, and every emoji you see there isn't from our operating system or platform. It is from the really awesome Twemoji project (**http://twitter. github.io/twemoji/**). There are many emoji libraries out there, so use whichever one you like if the native emoji support isn't what you are looking for.

? Ask a question: **https://forum.kirupa.com**

✔ Practice by building real apps: **https://bit.ly/coding_exercises**

Errors/known issues: **https://bit.ly/javascript_errata**

IN THIS CHAPTER

- Learn the basics of a web request
- Learn how to use both the Fetch API and the more traditional `XMLHttpRequest` approach

44

MAKING HTTP/WEB REQUESTS IN JAVASCRIPT

As you probably know very well by now, the Internet is made up of a bunch of interconnected computers called **servers**. When you are surfing the web and navigating between web pages, what you are really doing is telling your browser to request information from any of these servers. It kinda looks like this: Your browser sends a request, waits awkwardly for the server to respond to the request, and (once the server responds) processes the request. All of this communication is made possible because of something known as the **HTTP protocol**.

The HTTP protocol provides a common language that allows your browser and a bunch of other things to communicate with all the servers that make up the Internet. The requests your browser makes on your behalf using the HTTP protocol are known as **HTTP requests**, and these requests go well beyond simply loading a new page as you are navigating. A common (and whole lot more exciting) set of use cases revolves around updating your *existing* page with data resulting from an HTTP request.

For example, you may have a page where you'd like to display some information about the currently logged-in user. This is information your page might not have initially, but it will be information your browser will request as part of you interacting with the page. The server will respond with the data and have your page update with that information. All of this probably sounds a bit abstract, so I'm going to go a bit weird for a few moments and describe what an HTTP request and response might look like for this example.

To get information about the user, here is our HTTP request:

```
GET /user
Accept: application/json
```

For that request, here is what the server might return:

```
200 OK
Content-Type: application/json


{

    "name": "Kirupa",
    "url": "https://www.kirupa.com"

}
```

This back and forth happens a bunch of times, and all of this is fully supported in JavaScript! This ability to asynchronously request and process data from a server without requiring a page navigation/reload has a term. That term is **Ajax** (or **AJAX** if you want to shout). This acronym stands for **Asynchronous JavaScript and XML**, and if you were around web developers a few years ago, Ajax was the buzzword everybody threw around for describing the kind of web apps we take for granted today—apps like Twitter, Facebook, Google Maps, Gmail, and more that constantly fetch data as you are interacting with the page without requiring a full page reload!

Knowing how to Ajax it up and make HTTP requests is a very important skill, and this chapter will give you everything you need to be dangerous. Or, should I say… *dangeresque* (**https://homestarrunner.com/sbemail106.html**)?

The Example

Reading (or even thinking) about the HTTP and requests is boring…extremely boring! To help you both stay awake and understand what all is involved, we are going to be building a small example together. The example will look as follows:

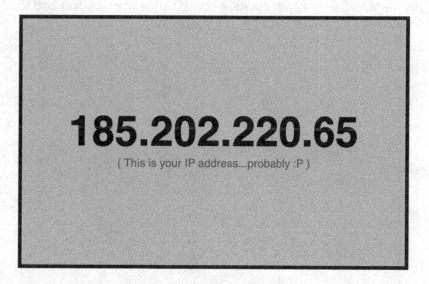

(This is your IP address...probably :P)

On the surface, this example seems just as boring as the underlying details of an HTTP request that I was hoping to make seem more exciting. Like, what are you going to do with this knowledge about your IP? However, this example hides some of the awesome underlying details relevant to what you are about to learn. Here is a sneak peek: We have some JavaScript that makes an HTTP request to a service (**ipinfo.io**) that returns a whole bunch of data about your connection. Using JavaScript, we process all that returned data and surgically pinpoint the IP address that we so proudly display here.

I don't know about you, but I'm totally excited to see this all come together. By the time you reach the end of this tutorial, you too will have created something similar to this example and learned all about what goes on under the hood to make it work.

Meet Fetch

The newest kid on the block for making HTTP requests is the fetch API. To use fetch in its most basic form, all we need to do is provide the URL to send our request to. Once the request has been made, a response will be returned that we can then process. To put all of these words into action, let's write some code and get our earlier example up and running.

Diving into the Code

If you want to follow along, create a new HTML document and add the following markup to it:

```
<!DOCTYPE html>
<html>

<head>
  <title>Display IP Address</title>
</head>

<body>

  <script>

  </script>
</body>

</html>
```

Inside the `<script>` tag, add the following code that makes up our web request:

```
fetch("https://ipinfo.io/json")
  .then(function (response) {
    return response.json();
  })
  .then(function (myJson) {
    console.log(myJson.ip);
```

```
})
.catch(function (error) {
  console.log("Error: " + error);
});
```

Once you have added these lines, save your changes and test your page in the browser. You won't see anything displayed onscreen, but if you bring up the console via your browser developer tools, you should see your IP address being displayed:

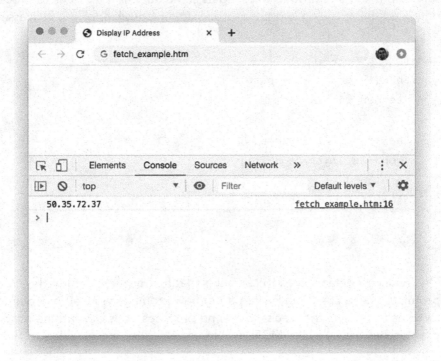

That's something! Now that you have your IP address displayed to your console, let's take a moment and revisit the code and see what exactly it is doing. With our first line of code, we are calling fetch and providing the URL we want to make our request to:

```
fetch("https://ipinfo.io/json")
  .then(function (response) {
    return response.json();
```

```
    })
    .then(function (myJson) {
        console.log(myJson.ip);
    })
    .catch(function (error) {
        console.log("Error: " + error);
    });
```

The URL we send our request to is **ipinfo.io/json**. Once this line gets run, the service running on **ipinfo.io** will send us some data. It is up to us to process that data, and the following two `then` blocks are responsible for this processing:

```
fetch("https://ipinfo.io/json")
    .then(function (response) {
        return response.json();
    })
    .then(function (myJson) {
        console.log(myJson.ip);
    })
    .catch(function (error) {
        console.log("Error: " + error);
    });
```

One really important detail to call out is that the response returned by fetch is a **promise**. These `then` blocks are part of how promises work asynchronously to allow us to process the results. Covering promises goes beyond the scope of this chapter, but the following MDN documentation does a great job explaining what they are:

https://developer.mozilla.org/en-US/docs/Web/JavaScript/Guide/Using_promises

The thing to know for now is that we have a chain of `then` blocks, where each block is called automatically after the previous one completes. Because this is all asynchronous, everything is done while the rest of our app is doing its thing. We don't have to do anything extra to ensure our request-related code doesn't block or freeze up our app while waiting for a slow network result or processing a large amount of data.

Getting back to our code, in our first `then` block, we specify that we want the raw JSON data that our fetch call returns:

```
fetch("https://ipinfo.io/json")
  .then(function (response) {
    return response.json();
  })
  .then(function (myJson) {
    console.log(myJson.ip);
  })
  .catch(function (error) {
    console.log("Error: " + error);
  });
```

In the next `then` block, which gets called after the previous one completes, we process the returned data further by narrowing in on the property that will give us the IP address and then printing it to the console:

```
fetch("https://ipinfo.io/json")
  .then(function (response) {
    return response.json();
  })
  .then(function (myJson) {
    console.log(myJson.ip);
  })
  .catch(function (error) {
    console.log("Error: " + error);
  });
```

How do we know that the IP address is going to be stored by the `ip` property from our returned JSON data? The easiest way is by referring to the **ipinfo. io** developer documentation (**https://ipinfo.io/developers/responses#full-response**)! Every web service will have its own format for returning data when requested. It's up to us to take a few moments and figure out what the response will look like, what parameters we may need to pass in as part of the request to tune the response, and how we need to write our code to get the data we want. As an alternative to reading the developer documentation, you can always inspect the response returned by the request via the developer tools. Use whichever approach is convenient for you.

We aren't done with our code just yet. Sometimes the promise will result in an error or a failed response. When that happens, our promise will stop going down the chain of `then` blocks and look for a `catch` block instead. The code in this `catch` block will then execute. Our `catch` block looks like this:

```javascript
fetch("https://ipinfo.io/json")
  .then(function (response) {
    return response.json();
  })
  .then(function (myJson) {
    console.log(myJson.ip);
  })
  .catch(function (error) {
    console.log("Error: " + error);
  });
```

We aren't doing anything groundbreaking with our error handling. We just print the error message to the console.

Wrapping Up the Example

What we have right now is a blank page with our IP address being printed to the console. Let's go ahead and add the few missing details to get our current page looking like the example we saw at the beginning of the chapter. In our current HTML document, make the following highlighted changes:

```html
<!DOCTYPE html>
<html>

<head>
  <title>Display IP Address</title>
  <style>
    body {
      background-color: #FFCC00;
    }
```

```
    h1 {
      font-family: sans-serif;
      text-align: center;
      padding-top: 140px;
      font-size: 60px;
      margin: -15px;
    }

    p {
      font-family: sans-serif;
      color: #907400;
      text-align: center;
    }
  </style>
</head>

<body>
  <h1 id=ipText></h1>
  <p>( This is your IP address...probably :P )</p>
  <script>
    fetch("https://ipinfo.io/json")
      .then(function (response) {
        return response.json();
      })
      .then(function (myJson) {
        document.querySelector("#ipText").innerHTML = myJson.ip;
      })
      .catch(function (error) {
        console.log("Error: " + error);
      });
  </script>
</body>

</html>
```

The biggest changes here are adding some HTML elements to provide some visual structure and the CSS to make it all look good and proper. Notice that we also modified what our second `then` block does. Instead of printing our IP address to the console, we are instead displaying the IP address inside our `ipText` paragraph element.

If you preview your page now, you should see your IP address displayed in all its dark text and yellow backgrounded awesomeness.

Meet XMLHttpRequest

The other (more traditional) object that is responsible for allowing you to send and receive HTTP requests is the weirdly named `XMLHttpRequest`. This object allows you to do several things that are important to making web requests:

- Send a request to a server.

- Check on the status of a request.

- Retrieve and parse the response from the request.

- Listen for the `onreadystatechange`, which helps you react to the status of your request.

There are a few more things that `XMLHttpRequest` does, and we'll cover them eventually. For now, these four will do just fine. Next, let's set the stage for re-creating the earlier example so that we can see all of this action for ourselves. In your existing HTML document from earlier, delete everything that is inside your `<script>` tag. Your document should look as follows:

```html
<!DOCTYPE html>
<html>

<head>
  <title>Display IP Address</title>
  <style>
    body {
      background-color: #FFCC00;
    }


    h1 {
      font-family: sans-serif;
```

```
      text-align: center;
      padding-top: 140px;
      font-size: 60px;
      margin: -15px;
    }

    p {
      font-family: sans-serif;
      color: #907400;
      text-align: center;
    }
  </style>
</head>

<body>
  <h1 id=ipText></h1>
  <p>( This is your IP address...probably :P )</p>
  <script>

  </script>
</body>

</html>
```

With our document in a good state, it's time to build our example one line at a time!

Creating the Request

The first thing we are going to do is initialize our `XMLHttpRequest` object, so add the following line inside your `<script>` tag:

```
let xhr = new XMLHttpRequest();
```

The `xhr` variable will now be the gateway to all the various properties and methods the `XMLHttpRequest` object provides for allowing us to make web requests.

One such method is open. This method is what allows us to specify the details of the request we would like to make, so let's add it next:

```
let xhr = new XMLHttpRequest();
xhr.open('GET', "https://ipinfo.io/json", true);
```

The open method takes three-ish arguments:

- The first argument specifies which HTTP method to use to process your request. The values you can specify are **GET**, **PUT**, **POST**, and **DELETE**. In our case, we are interested in receiving information, so the first argument we specify is going to be **GET**.

- Next, you specify the URL to send your request to. These URLs are well-defined endpoints that know what to do when an HTTP request flies by. For our IP example, the path we will specify is **ipinfo.io/json**.

- The last argument specifies whether you want your request to run asynchronously. This value should be set to **true**. Running the request asynchronously will ensure your page is responsive, and the rest of your code continues to run while your HTTP request is taking its time to make its way around. At this point, setting this value to **false** is going to be ignored by most of the browsers, so...yeah.

- The "-ish" part of the "three-ish arguments" I mentioned earlier refers to the arguments for username and password. Typically, you don't want to specify your username and password in such a plain-as-daylight location like your JavaScript file, so you probably won't ever need to set more than the three arguments you've already seen.

Sending the Request

So far, we've initialized the XMLHttpRequest object and constructed our request. We haven't sent the request out yet, but that is handled by the next line:

```
let xhr = new XMLHttpRequest();
xhr.open('GET', "https://ipinfo.io/json", true);
xhr.send();
```

The send method is responsible for sending the request. If you set your request to be asynchronous (and why wouldn't you have?!), the send method immediately returns and the rest of your code continues to run. That's the behavior we want.

Asynchronous Stuff and Events

When some code is running asynchronously, you have no idea when that code is going to return with some news. In the case of what we've done, once the HTTP request has been sent, our code doesn't stop and wait for the request to make its way back. Our code just keeps running. What we need is a way to send our request and then be notified of when the request comes back so that our code can finish what it started.

To satisfy that need, we have **events**. More specifically for our case, that's why we have the readystatechange event that is fired by our XMLHttpRequest object whenever our request hits an important milestone on its epic journey.

To set this all up, go ahead and add the following highlighted line that invokes the almighty addEventListener:

```
let xhr = new XMLHttpRequest();
xhr.open('GET', "https://ipinfo.io/json", true);
xhr.send();

xhr.addEventListener("readystatechange", processRequest, false);
```

This line looks like any other event listening code you've written a bunch of times. We listen for the readystatechange event on our xhr object and call the processRequest event handler when the event is overheard. Here is where some fun stuff happens!

Processing the Request

This should be easy, right? We have our event listener all ready, and all we need is the processRequest event handler where we can add some code to read the result that gets returned. Let's go ahead and first add our event handler:

```
let xhr = new XMLHttpRequest();
xhr.open('GET', "https://ipinfo.io/json", true);
```

```
xhr.send();

xhr.onreadystatechange = processRequest;

function processRequest(e) {

}
```

Next, all we need is some code to parse the result of the HTTP request inside our newly added event handler.

As it turns out, it isn't that simple. The complication comes from the `readystatechange` event being tied to our `XMLHttpRequest` object's `readyState` property. This `readyState` property chronicles the path our HTTP request takes, and each change in its value results in the `readystatechange` event getting fired. What exactly is our `readyState` property representing that results in its value changing so frequently? Check out Figure 44.1:

Value	State	Description
0	UNSENT	The open method hasn't been called yet
1	OPENED	The send method has been called
2	HEADERS_RECEIVED	The send method has been called and the HTTP request has returned the status and headers
3	LOADING	The HTTP request response is being downloaded
4	DONE	Everything has completed

FIGURE 44.1

The values returned by `readyState` *to tell us what our request is doing*

For every HTTP request we make, our `readyState` property hits each of these five values. This means our `readystatechange` event gets fired five times. As a result, our `processRequest` event handler gets called five times as well. See the problem? For four out of the five times `processRequest` gets called, it won't be getting called for the reasons we are interested in—that is, the request has returned and it is time to analyze the returned data.

Since our goal is to read the returned value after our request has been completed, the `readyState` value of **4** is our friend. We need to ensure we only move forward when this value is set, so here is what the modified `processRequest` function would look like to handle that:

```
function processRequest(e) {
    if (xhr.readyState == 4) {
        // time to partay!!!
    }
}
```

While this seems good, we have one more check to add. It is possible for us to find ourselves with no readable data despite our HTTP request having completed successfully. To guard against that, we also have HTTP status codes that get returned as a part of the request. You run into these HTTP status codes all the time. For example, whenever you see a **404**, you know that a file is missing. If you are curious, you can see a full list of status codes at **https://www.webfx.com/web-development/glossary/http-status-codes/**, but the one we care about with HTTP requests is status code **200**. This code is returned by the server when the HTTP request was successful.

We are going to modify our earlier code slightly to include a check for the **200** status code, and the appropriately named `status` property contains the value returned by the request:

```
function processRequest(e) {
    if (xhr.readyState == 4 && xhr.status == 200) {
        // time to partay!!!
    }
}
```

In plain English, what this check does is simple: The `if` statement checks that the request has completed (`readyState == 4`) *and* is successful (`status == 200`). Only if both of those conditions are met can we declare that our request did what we wanted it to do.

Processing the Request...for Realz!

In the previous section, I used a whole lot of words to explain adding a simple `if` statement. I promise this section will be more to the point. All that is left is to read the body of the response that is returned. The way we do that is by reading the value of the `responseText` property returned by our `xhr` object:

```
function processRequest(e) {
    if (xhr.readyState == 4 && xhr.status == 200) {
        let response = JSON.parse(xhr.responseText);
        document.querySelector("#ipText").innerHTML = response.ip;
    }
}
```

Here is where things become a bit less general. When we make a request to the **ipinfo.io** server, the data gets returned in JSON format...as a string:

```
"{
  "ip": "52.41.128.211",
  "hostname": "static-52-41-128-211.blve.wa.verizon.net",
  "city": "Redmond",
  "region": "Washington",
  "country": "US",
  "loc": "46.6104,-121.1259",
  "org": "Verizon, Inc",
  "postal": "98052"
}"
```

To convert our JSON-like string into an actual JSON object, we pass in the result of `xhr.responseText` into the `JSON.parse` method. This takes our string of JSON data and turns it into an actual JSON object that is stored by the `response` variable. From there, displaying the IP is as easy as what is shown in the highlighted line:

```
function processRequest(e) {
    if (xhr.readyState == 4 && xhr.status == 200) {
        let response = JSON.parse(xhr.responseText);
```

```
        document.querySelector("#ipText").innerHTML = response.ip;
    }
}
```

I am not going to spend too much time on this section because I don't want this to become a discussion of how the **ipinfo.io** server returns data. Just like what we saw with fetch earlier, every server we send an HTTP request to will send data in a slightly different way, and each one may require you to jump through a slightly different hoop to get at what you are looking for. There isn't an easy solution that will prepare you for all your future HTTP requesting needs outside of reading documentation for the web service you are interested in requesting data from.

THE ABSOLUTE MINIMUM

Writing some code that makes an HTTP request and returns some data is probably one of the coolest things you can do in JavaScript. Everything you've seen here used to be a novelty that only Internet Explorer supported in the very beginning. Today, HTTP requests are everywhere. Much of the data you see displayed in a typical page is often the result of a request getting made and processed—all without you even noticing. If you are building a new app or are modernizing an older app, the fetch API is a good one to start using if your app needs to make a web request. Since a good chunk of your time will be reading other people's code, there is a good chance the web requests you encounter are made using `XMLHttpRequest`. In those cases, you need to know your way around. That's why this chapter focused on both the newer fetch and the older `XMLHttpRequest` approaches.

? Ask a question: **https://forum.kirupa.com**

✔ Practice by building real apps: **https://bit.ly/coding_exercises**

🖋 Errors/known issues: **https://bit.ly/javascript_errata**

45

ACCESSING THE WEBCAM

Accessing your webcam via your browser used to involve a plug-in (pardon the profanity). That's right. In order to connect to a webcam and gain access to its video stream, you had to rely on something primarily created in Flash or Silverlight. While that approach certainly worked for browsers that supported plug-ins, it didn't help for the increasing number of browsers that aim to be plug-in free. This inability to natively access the webcam without relying on third-party components was certainly a gap in the HTML development story—especially on mobile devices. At least, that was the case until pretty recently.

The W3C has been attempting to fill this gap by encouraging browser vendors to implement the proposals outlined in the **Media Capture and Streams** spec (**https://w3c.github.io/mediacapture-main/getusermedia.html**). This spec defines, among various other things, how to communicate with a webcam device using just a little bit of JavaScript. The good news is that, despite it being fairly new, almost all modern browsers across mobile and desktop forms support this spec.

By the time you finish this chapter, you will have learned how to take your webcam's video stream and display it in your web page.

The Example

Before proceeding further, let's first take a look at an example that is identical to what you will be creating. Navigate to the following URL for a live example: **https://bit.ly/webcamJS**.

You should see something that looks as follows (hopefully with you in the picture instead of me!):

A key part of being able to access the webcam is handling the permission prompt your browser will display, similar to what is shown in Figure 45.1.

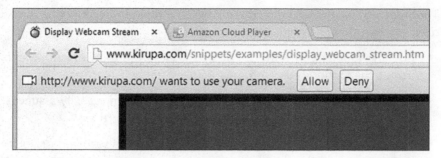

FIGURE 45.1

The permission prompt!

If you denied permission accidentally (or intentionally) when viewing the example, just reload this page to get a crack at acing this test again.

Overview of How This Works

To help make this code easier to write, let's look at an overview of how everything works using plain-old English. Two components do all the heavy lifting in getting data from your webcam displayed on your screen. They are the HTML video element and the JavaScript `getUserMedia` function:

The video element is pretty straightforward in what it does. It is responsible for taking the video stream from your webcam and actually displaying it on the screen.

The interesting piece is the `getUserMedia` function. This function allows you to do three things:

- Specify whether you want to get video data from the webcam, audio data from a microphone, or both.

- If the user grants permission to access the webcam, specify a **success** function to call, where you can process the webcam data further.

- If the user does not grant permission to access the webcam or your webcam runs into some other kind of error, specify an **error** function to handle the error conditions.

For what we are trying to do, we call the `getUserMedia` function and tell it to only retrieve the video from the webcam. I will cover the microphone in the future! Once we retrieve the video, we tell our success function to send the video data to our video element for display on our screen.

If this sounds pretty straightforward, that's because it actually is. Let's put all of this straightforward English-sounding description into HTML and JavaScript in the next section.

Adding the Code

In this section, let's go ahead and display our webcam data to the screen. First, let's add the HTML and CSS:

```
<!DOCTYPE html>
<html>
<head>
<meta charset="utf-8">
<title>Display Webcam Stream</title>

<style>
#container {
    margin: 0px auto;
    width: 500px;
    height: 375px;
```

```
        border: 10px #333 solid;
}
#videoElement {
        width: 500px;
        height: 375px;
        background-color: #666;
}
</style>
</head>

<body>
<div id="container">
        <video autoplay="true" id="videoElement">

        </video>
</div>
<script>

</script>
</body>
</html>
```

In a new document, go ahead and add all of the HTML and CSS that you see here. The important thing to note in this snippet is the `<video>` tag:

```
<video autoplay="true" id="videoElement">

</video>
```

Our `<video>` tag has an `id` value of **videoElement**, and its `autoplay` attribute is set to **true**. By setting the `autoplay` attribute to **true**, we ensure that our video starts to display automatically once we have our webcam video stream.

If you preview what your page looks like in your browser, you will see the following:

Yes, this looks pretty plain and boring now, but that's because we haven't added the JavaScript that ties together our video element with the webcam. We'll do that next!

Inside your `<script>` tag, add the following code:

```
let video = document.querySelector("#videoElement");

if (navigator.mediaDevices.getUserMedia) {
  navigator.mediaDevices.getUserMedia({ video: true })
    .then(function (stream) {
      video.srcObject = stream;
    })
```

```
    .catch(function (err0r) {
      console.log("Something went wrong!");
    });
}
```

Once you've added this code, save your HTML document and preview your page. Provided you are on a supported browser, you should see your webcam video stream after you've given your browser permission to access it.

Examining the Code

Now that you have a working example, let's go through our code line-by-line to understand how the verbal overview from earlier matches the code you just added.

Let's start at the very top:

```
let video = document.querySelector("#videoElement");
```

We first declare a variable called `video`, and it is initialized to our video element that lives in the HTML. We get our paws on the video element by using `querySelector` and specifying the `id` selector that targets it.

Next up is our code for accessing the `getUserMedia` API:

```
if (navigator.mediaDevices.getUserMedia) {
  navigator.mediaDevices.getUserMedia({ video: true })
    .then(function (stream) {
      video.srcObject = stream;
    })
    .catch(function (err0r) {
      console.log("Something went wrong!");
    });
}
```

The `getUserMedia` method is supported by most browsers, but it doesn't hurt to check first before starting to access properties on it. This `if` statement ensures that our media-related code only works if `getUserMedia` is actually supported.

The rest of our code is responsible for accessing our webcam and streaming the visuals to the screen. Before we go through and look at that, let's take a step back and talk about how `getUserMedia` actually works. It takes one argument that specifies what are known as **constraints**. Constraints allow you to control, among various things, whether video is allowed, whether audio is allowed, how big to make the video dimensions, whether to prefer a front-facing camera over a back-facing one, the video frame rate, and more. You represent these constraints as just objects and properties. Nothing fancy there.

In our code, you can see constraints in action in the following snippet:

```
if (navigator.mediaDevices.getUserMedia) {
  navigator.mediaDevices.getUserMedia({ video: true })
    .then(function (stream) {
      video.srcObject = stream;
    })
    .catch(function (err0r) {
      console.log("Something went wrong!");
    });
}
```

All we are telling `getUserMedia` is to specify a constraints object whose `video` property is set to **true**. This means that default settings will be used in capturing the visuals and displaying them. This isn't the most exciting constraint to set, but it gets the job done. To see the full range of constraints you can specify, refer to the following MDN article on `getUserMedia`, which goes through all the fun details: **https://developer.mozilla.org/en-US/docs/Web/API/MediaDevices/getUserMedia**.

Beyond constraints, there is another very important detail we need to know about the `getUserMedia` method. What it returns is a promise that resolves to an object of type `MediaStream`. When the promise successfully resolves, you can access the underlying media stream and perform any additional actions.

In our code, we are keeping things simple and just setting our stream to our video element's `srcObject` property:

```
if (navigator.mediaDevices.getUserMedia) {
  navigator.mediaDevices.getUserMedia({ video: true })
    .then(function (stream) {
      video.srcObject = stream;
    })
    .catch(function (err0r) {
      console.log("Something went wrong!");
    });
}
```

If there are any failures, the `catch` block will kick in.

 TIP Stopping the Webcam Stream

If you want to stop the webcam stream, you need some code that looks like this:

```
function stop(e) {
  let stream = video.srcObject;
  let tracks = stream.getTracks();

  for (let i = 0; i < tracks.length; i++) {
    let track = tracks[i];
    track.stop();
  }

  video.srcObject = null;
}
```

See the thread **https://bit.ly/stopWebcamStream**, which goes into more detail on what you should do as well as provides a working example.

THE ABSOLUTE MINIMUM

So, there you have it—a look at how you can access a user's webcam video stream and display it in the browser. Once you get the video to display, you can then do all sorts of things that you can do to videos in general. You can apply crazy filters, you can take a snapshot and save the image to disk, and much more, but that goes beyond the scope of what we are doing here.

The main takeaway is this: The getUserMedia method is our friend and is the gateway to many of the basic and advanced capabilities available to us when trying to display our webcam feed in our browser.

? Ask a question: **https://forum.kirupa.com**

✔ Practice by building real apps: **https://bit.ly/coding_exercises**

Errors/known issues: **https://bit.ly/javascript_errata**

ARRAY AND OBJECT DESTRUCTURING

A lot of the improvements made to JavaScript revolve around adding missing capabilities, such as being able to access the webcam, using cool new data structures such as sets, interacting in more creative ways with the DOM, and more. Some improvements fall purely on the side of convenience. There are many highly inconvenient JavaScript tasks we regularly perform that either take too much code or require too many "gotchas" to work properly. One such task involves taking values from arrays or objects and storing them in variables. Allow me to elaborate. Let's say that we have an array and it contains the following items:

```
let winners = ["bear", "cat", "dog", "giraffe", "unicorn"];
```

What we want to do is store the first three items from this array. The common approach we would use is one that looks like this:

```
let winners = ["bear", "cat", "dog", "giraffe", "unicorn"];

let firstPlace = winners[0];
let secondPlace = winners[1];
let thirdPlace = winners[2];

console.log(firstPlace); // bear
console.log(secondPlace); // cat
```

If we wanted to store every item in our array in its own variable or store the remaining items that aren't the first three values, we would be required to do a lot more array manipulation and/or copying and pasting. Tasks such as this extend to objects as well, where we may want to store certain properties in their own variables, as shown here:

```
let returnedData = {
    "id": 54901,
    "name": Laserific Spoon 2000,
    "price": $5.00,
    "inStock": false,
    "inventor": Dr. Atom
};

let productID = returnedData.id;
let inventor = returnedData.inventor;

console.log(productID); // 54901
console.log(inventor); // Dr. Atom
```

As our web apps become more data intensive, with us relying more and more on JavaScript to process this data, the traditional approaches for accessing data and storing it in variables become clunky. That is where the star of this chapter comes in: **destructuring**. Destructuring is all about making it *easy* to go from a chunk of data, stored either in an array or an object, and unpacking that data into variables. We'll look at what all of this entails in the following sections.

Destructuring Examples

The concepts behind destructuring are not very deep, so the best way to learn how it works is by just looking at a bunch of examples spanning across both arrays and objects.

General Overview Using Arrays

Let's go back to the array example we started with earlier:

```
let winners = ["bear", "cat", "dog", "giraffe", "unicorn"];
```

If we want to store the first three items from the array in their own variables, here is how we can do that by using destructuring:

```
let winners = ["bear", "cat", "dog", "giraffe", "unicorn"];

let [firstPlace, secondPlace, thirdPlace] = winners;

console.log(firstPlace); // bear
console.log(secondPlace); // cat
console.log(thirdPlace); // dog
```

We use this bizarre array-like syntax as part of the variable declaration to define the three variables (`firstPlace`, `secondPlace`, `thirdPlace`) that will store the first three items from our `winners` array. One of the other activities mentioned earlier is how we can store the remaining items from the array that aren't in the first, second, or third position. Well, as it turns out, there is a special operator called the **spread operator** (...) that allows us to do that very easily:

```
let winners = ["bear", "cat", "dog", "giraffe", "unicorn"];

let [firstPlace, secondPlace, thirdPlace, ...others] = winners;
```

```
console.log(firstPlace); // bear
console.log(secondPlace); // cat
console.log(thirdPlace); // dog
console.log(others); // [giraffe, unicorn, dinosaur]
```

Notice that we have the ...others expression, where we pair the spread operator (...) with a variable called others. The output is the remaining array values after firstPlace, secondPlace, and thirdPlace get mapped.

If we had to visualize all this, we would see something similar to what's shown in Figure 46.1.

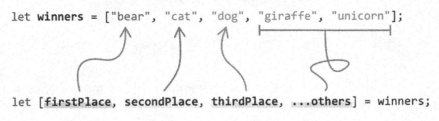

FIGURE 46.1

A visualization of how variables and the spread operator map to the data stored in the array!

Really cool, right? Now, what we have seen is the elevator pitch for what destructuring looks like and the syntax we will rely on. What we will do next is go even deeper and look at more examples that touch upon the edge cases we run into.

Skipping Items with a Comma

We sorta kinda see the importance that the comma plays in destructuring. Each variable is comma-separated, and the comma helps indicate when we jump from one item in our array to the next in sequential order. This knowledge is handy if we want to skip an item from being assigned to a variable. To skip an item (or many items), we need to specify a comma but no variable to pair with the comma.

Take a look at the following example:

```
let [a, , b] = [1, 2, 3, 4, 5, 6, 7];


console.log(a); // 1
console.log(b); // 3
```

Notice that we specify an empty comma after the a variable. This ends up appearing as two commas, and the result is one where we map only the first item and the third item. The second item is skipped since there is no variable to store that item.

When There Are More Variables Than Data

Sometimes we may be trying to map more variables than there is data to map to them. Take a look at the following example:

```
let [first, second, third] = ["Homer", "Marge"];


console.log(first); // "Homer"
console.log(second); // "Marge"
console.log(third); // undefined
```

The array we are trying to unpack into variables only has two items, but we have three variables. When we have a variable that doesn't have any data associated with it, that variable is given a value of **undefined**. That is what we see happening when we inspect the value of our third variable.

If the **undefined** value is undesirable, we can specify a default value to override that behavior:

```
let [first, second, third = "Person"] = ["Homer", "Marge"];

console.log(first); // Homer
console.log(second); // Marge
console.log(third); // Person
```

In this variation, notice that the value for third is set to the default value of **Person** because it doesn't have a defined value in the array.

Separating the Declaration and Assignment

Just like how we can separate the declaration and assignment activities when working with variables, we can do the same when destructuring. I will warn you, though, that it is going to look a little strange at first, but it is totally legit:

```
let foo;
let bar;
```

```
[foo, bar] = [1, 2];

console.log(foo) // 1
console.log(bar) // 2
```

Notice that we declare our `foo` and `bar` variables first, and we then assign those variables later when we destructure the contents of our array.

Destructuring with Objects

In past few sections, we saw how destructuring works with arrays. Destructuring also works with objects, and a lot of what we saw earlier applies fully in this objectified world. Take a look at the following object:

```
let chair = {
  brand: "Le Chair",
  legs: "4",
  material: "Wood",
  inventory: "42",
  price: "$29.99",
  color: "Blue"
};
```

We have an object called `chair`, and it contains a bunch of properties. If we want to extract and store the values of just the `brand` and `price` properties, we can do so via destructuring:

```
let chair = {
  brand: "Le Chair",
  legs: "4",
  material: "Wood",
  inventory: "42",
  price: "$29.99",
  color: "Blue"
};
```

```
let {brand, price} = chair;


console.log(brand); // "Le Chair"
console.log(price); // "$29.99"
```

In our variable declaration and assignment, we are declaring two variables called brand and price whose names match the property names inside the object we are unpacking. The end result is that we are able to work with the values stored by brand and price properties as their own individual variables.

As we can see, our chair object contains more properties than just brand and price. If we wanted to access the remaining properties without any manual book-keeping, the spread operator exists in this context as well:

```
let chair = {
    brand: "Le Chair",
    legs: "4",
    material: "Wood",
    inventory: "42",
    price: "$29.99",
    color: "Blue"
}


let {brand, price, ...rest} = chair;


console.log(brand); // "Le Chair"
console.log(price); // "$29.99"
console.log(rest); /* {
                        legs: '4',
                        material: 'Wood',
                        inventory: '42',
                        color: 'Blue'
                      } */
```

The `rest` variable stores the results of destructuring our object using the spread operator. What gets returned is a new object whose properties are the **ones we haven't unpacked**. In other words, this new object contains everything except the `brand` and `price` properties. Really cool, right?

Destructuring Differences Between Arrays and Objects

In this happy world of destructuring, what differentiates what we see here with objects from what we saw with arrays previously are three big things:

- The destructuring assignment for arrays involves brackets:

```
let [a, b] = [1, 2]
```

The destructuring assignment for objects involves curly braces:

```
let {a, b} = { a: 1, b: 2 }
```

- With arrays, the order of our variable names during assignment mapped to the order of our items in the array. With objects, order doesn't matter. The variable names determine which of our object property values get mapped.

- With arrays, the spread operator returns a new array whose contents are a *consecutive* list of array values starting right after the ones we had already mapped. With objects, the spread operator returns a new object made up of the properties we haven't already mapped. The order of how the properties are defined inside the object doesn't matter. The only thing that matters is which properties have already been mapped and which ones haven't.

There are a handful of other subtle differences, but these are the big ones.

Assigning to New Variable Names

In our earlier snippets, the variable names mapped to the property names we are accessing inside the object. That is the default behavior, but we may often want different variable names that are decoupled from the internals of an object's property naming. Fortunately, we have a way of doing that. Take a look at the following example:

```
let chair = {
  brand: "Le Chair",
```

```
    legs: "4",
    material: "Wood",
    inventory: "42",
    price: "$29.99",
    color: "Blue"
};


let {brand, price: cost} = chair;


console.log(brand); // "Le Chair"
console.log(cost); // "$29.99"
```

Pay attention to our destructuring assignment. Notice that we have the `price` property mapping to the value in the `chair` object we are trying to access *but* we remapped the variable name to be `cost` instead. We did this by using a colon character between the variable that maps to the object property name and the name we specify as the new variable name. The end result of this snippet is that we can use the `cost` variable to access the value of the `price` property instead of using the `price` name.

 NOTE There Are More Cases!

As with anything as general purpose as destructuring, there are many more cases covering uncommon (yet very important) scenarios than what we have covered here. For a full list of all the destructuring shenanigans that one can see with arrays and objects, the MDN documentation on this topic is perfect: **https://mzl.la/3I2Lbre**.

THE ABSOLUTE MINIMUM

Destructuring is one of those topics that has the potential to greatly simplify how we map variables to data stored inside our arrays and objects. It is important for us to understand the slightly bizarre-looking syntax made up of brackets, curly braces, and periods. Even if you and I have no plans of ever using it in our code, destructuring has gotten so common (especially in frameworks like React and Vue) that we'll find ourselves forced to use it or needing to review/read code written by someone else that heavily relies on it.

? Ask a question: **https://forum.kirupa.com**

✔ Practice by building real apps: **https://bit.ly/coding_exercises**

📋 Errors/known issues: **https://bit.ly/javascript_errata**

47

STORING DATA USING WEB STORAGE

Just like Las Vegas, often what you do in a web page stays in the web page. Let's say you have a simple application (**https://bit.ly/kirupa_todo**) that allows you to maintain a to-do list:

My To-Do List

1. Finish local storage article.

2. Mow the lawn.

3. Save the world.

Save Reset

If you accidentally navigate to another page or close the tab this page was on, the default behavior when you return to this page would be to empty the to-do list.

Web pages do not persist data by default. Fortunately, you have a bunch of approaches you can take for solving this problem. In this chapter, we are going to look at one of my favorite ways of storing data by relying on what is known as the **Web Storage API**. This API allows you to write just a few lines of code to handle a lot of tricky storage situations, so it's going to be a fun one!

How Web Storage Works

The Web Storage API sounds complicated and scary, but it is mostly a pushover. It is exposed to us via two global (attached to window) objects called `localStorage` and `sessionStorage`. You can use these two objects to specify what data to store as well as what data to retrieve, update, permanently remove, and perform a whole bunch of other storage-related activities. Let's go a bit deeper in our understanding of what happens.

What Exactly Goes on Inside

For the sake of simplicity, I am not going to focus on both local storage and session storage at the same time. They are very similar, so I am going to flip a coin and pick...our `localStorage` object.

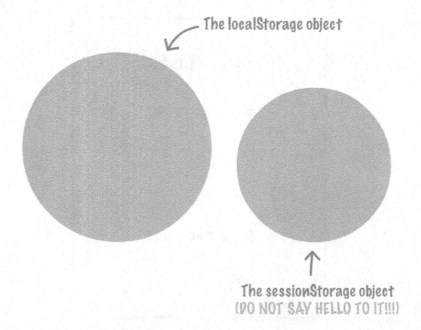

The localStorage object

The sessionStorage object
(DO NOT SAY HELLO TO IT!!!)

If you take a peek inside this object, you will see a well-oiled machine that is designed for storing data. It stores data by neatly organizing it **into key and value pairs**. If you aren't familiar with this approach, take a look at the following visualization:

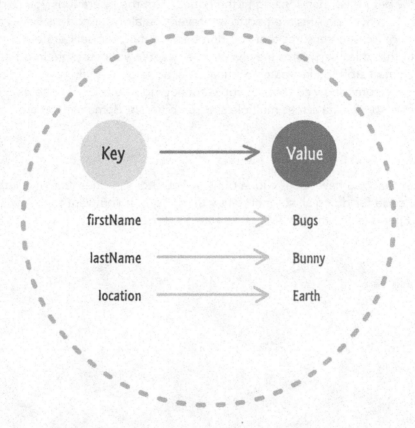

I am storing information about one of my favorite cartoon characters, and the data I want to store is indexed by an easily identifiable key value. More specifically, you can see that there are three pieces of data I am storing:

- The `firstName` key with a value of **Bugs**
- The `lastName` key with a value of **Bunny**
- The `location` key with a value of **Earth**

The key serves as the identifier, and the value is the data associated with it. As you will soon find out, almost all operations you perform using our storage objects will involve the key, the value, or both!

Web Storage Data Is Tied to Your Domain

We are almost done with the explanation. There is one last detail you need to know before we start looking at the code. All of the operations you perform with the Web Storage APIs are tied to whatever domain your code is being run on. This level of isolation ensures that you don't accidentally (or deliberately!) modify any data that third-party sites may have already set in your storage. In other words, any data I store on **kirupa.com** is inaccessible to code that may be running on **google.com**, and vice versa. If you were hoping to use local or session storage to persist some data across multiple sites on different domains, you are out of luck!

Getting Your Code On

Now that you have a basic idea of how Web Storage does its thing, let's look at the code for doing all sorts of data-y things to it. If you want to follow along, all you need is an empty HTML page with a `<script>` tag:

```
<!DOCTYPE html>
<html>

<head>
  <title>Local Storage</title>
</head>

<body>
  <script>

  </script>
</body>
</html>
```

There is no user interface (UI) for what we are doing here, so it's all inspecting the state of our `localStorage` or `sessionStorage` object using the browser developer tools.

Adding Data

If you've never done anything with local storage before, let's start by adding some data into it. The method you use for adding data lives off of your `localStorage` object, and it is called setItem. This method (unsurprisingly) takes two arguments made up of your **key** and **value**:

```
localStorage.setItem("key", "value");
```

Here is an example of the setItem method in action where I am storing the details of the (totally sweet!) music I'm listening to right now while writing this:

```
localStorage.setItem("artist", "Tycho");
localStorage.setItem("album", "Awake");
localStorage.setItem("track", "Apogee");
localStorage.setItem("year", "2014");
```

With each line, we are pushing data into our localStorage object. At the end of all this, the data in your localStorage object can be visualized as follows:

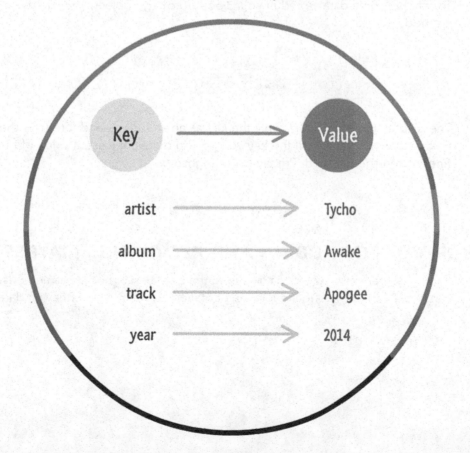

As you can see, the way you add entries is by using `setItem` and specifying a key that you haven't used before. If you specify an existing key, the existing value the key is pointing to will be overwritten with your new value:

```
// overwriting some data
localStorage.setItem("track", "Apogee");
localStorage.setItem("track", "L");
```

Now, here is one more important detail you should know: **Your keys and values must be strings**. That's right. If you want to store a snazzy custom object for retrieval later, you are completely out of luck under Web Storage. Basically, use string values and rely heavily on methods like `toString()` and `JSON.string-ify()` to ensure you are storing any complex data in the form of a string you can (hopefully) un-stringify later.

Retrieving Data

To retrieve some data stored in your `localStorage` object, you use the `getItem` method:

```
let artist = localStorage.getItem("artist");
console.log(artist); // will print out 'Tycho'
```

The `getItem` method takes only the key as an argument, and it returns the value associated with that key. If the key you pass in does not exist, a value of **undefined** is returned instead. Pretty simple, right?

A SHORTCUT FOR ADDING AND REMOVING...MAYBE?

If for whatever reason you don't like using the `getItem` or `setItem` methods, you can bypass them by using the following notation for setting and retrieving data:

```
// storing data
localStorage["key"] = value;
// retrieving data
let myData = localStorage["key"];
```

This is a notation you may have seen (and possibly even used!) when working with objects and associative arrays. That same technique can be used with your `localStorage` and `sessionStorage` objects as well. There is no right or wrong way to access your data, so use whichever approach speaks to your soul.

Now, back to our regularly scheduled programming.

Removing Data

There are two extremes to removing data from your local storage. You can remove everything scorched-earth style, or you can selectively remove a key and value pair individually.

Because *Scorched Earth* is an awesome video game, let's look at this method first. To remove everything from your local storage, you can call the `clear` method on your `localStorage` object:

```
localStorage.clear();
```

This will remove all traces of any data you may have stored, so use it cautiously if you have several pages on your site that each write to the `localStorage` object independently and rely on data stored there actually being there.

To remove only select key and value entries from `localStorage`, you can use `removeItem()` and pass in the key name associated with the data you wish to remove:

```
localStorage.removeItem("year");
```

In this snippet, the **year** key and its value will be deleted while leaving all of the other data intact. This is the safer option if you are working on an app that has many components that rely on storing data using Web Storage.

Dealing with File Size

For reasons I don't know, all of the browsers give you have a fixed size of 5MB for each domain your local storage is tied to. If you try to add more data after you have exceeded your 5MB quota, a **QUOTA_EXCEEDED_ERR** exception will be thrown.

Handling this exception is pretty straightforward by using a `try/catch` statement:

```
try {
  localStorage.setItem("key", "some data");
} catch (e) {
  if (e == QUOTA_EXCEEDED_ERR) {
    // do something nice to notify your users

  }
}
```

This ensures that your code fails nicely while still giving you the option of notifying your users that their data can't be saved. **With all of that said, you really should never have to do this**. Remember, all of the data you store is in the form of strings. Five *megabytes* is a lot of text-based data to store. If you need to store that much data, Web Storage may not be your best solution.

Detecting Support for Web Storage

Ironically, one of the last things we are going to do is talk about detecting whether or not someone's browser supports local storage. According to the **Caniuse.com** statistics on local storage (**https://caniuse.com/?search=local%20storage**), pretty much everybody (and their mothers) is using a browser that supports it. There is another, *better* reason outside of browser support why you want to do this.

Web Storage, just like cookies, allows websites to leave behind traces of themselves on your machine. When users are browsing using a "private" mode like the kind offered by all your major browsers, the goal is to avoid dealing with these traces of data. This means that your browser totally supports local and session storage, but it may have this feature disabled or severely crippled to respect user privacy. Trying to add some data into your local or session storage will either result in an error or your data will simply be wiped out the moment you end your browsing session.

For the "private" mode case, it is a good idea to check whether Web Storage is *usable* on the user's browser. The code for doing this check looks like this:

```
function isLocalStorageSupported() {
  try {
    localStorage.setItem("blah", "blah");
    localStorage.removeItem("blah");
    return true;
  } catch (e) {
    return false;
  }
}
```

A call to the `isLocalStorageSupported` function will return a value of **true** if local storage is usable, and if local storage isn't supported, you will see a value of **false**.

This code snippet is based entirely on the following Gist, which also outlines the brief history of local storage feature detection: **https://gist.github.com/paulirish/5558557**.

What About Session Storage?

Earlier I stated that we are going to focus on the `localStorage` object and that we will focus on the `sessionStorage` object later. Guess what? Later is here, so it's time to shift gears and look at session storage! For the most part, you use local storage and session storage the same way. Everything you saw for the `localStorage` object in the previous sections applies to the `sessionStorage` object as well. The way you add, update, and remove items is even unchanged. The only difference is the syntax where you specify the `sessionStorage` object instead of `localStorage`:

```
// adding items
sessionStorage.setItem("artist", "Tycho");
sessionStorage.setItem("album", "Awake");
sessionStorage.setItem("track", "Apogee");
sessionStorage.setItem("year", "2014");

// removing item
sessionStorage.removeItem("album");
```

As you can see, things are very similar from a code point of view! If they are so similar, why would the Web Storage API expose both of these objects for you to use?

As it turns out, the major subtle difference between `localStorage` and `sessionStorage` is **persistence**. When you store data using local storage, your data is available across multiple browsing sessions. You can close your browser, come back later, and any data you had stored will still be accessible by your page. When you are storing data via session storage, **your data is only available for that browsing session**. There is no long-term persistence. You close your browser, come back a few moments later, and you'll find that all of the data stored in your `sessionStorage` object is gone.

The takeaway is this: If you want to persist some information for just a single browsing session, you should use session storage. If you want to persist information (theoretically) forever, use local storage. For everything else, there is Master-Card. Oh, snap!

THE ABSOLUTE MINIMUM

The Web Storage API addresses a long-running wish by designers and developers to have client-side storage that is more flexible than cookies and easier to use than WebSQL or IndexedDB. As you can see, local storage (or session storage) is fairly easy to use. A handful of `setItem` and `getItem` calls is all it really takes to be up and running.

? Ask a question: **https://forum.kirupa.com**

✔ Practice by building real apps: **https://bit.ly/coding_exercises**

▨ Errors/known issues: **https://bit.ly/javascript_errata**

IN THIS CHAPTER

- Understand the relationship between when a variable is declared, initialized, and used

- Impress your friends with knowledge about the temporal dead zone, a source of many a gnarly error!

48

VARIABLE AND FUNCTION HOISTING

One of the quirkiest things about JavaScript is this thing known as **hoisting**. We'll get to what it means in a bit, but let's set the stage for it by looking at some examples and figuring out what the right behavior should be. For our first example, take a look at the following code:

```
function foo() {
  return "Yay!";
}


console.log(foo());
```

What do you think is going to be displayed in our console when this code runs? Here are three choices:

1. undefined

2. Error—foo isn't referenced

3. Yay!

If you guessed **Yay!**, you would be right. There wasn't anything tricky here, so it was pretty straightforward. Let's kick things up a notch and take a look at a slightly modified version of our earlier code:

```
console.log(foo());

function foo() {
  return "Yay!";
}
```

In this case, we are logging the value returned by our `foo` function *before* we actually even defined it. What do you think is going to be displayed in the console now? Will it be the same as before? Will it be something different? As it turns out, the answer is the **same as before**. Our console will print out **Yay!** as the output. Hmm....

It's time for our last example. Take a look at the following code:

```
console.log(bar);
let bar = 100;
```

This seems similar to what we've seen so far, right? You would expect the value **100** to be printed to the console. The actual answer is a whopping **undefined**. What is going on here? By the end of this chapter, you will know all about what's happening and the role this hoisting thing plays.

JavaScript and Compiler Behavior

When you are running JavaScript, you have a JavaScript engine that takes the code you write and turns (that is, *compiles*) it into the stuff that your computer understands and knows what to do with. As part of turning your code into something your computer understands, the *compiler* (aka the thing that does the turning) performs a variety of steps. One of these steps has to do with what happens when our compiler runs into any variable and function declarations. Depending on whether the declaration is for a variable or a function, the behavior is a little different. Let's look at each case separately.

Variable Declarations

Whenever our compiler encounters a block of JavaScript, the first thing it does is scan the entire block for any variable or function declarations. Take a look at an example from earlier:

```
console.log(bar);
let bar = 100;
```

Our compiler looks at both of these lines, but before anything gets executed, it hones in on the variable declaration where we declare the bar variable:

```
console.log(bar);
let bar = 100;
```

At this point, what it does is *promote* the variable declaration to the beginning of the scope it is looking at. From the compiler's point of view, our code will look a bit like this:

```
let bar;
console.log(bar);
bar = 100;
```

This promotion of the declared variable is known as **variable hoisting**. The important thing to note is that only the declaration is hoisted. The initialization where we set bar's value to **100** remains in the exact same spot. That explains what was going on with our example earlier and why we were printing an **undefined**. Because of hoisting, the bar variable exists when we try to log it. Because the variable isn't initialized at this point, what gets logged is a value of **undefined**.

Function Declarations

The behavior you saw with variable declarations is similar for functions as well. The major difference is that the entire function is hoisted—not an empty shell of it. Let's revisit our earlier example:

```
console.log(foo());

function foo() {
  return "Yay!";
}
```

When our compiler scans this block of code, it hoists the foo function to the top. This is known as **function hoisting**. What you have is something that ends up looking like this:

```
function foo() {
  return "Yay!";
}

console.log(foo());
```

That is why the output for this example is **Yay!**, just as it would be if we wrote our code with the function definition specified before we try to call it. Pretty simple, right?

Some Hoisting Quirks

We are almost done here. Just because we understand how hoisting works doesn't mean there aren't some exceptions to what we've seen.

Function Expressions Need Not Apply

First, hoisting doesn't apply to function expressions. Look at the following example:

```
console.log(foo());

let foo = function() {
```

```
    return "Yay!";
}
```

The output isn't going to be **Yay!** like we saw with plain-old functions earlier. It is going to be a **TypeError: foo is not a function**.

The Temporal Dead Zone

There are cases where hoisting applies but the value is never initialized to something like **undefined** as we've seen with var. Those cases occur when you are working with let, const, and class. Take a look at the following block of code:

```
console.log(answer) // ReferenceError
let answer = "Correct";

console.log(ROLE) // ReferenceError
const ROLE = "user";

let foo = new AwesomeSauce(); // ReferenceError

class AwesomeSauce {
  constructor() {
    console.log("I exist!");
  }
}
```

In all these cases, we would expect the variable or class to exist but simply not be initialized. However, that isn't the case. What you get with each example is a **ReferenceError**. It doesn't mean that using classes or variables defined using let or const don't get hoisted. They certainly do! The difference is that they remain **uninitialized**. This time between them getting declared and initialized has a pretty awesome name—the *temporal dead zone*.

THE ABSOLUTE MINIMUM

For the longest time, we've been told to declare our variables and functions first before initializing them. We've also been told to only *use* a variable or function after it has been initialized. None of that guidance changes. Just because JavaScript has a behavior around hoisting declarations to the top of the current scope doesn't mean we should make our code more difficult to read by relying on it. Think of hoisting as a warning for you to fix your code. It isn't intended to be something you look forward to using.

?   Ask a question: **https://forum.kirupa.com**

✔   Practice by building real apps: **https://bit.ly/coding_exercises**

🖋   Errors/known issues: **https://bit.ly/javascript_errata**

49

WORKING WITH SETS

When it comes to storing a collection of data, arrays probably come to mind first. They've been around forever, are very flexible, and contain a boatload of properties that make using them a breeze. Over the past few years, JavaScript gained another way to store a collection of data. That way is via this mysterious array-looking creature known as a **set**. On the surface, arrays and sets look similar:

Yep. Totally look similar. Totes!

But there are a bunch of characteristics that make them different. The biggest characteristic is whether or not duplicate values are allowed to be stored. **With a set, we can only store unique items**. This means we can use a set to store whatever we want (like an array), but we can store that item only once (unlike an array). If we try to add a duplicate of an item that is already a part of our set, that item is ignored and not added to our collection. Nifty, right?

In the following sections, we'll go into more detail on what sets are and how to use them like a professional ninja!

Creating a Set, Part I

Before we can use a set, we first need to create it. There isn't a whole lot of drama here. The only way we can create a set is by calling on the `Set` constructor:

```
let mySet = new Set();
```

When this code runs, we will have created an empty `Set` object called **mySet:**

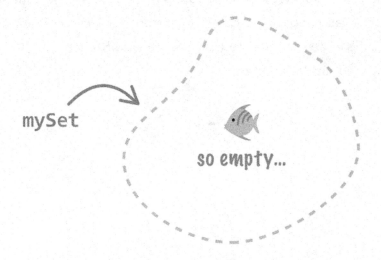

Now, you may be wondering if there are other, cleverer ways to create sets outside of typing in a new `Set()` like an animal. The answer is *nope*.

Adding Items to a Set

Once we have a set, we can add items to it by using the add method:

```
let mySet = new Set();
mySet.add("blarg");
mySet.add(10);
mySet.add(true);
```

Now, here is where the *uniqueness enforcement superpowers* of sets come into play. Right now, our set contains the text value **blarg**, the number **10**, and the boolean **true**. If we try to add a new item that already exists in our set, nothing new will get added. Take a look at the following highlighted line:

```
let mySet = new Set();
mySet.add("blarg");
mySet.add(10);
mySet.add(true);
mySet.add("blarg") // rut-roh
```

We are trying to add the text **blarg** one more time to our set. The **blarg** item already exists, so our set won't add this duplicated item.

Reacting to duplicate elements without making a fuss is one of Set's strongest differentiators compared to other data structures like arrays. When our set encounters a duplicate item, it just ignores it, and the rest of our code executes as if nothing out of the ordinary happened.

How Checking for Duplicates Works

For every item we add, our Set object has a really fast way of checking whether the item we are adding is equal to another item already in the set. The way our Set will check for equality with another item is by using the strict equality (===) approach. This is an important detail to call out, because it may be the source of some frustration if we aren't careful. By relying on ===, our set is checking for equality of **primitive values** and **object references**. The primitive value part is what we have been seeing so far in our code, where we added some text, a number, and a boolean. Something like the following doesn't have any surprises:

```
let sayWhat = new Set();
sayWhat.add("Lobby!");
sayWhat.add("Lobby!");
sayWhat.add("Lobby!");
sayWhat.add("Lobby!");
sayWhat.add("Lobby!");
sayWhat.add("Lobby!");
sayWhat.add("Lobby!");
sayWhat.add("Lobby!");
sayWhat.add("Lobby!");


console.log(sayWhat); // Lobby!
```

Now, here is where things get a little bit interesting. Take a look at the following example:

```
let anotherSet = new Set();
anotherSet.add(true);
anotherSet.add("abc");
anotherSet.add([1, 2]);
anotherSet.add([1, 2]);
```

What do you think the contents of our `anotherSet` object will be? The answer is **true**, **"abc"**, **[1, 2]**, and **[1, 2]**. The part that might seem trippy is the two **[1, 2]** arrays that we are adding. To us human beings, both of those arrays seem the same. They are representing what looks to be identical things. To the === check that our set performs, those two arrays are distinct. What our set will declare as equal are object *references* that refer to the same thing. The following snippet highlights this:

```
let myArray = [1, 2];
let anotherSet = new Set();
```

```
anotherSet.add(true);
anotherSet.add("abc");
anotherSet.add(myArray);
anotherSet.add(myArray);
```

In this case, we have our `myArray` object that stores our array values of **1** and **2**. It is this object we are now adding twice to our set, and since we are adding two `myArray` object references, the === operator will say that they are both the same. The end result will be that our array will end up getting represented inside our set just once. The contents of `anotherSet` in this situation will be **true**, **"abc"**, and **[1, 2]**.

Creating a Set, Part 2

Earlier, we saw how to create an empty set that we then added items to. There is another way we can create sets. It still involves the new keyword, but we can pass in an existing collection of data when creating our set to pre-populate it:

```
let someValues = ["a", "b", "c", 10, "a", "c", false];
let newSet = new Set(someValues);
console.log(newSet); // "a", "b", "c", 10, false
```

In this snippet, we have our `someValues` array that contains a handful of items, and some of the items like **a** and **c** are duplicated. When creating our `newSet` object, we still use the new `Set()` expression, but we pass in the `someValues` array to our `Set` constructor. When our set gets created this time, it isn't empty. It contains the *unique values* from the items we passed in when creating our set. Our duplicate items get filtered out.

This might bring up another question: What sorts of item collections can we pass in to the `Set` constructor when creating a set? The answer is **any iterable object**, which means any object that provides a way for us to cycle through all of its values. An array is one example of such an object. Text (Strings), `TypedArray`, `Map`, other `Set` objects, `NodeList`, and a handful more fall into the iterable object bucket. There are few really technical things an object must also satisfy to be considered iterable, and you can read more about that in this excellent MDN article on this subject: **https://developer.mozilla.org/en-US/docs/Web/JavaScript/Reference/Iteration_protocols#the_iterable_protocol**.

Before we wrap up this section, take a look at the following code, where we pass in a string (aka an iterable object!) as part of creating our set:

```
let textSet = new Set("diplodocus");
console.log(textSet); // d, i, p, l, o, c, u, s
```

We pass in the word *diplodocus*, and what gets stored by our set are the unique characters from it. Notice that each letter ends up becoming an individual entry in our set. Whenever an iterable object is passed in, each individual value from that object is evaluated for uniqueness and added to our set if that value is indeed unique.

VERY RELEVANT TIP

Did you know that a Diplodocus is the longest type of dinosaur we've discovered so far? Yeah, share that in your next standup routine!

Checking the Size of Our Set

To figure out how many items live inside our set, we have access to the handy `size` property:

```
let setCount = new Set();
console.log(setCount.size); // 0

setCount.add("foo");
console.log(setCount.size); // 1

setCount.add("bar");
```

```
setCount.add("zorb");
console.log(setCount.size); // 3
```

The value returned by the `size` property gets updated each time we add or remove (see next section) items from our set.

Deleting Items from a Set

To delete or remove an item from a set, we can use the appropriately named `delete` method and pass in the value of the item we are looking to remove:

```
var robotSounds = new Set(["beep", "boop", "who dis?"]);
robotSounds.delete("who dis?");

console.log(robotSounds) // "beep", "boop"
```

When you delete an item, the deleted item is both removed from the set and a value of **true** is returned:

```
let robotSounds = new Set(["beep", "boop", "who dis?"]);

if (robotSounds.delete("who dis?")) {
  console.log("Item successfully deleted!");
}

console.log(robotSounds) // "beep", "boop"
```

If we attempt to delete an item that doesn't exist, our set remains unchanged and **false** is returned by our `delete` method instead.

While deleting items individually is handy, there may be times when we just want to fully empty all items from our set. We can do that by using the `clear` method:

```
let vegetables = new Set(["🥕","🫛", "🥦", "🌽", "🧄"]);
console.log(vegetables.size); // 5
```

```
vegetables.clear();
console.log(vegetables.size); // 0
```

Another way to clear all the items from the set is by doing a new `Set ()` to re-create our `Set` object. It turns out that it isn't actually faster, so we should just stick with the `clear` method for efficiently emptying all items from our set.

Checking If an Item Exists

Not only is a set really fast at checking for duplicates, it is also really fast at checking if an item exists in its collection in the first place. To check whether an item exists, we can use the has method:

```
let ingredients = new Set(["milk", "eggs", "cheese", "tofu"]);
```

```
if (ingredients.has("tofu")) {
  ingredients.delete("tofu");
  ingredients.add("bacon");
}

console.log(ingredients); // "milk", "eggs", "cheese", "bacon"
```

The has method takes the item we want to check for as its argument. If the item is found, it returns a **true**. If the item doesn't exist in the collection, it returns a **false**. The way the check works, as we saw earlier as part of identifying duplicates, is by testing for strict equality (===).

Looping Through Items in a Set

There will be times when we'll need to loop through the items in a set. We can do this by using the `for...of` looping pattern. Take a look at the following example:

```
let textSet = new Set("diplodocus");

for (let letter of textSet) {
  console.log(letter);
}
```

This `for` loop will run until every item in the set has been reached. The order in which the items from our set will be accessed *is the same* as the order they were added to the set in the first place. Unlike arrays, sets don't have any concept of index positions that we can loop through. We have to use this `for...of` approach.

Entries, Keys, and Values

Under the covers, sets store items in the form of **key** and **value** pairs. This is something that makes the most sense when visualized. Let's say we have the following code:

```
let animaniacs = new Set(["Yakko", "Wakko", "Dot"]);
```

Inside our `animaniacs` set, the items **Yakko**, **Wakko**, and **Dot** will look a bit like the following:

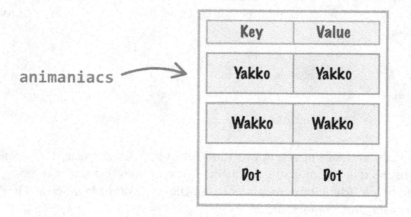

Think of the internals of our set being like a database or a spreadsheet with two columns. One column is labeled **Key**. Another column is labeled **Value**. Each row represents the item we are trying to store. The thing that makes sets a bit interesting when compared to other key/value storage arrangements (like a hashtable, for example) is that both keys and values store the same data. That is why in our example, **Yakko**, **Wakko**, and **Dot** appear in both key column as well as the value column. All of this is a bit strange, but, as the kids say these days, *whatevs!*

The reason why we spent this time looking at this key and value malarkey is that the `Set` object provides us with a handful of methods that return all the keys, values, and actual key/value pairs (called **entries**) that make up a set. Take a look at the following snippet:

```
let animaniacs = new Set(["Yakko", "Wakko", "Dot"]);


console.log(animaniacs.keys());
console.log(animaniacs.values());
console.log(animaniacs.entries());
```

The names of these methods should help clarify what type of data they will return. The `keys` method returns all the keys, the `values` method returns all of the values, and the `entries` method returns the key/value pair for each item in our set. The way the data is returned is not in the form of something like an array or generic object. The data is returned in the form of an Iterator object. This means the way you can access the items is by using the similar `for...of` approach we saw earlier:

```
for (let item of animaniacs.keys()) {
  console.log(item); // "Yakko", "Wakko", "Dot"
}
```

Iterators are really neat and provide a lot of cool functionality for iterating to items, so take a look at the following article on iterators and generators: **https://developer.mozilla.org/en-US/docs/Web/JavaScript/Guide/Iterators_and_Generators**.

THE ABSOLUTE MINIMUM

If you read through every section, you learned almost everything there is to know about the Set object and the various properties and methods you'll likely end up using. What makes sets really useful is their lightning-fast way of detecting duplicate items and ensuring only unique values are stored by them. You'll find yourself relying on sets more and more for a variety of simple and not-so-simple data-related tasks.

? Ask a question: **https://forum.kirupa.com**

✔ Practice by building real apps: **https://bit.ly/coding_exercises**

☢ Errors/known issues: **https://bit.ly/javascript_errata**

50

CONCLUSION

Well, now you've done it! You just couldn't stop binge reading and now you are nearing the end. How does it feel knowing that you won't have any more new content to look forward to until the next season?

Anyway, if you've been following along from the very beginning, you'll agree that we covered a lot of ground. We started with this:

```
<script>
  console.log("hello, world!");
</script>
```

We ended up with examples and snippets that had many more lines of more complex, useful, and far cooler code.

The thing you should remember is that writing code is easy. Writing *elegant* code that actually solves a problem is hard. This was best captured by one of my favorite lines from *Scarface* where Tony Montana delivered the following line (exact wording may be off a bit...it's hard to understand him sometimes, as you know if you've seen the film):

...you gotta learn the basics first.

Then when you learn the basics, you get to solve interesting problems.

Then when you get to solve interesting problems, then you get the bubble tea.

That's a TOTALLY sweet Al Pacino depiction!

This book is all about the basics. The way you go from the basics to the next step is by continuing to write code, trying out new things, and learning more along the way. This book described all the various tools and provided short examples of how they fit together to help you build small things. It's up to you to take this knowledge and apply it toward building all the cooler non-small things you often see associated with JavaScript. If you are feeling up for it, take a look at some of the more involved tutorials and examples under "Coding Exercises" on https://www.kirupa.com.

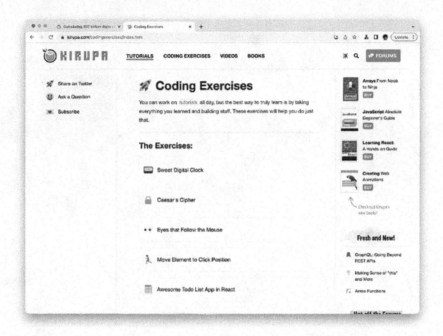

So with that, see you later. Feel free to drop me a line at **kirupa@kirupa.com** or find me on Facebook and Twitter (**@kirupa**). Like I mentioned in the introduction, I enjoy hearing from readers such as you, so don't be shy about contacting me. If you have any questions (big or small), take a moment and post them on **https://forum.kirupa.com**.

Also, I know you have a lot of choices in books for learning JavaScript. Thank you for choosing this book and allowing me to live vicariously through your code editor.

Cheers,

Glossary

A very casual look at the various terms you will encounter in this book and beyond.

A

Arguments The values you provide (or pass in) to a function.

Array A data structure that allows you to store and access a sequence of values.

B

Boolean A data structure that represents true or false.

C

Cascading Style Sheets (CSS) A styling language used primarily for changing how the content in your HTML page looks.

Closure An inner function that has access to an outer function's variables (in addition to its own and any global variables).

Comments Human readable text (often separated by // or /* and */ characters) in your code that is completely ignored by JavaScript.

D

Developer Tools In the context of browsers, they are extensions that help you inspect, debug, and diagnose what is going on inside your web page.

Do...While Loop A control statement that executes some code until a condition you specify returns false. (This is great if you don't know how many times you want to loop!)

Document Object Model (DOM) The JavaScript representation (often in a tree-like structure) of your HTML page and all the things inside it.

E

Event A signal that travels through your DOM to indicate something has happened.

Event Bubbling The phase where an event starts at the element that initiated the event and climbs the DOM back to the root.

Event Capturing The phase where an event starts at the root and traverses down the DOM until it reaches the element that initiated the event.

Event Listener A function that listens for an event and then executes some code when that event is overheard.

Event Target The element that is responsible for having initiated (aka fired) an event.

F

For Loop A control statement that executes some code a finite number of times.

Function A reusable block of code that takes arguments, groups statements together, and can be called on to execute the code contained inside it.

G

Global Scope Something declared outside of a function that is accessible to the entire app.

I

If Statement A conditional statement that executes some code if the condition is true.

If/Else Statement A conditional statement that executes different pieces of code depending on whether a condition is true or false.

IIFE (Immediately Invoked Function Expression) A way of writing JavaScript that allows you to execute some code in its own scope without leaving behind any trace of its existence.

Invoke A fancy way of saying the same thing as calling a function.

J

JavaScript A fussy and (often) inconsistent scripting language that, to everyone's surprise over the years, has grown to be quite popular for building apps on the web and the server.

L

Local Scope Something that is accessible only to the enclosing function or block.

Loop A control statement that allows you to execute code repeatedly.

N

Node A generic name for an item in the DOM.

O

Object A very flexible and ubiquitous data structure you can use to store properties and their values and…even other objects.

Operators A built-in function such as your friendly +, -, *, /, for, while, if, do, =, etc. words.

P

Primitives A basic type that isn't composed of other types.

R

Return A keyword that exits a function or block. In the case of functions, it is often used to return some data back to whatever called the function.

S

Scope A term indicating the visibility of something. In the real world, it is also a brand of mouthwash.

Strict Equality (===) Comparison Checks whether the value and type of two things are equal.

Strict Inequality (!==) Comparison Checks whether the value and type of two things are not equal.

String A sequence of characters that make up what we think of as text. It is also the name of a formal type for dealing with text in JavaScript.

Switch Statement A conditional statement that checks a particular condition against a list of cases. If one of the cases matches the condition, the code associated with that case executes.

T

Timer Functions Functions that execute code at a periodic interval. The most common timer functions are `setTimeOut`, `setInterval`, and `requestAnimationFrame`.

Type A classification that helps identify your data and the values you can use.

V

Values The formal name for the various types of data you'll encounter.

Variable Scope The term for describing the visibility of a variable in a section of code.

Variables A named bucket for storing some data.

W

Weak Equality (==) Comparison Checks only whether the value of two things is equal.

Weak Inequality (!=) Comparison Checks only whether the value of two things is unequal.

Web Browser A complex application that, at its bare minimum, helps you browse the Internet and display web pages.

While Loop A control statement that continually executes some code until a condition you specify returns false.

Index

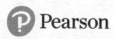